THE RETREAT OF AMERICAN POWER

Henry Brandon

THE RETREAT OF AMERICAN POWER

THE BODLEY HEAD
LONDON SYDNEY
TORONTO

Copyright © Henry Brandon 1972, 1973
ISBN 0 370 10662 8
Printed in Great Britain for
The Bodley Head Ltd
9 Bow Street, London WC2E 7AL
by William Clowes & Sons, Ltd, Beccles
First published in Great Britain 1973

To my wife, Muffie

CONTENTS

Thanks to . . .

When the idea of this book began to germinate it was only due to my wife's encouragement. She had insisted that I disprove a teasing remark made by Denis Hamilton, chairman of Times Newspapers, Ltd., and editor in chief of *The Times* and *The Sunday Times* of London, after my marriage: that in view of my new family responsibilities I would never again write a book. But my gratitude to her goes much further, for she not only thoughtfully adjusted home and family life to my needs and timed the birth of Fiona conveniently, she also helped with advice, criticism, even the typing. My stepchildren John, Elizabeth and Alexandra also showed remarkable consideration for the needs of a writer who had to spend his weekends with the typewriter instead of with them.

I am also deeply grateful to the many friends inside and outside the government who offered their knowledge, time and counsel, and for the encouragement, advice and support from Denis Hamilton and Harold Evans, editor of *The Sunday Times*.

Without the thoughtful assistance and editorial artistry of Oscar Turnill, an assistant editor of *The Sunday Times*, this book would not have been possible in the time it was done. Rita Feigenbaum, with the help of Harriet Alexander, was indefatigable in the preparation of the typescript.

Washington, D.C., August 1972

PREFACE

The changing place of the United States in the world can be illustrated in many different ways. One particularly startling one is a story John J. McCloy, the banker and elder statesman, remembers about negotiating with the Russians in 1962. President Kennedy had asked him after the Cuban missile crisis to get the Russians to remove not only their missiles from Cuba—to which they had already agreed—but also their Il-28 bombers which still sat on Cuban airfields. The man he negotiated with was Deputy Foreign Minister Vassilij Kuznetsov, and they met at McCloy's estate in Connecticut. Kuznetsov insisted that the talk be held in the garden so that nobody could record the conversation. Once in the garden, he lost little time in telling McCloy that the Soviet Union would withdraw all its bombers, but that this could only be an oral agreement, not a written one. He assured McCloy, however, that it would be carried out. Then he added, "And this is the last time the United States will be able to do that to the Soviet Union."

A decade later, much water has flowed down the Potomac and the Volga, and Kuznetsov's remark smacks less of braggadocio. The power relationship between the two countries has changed dramatically: Where once the United States enjoyed nuclear superiority, the Soviet Union has now, in a broad, general way, achieved nuclear parity. There was nothing the United States could have done about this—it was inevitable. And parity has been accompanied by many other developments which have led the United States to what can fairly be described as a retreat from power.

"Retreat" is a word of many meanings. It can be used to describe a withdrawal in the face of opposition, and that is what the United States has undertaken in Vietnam, even though the operation was camouflaged by an unprecedented display of American conventional power. It can simply be used to describe a drawing back to a new position, or it can imply diminution, reduction. The U.S. retreat that is now in progress is a mixture of drawing back from overextended forward commitments to less exposed and therefore more secure ones, and of the recognition that even the richest country in the world needs to husband its resources at home and abroad more economically and more effectively.

In my twenty-three years in Washington as chief American correspondent for *The Sunday Times* of London, I have enjoyed a privileged view both of the rise of the United States to world hegemony and its realization that such a position could not be held indefinitely. The Nixon administration, by seeking to make the withdrawal a carefully controlled one, has changed the concepts implicit in American foreign policy far more than is as yet generally recognized. I have tried to analyze in this book the play of the forces of change as they are influencing the American position around the world geographically, militarily, diplomatically, psychologically and economically, and to draw certain conclusions for the future. These forces should not be underrated; but neither is there reason to be panicked by them.

What follows is thus a selective retracing of the footsteps of President Nixon and his chief foreign policy adviser, Dr. Henry Kissinger, and an attempt to analyze in which direction they have headed the United States ("selective," because almost any chapter could itself have been developed into a volume). It is an account of a President deeply concerned that the retreat of American power should strengthen rather than weaken the country and of the many-splendored support his chief foreign policy adviser rendered him. Between them they set a pattern for a new phase of history, shaping out of the legacies of the sixties the policies the United States will adopt toward its allies and rivals in the seventies.

The book is limited to the evolution of foreign policy as seen by an outsider with access to a great deal of new information gleaned from the principal actors. This condition has its disadvantages, but, as a White House insider consolingly put it to me, "The only thing that is worse than not having the historic documentary record in front of you is having it in front of you."

CHAPTER ONE—THE NATION FACES
PRESIDENT NIXON

The task facing President Nixon as he was ceremoniously sworn in as President of the United States by Chief Justice Earl Warren on the steps of the Capitol would have daunted many bigger men. Not since the Civil War had the country been more dangerously divided, not since the Depression had any President been confronted with the kind of national crisis that was staring Mr. Nixon in the face. Perhaps, as never before, Americans had come to wonder whether their duly elected leaders could control the country and whether the system that elected them was really still a workable system. There were those who wondered whether American democracy was, in fact, still functioning; there were others who had become convinced that the democratic tools forged by a liberal tradition were too weak to cope with this national emergency.

And as Americans looked abroad, the world seemed to them an unfriendly, ungrateful and increasingly hostile place. They had spent billions of dollars in foreign economic and military aid on rehabilitating the allies and the developing world, but when they found themselves in trouble in ·Vietnam or when their gold reserves began to dwindle, no one showed the kind of gratitude they expected. On the contrary, it was the United States that was blamed for most of the ills of Western civilization. Such ingrained qualities in the American character as humanitarianism, enthusiasm and idealism, which had aroused so much respect and admiration throughout the world, now gave way to disillusion-

ment and hurt self-centeredness, to a new nationalism and a
nagging distrust. Worst of all was the loss of faith in the traditional American values, carrying with it the seeds of social and
moral anarchy. It seemed that the end of American optimism had
arrived with Mr. Nixon's accession to power and no one expected
him to inspire its revival.

It was an unenviable time for any President to assume leadership: What handicapped Mr. Nixon even more was the knowledge
that only 43 per cent of the American people had given him
their vote, that he was not a popular man. For too many people
his winning the presidency was a shock and an inexplicable turn
of fate, considering that he had acquired the aura of being a
"loser" and considering how little respect people had for his
character. Rarely had a politician been crucified for his sins as
Nixon had, rarely had the news media been as unforgiving as
they had been about him, rarely had the mud of a phrase like
"Tricky Dick" stuck as indelibly on a man's face as on Nixon's.
And yet there he was now, in the White House and presiding
over what many Americans and foreigners had come to call a
"sick" society. Since it obviously wasn't a miracle, it was simply
a historical accident. Just as President Johnson would have never
made it to the White House had he not been Vice President
when John F. Kennedy was assassinated, so Nixon would not have
done so had the Democratic Party not become so unpopular
because of the war in Vietnam.

But Mr. Nixon, as he stood on the Capitol steps, delivering his
inaugural address and setting the tone of his presidency, showed a
remarkable political instinct as to what the times required in
terms of leadership. He spoke of the need of "lowering voices," of
new flexibility, of shifting the emphasis from the dramatic to the
practical and of ending the war in Vietnam. And he set the hall-
mark of his foreign policy with his phrase "moving from confrontation to negotiation."

TAUGHT TO SUCCEED, BUT NOT HOW TO FAIL

It was a bland enough phrase, but it heralded a dramatic redefi-
nition of America's relationship with the world. The retreat from

domination has been a very painful experience for all great powers throughout history. Now the United States is going through this searing and shattering experience, intensified in this case by the revulsion against the humiliation in Vietnam. Americans have always been proud, confident and optimistic people. They have been taught to look upon American power as close to absolute. They have placed a profound trust in all the values that they have learned to identify as truly American. Confident in their ability to create, employ and disburse wealth, they have also enjoyed the certainty that economically they will always be richer than anybody else: In their armory of so much that was best in the world, the dollar was almighty. The shock, therefore, that many of the old tenets in which lay the seed and root of the American way of life were open to question or even to be denied was devastating and found Americans ill prepared. By the very nature of being American they had been taught how to succeed, but not how to suffer failure.

The historic tests of the American character were of a different kind—the determination to overcome the challenges of the frontiers in the West; the contest between the South and the North; welding a single nation out of a diversity of immigrants; gearing industry to levels of consumption never even dreamed of elsewhere. There were ordeals as well as challenges, but they did not injure American pride and prestige and did not lead to failure. They were overcome.

The bitter transition from hegemony to mere leadership is therefore proving a traumatic and disconcerting experience to many Americans, even while to some it engenders a sense of relief. Those who feel this relief will say that it was inevitable, even that it was overdue because the postwar period during which the United States had properly assumed a global role had come to an end. Those who are deeply upset are perturbed not only by the decline of influence itself but also by the fact that the retreat of American power is happening faster than any other in modern history—faster even than the British or the French retreated from their imperial role. Moreover, it is taking place under the highly disturbed gaze of America's allies as they wonder how far it will go.

Is what is happening due to some new-found weakness in the American character, or is it the forced product of the times in which we live? Many Americans would insist that the United States is simply not cut out, politically, geographically or mentally, to exercise a policy of quasi imperialism or what Americans have come to call, more grandiosely, "globalism." Politically and economically, basic American instincts tend to be more isolationist than interventionist; and considering the sheer scope and size of the American homeland, this is understandable. One could adapt to U.S. globalism the words of Tenney Frank, the American historian of the Roman Empire—that it grew up despite the Americans. Unlike the French, Americans have neither desire nor talent to be rulers among nations; unlike the British, they do not find an overwhelming incentive in the prizes of international trade, having a home market vaster than anybody else's. And yet by a series of historical accidents, such as its involvements in World War II and in remaining the richest country fully intact throughout a war which impoverished almost every other country, the United States exercised, to the surprise of most Americans and for almost a generation, hegemony over much of the non-Communist world.

Some American Presidents have believed in and promoted a policy of American leadership in the world. Theodore Roosevelt did, Woodrow Wilson did; Franklin D. Roosevelt gradually came to accept it; Harry S. Truman saw that he had little or no choice; Dwight D. Eisenhower believed in conserving American gains; John F. Kennedy had no doubt of his country's global mission. Their outlook was born, not in the old European way of mercantilist self-interest or militant expansionism, but of a profound belief in the beneficial influence of American ideas and ideals allied (in the later cases) to an urgent fear of the motives and ambitions of the Communist bloc. They were inspired by the assumptions that Americans made: that they could succeed in everything so long as they put themselves wholeheartedly, mind and shoulder, to the task. Behind them, they confidently assumed, was an economy that could afford "guns and butter" almost without limitation, a basic generosity and a sense of (whatever Americans might call it) noblesse oblige.

THE ODDS FOR WORLD LEADERSHIP

Some of the historians of the future, in their learned debates on why America took the path to retreat, will maintain, as some do already, that in the second half of the twentieth century no single power could have maintained world leadership, and that the American attempt to create some kind of benevolent imperial rule was doomed to failure. The idea of empire has been relegated to the attics of history: The Soviet Union is still trying to control one, but it too will go the way of all empires. What is more, the American world role was inflated out of proportion even to American means, which led to exuberance, overconfidence and finally error by those who found themselves actually exercising world leadership. Had that fatal progression been avoided, the retreat could have come more gradually and less convulsively for Americans as well as for the rest of the world.

Among the roll of postwar Presidents, General Eisenhower stands slightly apart, for the reason that he was by instinct not a mover but a stabilizer. He did not doubt America's assumption of world leadership, indeed he was noted for his passivity toward domestic affairs; yet it was during his time in the White House that confidence in that leadership began to sag, largely because of the distrust his Secretary of State, John Foster Dulles, generated abroad. Dulles' mistaken maneuvers in the Middle East gave the Russian-aid salesmen their first opportunity to get a foot in the Egyptian door, and his and his brother Allen's secret manipulations unsuspectingly baited the trap for their country's later military involvement in Vietnam.

The American world role during the last quarter century has had the strong backing of the American leadership classes, often referred to as the Establishment—eastern financial and industrial interests, the great law firms that represent them and much of eastern academia. The members of this Establishment in those years have deeply believed in their duty to serve their government in the liberal Anglo-Saxon tradition and in their gifts and talents for leadership. It was their influence that helped to save Europe from fascism; it was their sense of generosity that led to the Marshall Plan for postwar aid to Europe; it was their anti-colonial prejudice that accelerated the dissolution of the British, French and Dutch colonial empires. It was they who stood in the vanguard of those advocating a United States of Europe, and it was their Wilsonian idealism that advanced the creation of the United Nations. Confidence in American military and economic power was part of their creative strength—and later their undoing. They badly misread the importance of Vietnam to American national interests, perhaps because they were too preoccupied with foreign affairs and not sufficiently sensitive to the rising tide of domestic problems. They did not realize in time that the American values they believed in, and which had given them their confidence and inspiration, had become close to illusory. It is interesting that as the Establishment became disillusioned with globalism, so, as with Victorian imperialism, its commitments proved later to have deeper roots among the American public than among its own members.

WHEN THE MULE REFUSED TO MOVE

When Lyndon B. Johnson came to office, American statesmanship and American economic and military power had dominated the world for more than a generation, and on the whole in a beneficent way. It had been the most demanding and most successful period in American history. From being a country inexperienced in the art of world leadership the United States had learned the intricacies of statesmanship faster than any other great power, and it had created a modern version of benevolent imperialism that contributed much to the preservation of Western civilization. Lyndon Johnson tried hard to carry on the legacies of that heroic period, essentially along the classical lines of the politics of Franklin D. Roosevelt, whose disciple he was. Domestic reform accorded with Johnson's instincts and it excited his passions; it also suited him for the further reason that he did not feel at ease in foreign affairs. He promised the nation not a New Deal or a Fair Deal or a New Frontier, but his own even more grandiose brand, the Great Society. This concept fitted into the world that mattered to him most, which he knew perhaps better than anyone among his predecessors, the world that began and finished at the two ends of the ceremonial boulevard Pennsylvania Avenue—in the White House and in Congress.

But it did not take long before foreign affairs, in the hazardous form of the war in Vietnam, imposed themselves as his major preoccupation and gradually engulfed his more congenial interests on the domestic front. He would have liked to shake off the burden but his so-called "Alamo spirit"—his typically Texan pride in American power—never permitted him even to consider cutting his losses in time in Vietnam. Nor did the Establishment, usually not inflicted with an Alamo spirit, help to detach him from it. Perhaps it was impossible to save him from himself, perhaps it was that the Establishment too was blinded by this pride in American power. And so both committed the fatal mistake of never seriously considering withdrawal—before the decision in July 1965, which led to engaging the full panoply of American power—or the obvious idea of giving the South Vietnamese a crash course to enable them to assume responsibility for the fighting. The United States military command, on the contrary, made the basic mistake of assuming that the war had to be won with American forces in the principal roles and with the South Vietnamese acting only as stagehands. As a result American prestige became fully engaged in Vietnam. And so Lyndon Johnson's presidential fate was decided not on Pennsylvania Avenue, but along the Ho Chi Minh Trail.

His intuitive assessment of American power and American national interest misled him; so did his inbred belief that what mattered most was whether government functioned, not whether the nation was in tune with it or with him. The nation to him had become a mule that had to be dragged along, if necessary flogged. But Americans, and especially those on Capitol Hill, had turned into a very stubborn mule indeed, one that in the end refused to move at all. It was high time for a change of leadership.

THE DEMISE OF AN OLD ORDER

During the last two years of the Johnson presidency the United States looked almost ungovernable; they were years of chaos and violence. Superficially the cause was the uprising of the blacks and the students. The despair with the war exposed weaknesses in virtually every facet of American society. These weaknesses, however, were part of a much deeper development; the decomposition of the old order and its replacement by a new one. The war may have accelerated this process, but it had been coming, gradually, for some time. The assumptions underlying American family life had been eroded for almost a generation, and with this lost inner strength went some of the vital elements that had molded American society. The churches, which had assumed many of the responsibilities the family was abdicating, also were losing their hold on Americans, and the schools, the last substitute for parental guidance, had become the center of social unrest. The old elite, who embodied and defended many of these old traditions, and who had led this country for more than a century, were also losing their grip and were being replaced by another elite, that of the faceless technicians, business managers, applied scientists, systems analysts and media men. By a process of gradual assertion this new order was pulling hard at the fabric of American society, weakening the resilience and undermining the stability of this great nation. But it is also part of the strength of American society that it is not rigid, and that when revolutionary trends strain to break free of the old order, safety valves open up to prevent total social upheaval. In other revolutions—the French, the Russian—one class planned the overthrow of another. In this one, it was the perpetually moving, what I call "American escalator" society, where people can be up today and down tomorrow, that was in revolutionary ferment.

No other country would have been able to withstand and sustain the internal rebellions that were trying to break down the stockades erected by the old order. It seemed to me by 1968 that four different revolutionary trends combined seriously to endanger the stability of the United States: There was the racial revolution, fired by black nationalism; there was the rebellion of the young against the life style and the values of their elders; there was the surging up of the opposition both on the Right and on the Left against a political party system that denied them the kind of leverage for their ideas they demanded; and there was a perceptive shift of the political point of gravity from the eastern seaboard, with its liberal traditions and its world view, to the middle and western American traditions with their more conservative, more inward-turned perspectives. All these revolutionary trends, fueled by the frustrations of the war in Vietnam, churned up bitterness and rebellion. President Johnson was mentally and psychologically unable to cope with these powerful forces. Instead he tried to ignore them, which only heightened their sense of utter helplessness and their hatred of those in authority.

THE FLAWS OF LEADERSHIP

To understand President Johnson's failure one must go deeper into past failures of American leadership, at least as far back as President Eisenhower. Eisenhower made a major contribution toward calming the ugly waves stirred up by the Communist witch-hunting of Senator Joseph McCarthy, but for much of his eight years in power he failed to grapple with the mounting American domestic problems. John F. Kennedy "got the country moving," but after his premature death, left a legacy of hope and expectations that—perhaps because it was too ambitious to be fulfilled quickly—only contributed to the rising discontent and disenchantment.

In international affairs results, however evanescent, were easier to come by, and as a consequence they got preferential presidential treatment. They offered publicity and prestige, and gave the nation a sense of accomplishment, power and pride. The more that problems at home remained neglected, the more insoluble they became. Finally, too many domestic pressure cookers blew up at the same time. Paradoxically, that was what really aroused doubts in the United States' ability to lead the world. The United States was still a nuclear superpower, but that alone does not ensure world leadership: It is an even less negotiable commodity than the gold in Fort Knox. It was the decline of the dollar rather than "parity" with the Soviets in nuclear weapons that weakened American influence in the world. More than any foreign policy it was the plight of the dollar that threatened Western unity, and that mistake must be laid again at the door of Lyndon Johnson; with his eyes on the next election, he failed to take measures against an inflation that in the end ran wild and gravely undermined the value of the dollar.

He was swept out of the political arena by his own errors and by historic trends he hastened, but could not control. He did have the wisdom, though, to read the writing on the wall and to depart voluntarily.

THE JOHNSON LEGACIES

By the time President Johnson had handed his baton in the presidential relay race to his Vice President, Hubert Humphrey, the Great Society, that unfortunate hyperbole of a slogan, was in disrepute. Racial and campus violence was still in full swing by the end of 1968: The San Francisco State College was reopened only after several hundred policemen moved onto the campus for a prolonged period, and other campuses such as Fordham and Howard universities and San Mateo College were also plagued by trouble. As student bitterness mounted, so too did bitterness against students, and the mood of the American people, according to opinion surveys, was edging to the Right.

The poor and the blacks probably still felt that Johnson's massive efforts to help them would prove to be preferable to what Mr. Nixon was likely to offer, but a basic mistrust of current welfare methods had set in. The criticism was simple: Poverty and hunger continued even though the number of persons living in poverty had fallen from 38 million in 1959 to 29.7 million in 1966 and was still falling. For a rich country like the United States, with its extraordinary high living standards, it looked like a problem out of control, with too many cooks using too many dishes and too many recipes.

After years of deliberate speed in civil rights and many gradual improvements, bringing a feeling of hope to civil rights-oriented Americans, the sudden blunt demands of the blacks, as they wanted to be called, for speedier attainment of equality in education, in jobs, in politics, in the news media and so on came as a hard blow. As never before, the black issue loomed large and heavy, and however depressing this already was, it was obvious that this struggle for equality would overhang the social scene for many years to come, and with nobody quite able to foresee its outcome.

Crime was perhaps the issue that most disturbed most Americans. Mr. Nixon's promise of more police gave satisfaction to many, but to others it raised the growing specter of a repressive society. However, when fear grips and crime mounts, as it did spectacularly toward the end of 1968, people will accept more police as the lesser of two evils. Crime was a nightmare much closer to home than the Vietnam war, and it affected everybody.

Because of this, Americans realized that it was difficult to reduce crime quickly; many, however, could not see why it was not possible to liberate them from the Vietnam nightmare. What lay at the root of their feelings was not simply a revulsion against the events of the war, but the resuscitation of their old, latent anti-imperialist, anti-colonialist sentiments. Once, full of moral rectitude, they had vented these on others in the world. Now, though they were scarcely aware that this was what they were doing, they vented them on themselves, with the added bitterness of self-recrimination. American casualties in Vietnam were still heavy, two hundred a week. (South Vietnamese casualties were heavier, but were not reported.) Military activity in the Demilitarized Zone was intensifying rather than decreasing; heavy air raids continued against the Cambodian border and Communist base camps in Laos and along the central coast; and a fifth American reconnaissance plane had been shot down since the bombing halt on November 1. Despite the peace talks in Paris, the agony of the war continued, with no end in sight.

The Congress, in its rebellion against the Executive, became emotional and occasionally blindingly furious. It felt impotent, cheated and humiliated by the way President Johnson had treated it. Its anger and lust for revenge were building up, and on December 19, 1968, the Senate Foreign Relations Committee retaliated by announcing the start of a major probe into the Gulf of Tonkin incident. The controversy was over whether the North Vietnamese torpedo boats had actually fired on the American destroyer *Maddox*, an alleged provocation that led the Johnson administration to bomb North Vietnamese territory for the first time. This was the beginning of the air war against North Vietnam: It was the incident that many senators felt President Johnson had used diabolically to inveigle Congress into supporting the war. It was this Tonkin Resolution which he used from then on to justify the escalation of the war and to handcuff Congress into sharing responsibility for it. Now, in 1968, the Senate Foreign Relations Committee was launched on a crusade to recover the powers it had lost to the Executive over the past twenty-five years.

Only the economy, thanks to the inflation, seemed buoyant. Unemployment in December 1968 was at a fifteen-year low of 3.3 per cent and the Stock Exchange was up 9.4 per cent from the previous year. However, consumer prices were rising ominously—121 per cent above what they were ten years earlier—the interest rate was 6½ to 6¾ per cent, and the New York *Times* and others accused the President of having caused rampant inflation by failing to take effective deflationary measures in time because it would have undercut people's patience with the war in Vietnam.

ANXIETY AROUND THE WORLD

The catastrophic war also nourished doubts abroad. Governments allied to the United States were more appalled by the upheaval it had caused at home than by the stalemated condition in Vietnam. For this reason the allies favored an American disengagement from that unwinnable war, but not by cutting and running.

What worried the allies most was the instability of American public opinion and the sharp reversal in outlook among men who had been convinced internationalists. So much of the world depended for so many years on American inner political stability that the turmoil, which at a distance looked even more disturbing than it did at home, raised in the minds of foreign governments many new questions no one had thought of asking earlier. How reliable an ally was the United States? How resilient was the American civilization? How stable were the basic American political and social institutions? How capable were Americans of facing and absorbing national disturbances? What would be the world outlook of the young who had lost faith in the American traditional values when they assumed the reins of leadership?

There was no doubt that the war in Vietnam had profoundly changed the image of the United States in the minds of the rest of the world. Herr Helmut Schmidt, then Minister of Defense of the Federal Republic of Germany, bluntly summed it up when he said to me, "The greatest change is the way the world looks at the United States. Nobody any more talks longingly about the American way of life."

"Unhappy is the land that breeds no hero," was Andrea's lament in Bertolt Brecht's *Galileo*, to which Galileo replied, "No, Andrea. Unhappy is the land that needs a hero." In 1968, this summed up only too appropriately the American state of mind. The United States was a profoundly unhappy land then; it yearned for a new hero, but the choice of presidential candidates was between two depressingly unheroic figures, Hubert Humphrey and Richard Nixon. It chose the latter by a narrow plurality, without conviction and without enthusiasm, *faute de mieux*. It was relieved to see Lyndon B. Johnson depart, but it was in a quandary whether or not to welcome his successor.

NIXON FACES THE NATION

Mr. Nixon understood that his historic task was to manage the American retreat from the high watermark of global commitments without undermining the security of the West and American interests generally. He wanted to end the war in Vietnam, but without the loss of prestige; he wanted to curb inflation, but without applying strong medicines; he recognized the need for racial integration, but at a slow pace; he wanted to calm violence, but unprovocatively, and he wanted to introduce a new realism that would help make public expectations more rational. Gradualism as a form of leadership is not heroic, and for him, as a one-time interventionist and a hardliner in most fields of political endeavor, it must have created some complex inner dilemmas. But being an insecure man, no doubt sincerely awed by the responsibilities of the presidency and chosen to govern at a time, as Walter Lippmann once put it to me, "when the world has never been more disorderly within memory of any living man," his inborn caution became his principal guide.

In those very early days after his inauguration, one of Mr. Nixon's speechwriters went to the President's office in the Executive Office Building next to the White House, which Mr. Nixon liked to use as a sort of isolation booth whenever he wanted to remain undisturbed. He found the President in a relaxed position, reclining in his chair with his feet resting comfortably on a footstool. What startled the aide was that under the President's shoes he saw a hand towel to protect the footstool. Nixon did not remain so protective of White House furniture as he gradually got used to living with it, but it was indicative of how overawed he was at the start by his surroundings, even though he had known them in his days as Vice President. Eisenhower never made him feel at home in the White House, never invited him to his private wing.

There is an endearing modesty, but also an obvious uneasiness, about his living in an environment alien to his background. Almost eighteen months later, the President took me and my wife through his Moorish villa at San Clemente. The villa was tastefully furnished, with a decorator's elegance, the setting idyllic, yet curiously impersonal. The President told us then that when he bought the house it had been dark and austere. Now it was white-walled with soft deep sofas, thick rugs, sumptuous curtains, mostly in pastel shades. The gardens were profuse with flowers, especially roses, and the tones of piped-in music wafted over the swimming pool. He gave Mrs. Nixon all the credit for the decoration of the house. Then he added, "I have never lived in a house like this, you know." He seemed somewhat ill at ease in the elegant surroundings, but he also spoke of them with a house-owner's pride, though pride muffled by genuine modesty, almost embarrassment.

He seemed pleased to be able to afford now a retreat worth half a million dollars, but he was still amazed at its being his own.

SMALL TOWN, NOT LOG CABIN

Perhaps had he grown up in a log cabin instead of in a suburban home on the edge of Yorba Linda, a small town in California, where ends were met but barely, it might have been different, his style more soaring, his character more generous, his outlook on life less conventional. Fate did not make life easy for him; everything became a hard struggle.

"Nixon would be quite a man if he could believe in himself," one of his aides said to me soon after the inauguration. "It has the advantage, though, that he never deludes himself about his public support or about himself, and this is one reason why he did not enter the White House on a wave of self-induced optimism."

Nixon, of course, had been measuring himself for the presidency ever since he became Eisenhower's Vice President. He always liked power—maybe from the day he became president of his class at Whittier College, Whittier, California—but at the same time he detested the public exposure of one's personality that the reach for power entailed. He might have considered this exposure less distasteful had he not been aware of his insecurities. Somehow, though, he had the will to conquer them. It required an enormous effort, extraordinary self-control and a very deliberate attempt to conceal these inner inequities, and as a consequence, he resented anybody who tried to find out about the inner Nixon, and became an even more withdrawn person, even as his influence as a public figure grew.

THE ENGINES OF POWER

Many thought, and perhaps he did too, that once in the White House he would forget his hang-ups, rise above his insecurities and feel like the President. But he has never quite given the impression, whether at a public or private occasion, that he was at ease with his exalted position. On the contrary, his ease has appeared contrived. Despite his satisfaction at being President, he has seemed convinced, still, that he had managed to get into the White House in spite of himself. He had more or less convinced the public of his capabilities for the presidency, but had he convinced himself? Yet he had demonstrated endurance and extraordinary will power in seeking the job. In 1960, for instance, he felt outclassed by John F. Kennedy. He knew that he could not outshine the Kennedy charisma with his own conventional attributes, yet at the same time he remained convinced that victory was possible simply by dogged persistence. One of the results of his inner uncertainties was his belief that in order to get along in the business of politics one must show toughness, if necessary, ruthlessness. Experience gave him knowledge, but success did not give him self-confidence or put him at ease with life. Nixon the man certainly presented as many puzzling and confusing contradictions as he entered the White House as he had earlier as a mediocre politician.

New Presidents are always given a period of grace and the traditional allowances were made for Mr. Nixon. Even Herblock, the brilliant hard-hitting cartoonist of the Washington *Post* who, with unconcealed loathing, used to draw Nixon with the heavy "five-o'clock shadow" that FBI photographs of wanted men are famous for, announced that he would give him a clean shave for the time being. The blacks and the students also seemed ready to give him a breather, though they saw in him a hostile advocate of "law and order" and a determined enemy who would not hesitate to adopt repressive methods against them. Something akin to hopeful expectation was in the air, and the man who in the past had engendered such deep partisan hatreds aroused something close to a bipartisan wish for success, at least in regard to the ending of the war in Vietnam. But this political honeymoon was more a truce than an armistice. He knew that he would not get much support from the liberals, the blacks, the Establishment, academia, the Jews—his constituency was middle America. He wanted to identify himself, in the words of Eric Sevareid, the Columbia Broadcasting commentator, "with the middle class, the middle-aged and the Middle West, not with Boston, the mind of America, or with New York, its adrenalin glands." But it was something more than that; it was that the "middle" was most congenial to Mr. Nixon's character, upbringing and outlook.

Washington, D.C., was not friendly territory to him, either. To him it was a city with strong pro-Democratic and anti-Nixon prejudices. But as Nixon rode in his presidential limousine down from Capitol Hill to the White House, it was the Washingtonians who trembled awaiting the executioner; those who did the trembling of course were mostly Democrats. The reason that Washington is so "infested" with Democrats is that they tend to stay on even after a Democratic administration is thrown out of office. They cannot bear leaving the seat of governmental power. They feel, out of power, like a big league footballer without a ball, but they enjoy the game so much that they want to remain at least in the bleachers. Republicans are different; they tend to flee Washington as soon as they have lost office. To them working for the government is something of a sacrifice. They prefer making money to exercising power, which they see more as a temporary stint, an act of duty rather than one of pleasure or dedication. Democrats are for doing things through government, and therefore come with a purpose; Republicans are against doing things through government and usually arrive without clear aims. Republicans, of course, are well aware that a majority in the civil service are Democrats—people for whom the capital is "home," for their working lives at least—and are therefore apprehensive (often unnecessarily) about their loyalty to a Republican administration. And even if they are not as non-partisan as perhaps British civil servants usually are, they tend to be more loyal than Republicans, in their dark suspicion, assume. But these were not the only reasons why Washington awaited Mr. Nixon's arrival with so much trepidation.

He was remembered not only as a shrewd, crafty, calculating politician—what is sometimes called a political con man—but also as a man with a nasty, vindictive temper. He also had a reputation as a cold-war warrior, a classic anti-Communist.

But the question on most people's minds in those early days was whether Nixon, the unpredictable politician, capable of blows above and below the belt, would give the seasoned statesman in himself a freer hand and control the political con man. Some of his aides were greatly encouraged when in one of his rare intro-spective moments, he told an early Cabinet meeting that he began his political career by being against things, that he had to pursue that line in 1952 when he campaigned against the Truman pro-gram, and later again in 1968 when he battled on his own behalf, but that since he had now attained his highest ambition, it was no longer (he emphasized) the issues that mattered to him, but the accomplishments, and he did not want to be too partisan about them either.

However, the Cabinet he chose was disappointing. It lacked men of experience, brilliance or flair and it looked more partisan than pragmatic. As James Reston summed it up with quiet sar-casm: "The bland were leading the bland." It was also obvious that Nixon failed to attract Democrats, independents and Ne-groes of stature, who would have given his Administration a broader outlook and wider appeal. Mr. Nixon obviously did not want men who might outshine him or who would not be good team players. All seemed conventional types, all seemed to have been chosen to help cool the atmosphere and to blend into the sober style of this new Administration. And on the instructions of the President, the grandiloquence, the high-sounding phrases of the Kennedy-Johnson era were banned.

A NEW NIXON?

Was there a "new Nixon," as many of his aides were telling the press? The veteran anti-Nixonites said there was not and there never would be; others cautiously and hopefully suggested there might be. What he himself said sounded promising: "We can bring peace and keep the peace in these next four years . . . we can bring our people together at home and bring law and order with justice . . . we can even have a new era of progress without inflation." For his working desk he chose one that had been used by Woodrow Wilson, whom he much admired as a man of princi-ple. When this detail of Mr. Nixon's office equipment was men-tioned to me by one of his advisers, I could not help pointing out that Wilson, for all his qualities of principle and eloquence, had misread the state of American public opinion with disastrous results for his policies.

Some time after he had settled down in the White House I tried to plumb the presidential personality of Mr. Nixon in a private interview. I had sent word to him that I was contemplating writing a book about American foreign policy in the seventies, and he was generous enough to put some time aside for me.

We sat in high yellow wing chairs in front of the fireplace, unlike an earlier interview when he remained seated behind his huge desk, ensconced in his high-backed leather chair, as if behind a fortification. Then he seemed to want to create a distance, remoteness and formality. This time, standing behind his desk, as soon as he had greeted me he walked over to the fireplace, shifted the two wing chairs into a position that made us sit with our backs to the fireplace, looking across the room toward his desk. He clearly meant to make this occasion as informal as he was capable of. He sat most of the time in the same position, dressed in a lightish blue suit, matching dark blue tie with small dots, white shirt, gold cuff links with a blue semiprecious stone in them, dark blue socks. Most of the time he looked straight ahead; occasionally he turned toward me, but he never quite looked into my eyes. His eyes under his short lashes were fixed somewhere on my left lapel; they were ringed red, an obvious sign of fatigue, yet he seemed as relaxed as I had ever seen him, and in a mood to please and be helpful.

I asked him first what presidential qualities he thought important for the conduct of foreign affairs and suggested that a Truman-style toughness, for instance, would not succeed nowadays because it sprang from thinking in too contrasting terms—good and evil, black and white. I wanted to know how he, a man who once himself thought in these contrasting terms, felt about them now.

He agreed with my premise. "Yes," he said, "that is true of Truman. We had some tough encounters, but I respected him. He was good for his period, but I agree that today he would not know how to handle foreign affairs. Boldness is not the quality one needs. Today one has to be more subtle, more careful, more circumspect. Others sometimes call it devious or deceptive." (This last parenthetical remark was an interesting and telling attempt to explain, or to explain away, the "Tricky Dick" syndrome as being not a weakness in his character, but his critics' misinterpretation of his political style.

"The men who influenced me," he continued, "and who I consider my mentors, as you put it, are hard to define. In the fifties I strongly supported the Dulles-Eisenhower policies, which were then derided as brinkmanship and massive retaliation. But they were viable policies in those days because we had nuclear superiority. In those days it was also still possible to feed this superiority into one's decision making. Eisenhower could rely on it. Kennedy could still base himself on nuclear superiority during the Cuban missile crisis—the only danger then was that a madman or an unrealistic leader would use nuclear weapons. Fortunately, the Russians are pragmatists, even a man as emotional as Khrushchev was. Now the nuclear equation is in balance, now you cannot rely on superiority in decision making any more.

"Churchill at the end of World War II saw the great forces in the world developing. Many of his geopolitical ideas are now fully accepted. But in those days it was easier even than in the Eisenhower days to be decisive and to rally people.

"You need to see the world as it is," Nixon went on, "and keep an open mind to enable you to change your views. You need an individual whose ideas are not locked in preconceived notions." This was indeed a new Nixon compared to the one we used to know in the Eisenhower-Dulles period.

"He should have a basic idealistic concept," the President continued, analyzing the qualities he thought a leader should have and which, no doubt, he hoped were also his own, "but I don't mean in the sense in which we Americans are sometimes foolish about our idealism. In times of peace we go overboard in believing that everything can be solved at the conference table or by discussions in the UN. The trouble with idealists is that they destroy their own cause with their impatience. What is needed is a sense of history, an enormous capacity to keep up to date and to be able to contemplate problems without getting tied down in nitpicking irrelevancies. One must also have the ability to recognize what the priorities should be. Woodrow Wilson was an idealist, but the world needs more the idealism of Teddy Roosevelt. He was as much of an idealist as Wilson." (Here was the definition of a pragmatist who would like to flirt with idealism of a sort, but simply did not really believe in it. The toughness inherent in Theodore Roosevelt's outlook on the world was more in harmony with Nixon's view, at least at that point in his presidential career. Later on, his almost evangelical drive for a "generation of peace" had Wilsonian overtones.)

Nixon spoke with great intensity of feeling and seemingly great concentration. He developed his thoughts easily and without much hesitation, though I had not sent my questions along in advance. Whenever he mentioned an opponent such as President Johnson or certain members of Congress, his tone of voice turned edgy, there was a terrible visible contrast between the cool politician and the uneasy human being. Still, he exuded much more self-confidence than I expected. His knowledge and grasp of problems were impressive, and so was the ease with which he discussed himself. I did not feel any surer about him, the human being, but as the President, I began to understand him and the problems as he saw them. Finally, he added a last thought to his definition of a leader: "A President must be cool, unflappable, mature, with a feel for what the nation needs. President Johnson was basically a strong man, but he was too emotional, and the worst decisions are made in an emotional state of mind."

No one, of course, knows better than Mr. Nixon himself that he too has an ambivalent streak and that it has tripped him up time and again. Few people see their life in terms of crises, but Mr. Nixon even wrote a book, *Six Crises,** about the ones that had shaped his own life. The book was an attempt at self-justification and self-therapy, but it also reflected his obsession with the idea of leadership. He is not a natural leader and he is honest enough to admit this to himself. He carefully studied such contemporary leaders as Churchill, De Gaulle and Adenauer and reached the conclusion that the model that suited his character best was De

* Doubleday & Company, Garden City, N.Y., 1962.

Gaulle's style of leadership. Such aloofness from the public and the press appealed to him. The idea of trying to surround himself with a sense of mystery and a special aura of surprise and expectation for those occasions when he went before the public also tempted him. But only a man of supreme confidence, not one suffering from a lack of it, could get away with such splendid remoteness.

Nixon, with his love for power and his desire to prove himself, studied the mechanics of leadership the way others might study a textbook on how to service or drive an automobile. He studied the engines of power, their history and their various makes. He was concerned about the braking system and how fast the latter could effectively operate. He looked into the ratios of acceleration, the risks of traffic accidents and how to avoid them.

The question at the start of his presidency, though, was not so much whether he would live up to his well-studied, well-rehearsed, well-thought-out ideas of leadership, but whether the American public would accept and tolerate them and his priorities, his view of the world. That was the principal problem, as he saw it, facing him and the one that clearly preoccupied him most. With the United States so obviously going through one of the worst periods of her history, this was also the question people were asking abroad. Nobody felt confident, one way or the other, about what to think of either the new President or the state of the American nation or where he was likely to lead it.

One man at least, however, was prepared to give Richard Nixon the benefit of the doubt: "I think he has a chance," he said to me, "of restoring a sense of government and order to this country." The cautious balance between optimism and pessimism was wholly characteristic of Dr. Henry Kissinger, soon to be the second most powerful man in America.

CHAPTER TWO—THE PRESIDENT'S FIRST MINISTER: DR. KISSINGER

Never before in American history have the intellectual and conceptual views of the world of one man, who was neither in an elected position nor a member of the Cabinet, influenced American policy as have those of Dr. Kissinger. Many of the individual ideas and essential decisions that gave Nixon's foreign policy its special flavor certainly were the President's own—he stayed in the driver's seat. But one only needs to examine the prolific writings of the former Harvard professor to realize how much Mr. Nixon's views happened to coincide with Kissinger's and to what extent these two in fact saw the world from a similar vantage point. It became an unusual collaboration between a man who got where he was thanks to the strength of his will power, and another whose constant preoccupation had been an intellectual approach to the concept that was to be at the root of American foreign policy at this crucial turning point of history.

The nation held no particular expectation of Nixon when he moved into the White House. It looked to him, as it looked to other uncharismatic Presidents, to set a path to "normalcy," to lower the temperature, to bring order into chaos. In the nature of things such a course ought to mean that there would be few surprises. There was no reason to expect the creative innovations of Nixon's foreign policy when he appointed, first, Rogers as Secretary of State, and second, Dr. Henry Kissinger as National Security Adviser.

What was notable about the Rogers appointment was his lack of experience in foreign affairs. The President looked on the State Department bureaucracy as an incorrigibly lethargic snail protected by a thick shell of tradition, incapable of creative ideas or firm action. It was therefore assumed that Rogers had been given something of a trustee role rather than a policy-making position. His appointment got a generally good press because he had a reputation as a decent and honest man, with a lawyer's experience of negotiation and a record of reasonableness rather than political partisanship. Gradually, however, the State Department learned that his appointment and that of Henry Kissinger's added up to a neatly calculated equation.

Rogers was to ensure that this bland, fickle, indecisive giant did not, as Nixon suspected it would like to, play mischievous games with him, trip him up, embarrass him or ruin his initiatives by the slowness of its procedural habits.

Kissinger, who shared the President's prejudices about the State Department's bureaucracy, was to become on the other hand the idea man, the policy taster, the man in charge of the fuse box in the White House that could short-circuit the entire bureaucracy, even the Cabinet. What no one saw at first, though, was that he would quickly become the President's closest confidant, his principal negotiator, his troubleshooter, his First Minister, overshadowing members of the Cabinet—would become, in fact, as Joseph Kraft, the thoughtful American columnist, put it, no less than the second most powerful man in the world.

Nobody was more surprised than Henry Kissinger himself when the President offered him—an adviser to Nixon's fiercest Republican challenger, Governor Nelson A. Rockefeller, a quasi member of the eastern Establishment and a certified intellectual—so intimate a role. Those familiar with Dr. Kissinger's views about Mr. Nixon were even more surprised when he accepted. I remember, for instance, having a long telephone conversation with Dr. Kissinger in Miami Beach after Mr. Nixon had been nominated by the Republican Convention. We discussed the candidate's character, his outlook and qualifications, and Kissinger not only confirmed all my fears and misgivings, but reinforced them in no uncertain terms. He shared my mistrust of the man and his character, and as he put it to me: "I'm very worried that Nixon's cold-war outlook has remained frozen since his vice-presidential years in the fifties and that therefore in the seventies, in the waning military pre-eminence of American power, it could lead him into taking undue risks."

How did Mr. Nixon come to choose Kissinger, and why did Kissinger decide to serve a man whom he "profoundly distrusted" and did not think had the inner confidence and security a leader needs?

HOW NIXON CHOSE KISSINGER

Dr. Kissinger had met Nixon only once before, for two min-utes at a cocktail party given by Clare Boothe Luce in her apart-ment in New York, and the conversation did not go beyond small talk. Years earlier, though, Kissinger's writings had aroused Nixon's interest. He wrote to him twice, out of the blue, to ex-press agreement with his views. Once, after the publication of Kissinger's book *Nuclear Weapons and Foreign Policy*,* and the second time after an article of his on the mood of Europe had appeared in the New York *Times Magazine* in December 1959.

For curiosity's sake and for the record, it is worth quoting what particularly appealed to the then Vice President in that article. Kissinger criticized President Eisenhower's European policy as "sterile" and "too defensive." "We seem to be the prisoners of circumstances rather than their creators," Kissinger wrote, and in discussing negotiations with the Russians he said, "We should always be ready to negotiate not only for substantive but also for psychological reasons: to convey our peaceful purposes to the world . . . only the purposeful can be flexible."

Mr. Nixon's first approach to Kissinger after the election was made after a warm recommendation to the President by Henry Cabot Lodge—not merely because Lodge himself hoped to become Secretary of State, but because as Ambassador to Saigon he had called in Kissinger to give him a secret analysis of the situation

* Published for the Council on Foreign Relations, Harper & Brothers, New York, 1957.

there, and remained highly impressed with his acumen. After the first contact, through John Mitchell, Nixon's campaign manager and Attorney General to be, Dwight Chapin, Mr. Nixon's private secretary, called to find out whether Kissinger would see the President-elect. Kissinger said he would, and Mr. Nixon then asked whether he would be prepared, at least in principle, without specifying the job he would offer him, to work in his Administration. Kissinger, in turn, suggested that if Governor Rockefeller, whose foreign policy adviser he was, were offered a job, it would make it easier for him to accept. More specifically, Nixon also asked Kissinger whether John Mitchell could consult him on some of the people under consideration for positions in the Administration. There was some discussion about the function of certain jobs, but nothing was actually said about what role Kissinger himself might play, and so it was not surprising that he did not realize a job had in fact been offered to him. It was characteristic of Mr. Nixon's tendency for indirectness. Next day Kissinger heard from Governor Rockefeller: the President-elect had been in touch with him, but only to tell him that he would not be offered a job in the Cabinet. This dispelled whatever expectations may have lingered in Kissinger's own mind about himself and the new Administration.

Much to his astonishment, he nevertheless got another call to see Mr. Nixon two days later. This time he was offered, unequivocally, the job of National Security Adviser to the President. The two talked in detail in the President-elect's suite at the Pierre Hotel in New York about the function of the job and about their outlook on foreign affairs. Kissinger, to his surprise and relief, realized that their outlook was very similar. Still, before departing, Kissinger said that he first would have to discuss the offer with Governor Rockefeller and also with his colleagues—this, as he put it to me later, was to make certain that they felt he could be true to himself in accepting the job. He asked Nixon for a week to think it over.

For Kissinger it was a monumental decision. He had garnered some experience in Kennedy's White House as a part-time consultant and helped Nelson Rockefeller for more than a dozen years on various foreign policy studies. But Mr. Nixon's offer meant a unique apotheosis, the elevation of a poor German refugee to the highest level of service for his adopted country. It was also a reaffirmation of the role of the intellectual in the highest councils of government.

BECOMING AN AMERICAN

Heinz Alfred Kissinger (his real name) spent the first years of his life in the German town of Fuerth. His father was a teacher in a girl's school and his mother was a devoted middle-class *haus-frau*. He grew up in the turbulent years under the Weimar Republic with anti-Semitism galloping and inflation out of control. Kissinger denies that his father's dismissal from his job and his own expulsion from the Gymnasium where he was a student, followed by forced entry into an all-Jewish school, have had the profound effect upon his outlook on the world that some people attribute to them, but inevitably they must have left some indelible marks.

When he and his family finally succeeded in getting out of Germany and to New York via London, Henry was fifteen years old. It was not an easy transplantation, but he and his family eked out enough of a living not only for their survival, but even for their basic contentment. Henry soon found mentors who sensed his talents and wanted to help him succeed. Nobody, of course, wanted it more than Henry Kissinger himself, though for a long time shyness kept him from giving his ambitions freer rein.

One of those who perhaps had a greater influence on his career than any other individual was Dr. Fritz Kraemer, also a German-American, whom he met in the Army in 1943. Kissinger was then nineteen and a buck private in the U. S. Infantry. Dr. Kraemer, a former lawyer, was also a private. Kraemer became a lieutenant and helped to install Kissinger in the city of Krefeld, Germany, in charge of reorganizing its municipal government, a job he carried out well. It was Kraemer, too, who next steered him—Kissinger was by this time a sergeant—to the European Command Intelligence School. There he gave instruction in legal procedures against former Nazis and did it so satisfactorily that his superiors offered him, on demobilization, a job at $10,000 a year to remain on the school staff. But Kraemer thought that Kissinger's talents deserved better use and persuaded him to undertake study at a university. Harvard was among the few willing to accept Kissinger. He not only graduated there, but returned to teach at its School of International Studies.

Harvard became his intellectual home: It taught him a lot, but not a Bostonian accent—more than a dash of his native German accent remains. This did, in fact, trouble him for many years, but he is self-conscious about it no longer and even jokes about his accent. I remember seeing him, for instance, at a Georgetown dinner party on the eve of President Nixon's crucial speech about his Vietnam policy of November 3, 1969, clutching a big manila envelope. When asked whether it contained the text of the President's speech, he replied sheepishly, "It's only the German version, the English translation is still in the works." And to explain why he had arrived so late, he added, "You mustn't forget that English is only my second language."

Henry gradually established a reputation as a foreign policy expert and military strategist. He traveled far and wide, and became a member of that ingrown world establishment of foreign policy experts. His work for the Council on Foreign Relations and on the Rockefeller reports gave him an added cachet. What catapulted him into public controversy was his book *Nuclear Weapons and Foreign Policy*,† which was an attempt to prove that the limited use of tactical nuclear weapons was a practical possibility. It gave him a hawkish reputation and by becoming a best seller it earned him money and also entry into many governmental inner sanctums. "It is the most unread best seller since Toynbee," Kissinger likes to say in his self-deprecatory way. A few years later, however, he admitted that some of his basic assumptions had been overtaken by developments.

He was then married to a pleasant, German-born girl, not an intellectual, and she bore him a boy and a girl. They lived modestly in a small house in Cambridge, but by the time Henry began his

† Op. cit., p. 25.

short-lived career as a member of President Kennedy's White House entourage, the marriage had been dissolved.

Kissinger as a part-time consultant in Kennedy's White House was edged out early because, as McGeorge Bundy, one-time assistant for National Security Affairs to Presidents Kennedy and Johnson, later told me, "He tried to be a private consultant and a public soothsayer at the same time, and the two are incompatible." Kissinger himself admits that his behavior in those days left something to be desired—his ego, he says with a puckish smile, was much less under control than it is today. However, he returned to the government sidelines in 1965 when Ambassador Lodge invited him to Vietnam, and later on he acted as a go-between in one of the peace feelers between the Johnson administration and Hanoi. The discretion and the skill with which he carried out these missions aroused much admiration inside the Johnson administration.

OUT-HORATIOING ALGER

Now Kissinger took his uncertainties about Mr. Nixon's firm offer of a return to the governmental arena to Governor Rockefeller, who strongly recommended his accepting. So did his colleagues at Harvard, including McGeorge Bundy, by this time president of the Ford Foundation, who remained his admirer, if a grudging one; they felt relieved that Mr. Nixon should have shown better judgment than they expected. It did not seem to matter to Nixon whether Kissinger considered himself a Republican or not; he never inquired into his party affiliation. Governor Rockefeller, for whom Kissinger had worked for fourteen years, told me that he too had never tried to find out whether Kissinger was a Republican. When I asked him to speculate about Kissinger's political convictions he said, "He does not belong to any category or party. In our case the personal superseded everything else. Henry used to be totally apolitical, but I think he is now politically more aware. I would define him as a pragmatic realist, tough, disciplined, dedicated and willing to take responsibility. He is very good at taking responsibility, but not so good at working with people. He is very temperamental. In a fit of temper he once resigned from a job he was doing for me, but after a few months we made up and he came back. What is important to keep in mind about Henry is that he likes to create events, while others prefer reacting to them."

Kissinger also telephoned his old friend and mentor Dr. Fritz Kraemer to get his advice on whether to accept the President's offer. Kraemer's reply was characteristically long-winded but nevertheless clear and direct. "From your personal point of view," he said, "you would be best off by choosing the job of Assistant Secretary for International Security Affairs in the Pentagon. You would be your own boss, you would have time to develop your own ideas and you would have a certain if limited amount of power and influence. In the White House, on the other hand, you would be a slave and under the relentless pressure of never finished business." Then he added, "But from the point of view of national interest you must accept the President's offer. There is no one more qualified for the White House job than you."

Kissinger decided to accept and actually called Nixon before the week was over, after only three days' delay. Looking back now, Kissinger says, he feels ashamed of having hesitated, for the President took an even greater risk with him than he did with the President. I asked Kissinger at a meeting before the President took office whether he had received some sort of assurance from Mr. Nixon that had convinced him that things would work out. Kissinger replied, "You can't make a treaty with the President."

He still admits, however, that he remained distrustful until he actually began to work for the President; from then on their relationship grew into something unprecedented in American history: Kissinger became the President's de facto Secretary of State. Never before had a President depended on a foreign policy adviser who, in fact, did not hold that office. Woodrow Wilson's Colonel House did not hold a formal job and, though his relationship with the President was intimate, Wilson did not rely on House as heavily as Nixon did on Kissinger. Also, the global role of the United States in those days was not by any means as crucial and all-pervasive as it is today. Franklin D. Roosevelt's Harry Hopkins, according to Ambassador Averell Harriman, who was intimately acquainted with him, was more a catalyst of presidential decision making, more a warm personal friend and associate than a brain truster, negotiator or policy maker. Like Kissinger, though, he communicated with the President directly (in those days via the Navy's signal lines) to bypass the State Department. President Kennedy's McGeorge Bundy became a policy maker, but not by any means to the same extent as Kissinger.

For a German-born Jew, it was a unique rise to power and fame even in a country where Horatio Algers abound. Few, if any at all, would have predicted that so close a relationship could develop between two men of such different backgrounds: an intellectual with an outlook more European than American, and a middle American suspicious of intellectuals, especially the Harvard variety. But as time would show, the two had more in common than met the eye.

WHAT KISSINGER AND NIXON HAD IN COMMON

First of all, Nixon shrewdly recognized that Kissinger would not only be an asset to him as the only recognized and respected intellectual in his presidential environment, but that he would also provide him with the kind of raw and finished material and the concepts policies are made of. "Lawyers," Kissinger once wrote (and Nixon was a lawyer), "at least in the Anglo-Saxon tradition, prefer to deal with actual rather than with hypothetical cases, they have little confidence in the possibility of stating a future issue abstractly. But planning by its very nature is hypothetical. Its success depends precisely on the ability to transcend the existing framework." Kissinger obviously saw himself as the chosen instrument that would compensate for these weaknesses inherent in lawyers.

Nixon also knew Kissinger's writings, which told him that they held a shared view about how the United States should deal with the Russians and the Chinese—not as ideological powers, but on the basis of a mutual interest with which no middle power should be allowed to interfere. They also shared the conviction that negotiations with Communist powers must be conducted on a strictly *quid-pro-quo* basis. They were soulmates too in their distrust of the State Department and in their disdain of bureaucracy.

And they shared a conspiratorial mind, a penchant for secret diplomacy and the *coup de théâtre*. To such an approach to diplomacy bureaucrats can be a positive hindrance; an "eyes only" top secret document, for instance, which was the smallest distribution, nevertheless is circulated in sixty copies; this obviously makes it difficult to ensure its secrecy. Sudden action goes against the bureaucratic outlook and tradition, which are much more based on the idea that if you are willing to wait long enough the problem will disappear. If Nixon meant to pursue a foreign policy punctuated by threats and acts of surprise, he could not do so through a Secretary of State who, because of his own limited experience in foreign affairs, was dependent on the multiple advice of the State Department machinery. Secretary Rogers' function, as it evolved, was not the development or the conduct of foreign policy, but the protection of the President from the self-assertions of the bureaucracy. He needed Kissinger to enable him to act freely in establishing and effecting his own new policies. "Bureaucracy," Kissinger once wrote, "considers originality as unsafe."

All this explains why Nixon and Kissinger, to satisfy their basic instincts as well as their own convictions, preferred to conduct foreign policy by stealth. Kissinger, particularly, in his nineteenth-century outlook of "the public be damned" ideally would prefer to conduct policy out of sight of the public, of Congress, of the bureaucracy, but he has become enough of a realist to know that he has to accept compromises and does. He is in fact very good at public justification of policies and at discussing them with their critics.

Nixon, though accepting the need for accountability and despite his schooling in the world of politics, also prefers to play his hand close to his chest. This affinity of view explains how Kissinger came so much to care for the President and became his loyal, most personal, most dedicated servant rather than, as one cynical comment put it, his Rasputin. A psychological bond developed between the two, some of Kissinger's academic colleagues believe, for both men saw themselves as social outsiders, tolerated rather than accepted by the ruling class.

KISSINGER, ACTOR OR DIRECTOR?

After the President and Henry Kissinger had settled down to the making of policy it became very difficult to determine later who had had the original idea and who had influenced whom in developing it. Kissinger himself once confessed to me, "Often I don't know whether I am the actor or the director."

On the whole, he was careful to ensure that the President would harvest the ultimate credit for all foreign policy achievements, but the spectacular visibility and fulsome credit he was given by the news media after a time began to grate on the President. Some men of the President's inner circle resented the massive publicity even more than Mr. Nixon. As Pete Peterson, the gentle-witted Secretary of Commerce once put it: "Henry's relation with the White House staff is as intimate as was that between Caesar and Brutus."

Kissinger's strength from the start was that he was able to give the President's foreign policies a conceptual coherence. His ability to explain to the President where he might be likely to find himself after the next half a dozen moves gave Mr. Nixon the kind of intellectual sense of security he needed. Sir Burke Trend, the former Secretary to the British cabinet, defined Kissinger to me as "a conceptual shrewd thinker with long-term views, flexible enough to change his mind in order to keep several options open."

During the first few months in the White House, Nixon and Kissinger met every day at 9:30 A.M. to discuss their long-range objectives. Kissinger refrained from turning matters of policy into personal affairs, which seemed to impress Nixon, who likes detachment in himself as well as in others. Seventy per cent of those conversations were philosophical or historical, and this bent in Kissinger stimulated the President's philosophical interests. Frequently the behavior of intellectuals came up. Both basically mistrust them, yet to Kissinger's surprise the President's estimate of them was higher than his own. When the campus turmoil erupted at Harvard University, for instance, the President suggested that it was a fortunate thing that it had happened at Harvard, for, being the best university in the country, it would know how to deal with such a situation. Nixon was astounded later on when this proved not to be so. Often the President called in Kissinger during his lunch hour—a free hour for Mr. Nixon, for he hardly ever eats lunch. Their relationship grew in intimacy and yet retained a formality which neither ever dropped because, again, it is a characteristic they share.

They are also both loners, and in a theatrical sense, tragic figures who have achieved more than they ever expected, and yet lack the contentment and happiness it ought to bring. Neither can come close to anyone for fear of being unable to meet the demands of friendship or intimacy. They hold enormous power in their hands, but they remain in isolation. Both suffer from insecurities and feel the need of reassurance, but both have gained confidence from the use of power. Kissinger has been accused of displaying an arrogance of power, but if anything his fault is an arrogance of intellect which makes him believe that he can control and manage reality. This also leads him, if the facts do not vindicate his theories, to believe that the facts are wrong. His insecurities also develop from a sense of being disliked, of being surrounded by enemies, or of losing support among those he cares about, and from attacks in newspapers which tend to upset him as much as they do other public personalities. His most obvious insecurities, however, are his total dependence on getting his ideas accepted and his need for protection from his adversaries, of which he has as many as most eminence grises did in history.

Early in 1970, Henry Kissinger gave a friend for his birthday the one book he said he had read that year, a new book about Hannibal. The recipient naturally wondered what had attracted Kissinger to it. On reading it, he concluded that the melancholy Kissinger may look on Hannibal with a certain envy; for the Carthaginian is a great figure of history whose hopes were dashed by fate, but who at least lived in an age when heroism was appreciated as an end in itself.

KISSINGER'S OUTLOOK

Kissinger's disinterest in political or party power gave, no doubt, an important advantage in his relations with the President. He is interested more in order, stability, predictability and in a world in which people agree on the rules of the game rather than in doctrine or dogma. In fact, he tends to be critical of the rational conservatives of the early nineteenth century because he considers them too dogmatic. Prince Metternich (1773–1859), the great Austrian statesman who is one of Kissinger's idols of history, wrote that to be a conservative required neither return to a previous period or reaction, but carefully considered reform. True conservatism implied an active policy. Yet reform had to be the product of order and not of will; it had to assert the universality of law against the contingency of power. Kissinger's own definition of a true conservative is much less rigid. He is one who "will attempt to avoid unbridgeable schism, because he knows that a stable social structure thrives not on triumphs but on reconciliation."‡ He is a law-and-order man in the sense that "societies which contain fundamental schisms must rely on law, the definition of a compulsory relationship."* The reasons for Kissinger's relative freedom from ideology are to be found in his background. He suffered a youth profoundly upset by the experience of a Germany that came to epitomize to him utter chaos. Out of this shattering experience he could not help but develop, consciously or unconsciously, a basic mistrust of "shakers of the world." He fits into neither the world of Edmund Burke nor that of William F. Buckley. Kissinger's kind of conservatism and his vision of a world with a stable structure for peace led him to fall passionately in love with nineteenth-century nationalism and to admire that great architect of a structure for peace, the German Chancellor Bismarck (1815–98). But it is less the early Bismarck, who unified Germany, that he admires so much as the later one, who after he had unified his country tried to establish a secure and stable Europe.

‡ Kissinger, *A World Restored*, Grossett's Universal Library, New York, 1964.
* Ibid.

The amount of human tragedy Kissinger saw around him during his formative years accounts for his being a man given to occasional melancholy or perhaps *Weltschmerz*, and for being a convinced pessimist beneath a certain playfulness and levity. It is rather apocalyptic gloom that possesses him: thoughts about the inevitability of injustice and some sort of inescapable ultimate doom. He admits to a belief in the tragic element of history: "There is the tragedy of a man who works very hard and never gets what he wants. And there is the even more bitter tragedy of a man who fully gets what he wants and finds out that he doesn't want it." I am certain that the latter experience has been shared by both Mr. Nixon and Dr. Kissinger during their trials in the White House, even though they find occasional triumphs worth the agonies.

General de Gaulle too was obsessed with a similar apocalyptic gloom, which may be one reason why Kissinger felt sympathetic to the French President. To illustrate the general's tragic view of history there is the story of a dinner party De Gaulle held for the Danish Princess Margrethe, who has since succeeded to the throne and whose intellectual interests are not excessive. During dinner her host asked her whether she was interested in history; she replied, giggling, "I love history!" De Gaulle then asked, "Does it make you happy?" "Yes," she said, "very!" De Gaulle did not say another word to her for the rest of the evening.

In dealing with short-term problems of policy making, however, or as a negotiator and diplomatic manipulator, Kissinger can uncouple his underlying pessimism and think and act in ways inspired by confidence and hopefulness, even acquiring a hardy optimism. Like many clever and successful men he has been torn between a yearning for acceptance or at least approval by the Establishment and disdain for it. He worked for Governor Rockefeller because he took him to be a man who would stand firm in the face of popular political opinion or ignore it. Nixon, he told me in Miami in 1968, he feared would be tempted too much to mold his policy to the whims of public opinion rather than to principles. "I served Rockefeller to keep Nixon out," he said then, while his habitual gloom was focused on the Republican Party's future. He also mistrusts the Establishment because he sees its members as unaware of how difficult it really is to establish a stable order, as having too many scruples and being too inflexible to succeed in the subtle game of diplomacy, and also as too ready to believe that order can be created by "quick-mix" solutions. Ideas such as the Multilateral Nuclear Fleet, which was launched in the Kennedy days to give the Europeans and especially Germany the illusion of having a finger on the nuclear trigger, or the same Administration's counter-insurgency forces intended to challenge the North Vietnamese guerrillas, he considers as gimmicks devoid of *Realpolitik*.

Kissinger's anti-Communist outlook was inspired by Professor William Y. Elliott at Harvard, whose disciple he was. Elliott was a southern gentleman with a gentle nature, a powerful intellect and the physical presence of a Frankenstein monster. He branded all his students with his conviction that communism is the evil incarnate. But in the White House Kissinger's outlook on communism became more subtle. First, in his dealings with Soviet Ambassador Dobrynin, then with the Chinese and Russian leaders, the instincts of the *Real*politician and his belief in the concept of legitimacy made him separate the ideological from the practical. Legitimacy, as he defines it, means "an international agreement about the nature of workable arrangements and about permissible aims and methods of foreign policy." It implies the acceptance of the framework of a certain international order by the major powers— in his case his balance-of-power framework—which, he believes, does not make conflicts impossible, but limits their scope. However repugnant the internal political system of another state may be to him, what matters is whether the leadership is willing to participate in an international framework of order.

KISSINGER'S CONCEPTS

Kissinger himself provided the best insight into his thinking in that first impressive book, *A World Restored*. This study of Metternich's brilliant chess game of shifting coalitions and power politics in the aftermath of the Congress of Vienna is a masterly analysis of how the Austrian grand-scale manipulator, together with Britain's Castlereagh, not only checkmated Napoleon twice, but also how their maneuvers succeeded in maintaining peace in Europe for a century. Kissinger criticizes Metternich for his contention that a power equilibrium is something stable rather than something that had to be kept in balance all the time, and this criticism is indicative of Kissinger's own approach to diplomacy—"the manipulation of reality."

Both he and Nixon play a carefully calculated game. They move with caution and after they have considered all the options, but in Nixon there is also a gambler's instinct. This is a quality of the President that Kissinger, with his intellectual approach, must have worried about; yet he also admires it as an asset in a leader because it is an instinct that he lacks himself. He does, however, believe in an active, not a reactive, diplomacy, for he maintains that this is the best way to control events. He still holds that, as he wrote in his undergraduate thesis, "all truly great achievements in history resulted from the actualization of principles, not from the clever evaluation of political conditions." He has been very critical, for instance, of French strategic doctrine during the interwar years because it "exalted the value of the defensive and built its plans around the Maginot Line. However, the likely German attempts to overthrow the Treaty of Versailles could have been prevented only by French offensive action. By the time the Maginot Line could have proved useful, in other words, the Versailles settlement would have already been overturned. Thus French strategic doctrine contributed to the paralysis of French diplomacy."†

In order to be effective, he believes, a strategy must fulfill several requirements. It must be able to win a domestic consensus, both among the technical and political leadership, and that often depends on strong presidential leadership. It must be understood by its opponents to the extent needed for it to operate as an effective deterrence. During the Cuban missile crisis in October 1962, the United States conveyed an effective warning by dispersing SAC bombers to civilian airports. In September 1970, during the Jordan crisis, the United States reinforced the fleet in the Mediterranean

† Kissinger, "Reflections on Power Diplomacy," in *The Dimensions of Diplomacy*, E. A. J. Johnson, ed., Johns Hopkins Press, Baltimore, 1964.

and this provided the necessary warnings. What worries Kissinger, though, is what equivalent tactics can be employed when the American strategic forces are dependent entirely on missiles.

Another aspect of crisis management that troubles Kissinger is the human factor, the question of nerve. The Schlieffen Plan, for instance, designed in World War I, provided for every contingency except the psychological strain on the commanders. It failed largely, he believes, because the German leaders lost their nerve.

He saw, therefore, as part of his role to reinforce the President's "nerve." When Mr. Nixon came close to losing his composure during the Cambodian crisis, it gave Kissinger a crucial opportunity to prove his loyalty. From then on a certain dependence on each other developed between the two. The President not only came to rely on Kissinger to present him with the options to policies but also to relieve the loneliness of the presidency. Too much dependence on one man creates special loyalties, but it can also awaken a sense of frustration; both came to develop between the two.

Kissinger has the rare gift of being a conceptual thinker, a quality which separates the intellectual from the politician and which made Kissinger into a particularly valuable aide, for he was able to give the President's policy instincts intellectual content. The President is not a profound thinker, but he can ask profound questions, and Kissinger's ability to give him the answers, to explain to the President where he might find himself half a dozen moves from where he stood, gave Mr. Nixon the kind of intellectual sense of security he needed.

THE NEW EQUILIBRIUM

A further illuminating insight into his thinking was provided by Kissinger himself, before he got a chance to practice what he preached, in an essay written for a compendium sponsored by the Ford Foundation, called *Agenda for the Nation*. It was published late in 1968 as a guide and inspiration for the incoming President.

If we look for the bones in his essay, which is not easy, because he was still very much under the influence of what he later called "the obscurity that was often mistaken at Harvard for profundity," we find some of the essential principles underlying the Nixon foreign policy. We also find that in some cases he has failed to act according to his precepts.

Kissinger's essay proceeded from the premise that the international system, which had produced stability for a century, had collapsed under the impact of two world wars, and that the age of the superpowers was nearing its end. "For the first time a foreign policy has become global and not confined to continents. After tripolarity which had become a source of rigidity in foreign policy, multipolarity would now be the wave of the future." But "political multipolarity," he argued, "makes it impossible to impose an American design." For that reason, he went on—and it sounds like an early definition of the Nixon Doctrine—"To act consistently abroad we must be able to generate coalitions of shared purposes. Regional groupings supported by the U.S. will have to take over major responsibility for their immediate areas, with the U.S. being concerned more with the overall framework of order than with the management of every regional enterprise."

He further bolstered his contention for reduced American international responsibilities by arguing that in this nuclear age the major powers have great difficulty in translating nuclear power into a plausible threat. This was shown most convincingly in Vietnam.

He also warns of appeasement, because he sees it, as he says in A World Restored, "the result of an inability to come to grips with a policy of limited objectives." Thus, Vietnam is to him the result of a policy of "unlimited objectives" and the lesson from that experience will be that "American willingness to become involved in this form of warfare elsewhere is greatly diminished." In contrast to Walt Rostow, who held the same title in the Johnson White House, and who broadly believed in "unlimited objectives," Kissinger is endowed with a profound skepticism for great concepts. Therefore, Kissinger holds that "the major problem is to discipline power so that it bears a rational relationship to the objectives likely to be in dispute."

Kissinger also recommended in his article that "frequent unilateral changes of policy" would undermine allied unity, but this is one of those dicta that later on the Nixon administration violated too often. As a consequence, it lost much of the trust abroad that American administrations had built up over the last twenty-five years. Nixon, of course, saw this not as a transgression of his lieutenant's teachings, but simply as part of the great adjustment that was taking place in the ways Americans were now viewing the world. Powerful shibboleths of the past were beginning to lose their inviolability: the idea that the United States would have to accept nuclear parity instead of superiority, the possibility of resuming relations with Communist China, the devaluation of the dollar, the defusion of Berlin as the potentially explosive symbol of American commitment to the defense of Europe.

Neither Nixon nor Kissinger likes to give up positions of strength, but with superpower diplomacy in its death throes, there was a need for gradually withdrawing from positions that might decline into weakness. They therefore sounded the end of an era that had relied for its stability on rigid military alliances. As Kissinger put it: "Stability has always coincided with an equilibrium that made physical domination difficult."

When Kissinger wrote his essay in *Agenda for the Nation*, he certainly had no inkling that he would be called on to become the man to manage the advent of "political multipolarity" and what he had proclaimed as "a new period of creativity."

It became the task of the Nixon administration to navigate this new period of creativity and negotiate a new adjustment in American thinking about the relationship between power and equilibrium. First of all, the word "parity" imposed itself on almost every aspect of power diplomacy. The rhetoric of John F. Kennedy, who pledged in his inaugural address that the United States would fight anytime, anywhere, any enemy to defend liberty, sounded thrilling when he made the proclamation; now it would sound outdated and strident. Then, a certain altruism that had animated past American thinking was replaced by a strong emphasis on American national interest, by what Barnard Law Collier in a very perceptive profile of Kissinger called "benign selfishness."‡ The still-lingering idealism in American foreign policy was re-

‡ New York *Times Magazine*, November 14, 1971.

placed by a strong dose of *Realpolitik* and a conviction that "self-interest is not necessarily amoral," which is a European rather than American concept, but which proved congenial to Mr. Nixon. Bismarck, as Kissinger had noted, was also unencumbered by moral scruples. "His great strength was knowing how to restrain the contending forces, both domestic and foreign, by manipulating their antagonisms." Asked at a party whether it was true that he, Kissinger, made only foreign and not domestic policy too, he replied to his feminine questioner with an amorous twinkle, "I'm told to make love not war, but I'm trying to please everybody."

Kissinger is credited by many as a brilliant manipulator—both his admirers and detractors confirm it—and occasionally he prides himself on his expertise in this role. "Power is the ultimate aphrodisiac," he began saying when he came to realize the new attraction he exerted on women and took advantage of it. But power is more than an aphrodisiac; it is a temptation to test its effects in exercising it. Kissinger admits that he enjoys the exercise of power, and some have discovered this to their cost when they sought to interfere either with a course or a policy he considered vital or with his own status. What added to the inherent power of his position and his burdens was the weakness of two key Cabinet members, Rogers and Laird. Kissinger's very personal and conspiratorial approach to diplomacy, combined with Nixon's McLuhanesque electronic style, of using television for his dramatic *coup de thèâtre* announcements, provided a sort of surrealist vision of twentieth-century diplomacy. Together they made it work, but it is an unpredictable style and it disturbed political Washington as well as allies and foes. Yet Kissinger succeeded in defying an old Washington dictum that you can have in the capital visibility or influence, but not both. He acquired both, and more of either than any of his predecessors. At Harvard he is remembered as a shy, somewhat arrogant professor. "I was born arrogant," he says, and refers to himself as "an acquired taste." When I asked Kissinger, after his third year in the job, in what way he thought he had changed most, he said in the self-confidence he had gained. This self-confidence led him not only to test his own mettle to the limit, but also to enjoy living dangerously. Washington worships virtuosos, but it also strangles them with attention and blinds them with limelight. If the virtuoso is also powerful he is as much admired as feared, as much lionized as berated. Even his newly acquired humor was viewed with suspicion as well as amusement. Dr. Kraemer and his old Harvard colleagues remember Kissinger as humorless, almost too serious-minded to laugh at anything, least of all himself, and were surprised at the sudden wit and social ease his new-found self-confidence had inspired. To those who liked him it was an enjoyable new trait and a sign that this hard-headed, hard-driving egotist was becoming more human. To those who saw him still as Dr. Strangelove it was nothing but a clever device to put people off the scent of the real tough inner man. Governor Nelson Rockefeller, well acquainted with Kissinger's character, summed it up differently: "Every period has its Humphrey Bogart and the tough guy of our time is Henry Kissinger."

Kissinger has come to enjoy celebrities. Having become one himself, he can meet them on equal terms. He loves the power and fame of which he acquired more than he had ever dreamed, but he still chews his nails. His inner tensions and some of his insecurities persist behind a deceptively casual facade of geniality, self-deprecation, easy humor and aphoristic conversational skill. He felt at ease with Chou En-lai and Brezhnev, more perhaps than with Western political leaders, but he can still feel uncomfortable with people he thinks know him well. He can surprise his friends with his thoughtfulness and sensitivity, but may go further out of his way to keep his enemies disarmed—soothing them he regards as a challenge that he has been surprisingly successful at meeting. He maintains his old loyalty to Governor Nelson Rockefeller, but probably less for the appreciation of the man than for the safe harbor he continues to be to him. He has become more concerned than ever about what others say or print about him and caution is warranted when he says to a friend, "You are one of the few I don't try to manipulate." Publishers have offered him contracts in six figures, and yet he is worried about the future, less for its financial aspects than what kind of job he should seek and what the loss of power may do to him psychologically.

Kissinger's love-hates are the press and his Harvard colleagues, and both reciprocate these feelings. Yet there also exists a great mutual respect. In fact, he became the most appreciated and adroit press briefer in White House history. It is an extremely important role, which normally falls to the Secretary of State, but one which Kissinger also had to assume and in which his experience as a teacher and lecturer greatly aided him. His refusal to use the phrase "no comment" and his ability to illuminate or shrewdly obfuscate a situation aroused admiration as well as exasperation among the press. His habit originally was to make his briefings so-called backgrounders, which meant that he could not be identified except as a White House official; but then, partly under the prodding of Washington *Post* editor Benjamin Bradlee, he was persuaded to give his general briefings on the record and attributable to him, especially since Secretary Rogers rarely faced the press in public. Kissinger's press briefings were also an act of showmanship. He had an uncanny way of relieving the initial air of adversaries facing one another that always exists between the briefer and the reporters. He liked to open with a lighthearted but poignant anecdote, as for instance when he began by saying, "I understand that my job is to communicate with you. This reminds me of the story of a Christian who was thrown into the arena with a lion. He thought he had better start with a prayer before the ordeal. When he did this, he found that the lion was also adopting a rather reverential pose. He said, 'Well, thank God, at least I am communicating with you.' The lion said, 'I don't know about you, but I am saying grace.'" Or, on another occasion, "When I was at Harvard the thing that used to infuriate me most was tired bureaucrats who arrived to tell us that everything had been considered, that they knew so much more than we did, that any differences of opinion were due to gaps in knowledge, and that if we only knew as much as they did, of course, we would all agree with them. I just want to make sure, gentlemen, that you understand that everything has been considered by us. If you knew as much as we did, you would, of course, agree with us, but if you don't we will take it with the attitude that not even the press can be right 100 per cent of the time." Thanks to his gift of patience and his knowledge of the substance of the briefing, he always remained in control, however fierce and searching the questioning. "I am here to explain policy, not to debate it," he told one polemical questioner.

Sometimes correspondents complained, though, that in private briefings he tended to "shade" his interpretations to appeal to the political inclinations of the person he was addressing, whether that person was a Joseph Alsop or an anti-war priest. One must wonder what these reporters expected from a master diplomat who could be equally persuasive with the earthy, bullylike Leonid Brezhnev and the sophisticated mandarin Chou En-lai. Kissinger can fiercely resent what he considers unfair press attacks on him, but not for long. He quotes with glee from a review of one of his own books, "I don't know if Mr. Kissinger is a great writer, but anyone finishing his book is a great reader." He enjoys the company of talented and provocative columnists, whether or not their views are in sympathy with his or the Nixon administration's, though he may feel more comfortable with those whose are.

This ability to communicate became of enormous value to President Nixon, as it was a gift he lacked. Kissinger became the invaluable, and indefatigable and most loyal exponent of the policies he helped formulate and execute. And in the latter role he gained, in addition, greater personal fulfillment than any ever enjoyed by a senior presidential assistant. He had well-developed concepts and was presented with the opportunity, rarely given to an academic, to test them against practice, and he did it with a brilliance that led every head of state to recognize him not only as the President's first minister but also as his super-diplomat and plenipotentiary. He joined the President at the moment when the forces of change, so long suppressed, had begun to assert themselves. The question was how to manage a transition from relatively stable alliances to shifting coalitions in a world destabilized by the revolutionary manifestations of postindustrial society and by the changing military balances; how to effect the retreat or, as Kissinger preferred to call it, the retrenchment of American power in a way that would not weaken U.S. ability to hold her own in the world balance-of-power game.

The President immediately authorized Kissinger to recruit a staff
of the best available experts to service his National Security Council. Under his intellectual leadership, backed by the obvious approval of the President, the "Kissinger Operation" became the
most powerful foreign-policy instrument in presidential history.
Both Mr. Nixon and Kissinger were preoccupied with the power
and strength of the presidency and anxious to create an instrument that could enable them to make quick decisions. Very soon
the NSC became the fountainhead in the making of foreign and
military policies. Kissinger and his NSC staff superimposed themselves over the State Department, Defense Department, the Joint
Chiefs of Staff and the Central Intelligence Agency—to mention
only the most important arms of government—overriding and
cutting into the authority of the heads of those august departments. One result, as was to be expected, was a new set of interdepartmental (and personal) jealousies and antagonisms; but, as
one high official with years of experience in government put it
to me, "I would prefer to see the government without the Kissinger operation, but I can't." For Nixon's approach to decision
making, it was an ideal setup.

Different Presidents, of course, have different working methods.
Truman and Eisenhower chose strong Secretaries of State because
they wanted them to carry the load of decision making. A Dean
Acheson or a John Foster Dulles would not have tolerated a Kissinger in the White House. Kennedy and Nixon, in contrast, chose

to be directly in command of foreign policy; it was their most absorbing interest. Johnson was a special case. He inherited the Kennedy operation in the White House and did not want to change it, unsure, in view of his inexperience in handling foreign affairs, of how to improve it. He too believed in the traditional way of policy making, and reliance on the Secretaries of State and Defense. Gradually, however, his own personality asserted itself because he wanted to have his finger on every button, and his White House advisers, McGeorge Bundy and later Walt Rostow, were increasingly drawn into the policy-making process.

Nixon favored having his policy options laid out before him in writing, carefully, methodically and in great detail. In their presentation he preferred the advocate's approach. Eisenhower insisted on a departmental consensus before the recommendations reached him; Nixon did not want to drown the distinctions between different points of view.

"We try to identify the real issues for presidential decisions instead of burying them in 'agreed language,'" Kissinger told the congressional Subcommittee on National Security and International Operations. And in his report to Congress in February 1970, the President, in pithy and self-confident phrasing, which was obviously that of his National Security Adviser, defined the purposes of his National Security Council system by saying, "We do not want to exhaust ourselves managing crises; our basic goal is to shape the future. Our policy making must be systematic, our actions must be the products of thorough analysis, forward planning and deliberate decision. We must master problems before they master us. . . . I refuse to be confronted with a bureaucratic consensus that leaves me no options but acceptance or rejection, and that gives me no way of knowing what alternatives exist."

Kennedy and Johnson preferred the "inner circle" decision-making process of their Tuesday lunches. Kennedy, in fact, felt quite comfortable in turning over most of the decision making to Rusk and McNamara, leaving only the difficult tasks for himself and the Tuesday group. The regulars at these lunches used to be the Secretaries of Defense and State, plus McGeorge Bundy;

and later, under Johnson, Walt Rostow as well as Richard Helms, the director of the Central Intelligence Agency. One of the participants once told me that if Dean Rusk had only trusted his staff more, he would have been better prepared for these lunches and some mistakes might have been avoided. But he was too afraid that indiscretions might result from his drawing staff members into his confidence. McNamara suffered from a similar prejudice toward the military; he did not trust them as a group, and feared that they would leak decisions if they were given a voice in a so-called control group. He preferred the vertical way, which meant negotiating on issues with Dean Rusk directly, before they went to the President. Perhaps as a result, both Rusk and McNamara usually managed to avoid coming to grips with the real problems.

Again, according to one of the participants, the Kennedy-Johnson lunch groups did not thoroughly appreciate that they could not resolve the big issues over a meal without very careful preparatory studies. The familiar phrase "hand-to-mouth decisions" thus acquired new ironic overtones. The method tended to the assumption that all the options would be contained in their discussions and so—to give two surprising examples—no studies were made whether there existed an alternative to outright military victory in Vietnam or what the alternatives were to escalation in 1965.

MORE TO READ THAN IS HUMANLY POSSIBLE

Nixon rejected this haphazard approach. He wanted everything carefully laid out so that he could weigh the options methodically, carefully and in solitude. Kissinger therefore set out to give a systematic review and analysis of the problems at hand that would permit Mr. Nixon a rational and deliberate choice instead of his having to make tactical decisons under the pressure of events. This method of developing long-range policies, whether for Vietnam, the SALT (Strategic Arms Limitation) talks, the Middle East, China, etc., was slower than the Tuesday lunches—though at times of crisis it was speeded up. It involved more meetings than most of the participants liked to attend, and it meant reading more position papers than is, at times, humanly possible. Yet experience proved that negotiating positions were well prepared and, as a consequence, crisis management, too, was carried out with less nervous wear and tear for the government and for the American public. The idea, however, that the President or Kissinger would be able to avoid exhausting themselves "managing crises" was a forlorn hope, though the Nixon administration was relatively less haunted by crisis than most.

With his native *Gründlichkeit* (thoroughness), Kissinger first assigned an issue to an Interdepartmental Group, chaired by an Assistant Secretary of State. After it had formulated the policy options at hand, they were then examined by an Interagency Review Group of more senior officials presided over by Kissinger himself. Then the paper was readied for presentation to the National Security Council. That, however, was only the simple outline; the policy-proposing process was frequently much more complicated. Various specialist panels would inject into the position papers expertise thought to be necessary for the full understanding of the problems involved. Sometimes, at least to the weary readers, they included more detailed information than was necessary. The Verification Panel checked on all the data forming the basis of the policy decisions; this panel played a key role in the preparation for the SALT negotiations with the Soviet Union. The Vietnam Special Studies Group (VSSG) digested all the information concerning the situation in Vietnam. The Defense Program Review Committee reviewed defense policy and the programs underlying it. And the Washington Special Action Group was formed to deal with any sudden crisis; in between emergencies, it drafted contingency plans for possible crises, all designed to meet Kissinger's Wagnerian dictum of seeking to be masters of events, rather than at their mercy.

The new system gave more opportunities for the interested parties to have their say; it helped to observe due process and improved the quality of research; in the end, the issues looked well defined, if not overdefined, for presidential decision.

PUTTING THE MILITARY TO THE TEST

The old weakness of the NSC system—not enough civilian input—was largely remedied under the new regime. To their great delight, the civilians manning the NSC operation came to match wits with the representatives of the Joint Chiefs of Staff, who were forced into discussing their proposals with people from other departments. The military in turn learned from others what was on the President's mind, what troubled the CIA and others. It made them more aware of the existence of different points of view, for the military always know their own requirements, while usually remaining oblivious to the political and economic factors involved. What has always helped the military—and still did under the Kissinger regime, though less so than in the past—is that military solutions are usually easier to pursue and military decisions easier to make. They reflect strength, virility, prowess, all part of the western frontiersman that survives in almost every American. Opposition to such manliness tends to be interpreted as weakness, mushiness; and it is not easy, even for a Kissinger, to risk acquiring that kind of reputation.

The military had more opportunities to present their case than before, but their influence nevertheless suffered under the Kissinger system because their arguments became open to challenge. Even so, certain positions were obdurately held: For instance, the Air Force, in spite of so much proof to the contrary, refused to acknowledge that the bombing in Vietnam had only marginal utility. All the issues had to be fought out in discussion within committees, instead of between departments confronting each other in bitter argument: this reduced much of the bickering and helped to make people concentrate on the issues instead of on the process.

The power Kissinger acquired by building up his own micro-State Department was of immense help to Mr. Nixon, but it complicated the lives not only of members of the Cabinet, but also of foreign governments and diplomats. Every foreign statesman knew that he could get faster action through Kissinger than through the State Department; the temptation, therefore, to seek a short cut was great and created sometimes intolerable pressures on Kissinger or his aides. To complaints from American and foreign ambassadors that despite the elaborate way of decision making, decisions were often slow in being carried out, one NSC staff member remarked with a not-untypical feeling of superiority, "It's because we have no effective follow-through mechanism. The carrying out of decisions rests with the departments." And when asked how this could be remedied, he replied without hesitation, "Not short of abolishing the departments."

For a long time Kissinger maintained that he was neither a Secretary of State nor a Secretary of Defense, but only a co-ordinator for the President. However, the supremacy given him by a system through which all policy ideas have to be funneled was as undeniable as his intellectual pre-eminence among those around the President.

In the policy councils, he rarely advanced a definite position: He played the role of Socratic questioner and devil's advocate. "I am not arguing a position," he would say, "I'm just asking." Nor did he add his own proposals in writing when he passed position papers to the President. He preferred, when his opinion was specifically sought, to offer it in person in the privacy of the presidential office.

"People often see Kissinger as a Rasputin who is whispering into the President's ear and exercising an evil influence," Marshall Green, the Assistant Secretary for East Asian and Pacific Affairs, said to me in September 1971, "but that is not so. He prepares the options, or when he knows what the President wants he goes forcefully after getting it for him. He questions others, checks on contradictions and weak arguments, but he is not a man who wants to impose his own view, he only wants the President to get the best collective judgment the government can produce." Kissinger himself told me that he would go over the options with the President once the NSC had produced its conclusions, and that the President on these occasions wanted to know all the consequences of each alternative. "It would be rare if among senior people I did not agree with one of the options, since I helped to formulate them."

STUDY MEMO NO. 1: A REMARKABLE DOCUMENT

The cornerstone for the new NSC system was laid at the Hotel Pierre in New York, the temporary abode of the White House staff before the President's inauguration. It was here that Kissinger first wrote a long memo outlining what had been wrong with former National Security Council procedures and how he wanted to reorganize the Council. Then he got a group of experts—among them Daniel Ellsberg, who later rode to fame and notoriety as the source of the Pentagon Papers—to draft preliminary position papers on the alternatives in Vietnam. These are worth examining in some detail for the light they throw on the Kissinger process, as well as on the disparate views held at that time within the civilian and military bureaucracies.

The "Vietnam Policy Alternatives," drafted by two groups of experts representing a variety of viewpoints, offered eight options. They analyzed three possible approaches to negotiating victory; three to negotiating a compromise solution; and two to unilateral actions. These options variously involved military escalation aimed at negotiating a victory; a negotiated mutual withdrawal; a substantial reduction of the American presence while seeking a negotiated solution; the withdrawal of all U.S. forces within two or three years; and the withdrawal of all U.S. forces within twelve months. The advocates of these courses of action held views that were just as various: Some thought that the South Vietnamese Government had a fair chance of overcoming the Vietcong insurgency, others that the United States could accept a Communist take-over of South Vietnam since this was a civil war. A few thought that a direct territorial accommodation between Hanoi and Saigon was possible or that Hanoi might be willing to run the risk of leaving the Vietcong to fight it out with the South Vietnamese forces provided all U.S. forces were withdrawn. Another proposal for a solution was mutual withdrawal by both U.S. and North Vietnamese forces after three years—which might well have been the only one on which the United States and Hanoi could agree. (Some of those who worked on the so-called Pierre Vietnam Paper joined the permanent Kissinger staff, though not Ellsberg; others were either not asked or not interested.)

When the new National Security Council met for the first time on Saturday, January 25, 1969, the NSC staff broke new ground by firing twenty-eight questions to all those involved in Vietnam policy making. The result was NSSM-1 (National Security Study Memorandum No. 1). Everybody soon learned to refer to it as "Nissam-one."

The questionnaire had begun by invoking the President's authority and had landed in all the obvious places: the U. S. Embassy in Saigon, the U. S. Military Command in Vietnam, the Joint Chiefs of Staff, and the desks of Secretaries Rogers and Laird, CIA's Richard Helms and others. For the first time these individual duchies in the Vietnam policy-making process were forced to state their views separately, clearly and specifically. It helped to expose the basic differences that had more or less always existed between them but had never before been laid bare in quite so stark a fashion. The results were quite startling, even though many of the differences were predictable.

There was general agreement, assuming that the then current strategy would be pursued, that:

1. The GVN (South Vietnamese Army) and allied positions in Vietnam had been strengthened lately in many respects;
2. The GVN had improved its political position, but there was still great uncertainty whether it would survive a peaceful competition with the NLF (National Liberation Front) for political power in South Vietnam;
3. The RVNAF (local volunteer forces) alone could not then, or in the foreseeable future, stand up to the current combined forces of the North Vietnamese and the Vietcong forces;
4. The enemy had suffered some reverses, but had not changed his essential objectives. Nor had they (the United States and South Vietnam) sufficiently sapped the enemy's strength to

pursue these objectives. His forces were not suffering the kind of attrition that would help to overtake his ability to recruit or infiltrate replacements;

5. The enemy was not in Paris (for the peace talks) primarily out of weakness.

Basically, the Study Memo revealed two schools of thought within the United States Government. The military command in Vietnam, the commander in chief for the Pacific, the Joint Chiefs of Staff and the American Embassy in Saigon took the more hopeful view of current and future prospects in Vietnam. In contrast, the Office of Research and Analysis of the State Department and the International Security Affairs Office in the Pentagon were on the pessimistic side, assuming that the pacification policy was leading nowhere, that the Saigon Government was as corrupt as ever and that the enemy could turn on the pressure any time he chose to. The Southeast Asia Bureau in the State Department wavered, depending on the issues. The same applied more or less to the Central Intelligence Agency, though the estimators and current intelligence experts were in general more pessimistic than George Carver, special assistant to Richard Helms, director of the agency. Helms, unlike his predecessors Allen Dulles and John McCone, who had come under frequent criticism for playing too activist a role, stayed out of the making of policy. He preferred to stay in the background, playing the advisory role of the perfect civil servant.

In analyzing the enemy there was general agreement that under the then current rules of engagement, the enemy's manpower pool and infiltration capabilities could outlast allied attrition efforts indefinitely, and if Hanoi decided the NVA/VC forces had the capability for a large-scale offensive, it was prepared to bear the heavy casualties that would result. There was also agreement that the main supply channels were through the Laos Panhandle and the Demilitarized Zone, while the military, though not CIA, thought that Sihanoukville too was an important supply channel. (The decision taken later on to make the controversial "incursions" into Cambodia showed that the military view prevailed.)

As regards the South Vietnamese armed forces, there was general agreement that while the RVNAF was getting larger, better equipped and somewhat more effective, *it could not then, or in the foreseeable future,* handle both the VC and sizable NVA forces *without U.S. combat support.* Again, the military estimates were more optimistic than the civilian. The most pessimistic was the Office of the Secretary of Defense (OSD), which wrote that "it is unlikely that the RVNAF, as presently organized and led, will ever constitute an effective political or military counter to the Vietcong." (It was, in fact, Secretary of Defense Melvin Laird who pressed hard, if not hardest, for the United States to get out of Vietnam as soon as possible. He was first to suggest that one U.S. division be withdrawn by mid-1969, saying that President Thieu had responded favorably to the idea.)

Some of the most divergent views came to light about the progress of the pacification program. The authorities in Saigon saw the security of the countryside as better than it had ever been, while the OSD, CIA and the State Department were more pessimistic. The OSD estimated that at least 50 per cent of the total rural population was subject to significant VC presence and influence. The differences of view were sharp, and they divided the policy makers from the analysts, and both of them from the intelligence community. The implication of these divergencies could hardly have been more significant. To accept that the GVN had a high probability of success would lead to one policy, while a radically different one would be needed if it was accepted that the GVN had failed in the countryside.

As to the political situation, the conclusions were equally contradictory. The prospects for a continued non-Communist government in South Vietnam were regarded as impossible to predict, or chancy at best. No agency forecast "victory" over the Communists and all acknowledged the manifold problems facing the GVN as the United States withdrew. The CIA concluded that progress in South Vietnam had been sufficiently slow and fragile to mean that substantial disengagement in the next few years could jeopardize all recent gains.

Interestingly enough, in assessing the impact on South Asia the National Intelligence estimates, which are based on a combined analysis of all military and civilian intelligence sources, tended to downgrade the once popular "domino" theory. They allowed that a settlement which would permit the Communists to take control of the government in South Vietnam, not immediately but within a year or two, would be likely to make the dominoes of Cambodia and Laos fall into Hanoi's orbit at a fairly early stage, but that the process would not necessarily continue through the rest of Asia. The Army, Navy and Air Force intelligence and the Southeast Asian Bureau of the State Department dissented. They concluded that an unfavorable settlement would stimulate the Communists into becoming more active elsewhere and that it would be difficult to resist making some accommodation to the pressures this would generate.

NSSM-1 is a remarkable document. Most agencies replied with considerable frankness, and virtually all reflected the agonizing dilemmas and uncertainties they all faced in Vietnam, and the very limited odds given the South Vietnamese to remain under non-Communist rule unless "given sufficient" U.S. support. One thing at least on which they all did agree, in effect, was that if the United States withdrew, the South Vietnamese Government's chances of survival were virtually non-existent. Those on the spot (in every way) in Vietnam were trying to justify their past recommendations; the military, who had to be "can do" people, refused to admit that South Vietnam could not be held as long as the United States stayed in the fighting, and the civilians, more or less frankly, hinted at the hopelessness of the U.S. undertaking. And so this unprecedented document provided the policy makers with an extraordinarily illuminating picture of the shading of opinion within the government—a road map to the views held within the bureaucracy.

The NSDM (National Security Decision Memorandum) that finally emerged from these studies and from the intense discussions did not differ too much in substance from the Hotel Pierre paper, except that the alternatives were made pithier and more concise, and the option for "immediate and total withdrawal" was not included. The political options fell between:

(a) U.S. forces staying until victory.
(b) Mutual withdrawal without political accommodation, with both the United States and the North Vietnamese forces withdrawing from Vietnam on the basis of a sort of tacit understanding or agreement.
(c) Political accommodation, including mutual troop withdrawal, in a manner acceptable to both sides which would lead to the end of the military conflict. The negotiations would be between the United States and Hanoi, or Saigon and Hanoi, or Saigon and the Vietcong, with the possible assistance of an international force in the preparation of elections or in the creation of a coalition government.
(d) Terminating the war through a cease-fire, tacit or explicit, based on a limited territorial accommodation dividing South Vietnam into several large Vietcong and GVN (South Vietnamese) regions. Under this scheme American forces could be reduced and gradually withdrawn altogether as the threat from the NVA (North Vietnamese forces) declined.

Scheme "d" had become known as the "Leopard Solution," but it had few advocates. It would have left each side in control where it was at the time and given Vietnam, territorially, the pattern of a leopard skin. Its originator was Cyrus Vance, deputy to Ambassador Averell Harriman at the Paris peace talks. Three years later, in September 1971, Vance, by then back in private life, told me that he regretted that the United States had not offered this solution at the time President Johnson offered the bombing halt, because he thought the North Vietnamese would have accepted it then. Harriman, however, when I sought his views, did not agree.

In the NSC discussions, the view of the military that the NVA could be destroyed or driven out within one or two years was rejected because such a prolongation of the conflict was unacceptable to the American public. Mutual withdrawal without a political accommodation (the second option), it was agreed, could lead to an eventual victory by the Vietcong; and should that happen, the United States could argue that it was the result primarily of an indigenous conflict. This was rejected by the President who, rather than prepare excuses, still hoped to preserve the independence of South Vietnam.

In terms of military strategy, the alternatives were reduced by the NSC to a choice between (1) continuing the pressures on Hanoi by applying the current strategy, including threats of escalation or actual escalation; and (2) reducing the American presence in South Vietnam, with the South Vietnamese troops (ARVN) assuming an increasing responsibility, as another way of forcing Hanoi's hand at the negotiating table.

The fate of NSSM-1 is proof that policies are often determined on the basis of the convictions held by the President and not on the advice of the experts. When these estimates differ, then, of course, there is an added temptation—even if on balance the estimates tilt in the other direction—for the President to follow his own political convictions. This was particularly true in Mr. Nixon's case when he decided on his policy for Vietnam. He made his decision well before NSSM-1 was completed, which was only in March 1969, but did not tell his associates—except Kissinger —until a few weeks later; Secretary Laird, for instance, only learned of it before he departed on his first visit to Saigon that spring.

As the President saw it from the very start, his basic choice was between disengaging abruptly within the first six months or following the kind of policy he actually adopted. A quick withdrawal would have been tantamount to admitting defeat, and there was certainly a group in Congress and in the country at large that would not have been sorry to see the United States give up and accept defeat. To Mr. Nixon, however, such a policy looked a far more dangerous political and moral risk than a gradual withdrawal combined with a patient search for a negotiated settlement; the latter was much more in harmony with his own background and his own outlook on the Vietnam problem.

Had the situation on the ground been sharply deteriorating when he came to power he would have had to take a quick decision whether to give up or react harshly. Most likely he would have done the latter, in conformity with his deeply ingrained belief that a credible threat helps negotiations. However, with the military situation relatively stable, he was not under immediate pressure to act and had time to develop his combined strategy. To this he added a strong emphasis on making Vietnamization a reality as a warning to Hanoi that unless it agreed to a negotiated settlement, it might find itself confronted by a regime in Saigon strong enough to hold its own. He could leave, for the present, the decision whether to aim for total withdrawal or for leaving behind a residual force, as remained in South Korea, in case the peace negotiations failed. But the assumption was that if the United States had no other choice but total unilateral withdrawal without a political settlement, a long interval thereafter would make it impossible to escape the blame for the disintegration of South Vietnam. Only then could the United States claim that the disintegration was due to indigenous forces. Such were the ingredients of the Nixon-Kissinger strategy for dealing with the Vietnam war.

In the meantime, however, the President was not prepared to accept such a pessimistic interpretation of the situation. Rather than prepare excuses, he hoped to preserve the independence of South Vietnam.

ENDING THE WAR HONORABLY

Kissinger himself opposed the war on the basis that it was an overcommitment that destroyed American credibility. But it was also his view that the withdrawal of American forces had to be adjusted to the ability of the South Vietnamese to assume responsibility for their own defense, and he assumed that a residual U.S. force would remain as long as necessary.

Kissinger laid out his own ideas on ending the war in an article in *Foreign Affairs* called "The Vietnamese Negotiations" (January 1969), which to some extent reflected proposals sent to Ambassador Ellsworth Bunker in Saigon by the then Under Secretary of State Nicholas deB. Katzenbach, to which Kissinger had had access. No doubt one of the reasons why Kissinger and President Nixon hit it off well was that they essentially saw eye to eye on the strategy that was to govern the Vietnam policy. The principle that "ending the war honorably is essential for the peace of the world," as Kissinger then wrote, was also one that guided Nixon's thinking. Kissinger also recommended that "the withdrawal (of U.S. forces) should be over a sufficiently long period so that a genuine indigenous political process has a chance to become established; the definition of what constitutes a suitable political process or structure should be left to the South Vietnamese with the schedule for mutual withdrawal creating the time-frame for an agreement." Where Kissinger overrated the strength of the U.S. position was in arguing that "since it [Hanoi] cannot force our withdrawal, it must negotiate about it." He saw that Hanoi relied on American domestic pressures to accelerate the American withdrawal, but he did not take into account that the President had to commit himself and adhere to a phased *unilateral* withdrawal, which was bound to weaken his negotiating position.

The Nixon administration had assumed that Hanoi would come to realize that time was not on its side, because the longer it waited for a settlement the better the prospects became for the South Vietnamese to take responsibility for their own future, and the weaker therefore Hanoi's negotiating position. "The war will be settled when Hanoi becomes convinced that the American terms are fair to them as well as to us . . . in other words, that they can live with them," Kissinger said in October 1970. But the North Vietnamese were the toughest Communists left, and were not interested in a deal that would be "fair" to the Americans. What mattered to them was to gain control over the political process in Saigon even before it was set in motion. They did not want to take any chances. One of the very few concessions they were willing to make to Mr. Nixon's sensibilities was to offer, as they did during the secret negotiations with Kissinger, a hidden deal for removing President Thieu. It was rejected outright. Hanoi's stubbornness thus thwarted the U.S. hopes from unilateral withdrawals and succeeded in weakening the U.S. negotiating position.

The Kissinger article, though a shrewd analysis, did not avoid the mistake that had led to many earlier miscalculations, namely, to underestimate the staying power of the North Vietnamese and their pig-headed determination to unify Vietnam. However, it did uncannily foreshadow the strategy the Nixon administration followed.

President Nixon's speech in May 1969 was the first time that the United States put forward a serious peace offer. President Johnson never did; his policy was simply based on the idea that if the North Vietnamese left South Vietnam, the United States would withdraw. President Nixon emphasized that he did not seek military victory, and offered an eight-point plan that included provisions for mutual withdrawal of the "major portions" of U.S., Allied and North Vietnamese troops from South Vietnam and for internationally supervised elections to ensure "each significant group in South Vietnam a real opportunity to participate in the political life of the nation."

The Russians had been carefully briefed about the aims of this new American policy because Nixon was convinced that Moscow's intervention in Hanoi could lead to a settlement of the war. But he overrated Moscow's bargaining position, at least to the extent that he blamed the Russians for the failure of his first peace overture. He was shrewd enough, though, to follow up his speech with the announcement on June 8 that twenty-five thousand combat troops were to be withdrawn, and in August with the news that another twenty-five thousand would return home by the end of the year. These moves had the double aim of a token gesture to placate American public opinion and an attempt to gain time to strengthen the South Vietnamese military forces. The hope was that with its military capabilities strengthened, the Thieu Government could also be broadened politically and that this would improve the prospects for reaching an accommodation with the National Liberation Front. There was no talk at that time of total

U.S. withdrawal; it was simply a matter of reducing the number of U.S. troops, but with a substantial residual force staying on.

There is evidence that Kissinger would have preferred a faster withdrawal of American troops than was adopted, but neither the President nor the Joint Chiefs of Staff were willing to accept the risks this involved. He relied on the assumption that nevertheless the continued withdrawals in themselves would force a change in the military strategy and sooner or later the JCS would have to accept that. He also believed that an interval of about two or three years was necessary to shield the United States from events which could occur between the departure of the American troops and the collapse of the South Vietnamese regime. "What defense would there be against the accusations of the moms of all the soldiers who lost their lives?" Kissinger maintained.

But he disputed, as did Morton Halperin, who was Deputy Assistant Secretary for International Affairs in the Pentagon in the Johnson days, Averell Harriman's contention that the prospects for negotiated peace in Vietnam "were never more favorable than when President Nixon took office." Both insist that there was no concrete evidence to support this view unless Harriman meant a settlement that would have simply meant handing over South Vietnam to Hanoi. "It would have been bad for the record," Kissinger argued, "to have first overthrown Diem and then Thieu." Simply handing over South Vietnam to the Communists, he believed, would have caused a bad psychological letdown among Americans.

When it was suggested to him privately that the President should build a bipartisan coalition with the Democratic Establishment which would mean getting the support of important individuals in Congress, in the Democratic Party and in the universities, he replied that he did not think that such an agreement could be negotiated, especially in an election year.

Nixon knew that he had no option but to withdraw and that while he did so it was becoming "his" war. Yet he had changed American policy in a way that went well beyond the Peace Platform adopted by the Democratic Party Convention in Chicago a year earlier.

Thanks to Kissinger's dynamic leadership, the new NSC quickly came to provide all the basic material for decision making in the Nixon administration's foreign policy. It led to a greater conceptual coherence and to a more orderly process of policy making.

The NSC laid the groundwork for the new China policy, for the crucial arms control negotiations, for new approaches to European security; it studied in depth the situations in the Middle East, East-West relations and the problems with Japan. It reassessed the U.S. military posture, NATO policy, foreign aid, international monetary policy and the U.S. attitude toward Nigeria and Chile while it developed contingency plans for a variety of emergencies. In the first one hundred days Kissinger almost overloaded the government machinery by requesting fifty-five study memoranda, which came to be called "term papers," and by examining them rigorously and returning them if they failed to live up to his expectations. He set new and higher standards for the bureaucracy.

The complaints grew about an unnecessary surfeit of study memoranda, about too many contrived options in option papers, but few would deny the fact that Kissinger's NSC was superior to its predecessors. It tended to emasculate Cabinet ministers who lacked fortitude or expertise, but somehow the processes of reaching agreed policy recommendations were smoother and the product of higher quality.

THE ARCHITECT AND THE CONTRACTOR

The President gave Kissinger a great deal of latitude in running the National Security Council operation and in the execution of his foreign policy. He also left a wide range of decisions to him that other Presidents would have reserved to themselves. But it would be wrong to assume that he did not remain in charge. The extent to which he retained command remained a mystery even to those who had an opportunity to see the two together at various formal meetings.

What nobody knew was what went on between these two secretive men when they saw each other in private (and they did see each other at least once a day and talked frequently on the telephone), or what they had said to each other before they entered together to attend, say, a National Security Council meeting. Had Kissinger made up the President's mind or had the President made up his own? That was the question those listening to the two wondered. Even if they saw eye to eye on many decisions, what happened when they did not? Neither the President nor Kissinger offered any clues in front of others.

One high official who has attended many meetings with both present believes that the working relationship between them is comparable to one between an architect and a contractor. The decisions about the basic design were the President's, but Kissinger had great freedom on how to build the house. The President, for instance, decided that he wanted a solution to the Vietnam war which would ensure that the outcome would not lead to handing over South Vietnam to the Communists, and then Kissinger constructed the necessary strategy. The President decided he wanted to open relations with China, and Kissinger designed the road map to Peking and traveled there first to remove all possible hazards on the way. The President decided he wanted a summit meeting in Moscow, and Kissinger prepared various solid bridges so that the President would get there and score a success.

There is apparently never any doubt in the presence of the President who is in charge—in fact, the President's style in dealing with his entourage does not allow anyone to forget it. He may call Kissinger "Henry" or Haldeman, his personal aide, "Bob," but it is more a gesture than an expression of intimacy. He gives the orders always in a presidential, cool, no-nonsense tone. He makes it absolutely clear who is in command when important issues are up for decision. However, it was not the habit of the President to determine a policy in NSC meetings, though at times it was obvious in which direction his mind was running. He would commune with himself or have a last consultation with Kissinger alone before taking final decisions. He passed through a tough school in his quest for the presidency. He was Vice President to President Eisenhower, who never invited him to his private quarters; he was defeated by President Kennedy, and by Governor Edmund G. Brown for the governorship of California; and he had a lot of time in the wilderness to contemplate the world around him and the world at large.

His relationship with Kissinger found its basis not so much in personal congeniality as in a shared view of the world. Both are realists, without illusions about the basic ideological conflicts; both believe that "no national leader has the right to mortgage the survival of his people to the good will of another state," as Kissinger told congressional leaders in June 1972; they see the balance-of-power struggle in the world with almost identical eyes. They also agreed that they came to office at a time when the great powers, by fortuitous but also compelling circumstances, reached the independent conclusion that the time had come to lower tension.

CHAPTER FOUR—A NEW PERSPECTIVE

ON EUROPE

President Nixon's journey to Europe only a month after his inauguration pleased the Europeans. It seemed an indication that he was going to attach the same importance to relations with them as his predecessors had done ever since Roosevelt. What they did not grasp immediately was that behind the acceptable new shadings of his policy he was, in fact, contemplating a major adjustment in U.S.-European relations.

The hurried planning of the trip also signaled, in Washington, another major adjustment—the downgrading of the State Department as a policy maker. Asked to produce position papers for the trip, it delivered vast quantities of them, all defending the policies of the past, especially on how to fight the almost theological battle about the need for European economic integration and NATO's highest goal, military integration. But the new President was not in the market for either of these and became still more inclined to the view he already held, that in future, for this kind of briefing, he would rely on Dr. Kissinger and his NSC operation to prepare the position papers. His immediate actions indeed amounted to a vote of no confidence in the State Department, at least on these two issues of European integration.

By the time he departed on February 23, the American position had been decisively modified in the White House. Nixon determined that there was little he could do about European integration, even if he wanted to, and that he could more rewardingly concentrate on fighting the fires in Vietnam, on the Middle East, and on negotiations with the Soviet Union. For it was on what happened there that the success of his foreign policy would ultimately depend. As far as Europe was concerned he could afford to be less ambitious than either of his two immediate predecessors. He would not go to promote new policy agreements or consolidate old ones, but to make clear that he favored the Europeans working out their own form of co-operation with one another and with the United States. As the Europeans found their own identity a new special relationship with the United States would develop, based on a consensus of independent policies instead of deference to American ones. Specifically, he was eager to create smoother relations with France, an aim that would be assisted by his view that French failure to integrate with NATO was not the end of the world. This new perspective on partnership, he believed, would have much appeal to the Europeans, who had become impatient with Americans schoolmastering them, even though they retained the habit of American leadership, like pupils not yet quite ready to face leaving school. It would also appeal to Americans in their growing fatigue with global responsibilities and their rising resentment of the self-centeredness of the allies.

Moreover, the journey itself had, as he correctly calculated, an inbuilt double advantage: It made Americans feel that he was a respected President abroad, and it gratified the Europeans' desire to look him over at a close range. Instead of Tricky Dick they found a candidly spoken but sympathetic listener; instead of a hawk, an advocate of *détente* policies. They were impressed by his command of issues, his modesty, his courtesy and his capacity to put himself into the shoes of others. They were a little uneasy about the consistency of his flattery to each in turn of the countries he visited; some observers thought him too fulsome by half. There were slight misgivings, too, about the questions he was asked that he left unanswered. But, essentially, he inspired confidence. Europeans were relieved that he was neither a bully nor a weakling, and to see him strengthened at home and abroad was as much in their interest as his. It was particularly in their interest to make the Russians understand that he was a man of leadership quality, a man to respect, to take seriously. So they were relieved that they could comfortably co-operate in his build-up; his performance, indeed, exceeded all expectations.

NIXON'S LAST MEETING WITH IKE

American Presidents do not normally need an introduction to anyone, but shortly before leaving for Europe Mr. Nixon visited former President Eisenhower at Walter Reed Hospital. He asked him for advice, but also to write a letter on his behalf to General de Gaulle. Eisenhower was ailing—he had a pacer attached to his heart—but in his quietly deferential and unassertive way was anxious to help his former Vice President. He was modest in offering advice, yet impressively alert as he dipped into his recollections and the lessons he drew from his experiences. His memory was surprisingly fresh and lively, and his advice thoughtful and measured. Reinforcing the views of Mr. Nixon and Dr. Kissinger, who accompanied the President on what turned out to be his last meeting with Eisenhower before his death, he spoke at length about a President's need to run the machinery of government from the White House, so as to prevent departments from forming coalitions that might force him into a position where he would have to overrule one or more Cabinet members.

Only once did he become vehement, when he counseled Nixon to reject the new British Ambassador John Freeman, an ex-Labour Party politician, former British High Commissioner in India, and one-time editor of the *New Statesman and Nation*, the London political weekly paper. Eisenhower said he well remembered the scurrilous anti-American views this "sheet" purveyed even during World War II (when, truth to tell, Kingsley Martin, not Freeman, had been editor). The appointment of Freeman, who once wrote about Nixon that he was "a man of no principle whatsoever," was an insult, Ike declared. Nixon ought to make clear to Harold Wilson, then Britain's Prime Minister, he went on as his anger welled up, that Freeman would not be welcome in Washington.

Nixon, however, was used to dealing with people who had insulted him and decided to accept Freeman with good grace.

Later, in London, he even managed to turn the situation grace-fully to his advantage, when he welcomed the Ambassador-desig-nate with a conciliatory gesture during dinner at the Prime Minis-ter's residence at 10 Downing Street. It caught everybody by surprise. Bill Safire, the President's speechwriter, always quick with a timely witticism, earlier in the day had thought up the line to save Freeman's and the British Government's face. He suggested to the President that he should jokingly and casually mention to Freeman that he (Freeman) had become the "new diplomat" and Nixon the "new statesman." Nixon did not throw this graceful life line to Freeman lightheartedly, as had been suggested, but rather solemnly. Still, it cleared the air, and no one was more relieved, of course, than Freeman, who earlier had offered his withdrawal from the appointment. Freeman became one of the most successful British ambassadors, even though none of his predecessors had arrived with his kind of handicap.

A BOUT OF MUTUAL LOVE-MAKING

The Nixon visit to Europe included stops in Brussels, London, Paris, Bonn, Berlin and Rome and became something of a com-petitive act of mutual love-making. The President was wooed by everybody with rare intensity and he, in turn, was anxious to please all. He flattered Wilson by referring to the "special re-lationship" with Britain, which delighted the British, even though they pretended to be embarrassed by this remark. The Prime Minister cautioned the President not to press the British case for entry with De Gaulle—which Mr. Nixon did not intend to do anyway—but Nixon reassured him that British membership would be to the benefit of U.S. interests. In Paris, Mr. Nixon addressed De Gaulle with something close to deference. He had long admired the general with almost a schoolboyish awe, and therefore to confront him as an equal was a great moment in the new President's life. He obviously felt more than physically dwarfed by the towering Frenchman, who was well briefed in the op-portunity offered him by the encounter with Nixon and showed himself at his most affable and reasonable.

I remember De Gaulle, on arrival at the airport, welcoming Nixon with a few well-chosen sentences spoken without notes. Nixon, who does not like to be outclassed, even by a De Gaulle, promptly kept his prepared speech in his pocket and instead bravely ad-libbed as well. The result was a summary of his prepared speech, and the omissions gave the press an opportunity to harp on the differences between the prepared text they had been given earlier and what the President actually said.

When Bill Safire, at a reception, complimented De Gaulle on his extemporaneous remarks, he replied confidingly, "I first write my speeches out on paper and then I memorize them. Churchill used to do the same, but he never admitted it." Then he seemed to put Nixon in a slightly different category. "Your President remembers what he meant to say"

Nixon in his talks at the various capitals stressed that, unlike his predecessor, he intended to keep his allies well informed. For instance, there would be no secret agreements like the Nuclear Non-proliferation Treaty under Johnson without consultation. He also laid before them his broad plans for the withdrawal of American troops from Vietnam, based on Vietnamization and the pursuit of a negotiated settlement. He also explained his desire for changing American policy toward Communist China, and, in Paris, stated his intention of giving De Gaulle an opportunity to send word via the French Ambassador in Peking. (He did so, but the Chinese declined to believe it, and the Ambassador suffered a year-long loss of face until the White House made its own direct approach.)

In Berlin, Mr. Nixon came close to behaving like Kennedy, who made the emotional declaration of U.S. solidarity with the defense of the beleaguered city, "*Ich bin ein Berliner!*" But Nixon also, in a speech to factory workers, signaled to the Russians his readiness to search for a Berlin settlement when he said that the question was no longer the city's defense, but "how best to clear the way for a peaceful solution to the problem of a divided Germany." It was his direct intervention with Brezhnev that finally clinched the agreement in 1971. To be able to accomplish this, though, he had to make certain that NATO offered the kind of solid basis from which he could deal with the Russians.

CHALLENGING THE NATO ASSUMPTIONS

It almost sounded like "negotiation from strength," a John Foster Dulles slogan that had gone out of fashion, but Nixon himself disposed of this notion during his first press conference in Washington after his return. "When we talk about superiority," he said, contradicting the position he had taken during the election campaign, "that may have a detrimental effect on the other side . . . giving great impetus to its own arms race." Then he committed himself for the first time to the word "parity," which he later corrected to "sufficiency," as the new standard for the relationship between American and Soviet strategic power.

Sufficiency, which sounded less provocative than parity, had been underlying the Kissinger view of the world, and because of it he had been arguing that the reality of alliances was undergoing a change. "In the past a nation would come to the assistance of another," he wrote before he joined Mr. Nixon, "because defeat of the ally was either considered a prelude to its own defeat or involved a relative decline in its world position. The consequences of resistance seemed preferable to the risks of inaction." But, he went on to argue, with modern weapons it was not self-evident that the ultimate consequences of passivity would be worse than the immediate results of conflict. "If allied strategic doctrines relied on the threat of general nuclear war, the outbreak of a war involved risks which in the past were associated with total defeat. . . . One remedial suggestion has been to place greater reliance on the process of consultation. No doubt, we can and should improve formal consultative processes. But it is well to remember that even within our own government, consultation does not guarantee an identity of views."

This arrangement, which articulated the great dilemma among superpowers, was in the best tradition of the intellectual who sees his task in challenging deeply held assumptions, but neither Mr. Nixon nor the European NATO partners were as yet willing to admit it. It explains at least the theoretical willingness of Dr. Kissinger to support a Franco-British nuclear deterrent; it explains further Mr. Nixon's tolerance toward De Gaulle's independent-mindedness. But for the time being, Mr. Nixon did not mean to air theories about American support of NATO which would have a destabilizing effect. He had come only to reassure Europeans of the solidity of his commitment to NATO, which he considered the cornerstone of his military security policy. His flirtation with De Gaulle was not meant to imply that he accepted his ideas such as replacing the Common Market by a larger, more loosely organized European organization to which Britain could be admitted as an "associate," provided it renounced its "special relationship" with the United States. That was the proposal which De Gaulle offered Christopher Soames, the British Ambassador to France, as a basis for discussions with the British and which Harold Wilson ironically rejected as a possible trap designed to embarrass Britain's application for entry into the Common Market. Wilson, to prove the sincerity of his intentions toward union with Europe, told the Germans about it, which left many wondering whether Wilson or De Gaulle was the more perfidious. In view of Harold Wilson's *volte-face* toward the Common Market after his defeat by Edward Heath, he seemed to have won the race for the more perfidious in the posthumous finals.

Throughout his European journey, Nixon relied for expert advice on Kissinger; it was he who was always at the President's elbow, not Secretary of State Rogers. It alerted the diplomatic world to the importance of Kissinger, who quickly became the man to see and to know. He also became one of the greatest headaches for the world's diplomats and statesmen. The measure of ambassadorial success became the measure of access to Kissinger, because access to him, which was difficult, was the surest and quickest way to getting an authoritative answer or a quick presidential decision.

KISSINGER'S INTELLECTUAL ROOTS

Kissinger's intellectual orientation was Continental European, but it was the French he admired, not the British or the Germans.

He gave the British statesman Viscount Castlereagh (1769–1822) credit, in A *World Restored*, for introducing something entirely new in diplomatic relations of the major world powers, a vision of a European government; nevertheless, he faulted him and the British, generally, for their limited and selfish interest in European affairs. The conception of a Europe organized by anything other than a common danger, Kissinger wrote, "was simply beyond the scope of British mentality." The British, he felt, were willing to enter the European power struggle only when British interests were threatened. His sympathies were with the Continental powers, whose policy was "precautionary, their crucial battle was the first, not the last; their effort was to prevent an overriding danger from materializing." Continental statesmen tended to be natural activists and interventionists, and outstanding among them was Austria's Metternich, who from a weak political and military base was able to direct the peace-making process in Europe through clever deals, devious offers, threats and, above all, a shrewd assessment of the shifting power balances.

It is important to study Kissinger's intellectual roots and his philosophical commitment to the Continental approach, because it helps one to understand his policy concepts. It also explains why there is no British statesman in his pantheon. Those he has placed on pedestals are Metternich, Bismarck, Adenauer (West Germany's postwar chancellor) and De Gaulle. Churchill, although Kissinger admired his ability to rally the British nation during the war, is to him too much of a man who relied on intuition rather than intellect: He was not a chess player. Nor was Kissinger impressed by the over-all judgment shown in British policy since World War II. De Gaulle and Adenauer, on the other hand, were men who carefully calculated their actions, even if they did not create that impression. What he admired most in both, as in Bismarck, were their steely nerves and the all-inspiring way in which they embodied the state; in Washington, of course, where autocrats are viewed with great suspicion, this was a totally alien outlook. And so is the Metternich approach to diplomacy; it was, at least, in the postwar era when the fundamental principle was reliance on alliances. His guiding idea, as Kissinger has stressed, was that "the consciousness of having a greater range of choices than any possible opponent was a better protection than an alliance, because it kept open all options for the hour of need." The key to success in diplomacy, Metternich believed and Kissinger concluded, was "freedom of action, not formal relationships" between nations. The extent to which Kissinger might apply this principle to American policies quickly became a matter for general speculation, and increasingly a concern within the Western alliance.

Kissinger's admiration for De Gaulle was linked to the General's basic belief that the best way to control the Germans was to anchor them to France. The destruction of the Weimar Republic and its catastrophic consequences will always remain a nightmare to Kissinger, and he will never free himself of his distrust of the German capacity to maintain political stability and of the fear that in one form or another it could happen again. He admired Adenauer and De Gaulle not only because they were strong men who believed in stability above all else, but because they too shared the same doubt, and this was what had brought them together. And if Kissinger strongly counseled the maintenance of American military forces in Europe, it was not only for strategic reasons, but also because this looked like the best way of keeping a controlling hand over the Germans, rather than relying on them as autonomous actors in Europe.

When Kissinger, during the Nixon visit to Paris, suggested to De Gaulle that one of the advantages of Britain's membership in the European Community would be to make the control of Germany easier, the General replied abruptly, "We don't need Britain. We have controlled Germany in the past by war." The answer showed how much his aversion to Britain's entry into Europe distorted his judgment, even his common sense. A few weeks later, when Mr. Nixon and De Gaulle met again in Washington after former President Eisenhower's funeral and Mr. Nixon inquired into the prospects of Franco-German relations, the General replied in a similar if more poetic vein: "The Germans and the French have endured much together. We trudged through the desert in the scorched sun, we entered into forests surrounded by wild beasts, we crossed difficult streams together. Sometimes we opposed each other, but we were always looking for a mystical treasure. We discovered that instead of the treasure there was co-operation that would grow into friendship."

SHIFTING EMPHASIS FROM FRANCE TO BRITAIN

Kissinger, though he still held the French leader in high esteem, nevertheless had come sadly to the conclusion that while the General had been extraordinarily astute in spotting everybody else's weaknesses and turning them cleverly to his advantage, he had failed to offer anything constructive in their place. With France getting weaker and the Federal Republic getting stronger, with Franco-German relations increasingly at loggerheads, and with De Gaulle still barring Britain's entry into Europe, it became increasingly obvious that the General's policy concepts were unlikely either to survive his demise or to prove in retrospect to have been a constructive force in Europe. Consequently, Mr. Nixon and Kissinger put more emphasis on Europe. Harold Wilson was correct when he wrote in his account of his premiership, 1964–70, that Mr. Nixon had "the highest regard for the British tradition in world affairs, especially the judgment and experience of so many of our public servants." Kissinger's respect for the latter rose in dealing with them. I once heard him say that the IQ of French officials was higher than that of the British, but they got lost in trivia. The British officials, he thought, had a more open mind, especially as far as relations with the United States were concerned, and had a better grasp of the essentials.

A few months later, De Gaulle was voted out of office. To such firm believers in De Gaulle as Mr. Nixon and Dr. Kissinger, this shook their confidence in France's future stability. The French populace obviously thought differently. It trusted the future of France more than it trusted De Gaulle, even though there were enough precedents to show that the judgment of the French public was not a reliable oracle. With De Gaulle gone, Mr. Nixon and Dr. Kissinger attached greater importance to Britain's entry into Europe. They thought that her influence and administrative ability could redress the balance to ensure that the Western alliance remained solid and Germany firmly tied to it.

To many Europeans Mr. Nixon looked like a Babbitt, especially from the neck down. From the neck up he held his own, whether in Downing Street, at the Elysée, the Schloss Schaumburg or the Quirinale. He was no superman, but neither did he have horns. His decision to pursue a more passive foreign policy toward Europe suited the Europeans and it suited Americans, too, better than the grand old Kennedy idea of a "partnership of equals."

President Kennedy had developed the concept of a partnership of equals between the United States and Western Europe in his Independence Hall speech in Philadelphia on July 4, 1962. It was in the best tradition of romantic American leadership, but also in the old tradition of American oversimplification. It stirred Americans more than Europeans, who tended to take a more realistic and, therefore, a more pessimistic view of the prospects of developing the unity and the political will Kennedy's vision demanded. De Gaulle and the new nationalism that he was trying to inject into European relations loomed too large for most people to think of the Kennedy proposals as more than a faraway vision.

Now, anyway, it had lost its luster and, more importantly, its conviction, because the Europeans did not know what they really wanted. It was unclear what sort of a community they envisaged and what its internal and external policies were going to be.

SETTING THE SEAL TO TWO GERMANYS

The Nixon administration continued to believe that there were strategic advantages in European unification. Their doubts about the political ones surfaced only gradually. There was at first an uneasy reserve toward Chancellor Brandt's *Ostpolitik*, partly due to a distrust of the German socialist leader on the part of the conservatives in the White House, and partly due to a fear that it could be the beginning of the "Finlandization" of Germany which, many American experts believed, was the real goal of the

Russians in encouraging Brandt's overtures. But whether they liked it or not, the drive for a *détente* in Europe became inevitable once the Kremlin began vigorously to pursue such a policy. The four-power agreement in Berlin was something everybody had thought desirable for many years, and so was the rapprochement between the Federal Republic of Germany and the Soviet Union. However strong his earlier reservations, Kissinger was well aware that the new link between Bonn and Moscow was not the result of a weak-kneed Chancellor Brandt but that it was a historical inevitability. He remembered vividly that Chancellor Adenauer, who had been called "the Iron Chancellor" because of his un-yielding outlook toward communism, had once said to him, "Khrushchev and I have been waiting for each other, but the timing wasn't right."

Once the West Germans had signed their treaty with the Russians, the conviction grew that at least for the foreseeable future the Russian aim was not Finlandization but to establish an internationally recognized border between the two Germanys; in other words, to ensure their long-term division. By then the United States was also willing to admit this was preferable.

The pragmatism of U.S. policy toward Western Europe, which allowed for dealings on either a bilateral or a unified basis, created uncertainties that began to undermine the spirit of the Atlantic Alliance. Close consultations were largely limited to nuclear and military strategic matters generally. In fact, the very phrase "Atlantic Alliance" seemed to have fallen into disuse. A certain competitive discord between the United States and Western Europe began to set in as Europeans got the feel of becoming an independent economic power. On the American side, too, there were officials, especially in the Treasury, and the Departments of Agriculture, Commerce and Labor, who began to ask whether it might not make life easier for the United States if European economic unification were to fail; at any rate, it had ceased to be bad manners to think in such terms. European economic and political unity therefore still seemed to the United States worth some economic sacrifice, but not its active support.

Mr. Nixon's firm resistance to cuts of American troops in

Europe was the best proof of his support for NATO, but the concentration of his diplomacy on developing a new relationship with the Soviet Union detracted from that support. It created the impression in Brussels that this bilateral relationship had a higher status in Mr. Nixon's order of priorities. Kissinger, once a great believer in NATO, as a *Real*politician concluded that NATO's decline in the seventies is unavoidable. American troops are bound to be reduced and the Europeans are not going to do enough to make up for that lost strength. The long-term stability in Europe therefore will rest with NATO only in a limited sense; it will depend much more on European political and economic unity and on the Soviet Union's desire to maintain a *détente* policy with the United States.

CHAPTER FIVE—A DOCTRINE FOR ALL
SEASONS

Six months after he had taken office Mr. Nixon decided that the time had come to set the tone and state the broad objectives of his stewardship of foreign policy—what came to be known as the Nixon Doctrine. He chose to do so, appropriately, on the way to Vietnam because he knew he needed both to reassure American public opinion that his basic objective there was withdrawal and an end to U.S. involvement, and to reassure America's allies in Asia that this would not mean abandoning them. It was very much the personal product of the President and not sculptured by the National Security Council. As a consequence, the State Department had neither a hand in drafting the statement nor advance knowledge of the President's intention to deliver it to the world. Indeed, it took several days before the State Department received a transcript of Mr. Nixon's words. The occasion was an informal meeting in Guam, with the correspondents who accompanied the President on his first Asian visit, which included the Philippines, Indonesia, Thailand, South Vietnam, India and Pakistan, and was concluded with a special teaser for the Russians, a visit to Rumania, and a brief stopover in England.

To avoid having to repeat himself at various points along the way, Mr. Nixon had originally intended to have this important presentation in San Francisco before leaving for the Philippines. But at that point the Apollo 11 astronauts were still in the air and the President took advantage of their splashdown in the Pacific to start his own trip with a splash.

Some early pointers to his Doctrine could have been found in an article on Asia by Mr. Nixon published the previous year in *Foreign Affairs*, the house organ of the foreign-policy Establishment. Nixon had offered it to the magazine—it was not commissioned—and Hamilton Fish Armstrong, its then editor, remembers that he did not think too much of it at the time. He certainly did not expect that one day it would become a historic article, laying out the basic philosophy of the next American President.

The ideas outlined to the press on Guam, July 25, 1969, were relatively simple. The United States would not become involved in more wars like the one in Vietnam; it would reduce its military commitments in Asia, and while military assistance would be reduced, new forms of economic aid to the area would be considered.

To some, the Nixon Doctrine was a rationale for the retreat of American power; for others it was an exercise in rhetoric to justify the continuing U.S. involvement in the world. The ambiguity became obvious very soon, for after the first favorable comments interpreting Mr. Nixon's statements as heralding a withdrawal from the Asian mainland, the President seemed to contradict himself when, on his next stop in Thailand, he reassured his hosts that the United States "will stand proudly with Thailand against those who might threaten it from abroad or from within." In Manila, two days earlier, he had said in contrast, "Peace in Asia cannot come from the U.S. It must come from Asia. The people of Asia, the governments of Asia, they are the ones who must lead the way to peace in Asia."

UNDER COVER OF AMBIGUITY

One can have a great deal of sympathy for the doctrinal ambiguity. To lead the retreat of American power in a responsible way, fast enough to maintain support at home and slow enough not to lose confidence abroad or to tempt the enemy into wrong assumptions, is an extremely difficult maneuver. Anybody who thought that the Nixon Doctrine was a simple trumpet call of retreat was obviously wrong. As Justice Holmes once said, "General propositions do not decide concrete cases," and each case was bound to be decided separately on its merits.

But the Doctrine—a word that has lost its stature by many years of abuse—set a direction, set a tone and carried an implied warning. It also gave both Nixon's supporters and his critics an opportunity to interpret it the way that suited them best. In effect, it was a very clever way of telling the world that an end of an era had indeed arrived. The United States would still carry most of the burdens and responsibilities, but the rest of the world would have to shoulder more of them than in the past, many more. An internationalist by experience and outlook, even an interventionist, Mr. Nixon was charged by history to lead an orderly retreat from obsolete global commitments to safer and more solid positions and without serious adverse consequences on world security. It was also aimed at warding off an isolationist tide.

As he put it later in a conversation that Frank Giles, the deputy editor of *The Sunday Times* of London, and I had with the President in February 1970, the basic thrust of his foreign policy "must be seen as an effort to withstand the present wave of new isolationism as embodied in such moves as the Mansfield Resolution for the withdrawal of American troops from Europe. I don't say that this movement represents a majority, but it exists and it is growing. What we had to do first was to make it plain to the American people that in fact we cannot opt out of the world, and second, to seek their support in continuing a policy even though it is a revised policy of involvement."

DIPLOMATIC METHADONE

Thus, the Nixon Doctrine was at this stage as much a justification as a concept. It had the advantage, however disconcerting to friends and foes, that it injected a new uncertainty into diplomatic relationships, leading governments to re-examine their options and alternatives. In many cases there might not be any viable ones; in others, some might beckon. But this possibility did not disturb the Nixon-Kissinger outlook. The two intended that their allies should re-examine what was in their self-interest. They also expected them, however, after a realistic analysis, to conclude that their future continued to rest in co-operation with the United States. It was more psychological than factual, a kind of methadone treatment for a patient suffering from an overdose of Vietnam heroin, an attempt to alleviate damaging withdrawal symptoms to avoid a serious breakdown. For many in Congress it was too gradual and too vague. In their impatience they constantly sought to force the President's hand while he stubbornly adhered to his time schedule of withdrawal from Vietnam and resisted the reduction of troops in Europe, thus excluding Europe, at least temporarily, from his Doctrine.

Kissinger himself declared, in mid-1970, that "in many countries it looks as if the United States is in retreat. It is one of the big problems we face . . . We are doing what we are doing because we believe that if America is to remain related to the world it must define a relationship that we can sustain over an indefinite period. What has developed over the years is that precisely because there wasn't any coherent philosophy of what we were trying to do, everybody clung to whatever physical American presence existed as the tangible guarantee of American commitment . . . We are coming into a new period. No words can explain away the fact that when NATO was created we had an atomic monopoly, and today the Soviets have over a thousand land-based missiles. No presidential declaration can take away that change."

Later on, in the President's State of the World report in 1971, the Nixon Doctrine was further defined as "a strong but redefined American role," with others bearing a greater share in the definition of policy as well as the costs of programs. The "psychological reorientation" was more fundamental than the "material redistribution" on the theory that "when countries feel responsible for the formulation of plans, they are more apt to furnish the assets needed to make them work. . . . Thus while lowering our overseas presence and direct military involvement, our policy calls for a new kind of leadership. It must shape a new consensus for a balanced and positive American role."

He simply decreed, more or less, that the alliance systems had to become more "flexible" and much less reliant on American

prescriptions, American prodding, American assistance. By putting
the allies on notice that they should pursue a policy of greater autonomy, he also implied that the United States too wanted to have
greater freedom of action, be less chained to alliance policies and
be able to select from a greater variety of options. Keeping the
options open was a basic change, for in the past American policy
makers had been more anxious to make their allies feel safe,
through a secure knowledge of the objectives of American policy
and the benefits to be gained from constancy in co-operating with
the United States.

The Nixon Doctrine was a signal to everybody, heralding an
end to the containment policy against the Soviet Union and China
because the balance of power in the world was changing, the day
of immutable alliances was over. Nobody could be absolutely certain any more of American assistance, except where treaty obliga-
tions existed, and even those were undergoing a psychological re-
vision. And, of course, the Nixon Doctrine was not only the result
of a conscious effort to impose a new policy concept or revulsion
against the Vietnam involvement, but also a matter of budgetary
limitations, as the demands for a shift of funds to domestic programs became irresistible. The shortage of money became one of
the most potent American policy makers, just as its abundance
had been a generation earlier.

CHAPTER SIX—NIXON IN CRISIS:
THE CAMBODIAN TRAUMA

Mr. Nixon has a curious obsession with the psychology of crisis and its management. It is no accident that his only book is called *Six Crises*, and that he looks back on his past in terms of the adversities it has brought to him; this "exquisite agony" preoccupies him much more than his triumphs. This could be interpreted as a strong dose of self-pity, but it more truly reflects his profound conviction that these crises had the greatest influence on the formation of his character and that they are the keys to his success. He sees himself as a St. George with a compulsive need for combat with the dragons, battles which he relishes, giving us blow-by-blow analytical accounts even while the tournament proceeds. This reveals an extraordinary detachment, which enables him to observe and study himself as well as his opponent throughout. Every encounter is also a contest between his fears and his expectations, and there is an imaginative tendency to put the blame for the crises on the challengers. But he has already given the world ample proof that he has steeled himself in combat and has a will to survive that few politicians have ever matched. It may be because he could never envisage any other life or any other profession but that of a politician.

At the start of his presidency he instructed Kissinger to give him the kind of service that would make it possible for him to anticipate and avoid crises. It was the wise statesman and the realist in him speaking, not the St. George, the brinkman or the poker player who at times wins out and tempts him into provoking crises of his own. In the introduction to his book he wrote that his own attitude is best expressed in the way the word "crisis" is written in the Chinese language: Two characters are combined to form the word, and one brush stroke stands for "danger" and the other stands for "opportunity." He confesses, somewhat disturbingly, that the St. George in him could tempt him into a crisis in order to prove the strength of his character. It is this trait that has scared friends and foes, for it can turn the man of reason, the lawyer, into an unpredictable gambler. He also wrote, however, that his desire to avoid crises, while making for less dramatic government, makes for better government, "and in a nuclear age for much safer government." Later again, he says, "All too often, we concentrate only on the danger presented by a crisis. The fears of mankind go with those who recognize the danger; but the hopes of mankind go with those who seize the opportunity." There is in him a perpetual struggle between the man he is and the man he wants to be, and within it the constant temptation to test himself to discover whether he can seize the opportunity to prove himself.

NORTH KOREA: NIXON'S FIRST CRISIS

The first crisis involving the risk of confrontation that Mr. Nixon faced as President came on April 15, 1969, when North Korean aircraft downed a Navy EC-121 with thirty-one men aboard. The loss of the unarmed electronic "spy" plane hit the White House like lightning and led directly to the creation, on the President's orders, of the Washington Special Action Group under Kissinger as chairman. It has remained, ever since, the crisis trouble shooter. It also consolidated Kissinger's power, for up to then the State Department had been in charge of crisis operations and expected to be in charge again this time, but the hope soon was disappointed. Kissinger was calmly and firmly in the saddle.

After two days' urgent sizing up of the options, the National Security Council met under the President's chairmanship. As became his habit, he kept his counsel during the meeting, then retired to his own quarters to make his own decisions. He ordered a show of force in the area to keep all his options open. General

Earle Wheeler, chairman of the Joint Chiefs of Staff, favored an attack against a North Korean airfield. Secretary of Defense Melvin Laird's position was difficult to make out, even to the Council. Secretary of State Rogers, on the other hand, argued against retaliation because, he said, the bombing of an airfield had very little value unless one could at the same time destroy a lot of airplanes on it.

Kissinger did not express a view. He presented the options objectively and, while some at this stage at least had the impression that he was more receptive to the logic of Rogers' argument, later on some of his aides interpreted his thinking as more inclined toward retaliatory action. From then on, one of the favorite games inside and outside the Administration was to try and interpret "where Henry stood" on crucial policy decisions. But it was a difficult game to play, because Kissinger avoided taking sides or saying which option he favored. He reserved taking a position on an issue for the President, as he often repeated, only if the President ordered him to do so. Some tried to define his viewpoint from the questions he asked his advisers, but that could be misleading, as they often found out. As least one of those who later left Kissinger's team in disagreement over the President's decision to invade Cambodia said to me, with surprising loyalty to Kissinger, "I believe that for Henry to be able to function properly it is important to keep his views from the bureaucracy and the public, and those who work for him should not talk about what they thought he said to the President. I, too, used to be uncertain what he thought. Often he draws you out, but you can reach the wrong conclusion from this." Many of those who left Kissinger later did so after disagreeing with his or the President's policies or Kissinger's methods of operation, but all of them continued to respect his knowledge and skill.

A MENU FOR RETALIATION

What simplified the immediate decision on whether to retaliate against North Korea was that the United States lacked the military capability in the area to do so, except for the B-52s on Guam and

Okinawa which were capable of conventional as well as nuclear bombing. But to use them in this situation would have involved risks. The necessary fighter escorts were not available, and with the North Koreans known to have some four hundred MIG jets at their disposal, it would have been unwise to risk them with insufficient protection. The President, therefore, ordered all military contingency plans be reviewed in the White House in order to make certain that in future the necessary forces would be available.

WSAG, as the Washington Special Action Group became known, sat virtually all night developing estimates of military capabilities, the risks involved in retaliatory action, the targets worth hitting and the forces needed for a counterstrike. In the morning, Mr. Nixon was presented with a "menu," as the Kissinger insiders called it (and as, indeed, all the Kissinger position papers came to be called).

The NSC met again, and from that meeting it became clear that the President would not order an immediate retaliatory attack against an airfield, even though he thought that there was a good case for it. Even now it is hard to say whether the President really had retaliation in mind. What he did order, though, was an escalation of the show of force. The most powerful naval force ever assembled steamed into Korean and Japanese waters, and reconnaissance flights were resumed under heavy fighter escorts, but it took an entire week before the nuclear aircraft carrier *Enterprise* and the carriers *Ticonderoga* and *Ranger*, the battleship *New Jersey*, altogether a twenty-three-ship task force, had moved into position. Everything was in readiness for any major move that the President might choose to make.

While the task force was still assembling, however, Secretary Rogers told the annual meeting of the Association of American Newspaper Editors, four days after the plane had been shot down, that "the weak can be rash, but the powerful must be more restrained." He did not exactly exclude the possibility of a military response, but he did not expect it, and as things turned out reflected quite accurately the trend of the thinking as it evolved in the Administration. What reinforced the thinking was that there was no public clamor for retaliation and only a handful of voices were raised in favor of it.

When, the year before, the North Koreans seized the U.S.S. *Pueblo*, a floating spy ship, Mr. Nixon made it an almost jingoistic campaign theme for a while. When a "fourth-rate military power like North Korea takes on American naval power on the high seas, it is time for new leadership to restore respect for the United States of America," he used to say, but that was candidate Nixon. President Nixon, however much he felt emotionally inclined to retaliate, desisted. It is difficult to know whether it was simply due to the fact that he did not have the immediate military capability at his disposal or whether, as Mr. Rogers put it, the lesson of the past that impressed him was that being "a great power does not mean great freedom of action and decision. On the contrary, it means very narrow choices of action, and what we can do to influence events in a given case may be marginal."

In 1972, though, Kissinger was heard to say that if the United States had retaliated with limited force in one way or the other against North Korea after the shooting down of the spy plane, it might well have made a timely impression on Hanoi and become the kind of warning to them that might have had a beneficial influence on their Vietnam policy.

In the absence of retaliatory action, South Korean politicians in Seoul publicly expressed disappointment that Mr. Nixon had not lived up to his election campaign speeches. But Washington remained calm and impassive. Even the Russians remained unconcerned after the shooting down of the U.S. plane and, surprisingly, ordered two of their destroyers in the area to help in the search for survivors. Peking was mainly concerned with attacking the Soviet Union for doing so.

Had Mr. Nixon ordered his great armada to attack after a week's delay, however, it could have suddenly looked more like an American-made crisis than one caused by North Korea. Furthermore, the American public had by then almost forgotten the incident. Nobody from the Pentagon was called on the carpet by the President, even though the military, who were supposed to have kept an aircraft carrier in the area, were at fault in that they reduced the

President's options; maybe it was just as well. For a policy planner, though, it must have been a troubling experience. It was not surprising that about a week after the event, Kissinger was heard wondering in the corridors of the White House whether, with all their might, the United States and its military had not become muscle-bound. This limitation on big-power freedom of action, and the narrow choices of action available to them, came to impress Mr. Nixon and even more so Dr. Kissinger, and greatly influenced their thinking.

TRAP OR OPPORTUNITY

Just a year later, Mr. Nixon found himself with a new opportunity to test himself against crisis: This time, however, it was of his own making. In April 1970, he felt that his leadership was under challenge. He was in a strange, distressed mood. His defeat over his failure to get congressional approval for Judge G. Harrold Carswell's confirmation to the United States Supreme Court added to his feeling for the need to make a show of strength. It was partly this inner motivation that sucked him into the Cambodian crisis; he was concerned that if Cambodia fell to the Communists he would be blamed for it, though it was at the same time a calculated move to avoid risking a reversal of his policy of disengagement from Vietnam. "It was to save American lives," the President argued. He expected the Cambodian adventure to provoke a violent reaction from American students, but the intensity of their opposition shook him beyond all anticipation.

It did not look as if a crisis was imminent when Mr. Nixon announced, on April 20, plans for the withdrawal from Vietnam of 150,000 men over the next twelve months. In addition, the President seemed more concerned at the time about the misbegotten mission of the Apollo 13 astronauts whom he had gone to greet in Hawaii on April 18. But ever since Prince Norodom Sihanouk, Cambodia's unpredictable neutralist chief of state, had been deposed by Lieutenant General Lon Nol on March 18, the American military had been seriously flirting with the idea of cleaning out the enemy staging areas in the Cambodian sanctuaries to make South

Vietnam more secure from a new enemy build-up along that frontier.

Already, in the autumn of 1969, a great deal of resentment had begun to boil up—equally among the Cambodians—about the presence of North Vietnamese soldiers in the Cambodian sanctuaries. They were called sanctuaries because the enemy was safe there from American or South Vietnamese attacks, for neither wanted to violate the Cambodian borders and incur the wrath of the irascible Prince Sihanouk. Cambodia's own army was too impotent even to contemplate moving against the North Vietnamese. The only concessions Sihanouk had reportedly obtained from the North Vietnamese, in reply to his protest while in Hanoi for Ho Chi Minh's funeral, was of a ceiling on the tonnage of military material the North Vietnamese could land at the port of Sihanoukville. But Hanoi did not pay much attention to this understanding, and late in 1969 the Prince began to accuse the North Vietnamese of making promises and then breaking them.

In February 1970, after the Prince had left on a visit to Paris, anti-North Vietnamese demonstrations broke out in Pnom Penh, the North Vietnamese Embassy was sacked, and Sihanouk, obviously worried, cabled his mother from Paris to ask her what he should do next. She replied, with what was probably good advice, that he should stay in Paris. Nevertheless, he flew to Moscow where the news of his deposition caught up with him. Then he went on to Peking where his children went to school and where he was, at least initially, accepted with open arms. In his first public statements, he sounded much like Sihanouk. But the more he was denounced in his own capital, the more he sold his soul to the Chinese. From then on, his support at home declined rapidly and he became a rather useless exile from the Communists' point of view.

Washington, in the meantime, had become profoundly worried by the situation in Cambodia. Although some claimed that the CIA had instigated the deposition of Sihanouk, this was far from the truth; his fall did not bring much joy to the Nixon administration. True, with a more pliable regime in Pnom Penh it would have made it easier for the South Vietnamese and American forces to get facilities to police the North Vietnamese infiltration routes across the Cambodian-South Vietnamese borders, but it could also have meant the beginning of another involvement, in a country even less prepared to fight than South Vietnam. When the French proposed an all-Indochina conference on April 1, therefore, the United States was in favor of it, but did not say so for fear of scaring off the Communists. The delicacy of this position led to a certain amount of anguish, removed only when Sihanouk was finally and officially deposed by the Cambodian Parliament, and the negotiations became a hopeless undertaking. There remained, though, the Communist build-up in the sanctuaries.

On Tuesday, April 21, Mr. Nixon, having returned hurriedly from San Clemente, entered the Roosevelt Room where John Ehrlichman, his assistant for Domestic Affairs, was holding his regular morning staff meeting. The President delivered one of the homilies he likes to indulge in at times. He mused about the day-to-day chores and about the importance of not having one's long-range vision obscured, for it was the long-range results that mattered.

CRISIS DECISION MAKING

With this off his chest, the President went into a meeting with Kissinger and Richard Helms of the CIA, and was told about the urgent requests for aid from the Cambodian capital. He called a National Security Council meeting for the next day, April 22, and after being preoccupied with Cambodia all day, retired to the seclusion of his Lincoln sitting room, with its warm, old-world quality, one of the President's favorite sanctuaries. What clearly emerged next day from the debate in the National Security Council was that the newly installed government of Premier Lon Nol in Pnom Penh was in serious trouble, and some sort of consensus was reached that the United States, instead of sending aid to the Cambodians, should help them by letting the South Vietnamese troops intervene, possibly with U.S. air support. The idea of using U.S troops also came up, but not as a serious proposal.

The President ordered the preparation of planning papers for incursions against the sanctuaries; the Washington Special Action Group leaped into action. With Kissinger in the chair, U. Alexis Johnson, Under Secretary of State for Political Affairs; Richard Helms; David Packard, Deputy Secretary of Defense; General Earle Wheeler, chairman of the Joint Chiefs of Staff; and Marshall Green, Assistant Secretary of State for East Asian and Pacific Affairs, got to work on the options. The nub of the question soon emerged as to whether the military operations should be carried out with or without American troops. Marshall Green strenuously advised against the operation, or at least against the use of American troops, but his warnings had no effect. Equally it is not clear to what extent Secretary Rogers effectively reflected the reservations of his experts who thought the operation would have serious, unfavorable domestic repercussions. The State Department's influence, anyway, was only marginal. The fuzziness of the way Secretary Rogers expressed his views irritated the President and increasingly limited the effect of the State Department's impact on decisions. From then on, everything moved so fast that Marshall Green, who considered these days as the lowest in his career, described to me what was happening to him as follows: "I felt like on a surf board, trying to reach the shore, but being hit on the head constantly by one wave after another, preventing me from reaching the shore." His opposition was not made easier by the fact that his superior, Under Secretary of State U. Alexis Johnson, also an old Far Eastern hand, favored the operation. In retrospect, though, Green believes that he had been wrong and that the operation had the desired effect. The Joint Chiefs of Staff only thought in terms of whether the operation would succeed militarily. Mr. Laird also seemed to favor it.

The first decision was taken on Friday, April 24. The President decided that South Vietnamese troops should move, without American advisers, into Parrot's Beak, as one of the sanctuaries came to be called by the military.

Kissinger called in all on his National Security Council Staff who opposed a Cambodian operation much as Marshall Green did. He did not give them an inkling where he himself stood, but in characteristic style provoked them into discussion, either to determine how valid their objections were or simply to give them the satisfaction of being able to vent their violent opposition. They were six—all brilliant young men—Anthony Lake, William Watt, Roger Norris, Winston Lord, active members of the Foreign Service, Robert Osgood and Dr. Larry Lynn, a former "whiz kid" from the McNamara days in the Pentagon, hired by Kissinger for their highly rated expertise and intellect. No one at that point knew what the President's decision would be.

The next day Kissinger flew to Camp David where the President had gone the day before with his friend Bebe Rebozo, a Florida real estate operator who shunned the press and all publicity—one of the most discreet of presidential companions. Kissinger delivered the plans the President had requested for an additional incursion into the Fishhook area, another of the sanctuaries, so named because of its formation on the map. That evening, the President returned to Washington with Kissinger and, together with John Mitchell, they boarded the President's yacht, *Sequoia*. Secretary Rogers had been invited to join them, but was unable to go because of a speech he had to deliver in New York. After a four-hour cruise on the Potomac River, the President returned to the White House and relaxed watching the film *Patton*—for the second time—in his own theater. The story of this daring, head-strong World War II general who got a lift out of the brutal game of war and risk taking, but whose crises in life gave his career a tragic ending, mesmerized Nixon.

The next day—Sunday—the NSC met again at 4:30 P.M. They seriously reviewed the possible consequences of direct American troop participation on the basis of military estimates prepared earlier for contingency purposes. Then they debated whether once the risk was taken to move into one sanctuary, Parrot's Beak, it would not make sense to move into Fishhook at the same time. The public outcry would be about the same whether the operation included incursions into one or two sanctuaries. But once the operation assumed this magnitude, doubts arose as to whether the South Vietnamese troops could pull it off on their own, and whether it would not be better to play it safe and allow American forces at least to come to the aid of the ARVN should it run into heavy opposition. As usual, the President withheld his own decision, but he retired afterward in the solitary company of Kissinger.

On Monday, the President indicated to several aides and Cabinet members that he favored operations against both Parrot's Beak and Fishhook. Some of them warned that in view of the expected one thousand casualties the first week, this could set the campuses aflame again and outrage the Senate Foreign Relations Committee. General Creighton Abrams, who commanded the American troops in Vietnam, and American Ambassador Bunker in Saigon, in separate cables, were told that the President had not yet taken any decisions, but he wanted to have their views, which they were told would weigh heavily in making up his mind. That day the President also requested television time. He consulted with Attorney General John Mitchell, Kissinger, presidential assistants Robert Haldeman and John Ehrlichman, and two of his congressional liaison aides, talked privately to the Reverend Norman Vincent Peale, author of *The Power of Positive Thinking* and *You Can Win*, and to Mrs. Nixon, but he dined alone at his desk, thinking through all the implications of his gamble.

Decisions, in his handbook to leadership, are Nixon's own. Unlike Johnson or Kennedy, he never asks each adviser to state how he would vote, but only what he thinks. Meetings are not for telling everybody else what he thinks. He is a much less domineering man than was Johnson. But then comes the moment when he retires to commune with himself. He strongly believes that since he alone bears the responsibilities, he alone must make the decisions. But not, as one of his oldest aides put it to me, until he has the emotional assurance that he has debated it and thought it all through most.carefully.

His decision was to go in, but to avoid the risk of military failure the ARVN was to have every necessary American support, not merely advisers. It was to be the last time that American ground troops went into action. In the perspective of history, the Cambodian operation will go down not so much for its effect on the war in Vietnam as for the impact it had on Congress; it led to the formation of a permanent majority against the use of American ground troops in Vietnam.

NIXON EXPLAINS THE MOMENT OF TRUTH

About a year later the President described privately to me the agonies of the Cambodian decision:

"My two most anguished moments so far have been the decisions to deliver the November third speech on Vietnam [setting out his basic policy of phased withdrawal] and the decision to clean out the Cambodian sanctuaries. The first I did against the advice of my closest associates. I was alone in favor of it, well . . . not quite alone, but I won't tell you who said what to me. In any case, I decided against an announcement of my decision and instead delivered a speech." (In retrospect, although some of the rhetoric was appalling, the speech achieved its objective, which was to gain the President time.)

"As regards the Cambodian operation," he continued, "I was given the most dire predictions and estimates and they were persuasive, especially the warning that a public uproar was likely to occur. It was because of these warnings that I felt I had to go on television. I had concluded that we would be worse off if we did not fight in Cambodia, and that I had to risk the public outcry that would follow. North Vietnam would have extended its sanctuaries, reopened the port of Sihanoukville and disrupted our Vietnamization program and thus our orderly withdrawal.

"You listen to everybody's arguments, but then comes the moment of truth," he said quietly, almost as if speaking to himself. "Then I sit alone with my yellow pad and I write down on one side the reasons for doing it and on the other the reasons for not doing it. I do this before every important decision." He paused for a moment, smiled at some private thought and quickly turned serious again.

"In school we had fellows who loved bull sessions, sat around and talked about everything. I never did. I have bull sessions, only earlier. Some Presidents get more gregarious the closer they come to a decision. Johnson could not get enough papers, listen to enough people. But I think more clearly after I have heard everybody's point of view—then I retire and decide. I remained secluded at Camp David for two days and weighed the odds with not much sleep. Before the November third speech it also took me about two days of contemplation before I reached my decision."

Militarily, his decision to move against the Cambodian sanctuaries did what it was designed to do: It effectively helped to weaken the enemy's operations in South Vietnam. It was also aimed at getting across to the North Vietnamese the determination of the American purpose, the readiness not to rely on some surrogate (in this case, the South Vietnamese troops) and to demonstrate a U.S. capability of reacting strongly. To the Russians, it was a hint that the United States was unpredictable. But what mattered most was to ensure the success of the operation.

THE FRENZIED CLIMAX

It is one thing to expect troubles and another to experience them. What accentuated these troubles was the President's decision to go on television and to use the strident rhetoric which reflects the preacher and evangelist in him. ". . . if when the chips are down, the world's most powerful nation . . . acts like a pitiful, helpless giant, the forces of totalitarianism and anarchy will threaten free nations and free institutions throughout the world . . . If we fail to meet this challenge all other nations will be on notice that despite its overwhelming power the United States, when the real crisis comes, will be found wanting." And with a little gesture toward self-pity he said that it was "insignificant" whether or not he would become a one-term President because of this decision.

Some of his advisers had pleaded against the President's going on television—Kissinger especially—and for leaving the announcement to the Pentagon as just another military operation. But the President saw his decision as a demonstration of American power and determination and wanted the world to take note of it. But to many, especially in Congress, it came to symbolize Nixon's continued belief in the use of military power to prevent a Communist take-over in South Vietnam and it raised a specter—that he was preparing to accept a new commitment, the preservation of Cambodia. It led to the so-called Cooper-Church amendment in the Senate, aimed at cutting off funds for future U.S. military operations in Cambodia; it was voted into force only well after the operation was over, but it reflected the depth of opposition to any further Indochinese involvement.

The Cambodia adventure also led to a massive uproar on the campuses—448 colleges and universities had to close or went on strike—and massive demonstrations were quickly planned, which brought close to one hundred thousand protesters to Washington. The storm of outrage was further inflamed by the killing of four students at Kent State University in Ohio, victims of angry National Guard troop bullets.

The President in order to stem the protests held his first televised news conference in three months, conferred with leading educators and pledged that all U.S. ground forces would be out of Cambodia by the end of June. He made Administration personnel available for informal sessions with the throngs of student protesters that swarmed into Washington for Protest Day on May 9. In the midst of all this, it became known that Interior Secretary Walter J. Hickel had sent a letter to the President warning him of the alienation of the young from his policies and protesting the lack of consultation with Cabinet members. World leaders, too, were apprehensive. Britain's Prime Minister Wilson, on May 5, expressed the fear that U.S. forces might penetrate farther into Cambodia than the limits set by President Nixon and that this could cause a change in Washington's withdrawal of troops from Vietnam.

The President himself impulsively left the White House at dawn on the day of the protest march to talk to the students who had been camping on the steps of the Lincoln Memorial. He was clearly agitated and upset that morning. His mood reminded me of a sentence in his *Six Crises:* "Honoré de Balzac once wrote that 'politicians are masters of self-possession.'

Yet while we may show this veneer on the outside, inside, the turmoil becomes almost unbearable."

What he said and what he did that morning he left the White House to talk to the students at the Lincoln Memorial remained deeply etched in his memory. He remembered saying to them that he hoped that their hatred of the war, which he could well understand, would not turn into bitter hatred of the whole American political and social system, the country and everything it stood for. He remembered describing to them how excited he was as a young man, just out of law school and ready to get married, when Neville Chamberlain, the British Prime Minister, came home from Munich after his meeting with Hitler and made his now-famous statement about "peace in our time." "I had so little in those days," he told them, "that the prospect of going into the service was almost unbearable and I felt that the United States staying out of any conflict was worth paying any price."

In his efforts to convince the students of his good intentions he went on to explain that he was a Quaker, which made him as close to a pacifist as anybody could be, and that as a consequence Chamberlain at the time seemed to him the greatest man alive. "When I read Churchill's criticism of him, I thought Churchill was a madman," he added, "but in retrospect I realized I was wrong. Chamberlain was a good man, but Churchill was a wise man. Today the world is better off because Churchill had not only the wisdom but the courage to carry out the policies that he believed were right, even though there was a time when both in England and all over the world he was extremely unpopular because of his anti-peace stand."

Nixon then turned to the future and told the students of his great hopes that during his Administration, and certainly during their lifetime, the great mainland of China would be opened up and Americans would be able to get to know one of the most remarkable of peoples on earth, though Prague or Warsaw might be more interesting. "The point is that we are trying to build a world in which nobody will have to die for what he believes in," he continued telling his stunned audience, but then a student spoke up and said, "We are not interested in what Prague or Warsaw look like, we are interested in what kind of life we build in the United States!" To this the President replied, "The purpose of my discussing Prague and other places was not to discuss the city but the people. We are going to be living in all parts of the world and it is vitally important that you know and appreciate and understand people everywhere. Ending the war and cleaning the streets and the air and the water are not going to solve spiritual hunger, which all of us have."

By then the first rays of sunshine had begun to climb up over the massive needle of the Washington Monument and the President said he had to go. At that moment he noticed a bearded fellow from Detroit taking pictures as he tried to enter his limousine. The President still remembers that he asked him whether he himself would not like to get into the picture. The bearded fellow on the President's suggestion then handed his camera to the President's doctor, who had stood by, stepped next to the President, and the doctor obliged. It is the final impression that remains vividly in the President's mind: "The fellow seemed delighted—it was in fact the broadest smile that I saw on the entire visit."

Hardly any of the President's associates rallied around the President in the week that followed. On the contrary. Both Bill Rogers and Mel Laird let it be known among the press that they had reservations about the operation, that they might even have advised against it. This lack of loyalty enraged the President and from then on, he had reservations about both of them. Kissinger, who may have had some minor tactical reservation, most likely reinforced the President's thinking that a show of force was needed. Nixon had said so often in public that he would do something to prove that he was not bluffing, that in his and most likely in Kissinger's view, the time had come to show that he meant it.

SEALING A UNIQUE RELATIONSHIP

Kissinger, in the turbulent hours and days that followed, stood loyally by the President. Nixon did not crack, but at times he did not seem altogether in control of himself or the situation. Kissinger stood like a rock. He did not leave the White House. To his NSC staff he said, "We are the President's men and we must behave like them!" Kissinger was adamant in everything he said to his staff that they had to be loyal to the President in crisis. Some of Kissinger's staff resigned, and these to him were "the epitome of the cowardice of the eastern Establishment." Those who left him, and all did so in protest against the Cambodian decision, went without venting their feelings in public. Kissinger's firm support sealed the unique relationship between him and President Nixon.

The eruption of violent demonstrations triggered a profound rethinking at the White House. A majority of White House aides, who included John Ehrlichman, was now convinced that there was a real danger that the country could come apart at the seams, that not only students but others, too, would revolt, and that new shock waves would once again threaten internal stability. In view of this danger, a conservative minority, which included Robert Haldeman, the President's most personal assistant, and Herbert Klein, his communications expert, recommended a tough emphasis on law and order to protect the President from threats to his authority. The President himself seemed totally preoccupied with this threat.

Henry Kissinger gave me his reaction during those convulsive days of May 1970:

> I think it would be a great mistake if we believed that the unrest on the campuses today is exclusively or maybe even primarily caused by Vietnam. The unrest on the campuses has very deep, maybe even metaphysical causes, for it seems to me that it is the result of the seeming purposelessness of the modern bureaucratic state, of the sense of impotence that is produced in the individual reacting to decisions that far transcend him and that he does not know how to influence. It is the result of thirty years of debunking by my colleagues and by myself and by which the academic com-

munity has managed to take the clock apart and now doesn't know how to put it together again.

I don't think that we are helping the problem by encouraging the belief that emotional spasms are the way to make profound historical choices, however much I sympathize. Most of us in the White House have shown our sympathy by spending more time with students this week than we have on our primary jobs.

A month later at his own private birthday party, Kissinger mused about the aftereffects of Cambodia: "We are losing authority. The only man I can think of who would have understood how to preserve it was Bobby Kennedy whom we mourned this week. What is more important, the journey or the arrival? It is the journey and he knew how much this journey counted." By implication, he seemed to say that Nixon was an arrival man. He concluded by what obviously troubled him most, "There is a great need to rally behind our leader, for only then the plans for getting out of Vietnam will succeed." It was a refrain that he repeated at all crucial turning points of the American efforts to disengage from Vietnam; it was one of the basic convictions, that only if Hanoi saw the American nation backing the President, would it agree to end the war on acceptable terms.

Kissinger's words bring to life again the turbulence, the shock, the instability and the profound soul-searching the Cambodian adventure caused. But six months later, the President's decision, militarily, proved justified. The incursions forestalled the fall of Cambodia and bought valuable time, even increasing confidence in the capabilities of the South Vietnamese forces.

Even though the Cambodian crisis does not rank as an important event in the retreat of American power, it was the last time American ground troops went into action, and it greatly reinforced those forces, especially in Congress, clamoring for that retreat. This operation left a deep mark on Congress, deeper even than among students or the public. It further undermined the Nixon administration's credibility with Congress and aroused new suspicions that all the talk of getting out of Vietnam was a hoax.

INTO LAOS NEVERTHELESS

Yet only nine months later, Mr. Nixon, undeterred by the turbulence the Cambodian operation had created, decided on another "incursion," this time into Laos. The reason was essentially the same: to make South Vietnam more secure for the withdrawal of American troops. The concept though was different. In the hope of avoiding another damaging turbulence at home, American troops did not cross into Laos, their participation in the operation being limited to ferrying South Vietnamese troops into the battle zone by helicopter. There were no disagreements in the government as to whether this operation should be undertaken; there was only a discussion of its risks. But because the Cambodian operation had proved in retrospect a success, those who had opposed it did not want to repeat the same mistake. No one spoke up against the Laotian operation.

It is difficult to understand why those who participated in the decision did not see that for many obvious reasons, it had little prospect of success. There were the CIA estimates, essentially correct, which pinpointed the position of enemy regiments, including an armored one, that could quickly be thrown into this battle; there was the fact that the North Vietnamese had about thirty thousand men in the area up against some twenty thousand ARVN men, when it was the attacker who should have had the clear superiority; and there was the absence of direct U.S. military support. The military judgment both of the U.S. and ARVN command in Saigon was at fault. They underestimated the enemy's capabilities and overestimated the effect of U.S. air power, which they thought would give the ARVN superiority, even if outnumbered, and a mobility that would allow them to outflank the enemy. The Air Force time and again has overestimated its effectiveness and somehow no one dares to resist them—this has been the bane of successive U.S. administrations. The American military command was also wrong in its estimates of the reserves the ARVN could inject into a losing battle. It did not take into account that President Thieu would call a halt to the operation to avoid dire political repercussions for himself. There were in fact no more reserves available and there was a limit as to how far the South Vietnamese divisions could be moved from one place to another. The CIA had warned that in contrast to the experience in Cambodia, when the North Vietnamese withdrew as the United States and South Vietnamese advanced, in Laos they would fight "like hell." However, General Abrams and the Joint Chiefs of Staff were so optimistic that intelligence estimates were not given full weight.

CIA SPILLS THE MILK

It has been Richard Helm's experience that Presidents have a tendency to fall for what the Joint Chiefs of Staff say. President Johnson, who only too eagerly followed JCS estimates, once gave his view of the role of the CIA in front of Helms at a White House dinner: "Policy making is like milking a fat cow. You see the milk coming out, you press more and the milk bubbles and flows, and just as the bucket is full, the cow with its tail whips the bucket and all is spilled. That's what CIA does to policy making."

Mr. Nixon and his aides, basing themselves on the JCS predictions, not only oversold the operation but claimed in their briefings for the press and Congress that they would attain optimum targets when they should simply have said that they only hoped to disrupt the supply lines.

But the accounts of American helicopter pilots of the ARVN losses and the costly helicopter losses, graphically shown in television, aroused the public once again, even though American troops were not involved in the ground fighting. Secretary Rogers, who had made the initial announcement of the Laotian operation, held no more press conferences after it became increasingly clear that it would not be successful. Thus the weight for putting the best face on events fell on the White House and Kissinger in particular. "The trouble with every war," said Kissinger in one of his background briefings, "is that one general is always wrong."

When I saw President Nixon on March 26, 1971, it was clear that he, too, had put excessively much faith in the assessment of the military. He then said to me, "This morning, during the National Security Council meeting, people worried what the latest wire stories reported about the Laotian operation. I would never have ordered it for its short-range effect. I try to keep a perspective. One has to look down the road to what is needed next year." (The official purpose for the operation was to prevent the enemy from building up forces that would permit him to launch another Tet-type offensive in the spring of 1972.) "The Laos operation is for us the last major military effort in which we gave ARVN direct help with our helicopters. From now on, the Vietnam war will be wound down to its end as far as we are concerned. That's why it is important how the Laos operation will come out. It should assure us that next year will be the end of our involvement in the war."

In the end, the Laotian operation fell far short of expectations. Nor was it, as Mr. Nixon had confidently hoped, discounting the possibility of another major North Vietnamese offensive, the last time U.S. helicopters would fly in support of the ARVN. Its ill-starred ending proved one thing: that the South Vietnamese could not take the offensive, that at best they had the strength to defend themselves.

When I asked the President, during this private interview with him, whether he meant to take all Americans out of Vietnam by the end of 1971, he said that there would be something between fifty thousand and one hundred thousand men left. "That's the ball-park figure, but we want to get them all out." I wondered whether he was thinking of keeping an American "residual" force in South Vietnam, as there is still one in South Korea. For a moment he hesitated whether to answer my question, then he said, "There is a difference between South Korea and South Vietnam. In South Korea there are no guerrilla forces. The small American contingent therefore is safe there; but even in South Korea I will further reduce the number of American troops. The only thing that will keep American troops in South Vietnam are our prisoners of war held in the North." Then he suddenly added, "They will also stay as long as the North Vietnamese have not withdrawn from South Vietnam, Cambodia and Laos." It left open the question of what he really meant by complete withdrawal.

"I often feel like Michelangelo," Joseph Sisco, the Assistant Secretary for Near Eastern and South Asian Affairs, said to me in the
summer of 1970; "I am chiseling away but I have to be constantly
on guard that I won't split the sculpture down the middle." Sisco's
particular block of marble came from the eastern Mediterranean,
and from it he sought to hew a figure of peace recognizable to
both Israelis and Egyptians. He is a diplomat, but the very opposite of the stereotype that Americans like to characterize as a
"cooky pusher" or the "striped pants diplomat." Sisco's pants are
baggy, his coat rumpled, his tie askew, his voice jarring, his manner
forceful and at times even brusque. He is more barnstormer than
persuader; indeed, comparing the activity of this likable go-getter
to the delicate artistry of a Michelangelo may well strike those
who know him as rash hyperbole. The task which he assumed, of
bringing peace to the Middle East, was nonetheless one of the
most delicate faced by any policy maker in the State Department,
and spiked with as many hazards as there are quills on a porcupine.

In a Foreign Service that looked incapable of vigorous action,
Nixon saw Sisco as a welcome breath of fresh air and he gave him
wide latitude. He wanted to pursue an active policy, one initially
defined as more "even-handed" by William Scranton, the President's original choice for Secretary of State, after a fact-finding
tour to the Middle East before Mr. Nixon's inauguration. Nixon's
intention was to indicate that there was nothing sacrosanct about
past policies and that he did not want to be taken for granted. He

also wanted to make it clear that Zionist pressures would not affect his decisions; they could even have the opposite effect. He was willing to expose Israeli intransigence and turn world opinion against the Israelis. But things are never that simple in the Middle East.

President Nixon saw the situation in that region as one of the greatest hazards to world peace. American and Soviet interests there overlapped, and a confrontation between the two could develop even though neither of them wanted it. What unexpectedly heightened the danger of such a confrontation was the Kremlin's decision in late 1969 to station Russian troops and pilots in Egypt. This came as a total surprise because it was the first time in the history of the U.S.S.R. that it was willing to deploy its military forces in a country geographically remote from Soviet territory and outside the borders it considered essential for the defense of its own national security. Russia's infiltration was not a response to any American retreat, but the result of a positive Soviet decision to expand its military power and influence into an area that had been in turn a French, then a British and now an American preserve. It gave an entirely new twist to Russian foreign policy and, in view of the extent to which the United States, Western Europe and Japan depended on Middle Eastern oil, a very disturbing one. It presented a new and extremely difficult situation to American policy makers for it was obviously impossible to "expel" the Soviet Union, as Kissinger at one point incautiously, if oratorically, proposed at a background press briefing.

Even without the Soviet military entrenchment, the Middle East was a treacherous enough part of the world in which to try to bring peace. But William Rogers, the Secretary of State, was fretting in the shadow of Kissinger's command over U.S. foreign policy and zealous to make his mark on history somewhere. He was thus willing to risk his prestige and reputation on those shifting sands, partly perhaps because he did not fully realize what a diplomatic graveyard the Middle East has been, partly because he had at his elbow Joe Sisco, the outstanding activist among Assistant Secretaries of State, and partly, of course, because there was always the faint hope of achieving a settlement.

Kissinger, being Jewish, had his own hang-ups about American policy toward Israel, and so preferred to leave this crucial area to Rogers and his Michelangelo. Only when crises threatened, or as he once said to Soviet Ambassador Dobrynin, "If you have something really serious to negotiate about the Middle East," would he take over and assume responsibility. He, too, agreed with the pursuit of an active role in the Middle East—what Nixon described as bringing in the "era of negotiations"—but it was the challenge by the Soviet Union that concerned him above all. And so the Middle East became Rogers' hunting preserve for success. His aim was some sort of settlement between Egypt and Israel. Kissinger was more concerned with containing and counterbalancing the new Russian incursion into Egypt and its consequences.

Rogers is a thoroughly nice man with a casual charm, an ability to focus on the essentials, but no flair or real understanding of foreign affairs. He impresses not by his intellectual perceptions or analytical capabilities, but by his integrity, his patience, his reasonableness, his good looks and his willingness to play second fiddle. For a Secretary of State not to be really in command of the development of foreign policy requires either a certain self-delusion or a great sense of loyalty to the President or a disarming recognition of one's own limitations. John McCloy, once High Commissioner in Germany and a Republican who in President Truman's days became one of the symbols of the bipartisan character of U.S. foreign policy, was approached by John Foster Dulles in 1956 after President Eisenhower's re-election with the question whether he would be prepared to become Secretary of State. He added that it was President Eisenhower's idea. McCloy, a little surprised, said that he was interested but would like to think it over. Then it occurred to him to ask Dulles the not unnatural question of what were Dulles' own plans. Dulles replied that he would move to the White House. Whereupon McCloy without any further hesitation said, "Oh, that would mean that there would be two Secretaries of State," and rejected the offer.

Nixon had known Rogers for a long time—since the Truman days, when Rogers helped to expose the so-called bribery case of the "Five Percenters" in the Truman administration, as counsel for the Senate Executive Expenditure Committee. Whatever the job—as counsel, as Attorney General in the Eisenhower administration, or as a corporation lawyer—Rogers performed well but not brilliantly, with commendable restraint and little political partisanship. He had earned about $300,000 a year as a member of one of the leading New York law firms and among his clients were the New York *Times*, Washington *Post* and Associated Press. He was never an eager beaver, perpetually on the job. He liked to take a full weekend off, and continued the habit as Secretary of State. He preferred then to play golf rather than read policy papers. As a consequence, the high tension that pervaded the State Department in the days of his predecessor, Dean Rusk, who used to go to his office every weekend and never took a holiday, was relaxed into an uneasy calm. "The trademark of this Administration is to play it cool," Rogers said to me once in an interview. "We don't want to be intrusive. That was a mistake of the past we want to avoid. We were pressured from many sides, for instance, to intervene in Nigeria, but did not. We found ourselves in agreement with the British Government's attitude." At least outwardly, Rogers displayed the kind of detachment that was President Eisenhower's trademark in his devotion to golfing or fishing.

This casual attitude did Rogers no harm with the press, to whose opinion he was not indifferent. The newspapers treated him with a certain benevolence because he always conveyed the feeling that he meant well and because, being a moderate by nature, he was a dove on Vietnam—he wanted to get out of that war as soon as possible. This moderation and lack of partisanship also helped him with Congress. If his own knowledge and judgment did not seem to weigh heavily in the scales of decision making, his old friendship with the President remained a source of strength. Next to his own office, in a little cubbyhole, he had a special telephone linking him directly with Mr. Nixon, and whenever he had a visitor in his office and the President called him on the telephone, he withdrew to it. He did this even with his own close advisers.

He took no interest in reforming the State Department to meet or temper the President's criticism, nor did he really feel at home in the Kissinger-dominated National Security Council environment. He was not a man who enjoyed analyzing events or speculating about the future; in staff discussions he insisted that they stick to facts. In response to the constant refrain from the White House that the State Department was not producing new ideas, but only defending old ones, he did indeed often ask his staff to provide him with new ideas and promised to promote them with the President. But there was little evidence that he really did.

Rogers was handicapped not only by his lack of experience in foreign affairs, but also by his inability to assert the State Department role in the Nixon administration. He also developed the curious vanity of a man who, because of his sense of weakness, tries to compensate for it by seeking to pretend that he is strong. It is an old truth that the power position of a Secretary of State rises in parallel with the degree to which he can make the President feel that the State Department machinery is his instrument and not the Secretary's. Dean Acheson succeeded brilliantly in giving President Truman that feeling. Rogers, in trying to assert his strength in the beginning, attempted to make the State Department machinery his own spearhead. This only deepened the President's distrust of it, and the President's doubts about his Secretary's judgment. This picture of Rogers, it is true, differs from the impression frequently gained on the outside—that of a man almost too anxious to adopt the President's view rather than that of his own department—but after long discussions with those able to watch developments from more privileged and intimate vantage points, I have no doubt that it is a true one. It also helps to explain why the President's almost hysterical distrust of the bureaucracy, which infected the entire White House staff, got worse rather than better as time passed.

His friendship with Rogers persisted but, paradoxically enough, on matters other than foreign policy. Friendships tend to matter less to a President than the acquisition of reliable, informed advice and new ideas, and those Kissinger, rather than Rogers, was able to provide. As a consequence, Rogers found his power and influence with the President seriously cut down by the strong personality of Kissinger, who had foreign affairs traveling in his bloodstream. Inevitably, Kissinger's and Rogers' relationship became increasingly precarious. The State Department bureaucracy, of course, soon became aware of the weakness of their own Secretary, the difficulty he had in rowing his oar in the policy streams, and it badly undermined their morale. They were only too well aware that under the scheme of things, with the President wanting to be his own policy maker, wanting to keep the decisions almost entirely to himself and distrusting the bureaucracy anyway, they were in some kind of purdah.

A year before Kissinger was asked to join the White House, he explained his view of how to handle the bureaucracy in an essay for the Security Studies project at the University of California: "Some of the key decisions are kept to a very small circle, while the bureaucracy continues working away in ignorance of the fact that decisions are being made. . . . One reason for keeping the decisions to small groups is that when bureaucracies are so unwieldy and when their internal morale becomes a serious problem, an unpopular decision may be fought by brutal means, such as leaks to the press or Congressional committees. Thus, the only way secrecy can be kept is to exclude from the making of decisions all those who are theoretically charged with carrying it out." It became very obvious that Kissinger, once in government, was determined to translate his theories into practice. Even his own written communications to the President were highly impersonal and detached. He did not reveal his own thinking or (since other eyes would see his memoranda) some of those secrets he had decided were too delicate to share with anybody but the President. Rogers, though a stubborn man, could not contain Kissinger. The entire bureaucracy resented being ignored or kept ignorant by the President's right-hand man; it resented even more having a Secretary of State who was weak in asserting the State Department's power and influence.

It was wholly understandable, in such circumstances, that Rogers should seek to take the initiative where Kissinger did not, and so venture into that risky area of politics, the Middle East, where he pursued success with the zeal of a prospecting oilman.

JOHNSON'S GUILT FEELING

American policy toward Israel under President Johnson had been influenced by a great sense of guilt. After the 1956 Suez crisis, John Foster Dulles angrily threatened to vote United Nations sanctions against Israel unless the Israelis evacuated Sinai and the Gaza Strip captured during the fighting, but only when President Eisenhower, in a more moderate vein, gave the clearest assurances that the United States, come what may, would keep the Gulf of Aqaba open, did Israeli Premier Ben-Gurion in return order Mrs. Meir, then Israel's Foreign Minister, to inform the UN that Israel would withdraw.

Israel indeed withdrew, but the United States did nothing to live up to its promise when Egypt's Nasser refused passage for Israeli ships through the Suez Canal and blocked the Straits of Tiran and the Israeli port of Eilat. Memories of such a letdown die hard, if at all, and when the Israelis in 1967 put everybody on notice that war could become inevitable, President Johnson put no real pressure on Israel to desist. His conscience was nagged by the U.S. failure to protect Israeli interests by keeping the Gulf of Aqaba open; and he was afraid that he could stumble into war with the Soviet Union. He talked to the Russians and spoke of a four-power settlement and various other solutions, but he took no direct action; in fact, the whole problem was left to Israel. The combined guilt and fear that thus dominated Johnson's policies in the Middle East affected to some extent the thinking of Sisco, who in 1967 was an Assistant Secretary for UN Affairs, and then considered pro-Israeli.

After the Six-Day War President Johnson imposed an embargo on arms deliveries to Israel for four months, by suspending the arms agreements with Israel. He then tried to persuade the Russians to halt the arms race by entering into an arms limitation agreement for the entire Middle East. But the idea was doomed from the start, for it would obviously have undermined the Russians' position in the Arab world. When Dean Rusk had dinner with Mr. Gromyko, the Soviet Foreign Minister, on October 4,

1968, during the UN General Assembly, and told him that if they agreed to enter into an arms limitation accord the United States would postpone delivery of Phantom jets promised to Israel, Gromyko flatly rejected the idea. Then, on October 9, Johnson decided to sell the promised Phantoms to Israel, but the negotiations with Israel dragged on because he tried to attach to the sale the condition that Israel should commit herself not to use these planes in a nuclear war. Only two weeks before he left office, he signed the order for the fifty Phantoms he had promised Israeli Premier Eshkol in January 1968.

Nixon, by contrast, was free of Johnson's Israeli complex, just as he was of any dependence on Jewish political and financial support at home. To the pro-Arabs in the State Department, who had been chafing under the strong Johnson commitment to Israel, the future suddenly looked rosier and they began to press their case with new hope and vigor. Even the Pentagon, which was generally inclined to judge countries by their military capabilities and had therefore been inclined toward the Israelis and their requests for arms, began at least to hear, if not noticeably listen to, the pro-Arab voices of two or three high civilian officials.

MR. NIXON SHIFTS THE EMPHASIS

The obvious shift of emphasis was soon in the making. Johnson had given Israel strong diplomatic support, but had been loath to give them arms. Mr. Nixon gave them moderate support on the diplomatic front, but strong backing with arms to ensure that the balance of power would remain in Israel's favor.

The new policy making began during the transition period in December 1968, when the State Department was asked to prepare a Middle East policy paper. But at the first National Security Council meeting that dealt with this subject, early in February, the paper was rejected and instead an analysis requested of American interests in the area and of the options open to the United States. It was another clear indication that policy would be developed not in the State Department, but in the NSC.

The American options were whittled down: first, whether to

seek a solution with Russian co-operation or whether to oppose
their moves in the Middle East; secondly, whether to force Israel
to give up Sharm-El-Shek, which controls the entrance of the Gulf
of Aqaba; and thirdly, whether to make Israel give up all non-
mandate territories.

The motivation behind Nixon's and Johnson's assumptions,
however, was not very different. Both were convinced that if the
Arab-Israeli conflict was resolved by diplomatic means, the dependence of Egypt on the Soviet Union would decrease and the
Arab world would be accessible again to American interests.
However, if the Egyptians used force with Russian help, the Arabs
could regain their territory and American interests would suffer.
The return of the occupied territory, therefore, was seen as the
best bargaining card in the negotiations, so long as the United
States made certain that the balance of power between the Israelis
and Egypt was not upset and Israel's ability to defend herself en-
sured (though not overensured; there had to be no risk that Israel
would feel strong enough actually to defy the United States).

Inevitably, the question of how to make certain that Israel
could not be pushed back, yet would remain sufficiently dependent
on the United States and flexible and willing enough to negotiate
a settlement, became the permanent U.S. dilemma. One reason
for Israel's dependence on the United States was her need for the
Phantoms, and the question of how many of them should be
handed over was an almost constant preoccupation, with which
I will deal later. It was never a question, though, whether they
should or should not have them, despite the fact that they could
give Israel a potential nuclear capacity—for they could be used,
in desperate circumstances, to carry nuclear weapons to the Soviet
Union. Perhaps the Israelis and some in the Pentagon thought
that this would give the Russians some pause.

DOBRYNIN SUMMONS GOGOL TO THE CONFERENCE TABLE

To please General de Gaulle—since Nixon was anxious to improve relations with the French—the United States accepted a
French proposal that the search for a solution in the Middle East

be conducted on a four-power level among the Americans, the British, the French and the Russians. It was Sisco's idea to begin separate direct consultations between the United States and the Soviet Union about writing a contract between the two for a settlement which, of course, in the end would have to be imposed by the two on Egypt and Israel.

During these private talks, conducted throughout much of 1969 between Joe Sisco and Soviet Ambassador Dobrynin, the Russians first tabled their own peace plan, which was an interpretation of what they understood to be the meaning of United Nations Resolution 242, which had been unanimously adopted in the Security Council and ordered Israel's withdrawal from occupied territory. The United States, dissatisfied with the Russian proposal, advanced its own draft, which sought to combine what was acceptable in the Soviet position with the American one. After many frustrating meetings, including one in Moscow, Sisco finally impatiently produced a document with a complete outline of what could be called a U.S.-Russian contract settlement to bring the negotiations to a climax. It was based on total Israeli withdrawal from Sinai excluding the Gaza Strip and Sharm-El-Shek, but left the general terms to be negotiated.

At one particularly exasperating point during the negotiations between Sisco and Dobrynin, the latter, who likes to ease acrimony by cracking a joke or telling a good story, recalled a parable drawn from Gogol's novel *Dead Souls*. It was about a big landlord who used his many slaves for collateral with a moneylender. The slaves had to be registered in the big city, but when any of them died, the landlord never bothered to have the registrar cross them off the lists. One day, the landlord came to the city to raise a loan. The moneylender checked the registrar, found the landlord's claim as to the number of slaves in his possession confirmed, and agreed to give credit against the "living souls." He insisted, though, that he had to have the receipt for the slaves before he could hand over the money. The landlord retorted that he could hand over the receipt only when he had the cash in hand. They too had a long hassle, but finally managed to agree: One would move the money to the middle of the table, and the other would do the same with the receipt. Then each would quickly grab the part that was coming to him. Dobrynin, eyes twinkling, concluded, "We are facing a similar situation in our negotiations. The only trouble is that neither party is yet willing to move his contributions to the middle of the table."

That really remained the trouble throughout. Neither the Israelis nor the Egyptians were willing to move their chips into the middle of the table; nor were the Russians, though the United States went some distance.

After further endless fencing and fruitless discussions, "Jumping Joe" Sisco, as he came to be nicknamed, lost whatever patience he could still summon and scornfully gave up when the Russians rejected as unacceptable the "contract settlement," which he may have deluded himself had met their conditions.

Kissinger, meanwhile, was not enamored by the idea of a settlement to be accomplished by the United States putting pressure on the Israelis and the Russians on the Egyptians, since its outcome would depend mostly on how effective the United States alone managed to be. "Why should we let the Russians have credit for an agreement that is largely due to American pressure on Israel?" he used to ask.

THE ROGERS PLAN

Rogers made his first crucial move on December 9, 1969, when he combined the text of two American documents—one the outline for an agreement between Israel and Egypt, which he had first submitted to the Russians in private, and the other, between the Israelis and the Jordanians—and in a public speech unveiled them as the basis for a Middle East settlement. It came to be called the Rogers Plan. The Israelis tried unsuccessfully to persuade him not to commit himself so specifically to their withdrawal from occupied territory because, they said, it was all too public; it would undermine their bargaining position, enabling the Russians and the Egyptians to assess exactly the maximum concessions they would have to make, while they themselves would be unable to make any. Thus, the Rogers Plan became one of the most controversial moves of the Nixon administration. In Israeli eyes it was unacceptable because it gave them no "concrete security" and protection against future reversals of Arab policy. The Israelis did not deny that earlier their fundamental requirement had been peace, but admitted that their position had changed. Territorial security rather than peace had become the dominant criterion for Israel. What mattered to the Arabs was the return of all captured territory. That was the crux of the stalemate.

THE SISCO IMPRINT

Rogers and Sisco had pinned their faith on a bilateral (i.e., U.S.-Russian) approach, but probably overestimated the extent of agreement over common ground. Sisco, as one official close to these talks said to me later on, "suffers from a capacity of self-delusion and overoptimism. It has been a persistent strand, even at times when the talks were on the verge of a breakdown." Virtually the entire Washington diplomatic community watched his performance with incredulity. He was the outstanding example of that dying breed of American officials who remained convinced—contrary to what General de Gaulle used to say, that the best diplomacy could only mitigate problems, not solve them—that solutions were still to be found in diplomacy. Perhaps only this kind of psychology could keep him going in these "sandstorms" blown up by irate Arabs or Israelis. There was much open criticism that Sisco in his ebullient optimism and drive for action lacked the patience to narrow the gap in private preliminary explorations, finding out the most that would be acceptable to both parties before shifting the negotiations closer to the public arena. "Above all, not too much zeal," Talleyrand used to say. Bulldozers can move mountains, but they are helpless against shifting desert sands. And the more the Israelis came under public pressure, the more stubbornly they reacted.

Rogers' diplomatic maneuvers looked to some like pique over having been let down by the Russians, to others, designed to warn the Israelis not to take the United States for granted. The overtures to the Egyptians troubled the Israelis, but did not look convincing enough to Egyptians. The idea that the United States could upset Russia's "game plan" by making these overtures was, in the circumstances, too naive.

KISSINGER DISAGREES WITH ROGERS

Henry Kissinger, meanwhile, watched Rogers' and Sisco's initiatives with a growing sense of uneasiness. To him, the Sisco approach was all tactics without a basic strategy. Still he remained on the sidelines, asserting his own views only when he thought that those tactics began to affect American long-range goals. He worried about the growing inroads the Russians were making in Egypt and the Middle East generally, and the ground the United States was losing. He warned that too drastic a shift in U.S. policy would only extend a vacuum the Russians would keenly want to fill. He also feared that the more the United States was seen to be exerting pressure on the Israelis, the more the Egyptians would feel encouraged to accept greater risks with Russian involvement in Egypt, and that the more the United States became preoccupied with the relinquishment of territory by the Israelis, the more the Israelis would become preoccupied with holding on to it for fear that the United States was winding down her responsibilities for Israel's security. To the Russians, Kissinger felt, Rogers' December 9 speech did what they preferred and really wanted the United States to do—impose a solution on Israel. Rogers was thus seen to be telegraphing the wrong signal to Cairo and Moscow, by encouraging both to assume that American "evenhandedness" meant both that the United States was less preoccupied with Israeli interests and more anxious to pursue her own in the Arab world, and that the United States was increasingly unwilling to risk a confrontation with the Soviet Union in the Middle East. It was a strange situation, with Rogers galloping ahead and Kissinger, though holding the reins, preferring not to tighten them.

Instead the Russians, however gradually, began to see new opportunities beckoning to widen their foothold in Egypt, and by the middle of 1970 their ability to contain Israel had grown by leaps and bounds. The Israelis inadvertently helped them when they flew their Phantoms deep into Egyptian territory, dropping bombs as close as twenty-five miles to Cairo. They thus challenged the Russians' willingness to defend their client, and triggered a decision in the Kremlin which led to Communist Russia, for the first time in its history, building foreign bases—the kind of move for which they had castigated the United States for many years. Russian troops were now stationed outside their own traditional defense perimeter and for the protection of another country not contiguous to the Soviet Union. It was also a daring turning point in the history of Israeli-Egyptian confrontation. Soviet pilots had begun flying defensive missions against Israeli raiders and SAM-3 anti-aircraft batteries were being operated by Soviet crews along the Suez Canal. Suddenly the intermittent war had become a different ball game. The Israelis tried hard to prove that their deep penetration raids were not responsible for this drastic change in Soviet policy by arguing that the Russians already had various footholds on Egyptian territory, but the Israelis had said earlier that these raids were designed to show the Egyptian people that their government was incapable of protecting them, and this must have been too much of a taunt for the Kremlin to swallow. It decided to teach the Israelis a lesson.

CEASE-FIRE

A nasty crescendo of the war built up and in March 1970, Rogers announced new "serious initiatives" by the United States: efforts to secure a ninety-day cease-fire and a new attempt by Ambassador Jarring, the UN special representative, to seek another approach to negotiations. The initiatives were buttressed by another announcement that the United States would delay a final decision on the second Israeli request for Phantoms. The new diplomatic initiative was designed to finesse the biggest problem, face-to-face negotiations, which the Israelis insisted on and the Arabs refused to accept. Mrs. Meir was convinced that the Arabs would refuse and told Rogers in private: "If Egypt says yes, I lay my cards on the table afterwards." To everybody's surprise the Arabs, after checking in Moscow, accepted; and after much soul-

searching and five Phantoms lost in combat to the new Soviet
SAM ground-to-air missiles, the Israelis accepted too.

This was the moment when Arabs and Israelis were closest to
a *détente*. It looked like something of a triumph for Rogers and
the best moment to reach for a settlement. Had the United States
stumbled on the right formula?

The ink on the cease-fire agreement was hardly dry, however,
when the Israelis reported that the Egyptians were violating the
standstill agreement and with Soviet aid were moving SAM missiles close to the Canal. U-2 spy planes were not ready at midnight, when the cease-fire went into effect, to observe the truce, but
soon afterward the United States was able to confirm the Israeli allegations. Some sixty new missile sites had been built, the Israelis
claimed. A great controversy developed as to whether the Russians were guilty of having violated the standstill agreement or
not; and if they had, what were the implications and what should
be done. The State Department maintained that it represented
a gross act of bad faith and a direct defiance of an agreement to
which the Russians had committed themselves as, in a sense,
guarantors. Behind the scenes in the White House, however, the
issue did not look so clear-cut. There was some doubt whether
and to what extent the Russians had committed themselves orally
—they certainly had not signed anything. What troubled the
White House was that Sisco, who was the one who had shown Ambassador Dobrynin the cease-fire agreement, displayed a peculiar
self-consciousness about offering to show the paper he had given
Dobrynin to read. It made it difficult to determine what Dobrynin had seen, whether it was an early draft only or the final one,
and what exactly Dobrynin had said. He, at any rate, claimed
that he had given no undertaking and that the Soviet Union did
not consider itself either involved or a party to the agreement. It
therefore could not be accused of any violations.

It was a most unfortunate situation to which the hasty drafting
of the agreement had made a confusing contribution. At least, an
attempt should have been made to get the Russians to counter-
sign the document. They might possibly have done so for, after
all, they had nothing to lose after Egypt, Jordan and Israel had

signed it and after it had become clear that both sides viewed the cease-fire as in their interest. Had the Russians formally signified or declined approval of the cease-fire, then it would at least have made clear whether they were now in a state of grace or perfidy.

This confusion changed a hopeful situation into an unnecessarily contentious one, and whatever prospects for negotiation had appeared on the horizon now vanished. Whatever the doubts in the White House about the justification for the allegations against the Soviet Union, the fact remained that those missiles *had* been moved to the Canal and that the United States had no choice but to be upset by this and to react vigorously. After that experience, the President decided that it was impossible to secure a comprehensive agreement or a *détente* and that the best that could be hoped for was to keep things quiet and avoid a big-power confrontation. A background briefing of the White House correspondents by Kissinger reflected the new tougher attitude toward the Soviet Union. The idea that the United States and the Soviet Union had a mutual interest in negotiating an Arab-Israeli agreement which would remove the dangers of a confrontation between the two superpowers had obviously been abandoned.

THE CHIMERA OF THE NOBEL PEACE PRIZE

Israel was now facing the largest concentration of ground-to-air missiles in the world and Mr. Nixon, as a consequence, moved to provide Israel with the means to combat them; he also requested $500 million from Congress in supplemental appropriations for credit assistance to Israel. The easy passage of these measures in Congress proved that Israel continued to enjoy strong support among legislators. There was much relief in Jerusalem at the turn of events. The more the Russians antagonized the United States, the more the United States found itself limited to the one ally it had in the eastern Mediterranean, and the more it helped Israel, the less likely were the Arabs to respond to U.S. overtures for better relations. The crisis in Jordan, to which I have devoted a special chapter, in September and October preoccupied everybody in Washington. It further aggravated U.S.-Soviet suspicions, and even after it was all over, the prospect for mediator Jarring looked virtually hopeless.

The next initiative for negotiations did not come from the United States, although Rogers was still looking for a rather more limited approach, but from President Sadat. He publicly suggested an interim solution for the reopening of the Suez Canal and linked it to a partial withdrawal of Israeli troops from the Sinai side. What made a new effort seem worthwhile was the fact that Israeli Defense Minister Dayan had made a similar suggestion for reopening the Canal, except that he stipulated a mutual withdrawal of both Egyptian and Israeli troops from the Canal. Messages between Washington and Cairo seemed to flow easily then, even though diplomatic relations had been suspended, and the tone of the exchanges began to sound more cordial. As could be expected, relations with Israel became full of irritations—one cause was American delay in the supply of Phantom jets—and Jerusalem began to get anxious about the new turn of U.S. policy. Rogers, eager to avoid a hiatus in the progress to negotiations, reached for the interim agreement proposal like a thirsty traveler in the desert groping for a glass of water. So promising did the situation look to both Rogers and Sisco that in May 1971 they decided to fly to the Middle East. The visit, they thought, would please the Egyptians as well as worry the Russians and the Israelis, and perhaps this could be conducive to an agreement.

In Cairo, they were impressed by President Sadat and came away reassured that he wanted a settlement and that he had no pan-Arab ambitions. They also thought that his desire to get on better terms with the United States was genuine and that he was anxious to reduce his dependence on the Soviet Union. Indeed, they gained the impression that he would actually like to get rid of the Russians in Egypt and would take steps in that direction provided Rogers could pressure Israel into an acceptable peace settlement. Rogers, buoyed up by this thought, arrived in Jerusalem full of expectation.

He and Sisco suffered a rude shock on the first day when they met with President Golda Meir and her Cabinet. Each Cabinet member made a long speech about the injustices Jews had experi-

enced throughout history and their persistence still, and all expressed their opposition to total withdrawal; some even became
critical of U.S. policy. Rogers, despite his patient, amiable mien,
interrupted several times, complaining that he was forced to listen
to speeches about the past when he wanted to know about the future.

The following day the atmosphere changed. Dayan took the lead
and told Sisco privately that he did not want this visit to end on
a sour note. Then he began to discuss his own partial withdrawal
concept, stressing that under it Israeli troops would in no circumstances go beyond the passes on the high ground in Sinai. Much
of his presentation, however, dealt with Israel's need for additional military equipment. A later meeting with Mrs. Meir, too,
was much more businesslike, and key questions were asked. Would
the Egyptians start shooting if no agreement was reached? (It
would be sowing the seeds of war again, Rogers replied.) How
would the Egyptians take over the area evacuated by Israeli
forces? (Their maximum position was to send Egyptian forces to
reoccupy it.) Would the Russians agree to the idea Rogers had
thrown on the table, the creation of a UN-supervisory organization to water down an all-Egyptian presence? (Rogers did not
know.) Still, toward the end of the meeting, when he asked
whether he should send Sisco back to Cairo to get negotiations
for the interim solution going, Mrs. Meir's skepticism and reservation surfaced again. She replied that she did not want to
decide that. Irritated, Rogers replied that if she could not make
up her mind he would not send him back. "I'm trying to be
helpful; it is up to you to say whether you want help." Then
putting on a little more pressure with a veiled threat, he reminded
her that Israel had only one ally left in the world, the United
States, and if she lost that one where would Israel stand? To
encourage Mrs. Meir he added that he had come away from Cairo
with the impression that Sadat was fed up with the Russians. He
did not think that the Egyptians were under any real obligation to
them because they were paying for all the arms they were getting,
and so he thought an interim agreement was possible; it would lay
the basis for getting the Russians out of the Middle East—and

that was what was vital to the United States. Mrs. Meir expressed hopes, but made no specific commitments or concessions.

Rogers and Sisco returned to Washington nevertheless slightly intoxicated by the experience and by the prospects for advancing the cause of an interim agreement. At the first staff meeting on his return Rogers, giving an optimistic interpretation of the results of his mission, leaned over to Sisco and laughingly suggested, "We may still come to share the Nobel Peace Prize!"

AN INCURABLE SCHIZOPHRENIA

At whatever level one tries to cope with the Arab-Israeli conflict, the problems are enormous. Most difficult of all is to reach a conclusion on how to resolve the schizophrenia between the desirability of a peace settlement—which would mean putting pressures on Israel that could come close to strangling her—and making certain that in the face of the Soviet challenge, Israel would remain strong enough to be able to maintain a military balance.

As usual, the views about Israel differed according to emotional reaction. Thus, in one view she was shrewdly taking advantage of this situation; in another, she was making the best of a dangerous and difficult one. The best way to obtain the Israelis' co-operation was to give them what they needed and make them feel secure; or the only way to get concessions was to put heavy pressure on them. Israel had inadvertently helped the Soviet Union to establish a base in Egypt; or the Russians had put their foot in the door anyway and would have proceeded when the timing looked right. With the experts sitting on such seesaws, no one has convincing evidence to prove he is right. Most people, though, agree that if they were in Israel's shoes they would not play it much differently, for its current frontiers were the most defensible—so why budge? And where was there any international guarantee that Israel would find safer?

Hardly anything could have come as a greater surprise, however much one is used to the shifting sands in the Middle East, than President Sadat's temerity in suddenly ordering Russian troops out of Egypt. True, he had hinted at the possibility to Secretary Rogers, but he had firmly attached the unalterable condition of a peace settlement with Israel. All through the closing months of 1971 he had threatened at least once a week that he was about to go to war against Israel, but nobody took him seriously. All his efforts to persuade the Russians to give him the offensive weapons he needed to launch his attack were turned down in the Kremlin. On past experience the Russian leaders had had their confidence sapped in the Egyptian armed forces. They did not want once again to be confronted with the humiliation of an ally and the loss of precious modern Soviet equipment. Nor, of course, did they want to be dragged into the war to save a client state from the jaws of defeat. They now knew better than in the days before the Six-Day War in 1967, when CIA was amazed at how badly informed the Russians were about the capabilities of the Egyptian armed forces and their military leadership.

The inability either to go to war or to have a new peace had become intolerable to Sadat and his military; the one was frustrated by the Russians, the other by the Israelis. All the same, when Sadat did ask the Russian troops to go it was probably as much a surprise to the Kremlin as it was to the White House. Henry Kissinger's desire to see the Russians "expelled" from Egypt, as he had once incautiously put it, was being fulfilled for him, and quite gratuitously. It seemed to put the United States in a favorable strategic position, but however great the cheers in Washington, Sadat's self-assertive impulse came at an awkward time. An impending U.S. presidential election does not provide the most propitious climate for initiatives involving Israel. In that country, too, it represented an awkward development, for Mrs. Meir and her colleagues still felt that the *status quo post bellum* was better than any change.

The greatest achievement of Secretary Rogers' Middle East policy was to have maintained the cease-fire and to have created a situation which promised relative quiet before the presidential election.

However much the Russian military presence was reduced, Russia continued to have an economic stranglehold on Egypt, especially through the Russian agreement for financing rural electrification and their support of the local aluminum industry. The Kremlin's long-term bet is still on the Arab world. Russian influence in the area, actual and psychological, is still greater than it has ever been. The Russians were not put off when President Sadat provided the airlift that helped dislodge a Communist regime in the Sudan, or by their loss of influence in Libya or by the defeat of Syrian forces using Soviet tanks in Jordan, and they accepted their embarrassment over the expulsion of their military forces with restraint. They continue to have naval facilities and more warships in the eastern Mediterranean than ever before. Comparatively, of course, the mighty U. S. Sixth Fleet is still an overwhelming force, but it is shadowed by Soviet surface vessels and submarines, and is under aerial surveillance from Soviet TU-16s.

Russia's growing stake in the Middle East may, in fact, further her interest in peace. At least, that has been the experience of most imperial powers; the British, for instance, became increasingly responsible as their empire, and their respectability, grew.

President Nixon on entering the White House was assumed, as I have said, to be more pro-Arab than pro-Israel. His approach to the Middle East was to be "evenhanded." His aides did not think that he had many votes to lose among American Jews, and the Israeli Government, aware of that, was extremely worried about how Israeli interests would fare under a Nixon administration. But gradually it became obvious to Jerusalem that Mr. Nixon was in this case less influenced by domestic political considerations than by the challenging attitude of the Soviet Union. For as the prospects for a peace settlement between Egypt and Israel declined, so American concern grew over the Soviet challenge in the area. The inbuilt schizophrenia that haunts American policy in the Middle East became obvious again and the White House felt the need to shift the emphasis from befriending the Arabs to fortifying the Israelis, whose needs were determined not always by a military yardstick but sometimes by the kind of warning signals President Nixon wanted to send to Moscow. Yet when, in December 1971, he gave Israel additional Phantoms against Mr. Rogers' advice, this specific signal looked rather more directed toward the Jewish voters.

The Soviet Union could not crowd the United States out of the Middle East; in fact, it learned the lesson that the French and the British learned a long time ago about the treachery of the shifting sands of the Middle East sooner than expected.

Senator Mansfield believes, and he did so even before the Russian troops were ousted from Egypt, that the Sixth Fleet should not remain in the Mediterranean. He told me, "I think that there ought to be a multinaval force, composed of the nations rimming the Mediterranean on the European side, of which American ships would be part of the complement. I agree that this is a delicate area where the Soviet Union, with the opportunity to leave the Black Sea through the Bosporus and the Straits to go to the Mediterranean, is a good deal closer than we are; still, I believe that the primary responsibility should rest with the nations in this area." When I asked how such a shift in the balance of responsibility for the area would affect the security of Israel, he offered this view: "I doubt that such a shift has much to do with the security of Israel, because Israel by and large has gotten by pretty much on its own. There have been references to the time when the situation became tense and the elements of the Sixth Fleet were dispatched close to the coast of Lebanon. By implication it meant that this was done for the purpose of defending Israel. My private conversations with President Nixon do not confirm this supposition. It was the evacuation of Americans, should the situation get out of hand, that was the purpose of the dispatch of those elements of the Sixth Fleet."

Senator Mansfield's views notwithstanding, though, the American presence in the Mediterranean is unlikely to be reduced substantially, even after a settlement between Egypt and Israel, which will have to come some time in the seventies. This does not mean the U.S. power and influence in the area will not diminish relatively as the Soviet Union seeks to extend its own between the eastern Mediterranean and the Indian Ocean. The Middle East will remain a crucial testing for President Nixon's theory of self-restraint among superpowers.

CHAPTER EIGHT—INTERNATIONAL
POKER IN JORDAN

The American power position in the Middle East had never been challenged quite so seriously and aggressively by the Soviet Union as it was in September and October 1970. Soviet ground and airborne missiles were now operational in Egypt and pointed at Israel from across the Suez Canal, a growing Soviet fleet was running interference with the U. S. Sixth Fleet in the Mediterranean, and pro-Soviet regimes were in power in Syria and Iraq. The United States had one firm and militarily powerful anti-Soviet ally in Israel, and another in the pro-Western but militarily and politically weak King Hussein of Jordan, whose preservation seemed more a liability than an asset because the Palestinian guerrillas appeared to have gained greater control of Amman, his capital, than he had. His overthrow therefore became a temptation to the Soviets as well as to the Arab radical forces who saw in his non-hostility to Israel an obstacle to its destruction.

This temptation led to a showdown with Israel and the United States, which became Mr. Nixon's most serious international crisis up to that point. It also became a textbook case of brinkmanship, which succeeded because Nixon seemed to be good at calculating the odds in international poker. But he won, above all, because he held a trump card in his hand which the Soviets were unable to match among the Arabs—Israeli military power.

For months King Hussein had hesitated what to do about the Palestinian guerrillas, El Fatah, who in open defiance of his government of Jordan and his Royal Army, had come close to controlling the kingdom. The Royal Army's prestige had sunk so low that Jordanians preferred joining El Fatah to enlisting in the regular Jordanian forces. But in the end it was the Soviet-supported Syrian attempt to aid the fanatical Palestinian guerrillas gain control over Jordan that helped to lance this boil.

THE HUMAN CHIPS

It all began with the guerrillas focusing world attention on their irrationality and their terrorism when, during the first week of September 1970, they succeeded in hijacking three airliners, one Swiss, one American and one British. All three were forced to land, in what was a coolly planned operation, on the same desert airfield in northern Jordan, a World War II RAF base then known as Dawson Field, but rechristened Revolution Field by the guerrillas. Only their attempt to capture an Israeli El Al Boeing 707 failed. In that abortive hijack attempt, an Israeli guard on the plane killed the male Arab hijacker and arrested his Arab girl companion just before they landed in London. Drunk with the success of their brazen exploits, the guerrillas confronted the British, German, Israeli and Swiss governments with demands for the release of all Palestinian terrorists held by them in custody; the Americans held no terrorists, but the reason an American TWA plane was included in the hijacking operation was, no doubt, the influence they could exert on the Israelis. The chips in this first round of high-stakes poker were the lives of the passengers.

For all the governments involved the great issue at stake was whether to hold out against the terrorist demands and risk the lives of those innocent passengers or whether to yield to domestic public pressure and give in. On Monday, September 7, after a series of hurried meetings between Deputy Under Secretary of State U. Alexis Johnson and the ambassadors of Britain, the Federal Republic of Germany and Switzerland, it was decided in view of the seventy-two-hour deadline that the three governments should firmly demand the release of all the passengers and all the aircraft. The Americans moved fast and put on pressure after indications that the three governments were vacillating, and after rumors that they were exploring bilateral deals with the PFLP (Popular Front organization). However, the situation steadied when they agreed to the American proposal and it was put through to the hijackers via the International Red Cross.

The British Government at first played it cool and firm and refused to release Miss Leila Khaled, the Arab girl hijacker, who was in custody at a London police station. The Germans were wobbly, the Swiss remained steady, and the Israelis, in spite of the fact that the Jewish passengers were subjected to special threats, refused to accede to any of the terrorist demands. The Israelis held some three thousand Palestinian terrorists in their prisons. The cool of the British Cabinet, however, began to wane when public pressures at home mounted to obtain the release of the 127 passengers against the release of Miss Khaled. The American position hardened; Nixon did not want the Palestinians to win this poker game because, he thought, the ultimate price would be infinitely greater if they were allowed to do so, for their real aim was to shatter any chance that existed for a Middle East settlement. The audacious game of blackmail was not really directed against Israel, which was too hard a nut for them to crack, but Jordan and Egypt and those governments involved with the negotiations for a Middle East settlement, especially the American and the British. They hoped to prove by their success that they were the true representatives of Palestine and that their violent methods were more effective than negotiations. The first victim of their strategy would have been King Hussein.

THE BRITISH AMBASSADOR DEFIES THE FOREIGN OFFICE

The United States, consequently, pressed the British Government to hold firm. The British Cabinet, however, became increasingly impatient with the American attitude and seemed to be losing its nerve as pressure in Britain mounted for using Miss Khaled to get back the passengers of the BOAC plane. John Freeman, the British Ambassador to the United States, had come to sympathize with the broader argument advanced by the White House of the wider implications if the Palestinian guerrillas were allowed to succeed, but he had a hard time trying to convince London. There the Foreign Office was more concerned with the fate of the passengers; in its view, the only hope of maintaining a common front depended on the Americans managing to persuade the Israelis to release a number of hostages from among the 450 whom they had newly arrested without consulting any other government. The so-called co-ordinating group, which met in Berne with the Israelis as observers, tried but failed to persuade them to make some concessions to advance the release of the passengers, who were being treated with increasing cruelty.

The diplomatic activities during the weekend of the thirteenth reached something of a fever pitch. From Amman came urgent demands for the immediate release of Miss Khaled. From Washington Kissinger got in touch with 10 Downing Street, and his assistant Major General Alexander M. Haig, Jr., with the Foreign Office to persuade the British Government not to give in. The British Embassy in Washington also made every effort to explain the importance of maintaining a steady hand and why the Nixon administration had come to be so insistently opposed to any concessions. Freeman had come to the conclusion that to repeat again and again the instructions from London to press the Americans to press the Israelis would only aggravate the situation, but he became really perturbed when London hinted that unless some specific offer was made by the Israelis, the British Government would find it impossible to maintain the kind of common front against the guerrilla demands the White House insisted on. The Federal Republic of Germany, too, warned Washington that without Israel's co-operation it might have to proceed on its own. Both London and Bonn had become alarmed because the whereabouts of some of the hostages was unknown, the International Red Cross had no effective contact with the guerrillas, and the deadline set by the PFLP for the destruction of the planes had been reached.

It was during the night of the thirteenth that John Freeman, in an urgent late-night transatlantic call, once again explained to Sir Denis Greenhill, the Permanent Under Secretary at the Foreign

Office, that the White House, which by then had taken charge of the crisis, disagreed with the assessment in London. The Americans were convinced that the deadlines threatened by the fedayeen were being taken too seriously, and that it was unlikely that they would kill the hostages, for then they would deprive themselves of their only bargaining chips. The Americans also did not think it wise to force the Israelis into releasing those 450 Arabs they had arrested in reprisal, because they thought, based on past experience, that it would make them only more stubborn. They felt confident, though, that if everybody held fast against the guerrillas' threats, the situation would improve and then the Israelis too would become more co-operative. Freeman therefore pleaded for patience in London, questioned the wisdom of the instructions he had received from there and, in fact, made it clear that he would not carry them out. Sir Denis, in turn, used all his experience, and it was considerable, to implore Her Majesty's ambassador to carry out his instructions; in fact, it had not occurred to him that he would not, in the end. But Freeman balked. Finally, Sir Denis diplomatically left the decision to Freeman.

It was one of those unusual cases nowadays when an ambassador, convinced that he knew better than the government he represented what was the best policy for it, stood his ground and defied his instructions.

In the meantime, throughout those hectic and convulsive days, the Press Office of the Prime Minister gave the impression to the British press, correct in the beginning, that Mr. Heath was keeping his cool and firmly refusing to yield to the demands of the Palestinian terrorists. It was a case of "news management," inspired either by foresight or by a refusal to allow Mr. Heath's image as a determined, undeterred man to be tarnished until events proved otherwise. In the end, the Israelis released their hostages between the sixteenth and eighteenth and Miss Khaled was given her freedom on the thirtieth.

At the height of the crisis, the United States had been considering a military rescue operation of the hostages by dropping American parachutists on to the airfield. It seemed a particularly tempting idea because of the fighting that had broken out between King Hussein's troops and the PFLP, and this would have been one way of having an excuse to establish an American presence close to Amman which could be used to save the threatened existence of the Hashemite kingdom. Some policy makers were indeed advocating such a risky action, but no one was strongly in favor of it. Instead, to indicate that the United States was at least making contingency preparations for military intervention, two mobile units were readied in Turkey, twenty-five Phantom jets were moved to a U. S. Air Force base in Incivlik, Turkey, and so were six C-130 transports for a possible evacuation operation. In addition, a U.S. aircraft carrier and supporting ships of the Sixth Fleet were ordered to a position within reach of Jordan. The PFLP commandos, when rumors of possible American military intervention spread, seemed in panic.

KING HUSSEIN'S SHOWDOWN WITH THE FEDAYEEN

The crisis suddenly looked like it was assuming broader proportions when Henry Kissinger received a warning from British intelligence that the Jordanian Army was about to move against the fedayeen, a move that the United States had been encouraging but King Hussein hesitated to take. Kissinger was at Airlie House in nearby Virginia for an award ceremony honoring Secretary of Defense Laird, when King Hussein officially declared war against the fedayeen to "settle his account" with them, as he put it in his communications to the United States and British governments. About dinnertime, General Haig called from Washington to say that the Jordanian Army had begun moving against the fedayeen. Kissinger immediately returned to Washington, together with David Packard, the Deputy Secretary of Defense, Admiral Thomas Moorer, chairman of the Joint Chiefs of Staff, and Joe Sisco. It is difficult to assume that King Hussein did not have American approval for his move, even if the timing was left entirely to him. But now that the operation was in progress, Kissinger in talking to the assembled group of high officials in the White House said that this was a civil war, yet the United States had to make contingency plans for two possibilities: one for the United States to enter the fray, the other to let the Israelis do it. He also suggested that if King Hussein lost the war, it was for the United States to move first, for, Kissinger reasoned, if the Israelis went in, this would precipitate a war in the Middle East. The idea that Israel might be tempted into a desperate move was not well received—to put it mildly—by those present. President Nixon, at this moment in Chicago on a speaking trip, chose the occasion also to visit the editorial offices of the Chicago Sun-Times for a background talk, and to signal the Soviets that the United States did not intend to sit idly by in this crisis. He broadly hinted that if the situation required it, the United States might have to intervene militarily. For the benefit of the editors, he added that it might be beneficial if the Soviets thought the United States capable of "irrational or unpredictable" action. It was one of those basic dicta Nixon believed in. When the Sun-Times in a carefully worded story next day reflected this warning, he later congratulated the writer of the story for his skilled and careful handling.

That night the civil war between King Hussein's forces and the fedayeen began in the streets of Amman. There was much disagreement among the experts as to whether he could survive. The British, for instance, who once upon a time created the Hashemite kingdom, were much less confident than the Americans. Having held sway over the Middle East for so long and lost it, and yet also having retained certain imperialistic hang-ups or hankerings about it, the British offered expert but somewhat despondent predictions. The Americans, because of their superpower status and their stake in Israel, took a much more optimistic line. They estimated not only that Hussein had a good chance of survival, but also that if he could mow down the fedayeen, he would be able also to overcome the deep antagonisms that would follow. What encouraged King Hussein, who for so long had avoided dramatic action against the Palestinians, to action was the fact that the U.S. initiative for a cease-fire between Israel and Egypt had been accepted by Egypt and also had the support of the Russians. It put him into a better position for seeking a showdown.

NO CHEAP WAY OF OUTSIDE INTERVENTION

The basic problem Kissinger and his group were wrestling with at this point was not how to retreat from this hazardous situation, but how to preserve American influence in the area and how to prevent the Russians from broadening their power position. There was no cheap way of outside intervention, nor was there an easy answer as to how to strike a balance between keeping Israel from precipitate action and yet letting it maintain a posture that would deter the Russians from heating up the crisis further. As a first step, the United States decided to reinforce American military power in the eastern Mediterranean in an ostentatious-enough way to bolster Israeli courage and to warn the Russians. Troops were alerted in Germany in a way the Russians were bound to pick up; the 81st Airborne Division at Fort Bragg was ordered into readiness; and another carrier and helicopter landing ship were also ordered into the Mediterranean. The Israelis in turn had begun to mobilize—which must have become equally obvious to the Russians, too, as men disappeared from the city streets—and massed tanks near the Golan Heights; the Israeli Air Force was also placed on the alert.

On Friday, September 18, the United States received an urgent Russian note saying that the Soviet Union was doing its best to keep other countries from intervening. It sounded reassuring and made Kissinger think that the crisis was over. Mr. Nixon, however, remained dubious, and, as it proved, with reason. On Sunday morning, some three hundred Syrian tanks suddenly began to move into Jordan. They were Soviet made and their Syrian crews, Soviet trained; obviously, they would not have moved without Soviet approval. Instead of taking the issue to the UN Security Council, as some American officials and foreign diplomats proposed, the President decided that all the United States would do was to answer the Soviet note curtly and to point out that the Russians had been wrong to say, as they had claimed, they had used their influence to prevent others from intervening. After that the United States refused to communicate with Moscow. The expectation in the White House now was that the war would come to a head, that the Israelis would move, that Egypt would follow and that the Russians would then have to move as well.

On Sunday, Secretary Rogers called in Soviet Ambassador Dobrynin and thereafter the State Department announced that he had been told that peace in the Middle East was a common interest and that the Russians should do what they could to get their friends, the Syrians, to go back to where they belonged. Dobrynin again claimed that his government had made representations in Damascus.

CO-ORDINATING U.S. AND ISRAELI ACTION

President Nixon during those crisis days met every morning with Kissinger, Rogers, Laird, Helms and Admiral Moorer, weighing the options and giving directions. The proposal for U.S. troops to parachute into Jordan and shoot their way into Amman was turned down, but intervention by the U. S. Air Force was considered a real possibility so long as the Jordanian ground troops were able to hold their own. The preferred alternative, however, was to let the Israelis undertake the air strikes, with U.S. air power protecting their rear against possible Egyptian and Soviet intervention. U.S. intervention, it was agreed, might widen the war, while intervention limited to the Israelis might contain it, especially if two or three air strikes succeeded in turning the tide. In case the Syrians gained the upper hand on the ground, however, the United States would have been ready to let the Israelis move their ground troops into Jordan as well. All the various alternatives, realistically stated, were contained in an NSC paper, but no one knew what the President thought about it.

In the meantime close contact was established between Israeli and U.S. military intelligence, though as yet no joint operations had been formulated. An American COD intelligence-gathering plane ostentatiously established contact between the Sixth Fleet and the Israeli military command, with the mission of exchanging air target information. In Washington, diplomatic contact between the White House and the Israeli Embassy was such that both sides knew what each was thinking and although long-out-standing American assurances were reinforced that weekend, on the specific authority of the President, the Israelis were not given anything in black and white, so as to prevent them from inter-preting such guarantees as an incentive for intervention. What was clear, though, was that the United States encouraged Israeli inter-vention should the Syrians gain the upper hand on the ground.

Once the United States withdrew its objection and Israel moved its armor to the Syrian border, Syria and the Russians be-gan to realize that they were courting a serious confrontation. The only country that could have deterred Israel from moving was the Soviet Union, but by then it had become clear to Moscow that the United States would offer the Israelis a shield and escalate the war if necessary. At that point the Russians, knowing that the Syr-ians could not match Israeli fighting power, began to put pres-sure on Syria to withdraw.

On Tuesday night, as the war fever graph shot up dangerously high, Kissinger purposely chose to attend a dinner party at the Egyptian Embassy and made it quite obvious that he was availa-ble for private talks. Soviet Minister Counselor Yuly M. Voront-sev, who was also present, picked this up and sought him out. Again he tried to reassure Kissinger that the Soviet Union was doing everything to stop the Syrian tanks. He sounded tense, al-most incoherent. Kissinger replied coldly, "The last time you told me that the Syrians would send no more troops . . ." Vorontsev replied heatedly, according to Kissinger, "We didn't know the Syr-ians would cross the border, our own military advisers stopped at the border and went no farther." Kissinger ended the conversa-tion abruptly, "Your client started it, you have to end it." Voront-sev was correct in saying that the Soviet experts did not move with the tanks beyond the Syrian border, but it was also true that they had advance knowledge of the Syrian decision to intervene.

SYRIA GETS ITS NOSE BLOODIED

The Syrians, whose aims were a limited operation to help the fedayeen by intimidating the Jordanian Army, put up a poor show and lost no fewer than 130 T-54 tanks, close to half their force. They had the choice of calling in their air force in support instead of withdrawing, but they chose withdrawal. They knew that ordering their air force into the fray would have given the Israelis the cue for throwing in their aircraft and then the chain of events would have been rapidly extendable. King Hussein was also helped by the fact that the Palestinians proved weaker than expected, and that the loyalty of the Jordanian Army was greater than had been assumed. The Russians also began to restrain Damascus, to prevent the escalation of the war. The hijacked aircraft were destroyed, and their passengers gradually released.

And so it all ended up better than expected; the most serious crisis Nixon had been confronted with up to that point suddenly petered out.

Those directly involved in steering this crisis agree generally that the main credit for the success must go to the Jordanian Army, which inflicted decisive losses on El Fatah and on the Syrian tanks, and to the incompetence of the Syrians. King Hussein was also greatly helped by the rapid Israeli mobilization and the fact that the Syrians and the Russians knew Israel stood poised on the frontier ready to intervene; it was especially reassuring for him to know that Israel wanted this crisis sorted out and in his favor. The American saber rattling certainly helped and must have given the Russians pause.

What made a great difference in comparison with the June war in 1967 was the co-operation that obtained between Washington and Jerusalem, and which greatly helped to prevent Israel from going it alone. In all this the United States was also very conscious of the precedent of the Suez crisis of 1956, when Israel led France and Britain into an intervention from which they never quite recovered. Thinking back to 1967, one reason, I think, why the war between Israel and Egypt started was that President Johnson got himself involved in the situation to establish sufficiently the legitimacy of the Israeli complaint, but without then giving them enough help. This time Nixon fully supported the legitimacy of the Israeli moves, which not only gave them time to get into position, but also assured them of American military support should the Russians intervene and Israel's survival be in question. This, in turn, made it easier for the Israelis to agree to the condition that they would not attack unless they had given the United States advance warning.

Whether the President would indeed have been in favor of intervening had it proved necessary is difficult to know even for those closest to him. He is a very private man, especially in situations as risky as this one was. Certainly a mood of great caution prevailed at the White House throughout the crisis. Everybody, however, felt that intervention was not ruled out. Laird and Admiral Moorer were certainly not eager to get into another war. They saw all the stark liabilities ahead, with American military capacity already sorely strained and the repercussions of the involvement in Vietnam still in their bones. Israel, however, was ready to move if necessary, and though I doubt whether this would have provoked the Russians—who were militarily too weak in the area to risk challenging the United States—to intervene, if they had done so the United States would not have been able to stand idly by.

Mr. Nixon saw the situation in its broadest implications. Jordan to him was a microscopic spot on the map and yet he viewed it as having far-reaching implications on the worldwide stage and on American relations with the Soviet Union.

The idea that Soviet-American relations must be viewed as a chain with each link representing a test of the validity of relations as a whole was again uppermost in the President's mind. That was also the reason why he spent so much time seeking the right alchemy between the application of military strength and that of diplomacy.

Nixon decided to show his fist in the Middle East because he feared that the Russians interpreted his Doctrine as a policy of weakness. He used the Israelis, who were only too eager to be used, to impress the Russians that they could not gain any decisive advantage by using their Arab client states as proxies to change the balance of power in the Middle East. It may have helped to convince the Russians that mutual self-restraint is the best policy for the superpowers in this area.

CHAPTER NINE—UNITED STATES
CONGRESS: SPEARHEAD OF RETREAT

The Congress became the gadfly of the retreat of American power for two basic reasons: It sensed and reflected the mood of the public more accurately than the President, and it felt with resentment that it had been taken for granted by Presidents for almost a generation. Ever since the mid-sixties, a determination had been growing to reassert its constitutional powers in foreign affairs and to be less deferential to the White House. What gave the situation its touch of irony was that this resistance to the Executive welled up under a President who had been once the leader of the majority party in Congress and who had been thought of as one of the most astute, most experienced and effective parliamentarians: Lyndon B. Johnson.

He more than any of his postwar predecessors mishandled Congress by trying to manhandle it. Admittedly he obtained more than most from Congress in domestic legislation, and that reserves him a special place in history; but it was obtained at a cost. His pride in his legislative achievements and his utter self-confidence in his dealings with Congress made him insensitive to the growing impatience on Capitol Hill with the war in Vietnam and the steadily less willing assumption of the burdens of a world role that flowed from it. Johnson's nature did not admit of backpedaling; he failed to realize both that the public mood had begun to change and that the pendulum was swinging back from the Executive toward Congress.

Little less than twenty-five years ago a Democratic administration under President Truman succeeded in creating one of the most harmonious relationships ever achieved between the two on foreign affairs. Even if one takes into consideration the fact that President Truman was greatly helped by Stalin's policies and the profound fears of Communist expansionism that pervaded American public and political opinion, such monuments to statesmanship as the Marshall Plan (for aid to Europe), the Point Four program (for developing countries), and the NATO treaty were proof of how fruitful and co-operative the relationship was. The secret of that golden "buddy-buddy" era was the intimacy that first General Marshall and then Dean Acheson were able to develop with the powerful Republican Senator Arthur Vandenberg from Michigan and Democratic Senator Tom Connally from Texas. (It is a measure of how much things have changed that some today will readily categorize the senators' role then as "acquiescence" or even "subservience.") The intimacy went very far. Some of Vandenberg's and Connally's speeches were written in the State Department, and much of the legislation was formulated there, as were even some of the committee reports. Vandenberg insisted on being privy, as he once put it, to the "take off" of policy, and the State Department went far in obliging and in sharing vital governmental secrets. Thus key congressional hands had a sense of participation in the policy-making process and also of sharing in the responsibilities for these policies. It sounds rather like a fairy tale today, and it is justifiable to ask whether such co-operation does not entail some risk of undermining the valuable American system of checks and balances.

As the Communist threat became less intimidating and the harbingers of a *détente* began to appear, and as the Executive began to take intimacy for granted by short-circuiting the "advice and consent" relationship, so Congress became less deferential. In 1961, Senator William Fulbright, the chairman of the Senate Foreign Relations Committee, still favored strong executive leadership in foreign affairs. He was impressed then by the efforts of President Eisenhower and his new Secretary of State Christian Herter to thaw out the cold war, and annoyed by the endeavors of what were then called "captive nations" lobbyists to prevent Congress from supporting the presidential efforts toward *détente*. In an article published under the title "American Foreign Policy in the Twentieth Century Under an Eighteenth-Century Constitution" Fulbright wrote:

> The force of an effective foreign policy under our system is presidential power. This proposition, valid in our own time, is certain to become more, rather than less, compelling in the decades ahead. The pre-eminence of presidential leadership overrides the most logical and ingenious administrative and organizational schemes. The essence of our "policy-making machinery" and of the "decision-making process"—concepts of current vogue in the academic world—is the President himself, who is neither a machine nor a process, but a living human being whose effectiveness is principally a function of his own knowledge, wisdom, vision and authority. It is not in our power to confer wisdom or perception on the presidential person. It is within our power to grant and to deny him authority. It is my contention that for the existing requirements of American foreign policy we have hobbled the President by too niggardly a grant of power.*

Gradually, however, he turned from being one of the truest believers in presidential power to one of its most passionate detractors.

WHY FULBRIGHT TURNED AGAINST THE PRESIDENCY

What really triggered Senator Fulbright's rebellion was the deception he felt President Johnson had first perpetrated on him with the so-called Tonkin Resolution. When the President asked him on August 6, 1964, to introduce that resolution in the Senate and to obtain the quickest possible passage for it, he was convinced that it was based on incontrovertible evidence. Furthermore, he was so worried about the threat posed by Senator Barry Goldwater, that year's Republican nominee, that he did not want

---

* Fulbright, *Cornell Law Quarterly*, Fall 1961.

to deny President Johnson anything that could hurt his re-election campaign. Fulbright was still suffering from a conscience about his investigation into the scandals of the Reconstruction Finance Corporation in the early fifties, which Truman had angrily labeled "asinine," and which Fulbright later came to feel might have contributed substantially to Adlai Stevenson's defeat in 1952. The shocking revelations and the adverse publicity the report engendered hurt not only Truman but also the Democratic Party and thus Stevenson. Fulbright, having been the floor leader who advocated prompt passage of the Tonkin Resolution, came to see himself as having helped President Johnson to escalate the war, thanks to the authority the resolution gave the President. In their sympathetic biography, *Fulbright the Dissenter*, Haynes Johnson and Bernard M. Gwertzman wrote that Fulbright regarded his leading role in getting the Tonkin Resolution through the Senate as "his most humiliating moment in public life."†

Fulbright was further outraged when President Johnson ordered the Marines to go ashore in Santo Domingo on April 28, 1965, without consulting Congress and under what Fulbright thought were false pretenses. It was a decision that Johnson took in a fit of angry activity which those around him then still remember with a shudder: Nobody could calm him. It was the first official U.S. military intervention in Latin America since 1927. (Whatever one may think of the merits of this operation, at least in military terms and limited duration it was something of a model for this kind of intervention, especially in contrast to Vietnam.)

These two events, however, completely changed Fulbright's outlook and fueled his bitter, passionate crusade against both Presidents Johnson and Nixon, in which he became the leading advocate of the retreat from the arrogance of power.‡ Thanks to his position as chairman of the Senate Foreign Relations Committee and the attention he stimulated with the news media, which relish the drama of confrontation, the once very private Fulbright

† Johnson and Gwertzman, *Fulbright the Dissenter*, Doubleday & Company, Garden City, N.Y., 1968.
‡ He enlarged the theme into a book called *Arrogance of Power*, Random House, New York, 1966.

became a very public and very controversial figure. Despite his phlegmatic manner and outward diffidence, and his slow, lazy-seeming southern drawl, he became a star TV performer, a tenacious, ferocious and omnipresent crusader, a permanent presidential stumbling block.

THE POWER OF THE SENATE ARMED SERVICES COMMITTEE

The most effective challenger to the Senate Foreign Relations Committee, however, is not the President, but the Senate's own Armed Services Committee. It has a quieter way of operating. It prefers to avoid publicity and yet, in its own ways, it has been more effective than the Senate Foreign Relations Committee in what it wanted to achieve, mainly of course because it tends to support the Executive's requests. It has been traditionally the repository of hawkish sentiments and the defender of military and intelligence interests, which for a long time enjoyed greater support than *détente* policies. Its long-time chairman, Richard Russell, was a far more powerful man in the wings of Congress than Senator Fulbright, for he tended to have power and influence in the White House and was able to elicit favors others could not. President Johnson, for instance, and the Pentagon were able to get whatever they requested from that committee for the Vietnam war, at least until 1966 when even the members of the Armed Services Committee began to worry about American "overcommitments." This did not mean that Senators Fulbright and Russell, or Fulbright and Stennis agreed with each other. John Stennis, Democrat from Mississippi, was not unlike President Johnson in his belief in the need for arrogance of power, but worried that the instruments of power had become too thinly spread around the globe. President Johnson for a long time refused to read the writing on the wall and only saw the coonskin there, that symbol of victory ever since Daniel Boone.* President Nixon from the start of his Administration knew that he had to de-escalate the war, but since he also wanted an honorable end—and in this he

* See William Safire, *The New Language of Politics*, P. F. Collier, Inc., New York, 1972.

did not differ substantially from Johnson's psychology—he was for some time in two minds about how to accomplish both.

However isolated a President may be in the White House, he nevertheless can—if he wants to—sense the winds of public opinion and the pressures from Congress, and I have little doubt that both helped Nixon make up his mind.

The Founding Fathers had vested Congress with war-making powers—to declare war and to appropriate money for the military services—because of the way English monarchs, especially Charles II, involved themselves in wars for which Parliament had to pay. The fact that this check on power reposed in Congress had been side-stepped by President Truman when he involved the United States in the Korean war, by President Eisenhower when he landed troops in Lebanon and by President Johnson in the Dominican Republic and Vietnam. The favorite gambit was to request Congress to pass broad resolutions which would give the President wide war-making powers without having to consult Congress first. Thus, for example, the Eisenhower administration got the Formosa and Middle East resolutions. Both were important instruments for indicating to Americans and to the world that the Executive and Congress were united in their determination to pursue their declared policies, and this is so useful a function that it would be a pity if it could not be retained even if it had to be within resolutions more narrowly drawn up; in future, though, it will be much more difficult to persuade Congress to approve such resolutions.

Congress at first offered Mr. Nixon a longer honeymoon than anybody expected, but the mood for a showdown with the President soon asserted itself, and Congress was out to recoup some of its lost powers and authority. Symbolic of this trend (though of no greater significance) was a resolution, approved unanimously by the Senate Foreign Relations Committee, which stated that it was the sense of the Senate that the President should not commit the U.S. armed forces to hostilities on foreign territory without "affirmative action" by Congress. The full Senate passed this resolution in June 1969.

THE SHOWDOWN BETWEEN NIXON AND CONGRESS

However, by the end of that year it had become obvious that generalized resolutions reasserting existing congressional powers were not enough. A flood of resolutions was tabled and voted on in the Senate and the House, all designed to expedite the ending of that unwinnable war, all designed to express mistrust of official policy. In an interview with the Washington *Post*, the quiet but powerful chairman of the House Appropriations Committee, Representative George H. Mahon (Democrat, Texas), a long-time hawk and backer of the military, said, "There was a time when any member of Congress would hesitate to vote against anything proposed by the Joint Chiefs of Staff because he might be subject to the charge of being soft on communism. Now, since Vietnam that day is over." Then—after a pause—he added, "It could return."

When President Nixon ordered American troops into Cambodia without first consulting Congress, and only belatedly asked more than one hundred senators and representatives from both parties to White House briefings, his excuse was that this operation would not widen but shorten the war in Vietnam. He assured them that the American ground forces would be out of Cambodia before July 1, 1970, but the Senate reacted with an amendment proposed by Senators John Sherman Cooper and Frank Church to a foreign aid bill stipulating that the President could not use any funds to introduce American ground combat troops or military advisers into Cambodia, though it agreed to the Administration's request for more military and economic aid to that country.

The President could have taken the sting out of the Cooper-Church amendment by simply ignoring its implicit criticism and saying that it accorded with his own policies. Instead, he treated it as an insolent attempt to curtail the presidential prerogatives and made an issue out of it. He warned that only he could judge whether this operation was necessary to facilitate the withdrawal of 150,000 American troops by the following spring. He threatened, "If Congress undertakes to restrict me, Congress will have to assume the consequences." In fact, he made certain that American troops would withdraw from Cambodia by the deadline he had set.

The Cooper-Church amendment, barring the use of ground troops in Cambodia, was passed by the Senate and first rejected by the House of Representatives; it took almost seven months after the Cambodian "incursions" before it became law on December 29, 1970. By then it also included a provision barring the introduction of ground troops into Thailand and Laos, stipulating also that a 2.5-billion-dollar fund for Free World forces in Southeast Asia (another phrase for mercenaries) could not be used for military support in Cambodia or Laos. The extension of the ban to ground troops entering Cambodia, however, was deleted in the final version that became law.

This resolution certainly represented an unmistakable limitation on the President's powers and may have contributed to his decision not to use any American ground forces in the Laos operation, which he sanctioned the following February, but was left to be carried out, however poorly, by South Vietnamese troops. The Cooper-Church amendment thus became something of a landmark in the congressional challenge to the President.

Otherwise, though, the President pursued his own policy at his own pace. He kept the congressional opposition forces at bay, mainly by living up rigidly to his withdrawal schedule and by promising in advance to continue withdrawing at the same or at a faster rate and by stressing his doctrine of disengagement. This calmed public opinion and reinforced those senators who were reluctant to have a real showdown with the President. As Senator Stennis put it: "The basic question is, do we really want to relieve the President of his responsibility in the handling of the war?"

Senator Mark Hatfield from Oregon, who sponsored one of the withdrawal resolutions together with Senator George McGovern, maintained that Congress had a constitutional responsibility for the war and the power to bring it to an end. But this was not the majority view. Nor was it the prevailing view in the House of Representatives. Though more willing to be critical of the conduct of the war than in the past, in the crunch, House Speaker

Carl Albert, Majority Leader Hale Boggs and Thomas Morgan, chairman of the House Foreign Affairs Committee, protected the President. Albert in particular, while a loyal Democrat in domestic policies, is a strong believer that foreign policy should have bipartisan backing.

It is often said that the House, whose members must seek re-election every two years, reflects more accurately the state of public opinion and that, judging by the members' voting habits, it mirrors what Mr. Nixon calls the "Silent Majority," the constituency he likes to consider his own. It is more tolerant of presidential leadership, more patient with the Vietnam war, more willing to back American world commitments. It is a fascinating switch and confirms that the Silent Majority, once the backbone of isolationism, remains the steadier, more co-operative backer of an internationalist foreign policy, while the more sophisticated Senate, under stronger liberal influence, more globally oriented, now has strong withdrawal symptoms from world responsibilities. The symbols of sophistication have their own change of fashion.

The Senate saw its opportunity in the public distrust opened up by Nixon's presidential leadership. Fulbright and his equally suspicious colleague Senator Stuart Symington from Missouri decided to take advantage of it and to send out their own investigators instead of relying on testimony by members of the State Department. The results startled the Senate Foreign Relations Committee and caused much embarrassment to the Executive. A secret defense pact with Thailand was uncovered which the United States had signed in 1965, new facts about the extent of the U.S. involvement in Laos and about U.S. base commitments in Spain came to light; all this led to intensive questioning of State Department officials and to various new curtailments imposed by Senate action. Some of them such as the amendment prohibiting the use of American troops in the defense of Thailand and the financial restrictions on mercenaries were indeed limiting presidential power in specific situations; others had a certain psychological value as a veiled warning to the Executive not to act thoughtlessly or incautiously.

But the assertive and critical congressional mood of retrenchment extended to many other issues. The Senate, for instance, not
only heavily cut the foreign aid bill, but in November 1971 did
something it had never dared to do before: completely rejected the
foreign aid authorization bill. Even though it later passed a
badly truncated bill, it nevertheless symbolized the declining
American interest in playing a responsible role in this field. With
American cities in full cry about the need for more federal aid,
members of Congress felt increasingly inhibited from voting for
an unpopular bill, and with the disenchantment among liberals
over the way foreign aid had been used to provide military sub-
sidies, and with the traditional fiscal conservatism among South-
erners and Republicans, who never had much sympathy for foreign aid, the Senate's willingness to continue it was rapidly
declining.

All this was virtually beyond a President's powers to reverse.
Foreign aid had been "sold" to Congress for so long as a cold-
war measure that it became impossible in times of international
détente to find enough reasons to explain the continued need for
it. But the less the United States, the richest nation, is willing to
aid the developing nations, the wider will grow the chasm between
the rich and the poor. A commensurate American contribution—and it is now in terms of the gross national product relatively lower than that of any of the industrialized nations—is
particularly needed at a time when American military influence
around the world is declining. Also, the more frustrated and
hostile these nations become, the more they will consider how to
retaliate. Their weapons in this fight for survival are their basic
raw material resources essential to the industrial countries.

Congress is hard put to see the light. It is willing only to view
the situation from a very narrow perspective, and willing only to
consider the present. For this reason, and because it is a far too
disunited body with too many diverse special interests and no
strong leaders, it cannot assume the kind of foreign policy-making
role it would like to appropriate to itself.

RESTRICTING THE WAR POWERS

The most far-reaching attempt to restrict the President's constitutional powers is the so-called War Powers Act of 1971, designed to forestall the President's leading the nation into undeclared hostilities. Its architects are one of the most liberal, most enlightened among senators, Jacob Javits of New York, and the conservative hawkish Senator Stennis. The oddness of this combined sponsorship is also indicative of the trend of senatorial opinion. But, I believe, there is a limit to which Congress can go in creating a formal set of restrictions on the President. In the case of the War Powers Act, the thirty-day authorization period, after which the President could not continue a military involvement, does not sound practical in our time. It would mean arguing the case for some twenty days in Congress, and the consequences of such a discussion on the credibility of international American commitments is easily visualized.

Even without the War Powers Act, though, trust in American overseas commitments has been badly shaken by various congressional actions. The more Congress turns against the Executive the more uncertainty this injects into American foreign policy, and the more difficult it becomes for foreign governments to rely on governmental promises or to assess the future course of American foreign policy. The Mansfield resolution for a partial withdrawal of American troops from Europe, for instance, may have enabled the Administration to obtain a bigger contribution to American troop costs in Europe, as some officials believe. But the opposite may also be true, that the uncertainties created by Mansfield have made European governments reluctant to accept a greater share of troop costs.

Congress is also forcing the pace of the American retreat of power by cutting heavily into the defense budget and by defeating the President's proposals for the financing of the supersonic transport plane. It is part of the psychology of the retreat that this country, which always wanted to be first in everything, now does not care as much whether it will be outdone by Anglo-French or even Russian competition, at least in this controversial field. It is a far cry from the days when the United States bent every effort to catch up with Russia's sputnik.

Many think that to impose budgetary limitations on the President is a healthy safeguard. But if it means depriving him of his flexibility in matters of policy, it could handicap him seriously. Walter Lippmann said that "to make our system work, it is essential that the initiative of the President be respected by Congress," and spoke of "the simple-minded fallacy that because Congress appropriates the money it can and should run the government. . . . Congress is trespassing upon the constitutional prerogatives of the President in attempting to determine foreign policy by legislative injunctions and prohibitions." These are fighting words, but anyone who has followed the haphazard efforts of Congress to legislate in the field of foreign policy will have much sympathy with the Lippmann view.

The record of Congress in the field of foreign policy making is far from reassuring and at times highly disturbing by its inconsistencies and misjudgments and even blindness. It would therefore not be a service either to Americans or the world at large if Congress, in its drive to force the pace of the American retreat, tried to impose its will on the President. There are enough signs that this will not happen. In a real emergency the President always has an immediate ability to sway Congress and to obtain its backing. He has the means to execute the kind of shock treatment Congress still reacts to, especially with television at his disposal. But the aggressiveness of Congress and its efforts to penetrate more deeply into the policies behind the President's policies has also caused the Executive to become even more reticent and secretive. Congress should be an intelligent and watchful critic and brought more into the confidence of the Executive, but it cannot expect to assume a greater policy-making role. It does not have the expertise, it does not have the staff. A telling detail of how ill-equipped it is by comparison with the Executive is the fact that while the Administration employs four thousand computers in the collection and examination of facts, Congress has only four, and at least two of those are busy with administrative chores.

The pendulum of power, of course, tends to swing between the Executive and Congress, and it will do so again. Senator Fulbright has been trying to establish a foreign policy-making role for the Senate through the Senate Foreign Relations Committee, and in the wake of the catastrophic experiences of the war in Vietnam he made a certain amount of headway. Senators Javits and Stennis by getting acceptance of their War Powers Act have enshrined symbolically the mood of the seventies in the Senate. But once the memories and consequences of the Vietnam war have faded and crusader Fulbright is gone, the doctrine he has been trying to establish will prove to have been impractical. In my view, the change in a conservative like Senator Stennis is more significant and, as I have said earlier, the Senate Armed Services Committee has always been more effective than the Senate Foreign Relations Committee in what it tried to achieve. The new mood in the Senate Armed Services Committee, therefore, is more important and so is the concrete power it holds over military budget making and management. It can limit the number of aircraft carriers the United States will build or determine whether the Pentagon should be permitted to escalate the arms race another notch into a new generation of weapons, and it, no doubt, took courage from a Gallup poll that showed that a majority favored cuts in the defense budget.

It is still a novelty for the Congress to impose its will on matters of military strategy because for years it had become used to authorizing them as a matter of course. World War II, the Korean war and the Cuban missile crisis induced a sense of insecurity among Americans that frightened Congress into sanctioning almost everything the military asked for, and without much expert scrutiny. But the mistakes of the military, which I analyze at length in a later chapter on the Pentagon, have changed that. The *détente* fostered by the Kremlin, the White House and Peking has also had its effect on Congress. It has become less intimidated by the expertise of the military and begun to acquire its own. Experts in Washington always gravitate to where power is, and since Congress has been trying to wrest some of the powers from the Executive, more of these experts are willing to work for congressional committees, especially the Senate Armed Services Committee, which used to be content with hiring former military men, whose views differed little from those they held while in uniform. Helped by the swing in American public opinion, military budgets in the last two years have shrunk in terms of stable dollars. Indicative of cuts in defense spending was the fact that over a million defense jobs were eliminated. Most of it was done by the Executive—Deputy Secretary of Defense David Packard deserves much credit for this—but Congress too helped to trim the defense budget both in 1969 and 1970. What made these cuts particularly significant was that they occurred while the United States was still engaged in a war.

Barring another war, the continuing shift of emphasis from foreign to domestic preoccupations will be particularly noticeable in Congress in the seventies. With expenditure for domestic social legislation skyrocketing, new limitations are bound to be imposed on military spending. It will be much more circumspect in appropriations for weapons and virtually make it impossible for the President to assume new overseas commitments. It will continue to seek a reduction in existing commitments and thus will remain the spur to the retreat of American power.

CHAPTER TEN—THE END OF SPECIAL
RELATIONS

Henry Kissinger wrote, in 1965, in his book A *Troubled Partnership*:

> . . . the "special relationship" [Anglo-American] has never had the same psychological significance for the United States that it did for the British. . . . As the postwar period progressed many influential Americans have come to believe that Britain has been claiming influence out of proportion to its power. Consequently they have pressed Britain to substitute close association with Europe for the special ties across the Atlantic. This school of thought has objected to giving Britain a preferential voice or even the appearance of it.*

With the relatively simple world that had emerged from World War II changing from confrontation between the Atlantic alliance and the Soviet bloc to a more varied pattern of multipolarity, and with coalition diplomacy being replaced by a new larger balance of power diplomacy, special relationships in the Western alliance were also undergoing some basic readjustments. The one most obviously affected was the so-called Anglo-American special relationship, but the U.S.-West German and the U.S.-Japanese relationships, although of a very different hue, were also undergoing a transformation.

* Kissinger, McGraw-Hill, New York, 1965.

Kissinger was correct in claiming that psychologically the special relationship was more important to the British than to the Americans. After all, the Americans emerged from the war as the victors in name as well as in fact, while the British were only victors in name. The United States was now the most powerful nation in the world with world-wide commitments, while the British had suffered cruel physical damage and lost far more of their military, economic and financial power than they realized at the time. Churchill most probably sensed it and therefore decided that the only way the British could continue to play a leading role in the postwar world was to perpetuate the wartime relationship with the United States. In discussing the Anglo-American alliance on his first visit to France after the liberation, he explained to General de Gaulle the difference between the British and the French approach to influencing the Americans. The British, he said, were convinced that the best way to achieve this was by working with them as closely as possible. The French, he went on, and no doubt he meant De Gaulle, believed that the best way was to oppose them.

What aided the British in this endeavor was the fact that the United States Government was still uncertain of the leadership role that had suddenly been thrust upon it; it felt that the British with their centuries of experience knew more about the world and Western civilization and how to preserve both than the United States. It wanted company in the lonely business of being the world's leader, especially when the world immediately after one great war looked as if it might risk another confrontation, this time with communism and the Soviet Union. Even though the British were only able to play the junior partner in sharing those responsibilities, the United States saw a real advantage in preserving the wartime alliance and continuing it as a special relationship, unique among modern nation-states. There was no need for a written agreement, the basic rules were obeyed as they are in Britain under an unwritten constitution.

For some years after World War II, the United States was short on specialist expertise in foreign affairs, intelligence and economic and monetary matters, and British power still held sway over some crucial areas in the world. In those early postwar years, Britain still shared, at least relatively, 50 per cent of the burdens with the United States. But year by year, the debilitating effects of the war asserted themselves, even though the true facts of Britain's weakness, militarily and economically, remained camouflaged for longer than was good for Britain. Yet in the late forties and early fifties, the British and also the Americans saw advantages in inflating the appearance of British power through the aura of the special relationship. It worked in oddly devious and counterbalancing ways. At times the anti-colonialism implicit in American thinking expedited the retreat of British power: This was especially so in Africa, as Americans later discovered to their detriment and the British concluded to their advantage. At others, British politicians allowed the illusion of Britannia's power to blind them to their own and their country's detriment, and this was especially so in the case of the Suez adventure.

THE HURT OF SUEZ

Suez was the lion's last, strangled roar and it dealt a fatal blow to the intangibles of the special relationship. The British had been accustomed to reminding the Americans of its unwritten rules whenever they found that they were not getting the co-operation they felt they deserved: Now they were the ones who broke the rules by misleading Washington about what they were up to. Eisenhower flew into such a rage that he instructed John Foster Dulles, who was if possible even angrier, to side with the Soviet Union against the British in the United Nations, and Britain, in turn, used her first veto—against the United States. It was the blackest week in Anglo-American relations since the active alliance had begun with Pearl Harbor. In my diary I wrote at the time: "From now on the U.S. will decide for herself how to deal with Russia and other problems. It will seek solutions without consulting Britain." And although this was still not quite correct because the mystery of the special relationship proved to have a greater resilience than I and perhaps anybody at that time supposed, the Suez crisis nevertheless left an indelible mark of hurt and basically shattered confidence between the two governments. The permanent officials of the State Department in particular never forgave the British for it. The politicians who moved in and out of the United States Government were, however, more flexible. Thus Eisenhower swallowed his anger and bitter disappointment later when Harold Macmillan, his old wartime chum, became Prime Minister; the passing of John Foster Dulles and his replacement by Christian Herter also helped.

In Dulles' mental handbook to diplomacy, expeditions of the Suez kind as tools in the exercise of power to attain political ends were, I am certain, not excluded. In fact, he proved this a year later with the U.S. landing in Lebanon, and in Eden's place might well have chosen the same path, however differently he might have staged it both diplomatically and militarily. At a dinner party I gave for H. V. Hodson, then editor of my own newspaper, *The Sunday Times* of London, six weeks before the fatal Suez operation began, Dean Acheson challenged Hodson to present a convincing case why Britain should resort to the use of power, as he had been editorially advocating. Hodson in his quiet and scholarly way—and, be it admitted, a way much to Acheson's taste—made his case. Acheson had earlier in the conversation seemed to disagree with the proposition, but now he replied, "You have persuaded me. I would have backed your case." Then he paused and added, "If you succeeded."

What really upset Eisenhower was that Eden proceeded in stealth and with the obvious intent of timing the operation to coincide with the American elections in the hope that this would prevent the Eisenhower administration from interfering with it. The mutual antagonism Eden and Dulles felt for each other may also have made its contribution. Dulles was an intellectual of sorts, whether one agreed with his outlook or not, who thought deeply if often wrongly about the problems at hand, and tried to apply his own rationale to them. Eden, though long experienced in international affairs, was an intuitive, impetuous man who relied on his hunches. He was easily bored with intellectual analysis, especially Dulles' way of debating problems, and as a consequence, whenever the two met they usually managed to part in greater discord than when they had begun. Their disagreement about the usefulness of summitry with the Russians, for instance, was quite fundamental and caused much mutual antagonism. After Suez there was no longer any pretense about the true evaluation of British power and her usefulness from the American Government's point of view.

MYTH OR REALITY

The question, however, whether the special relationship was in truth more a myth than a reality went much further back. Leafing through my diaries of the fifties, I was surprised to recall how many serious disagreements buffeted Anglo-American relations during those postwar years, and yet how much reality the myth had assumed. My surprise proves how tolerant both sides were of these differences—it was a flexibility no other two nations were capable of. Co-operation in the nuclear weapons field between 1945 and 1955, for instance, was suspended, and so was co-operation in diffusion and centrifusion technology. Despite the manful efforts, which he described in his book *Present at the Creation*,† Dean Acheson failed to get Congress to co-operate with the British, although a Special Committee of National Security chaired by him recommended full collaboration on all atomic energy matters, including weapons. The congressional opposition weakened at a meeting in October 1949, after the Russians had exploded their first nuclear bomb, but on February 2, 1950, just as things looked like moving forward toward a new agreement, Klaus Fuchs, the British nuclear physicist, was arrested and charged with passing information to the Russians. Fuchs's treachery confirmed all the congressional prejudices about British security and the prospects for an agreement between London and Washington again vanished.

The differences between Britain and the United States on Middle Eastern policy, even before Suez, were also profound. The Middle East in the early fifties hardly existed in the minds of American strategists, and the outlook at the United States Embassy in Cairo was so anti-British and pro-Egyptian that it in

† Acheson, W. W. Norton, New York, 1969.

effect encouraged Egyptian resistance to British policy. In the Far East, the Americans were deeply upset when Britian, despite American pressures to the contrary, recognized Communist China. The British refused to co-operate when John Foster Dulles tried to save Indochina for the French. In Europe, disagreement over the rearmament of West Germany was a traumatic experience. The controversies over sterling balances were also fundamental. My diary notes reflect the fact how *un*special the relationship was, even when the official relationship was at its height.

On January 10, 1950, for instance, after a private conversation, I quoted Sir Oliver Franks, the then British Ambassador to the United States, as follows:

We are in a difficult transitional period in which the momentum of Anglo-American co-operation must not be lost, though it is evident that it already has lost some of its impetus. The great danger at present is the absence of a broad policy on both sides, and with each side waiting for the other to produce something new, smaller problems are accentuating a growing irritation. The Truman administration has allowed itself to become too much the prey of fears of congressional reactions and intimidations and is in danger of losing its constitutional initiative. On the other hand, the momentum of British policy initiatives has gone too. What makes me pessimistic about the future of Britain and Anglo-American relations is her economic situation. We need to work up some courage to propose a solution of our sterling balance problem (sterling held in escrow [on deposit] for many countries, which if dumped on the market could seriously threaten the value of sterling on which in turn depended the functioning of the so-called sterling area) and to increase our productivity.

Shortly before leaving Washington in 1952, Sir Oliver sounded more upset than he would normally have liked to admit:

The American mistake is that they are trying all the time to impose their own way of doing things on the Europeans. If it isn't German rearmament it is European unity, if it isn't their view of the Middle East it is their view of China. They have acquired a habit of putting on all the pressures whenever the Europeans do not follow, but the Europeans cannot be badgered like that because they have a more co-ordinated way of evolving policy than the Americans. Americans behave in Europe as if it belonged to them.

I was surprised at the time to hear one of the most pro-American among British ambassadors to Washington leave the post he had ennobled with unusual distinction, on this angry, disappointed note.

U.S.-EUROPEAN DILEMMA

Dean Acheson, one of those who emotionally, if not intellectually, believed in the special relationship, wrote in *Present at the Creation*: "Of course, a unique relation existed between Britain and America—our common language and history insured that. But unique did not mean affectionate. We had fought England as an enemy as often as we had fought by her side as an ally. The very ease of communications caused as many quarrels as understandings." He made those comments during some Anglo-American staff talks in London in preparation for a Foreign Ministers' meeting between the United States, Britain and France, when a paper was produced by British officials, defining the special nature of Anglo-American relations, which in his view could have caused serious trouble with the French. The British had produced it, ironically enough, because the Americans were reluctant to acknowledge the partnership officially!

At that time, in May 1950, the French Foreign Minister Robert Schuman and Jean Monnet authored together the Coal and Steel Community plan, which Acheson saw as a kind of mild forerunner to European unity. Later he wrote that "the refusal to join it was Britain's great mistake of the postwar period," indicating that in his view Britain had a more important future in close association with Europe than tied to the United States. Sir Oliver at that time still had illusions about the Anglo-American relationship, for he said to me that those relations were safe because Britain was the only country the United States could rely on in an emergency. That was true, he said, for two reasons: It was politically the most stable country in Europe, and the United States was not quite ready to pay the price of world leadership. Both men's estimates were, as it happened, accurate ones. But Acheson did not take account of the strong conviction then still prevalent in London that Britain would be playing a secondary role as part of Europe; while Franks did not go so far as to confess that in partnership with the United States Britain would not only preserve a quasi-independent power position, but could still hope to recapture a genuine one. For Britain, partnership with the United States was only to be set against her relations with the erstwhile Empire, the new Commonwealth. For Americans, however, there were other special relationships to be considered.

Both Acheson and Dulles also had a special respect for Germany's postwar Chancellor Konrad Adenauer. They knew they could rely on him for support of their policies, and their view of Europe was very much akin to his. When I met Adenauer in 1951 he explained that view to me as follows: "Look at Europe—what does it consist of? Britain? Aloof. France? Politically unstable because of its influential Communist Party. Italy? Economically unstable. And Benelux does not count." He paused for a moment, raised his non-existent eyebrows and then asked rhetorically: "What does Europe therefore consist of—the Federal Republic of Germany." In many ways Dulles and Acheson shared this view, and they therefore felt strongly that the power of Europe had to be based on a stable Germany. They also accepted Adenauer's view that a strong West Germany would act like a magnet, as he put it to me, and, by attracting East Germany, lead to German unification. But the essence of U.S. policy was, as George Kennan, then head of the State Department Planning Staff, put it to me in 1950: "We must build a home for Germany to prevent it from going its own independent nationalistic ways." The house was built, but inevitably it had a view in two directions: to the West and the East. The view to the West had its discouraging aspects because the division between pro-American and pro-French factions created an unhealthy split, and because the United States was constantly threatening to reduce its military presence in Germany. The view to the East gained in attraction the more the Russians played their *détente* card and the more the future of American policy was being questioned among West Germans. It was of course possible to remain a faithful member of the NATO alliance and to seek a *détente* with Moscow; indeed, Chancellor Brandt always maintained that the close relationship with the United States and with NATO made it possible for him to negotiate from a position of relative strength with the Soviet Union. However, the special relationship between Washington and Bonn, which is not a sentimental one but based coldly on common security interests, will very much depend on the extent to which the Federal Republic of Germany will give priority to advancing Western European unity over a policy of accommodation with the East.

It might be supposed that British sympathy to American urgings toward Europe ought to have been implicit in the special Anglo-U.S. relationship itself, but the fact was that for some years after World War II, the British Government was convinced that American public opinion favored its view that Britain could not associate itself exclusively with a European union. Moreover, American pressures did not take into account either the strength of British public feeling, which contrasted even the self-aggrandizing Americans warmly with late allies and enemies across the English Channel, or the difficulties that British politicians felt they faced in any move toward Europe. These feelings were shared by both Labour and Conservative parties. Shortly after Harold Macmillan became Prime Minister in 1957 I had a private talk with him at 10 Downing Street, and asked him why he had not lived up to his convictions and led Britain into Europe. Without raising an eyebrow he said, "As Foreign Secretary I thought of it and tried, but I came to the conclusion that the Civil Service was too much against it. Then when I moved to the Treasury, I thought I could do it by way of economics, but I didn't stay there long enough, only nine months. And now that I am Prime Minister, I have found that it is impossible."

It was the British, above all, who deceived themselves in spite of American pleading to accept the logic of the situation. Dean Rusk, when he was Secretary of State in the Kennedy days, enjoyed telling a story to illustrate the strenuous American efforts to persuade Britain to enter Europe. A girl was dreaming in her bed when suddenly a hulk of a strong handsome man entered her room through the window. The girl, frightened, pulled her blanket over her eyes and asked the man, "What are you going to do to me?" "That's for you to decide," the man replied, "it's your dream."

THE MAGIC OF PERSONAL RELATIONS

When Harold Macmillan took over from Eden he managed brilliantly to overcome the profound division the Suez affair had created among the British public by sweeping it under the rug; the Americans, in contrast, believe in catharsis as the cure after a great crisis; there is no better illustration than the agonies over Vietnam.

Macmillan was determined to hang on to the special relationship, and the fluke of his special personal relationship with President Eisenhower and later with Kennedy helped to resuscitate it; certainly it was by this time no longer sustained by any underlying realities. Britain could no longer uphold the power position Churchill had sketched for it after the war. Britain, in his view, was in a unique position to promote strength and unity in the Western world. He saw it at the center where three circles cut across each other: the Commonwealth, Western Europe and the Americas. It was this continuing world role that Churchill emphasized, one that even the Labour Party, though it began Britain's disengagement from "world policemanship," as the Americans call it, did not want to shed. But by 1947, Britain was too weak to sustain the three-circle policy. Dean Acheson realized the dangers of a British collapse and with others in the Administration mounted the Marshall Plan. Successive American administrations, however, made it difficult for British governments to overcome their dilemma. On one hand, they pleaded that Britain should go into Europe, on the other, they wanted it to continue to help carry the burden of world responsibilities. Those Americans who argued that the two were compatible simply did not want to face the dilemma either. And so successive British governments hung onto the special relationship, especially after General de Gaulle came to power again and frustrated Britain's attempts to seek entry into the Common Market.

I remember seeing Harold Macmillan at 10 Downing Street shortly after John F. Kennedy's inauguration as President in January 1961. What troubled him more than anything at the time was how he would be able to establish a close personal relationship with the new President. "It was easy with President Eisenhower," he said to me at the time. "We got to know each other in Algiers during the war, we became friends and then remained friends. We also belonged more or less to the same generation. But now with this young, cocky Irishman in the White House, how can I create a new, close personal relationship?" He looked at me as if in real despair. Then he added, "We belong to different generations, and on top of it he is an Irishman. He will be difficult to deal with." However, even though their first meeting in Palm Beach, when President Kennedy sought the Prime Minister's support in the Laotian crisis, did not go well, they later became fast friends. Macmillan mesmerized Kennedy, with what the President considered his foxy, casual Britishness and his political craftiness, and the President became genuinely fond of him. Kennedy, in fact, proved a better friend of Britain's than Eisenhower. During that period one of the worst misunderstandings between Washington and London occurred. The United States decided to abandon Skybolt—a missile to be launched from a bomber, which the British had been promised to prolong the life of their Canberra bombers—but forgot to consult with the British and to check how this would affect them. The reaction was so devastating that President Kennedy, against the advice of his closest aides, went further than he intended and agreed to give Harold Macmillan the Polaris missile together with the designs for the Polaris-carrying nuclear submarines. It was a remarkable concession on the part of the Presi-

dent in order to rescue the special Anglo-American relationship—
and to make up with his aggrieved friends Sir David Ormsby
Gore, Ambassador in Washington, and the British Prime Minister. It was a clear case of personal relations saving the special relationship from another mortal blow. The reason the misreading
on both sides occurred, in spite of the closeness of the President
and the British Ambassador, was well defined by Professor Richard
Neustadt in his book *Alliance Politics* when he wrote that "those
who play at governing in London or in Washington are playing
different games by different rules. However much they mingle
with each other, every player carries in his head the rules of his
own game."‡

And yet it was also under the Kennedy administration that the
most determined effort was made, at least by the then highly activist State Department, to force Britain from a preferential position with the United States into equality with the rest of Europe.
George Ball, the Under Secretary of State, and Walt Rostow,
chairman of the State Department Planning Staff, tried persua-
sion, even coercion, to achieve their goal. It was also under that
Administration that the utility of the British independent nuclear
deterrent was publicly deprecated and yet it was also this Administration which at the Nassau conference helped to prolong it for
fear that the United States Government and Kennedy could be
blamed for the fall of the Conservative government.

FRIENDS TO KEEP SECRETS FROM

By the time Mr. Nixon came to power, Britain still meant more
than the other European allies to him. Kissinger at the time said
to me that he did not see anything immoral about insisting publicly that there was still a "special relationship," or that this would
disqualify Britain from entering Europe, where he thought it belonged, because it was due to General de Gaulle that Britain was
still cooling her heels on the European doorstep. The professor, as
he still liked to be called, had by then sadly tempered his admiration of the General with the conclusion that while De Gaulle had

‡ Neustadt, *Columbia University Press*, New York, 1970.

been extraordinarily astute in spotting everybody else's weakness, he had failed to come up with anything constructive himself. Kissinger thought that De Gaulle had created an intolerable situation and that the anchor of Europe could not be shifted to Germany without its becoming the target of everybody's resentments. Because of this constellation, Britain's role as the balance wheel in Europe gained meaning to Kissinger. Thus Britain kept a somewhat preferential position in the Nixon administration. The British Ambassador still had easier access than any other—perhaps with the exception of those representing countries that had special crisis relationships with the United States such as Soviet Ambassador Dobrynin and Israeli Ambassador Itzhak Rabin—and secret information was still given more readily to Britain than any other country.

Much was also still being made, especially in the minds of jealous countries not so favored, of the fact that secret intelligence cooperation continued to give validity to the special relationship. But those Americans who ought to be able to assess that aspect best, while allowing that it still had some usefulness, also frankly admit that British co-operation in that field had ceased to be of such importance that the United States could not do without it. One of the ironic consequences of this exchange was, as one knowledgeable American put it, that the British Government, used to taking its own intelligence reports seriously and acting in accordance with them, read the American reports with the same sort of seriousness, at least until they learned that the American Government did not. This was proved time and again in the case of the CIA reports out of Vietnam. For a while, therefore, the British wondered in their "wrongheaded" way why American policy did not reflect the conclusions of its intelligence reports. U.S.-British intelligence exchanges about the targeting of the American nuclear strategic forces were relatively intimate. Such information—about China—was given at first by the United States to Pakistan, but when it became evident that this information got into the hands of the Chinese with hardly any delay (or none at all), outdated information was substituted.

When Mr. Nixon first visited London as President in 1969 there were still a few remnants of common Anglo-American interests, but it was mainly memories that were left. He resurrected the "special relationship," however," by calling it that, giving a certain amount of pleasure but also causing some embarrassment and eyebrow raising. Many people in Britain by then had accepted that the special relationship had become a myth.

This was even more true by the time Prime Minister Heath and President Nixon met in Bermuda, just before Christmas 1971. Too much had happened for either to pretend that even their own personal relationship could still be called "special." What had badly undermined it in the Prime Minister's view was the President's failure to take him into his confidence on the Kissinger visit to Peking—Kissinger had spent a few days in London shortly before departing for Peking, but had given no hint of his planned visit— or about his decision to end the convertibility of the dollar into gold. Mr. Heath suddenly felt himself treated like any other ally; he was particularly disappointed because he and Nixon had had a fairly long-standing personal relationship. He had made a point of seeking out Nixon on his private visits to the United States while he was in opposition and Mr. Nixon was still in the political wilderness. Nixon appreciated such attention at a time when much of the world ignored him; he admired Heath's determination and decisiveness; and both, as strong partisan conservatives, felt a political kinship with one another. Their relationship was such that Heath, while still in opposition, was able to send President Nixon messages regarding U.S. policy toward Rhodesia, which in fact went against Harold Wilson's policy.

Heath, unlike his predecessors whether Conservative or Labour, never had a special emotional attachment to the United States; he was a latecomer to the idea of the special relationship. He did not feel comfortable with it, except so far as it meant his own with Nixon, which was not in truth very far for the simple reason that neither man understands the real meaning of personal relations. Both are loners, introverts, inclined to put political self-interest above almost everything.

And so in contemplating the virtues of the special relationship with the United States, Heath, who had hardly acquired the taste for it, had already lost it. He did not believe in perpetuating a myth in which neither he nor the Americans any longer saw real profit. Also the outlook on Britain's role in the new Europe was undergoing a change. Kissinger once wrote that "Where Britain tended to exaggerate its special influence in Washington, the United States may have overestimated the extent of Britain's pliability. It became an axiom of United States policy that Britain's entry into a supranational Europe would be a guarantee of Atlantic partnership. This is why Washington championed Britain's entry into the Common Market so ardently and why it was so outraged when this policy was thwarted."*

President Nixon was not an activist for Britain's entry into Europe. If anything, he was more ambivalent about this than his predecessors for the simple reason that more people in the United States Government had come to have doubts about the extent to which it was still in the American interest.

The problem that preoccupied the British Embassy in Washington by the time Mr. Nixon assumed the presidency was how Britain, as part of the Common Market, could still act as a bridge between the United States and Europe. The hopeful answer then seemed to be that Britain could possibly fulfill this function by defending some of the U.S. economic interests in Europe and by asserting its political leadership in Europe. But the idea of playing the "Trojan horse" in Europe for U.S. interests had disappeared (if it ever existed), for at least in the view of Prime Minister Heath Britain's first interest was to help make the European Community into a new European power. Britain, to adapt Dean Acheson's famous aphorism, had found a new role while the United States, by a fluke of history, was groping for one.

UNNATURAL FRIENDS, UNWELCOME RIVALS

Next to the special informal relationship with Britain and the realistic relationship with the Federal Republic of Germany (though there is no separate, bilateral treaty), the United States also had a formal treaty relationship with the former enemy Ja-

* A *Troubled Partnership*, op. cit.

pan. Its purpose was to protect Japan's national security and to ensure that it would not seek a nuclear military capacity. For years
this was a relatively stable, if somewhat patronizing relationship,
at least while Japan was willing to play it by the established rules.
But when Japan, intent on nothing else but how further to spur
its own galloping gross national product, how to increase exports
and general prosperity, came into serious conflict with American
economic interests, this relationship changed. The Japanese in
their productive zest and brilliant inventiveness had overrated the
patience of American big business and Mr. Nixon's relationship
to it. Angry that the Japanese Government, despite its promise to
do so, did not place voluntary restraints on its exports, Mr. Nixon
deliberately affronted Japanese Premier Sato by giving him no
hint of his new policy toward China. And when the Japanese refused to revalue the yen voluntarily, he forced this on a short-
sighted government by his new monetary policy of August 15. After that, Mr. Nixon's great gesture of the return of Okinawa was
quickly forgotten and a crisis of confidence developed whose aftereffects may prove to be lasting. The difference is that while the
American special relationship with Britain was, as Mr. Heath preferred to call it, a "natural" one, the one with Japan is an "unnatural" one, for Japan's historic affinity is to China. But however unnatural it is, there are some basic inevitabilities that force the
United States and Japan into close co-operation. Japan has developed the kind of sophisticated export production since World War
II that will have to rely for years to come on the American market.

For some hundred years, ever since the Meiji era, Japan's trouble has been its economic weakness. Now it is its economic
strength. Among Americans it has led to fears that Japanese competition could become a serious threat to American industries. A
similar fear has gripped the Europeans, and Prime Minister Heath
once told me that he had warned the Japanese privately not to try
and swamp Europe with the goods it cannot sell in the United
States because it would only lead to new protectionist measures.
In Peking, the fear is that this industrial power could easily be
translated into military power.

The Japanese-American Security Treaty has been extended

without any serious objections by Japanese public opinion. But the extension ties Japan to no fixed term, and symbolizes that, after having been closely linked with the United States, she has now started on her "age of choice," as the Japanese themselves call it. This new "age," however, also coincides with the introduction of the American version, the Nixon Doctrine.

Both to the Europeans and the Japanese the United States is preaching that they must assume greater responsibilities for their own security. The British nuclear deterrent remains closely linked to the American; the French is not, but the two could be combined into a European deterrent within a European defense community and assume a certain independence of the American. The British would like to have it both ways, but their basic goal, I believe, is above all to keep the United States as closely tied to Europe as possible. The Japanese are relying on a security treaty with the United States for their nuclear protection. But there are some powerful voices inside the American Government which are convinced that in the long run Japan will not be able to resist the realities of its world power status and will decide to develop its own nuclear deterrent. Some Americans such as Kissinger, for instance, say that some of the detachment that has crept into the American attitude toward Japan is due not only to its economic policies—its export drive and the protectionism that shields its own industries —but also to the need to make Japan realize that it cannot indefinitely hold on to the American apron strings, that it must assume greater responsibilities in the Pacific and develop its own conceptual view of its future.

However, I believe that since it will be in the interest of both the United States and China to prevent the proliferation of nuclear weapons in Japan, the United States will and should resist as long as possible Japanese temptations to build their own nuclear weapons. Japanese defense forces will gradually replace American troops in Japan, and that should help rather than hinder relations. What would be more controversial would be a total American withdrawal from Korea because Japan will remain fearful of a Communist take-over of South Korea.

Mr. Nixon did not make friends in Peking—that would have

been too much to expect—but neither, by going to Peking, did he make real enemies in Japan. National interests in the end prevail and Japan's national interests will continue to rely on U.S. power and American markets during the seventies.

Mr. Nixon said in his inaugural address on January 30, 1969, "We cannot expect to make everyone our friend, but we can try to make no one our enemy." This dictum may not be altogether reassuring to those who consider themselves allies of the United States. No doubt a measure of uncertainty has a lot to recommend it, but much also depends on the character of those involved. In real life some married couples' happiness thrives on the certainty of their dependence on each other, others need uncertainty to preserve their relationship. Uncertainty can also lead to miscalculations, even though, it is true, it tends to impose greater caution on decisions and actions.

In a world, however, where anti-communism is not any more the cement of the Western alliance, where the major powers are becoming more concerned, as Harvard's Professor Stanley Hoffmann put it, with "the designs of equals rather than about the tantrums of the pygmies," and where the United States is emphasizing the retrenchment of its power and of its commitments, special relationships are bound to lose their significance, to peter out.

What applies to real life generally can also apply to diplomacy: In a world that has come to believe more and more in free love, the courtesans lose their attraction and their *raison d'être*.

President Nixon seemed a little nervous and distracted as he and my wife and I stood in front of the big picture window in his study at San Clemente. Below us spread a beautifully lush garden and beyond was the vista across the blue-green Pacific. Suddenly, without turning his head, but looking out into the faraway, the President said, "We shall have a very important announcement to make this evening. Just remember this room and this view when you hear it."

It was not only his remark that came unexpectedly but actually finding ourselves the President's guests in his private villa. Originally we had come to the presidential compound on Henry Kissinger's invitation. He had just returned from a tour around the world which had taken him to South Vietnam, India, Pakistan and Paris—at least as far as we knew then—and had kindly asked us to lunch on the little restaurant terrace a few steps from his own office. He looked tired, unusually pale and jowly. He had just spent his first twenty-four hours briefing the President and also Mr. Rogers on his findings and had written a voluminous report as well, yet now he talked with gusto. His outer calm seemed to hide a deep excitement about his experiences. The professor sounded at times like a statesman, at times like a reporter. He is a brilliant raconteur and was at the top of his form, mixing wit and wisdom, perception and perspective with ease—amusing, serious, sardonic, biting, malicious, generous and diplomatic, all it seemed in the same breath.

The situation in South Vietnam looked to him more reassuring than he had expected; Yahya Khan, the Pakistani President, evidently bordered on the stupid; Mrs. Indira Gandhi, the Indian Prime Minister, was obviously not the type for one of Kissinger's quiet dinner dates; there was no substitute for on-the-spot talks, and he chided those who staged the U.S. coup against Diem by cable from Washington in 1963. Then he launched into one of his favorite subjects: excessive activism of liberal intellectuals in government and their excessive negativism outside it as far as foreign affairs were concerned. Like so many in government, he was upset about the lack of outside understanding for his own difficult position and the minimal sympathy and support he was given. The constant harping by the New York *Times* and the Washington *Post* that he did not seize the initiative in the negotiations with Hanoi quite obviously irritated him beyond words and, he complained, made it only more difficult to get anywhere with the North Vietnamese.

Only six months later did we realize why he was so obsessed at that moment with this idea. It was on his last stop in Paris that he had one of his secret and relatively hopeful get-togethers with the North Vietnamese. Negotiations with Communists are difficult enough in themselves: To conduct them in absolute secrecy must be nerve-wracking, and not to be able to defend oneself against public criticism, when one in fact is doing what the critics advocate, must be the ultimate in exasperation. But all he said now, on the terrace at San Clemente, was, "I'm absolutely certain that we know what we are doing and that this Administration is not going to make the same mistakes as the Johnson administration. We are going to continue negotiating with the North Vietnamese, we have a plan," and there was no mistaking his determination.

Once Kissinger's dander is up, various other of his annoyances are apt to surface, and I was not surprised when he recalled how a few weeks earlier he had gone to Endicott College in Boston to a panel discussion sponsored by the Massachusetts Institute of Technology and how he had got into a bitter argument with Daniel Ellsberg (who had then not yet confessed to being the source of the leak of the Pentagon Papers). Kissinger had gone to Boston to defend the Administration's Vietnam policy, with Cyrus Vance speaking for the opposition in, as he said, a most civilized and reasonable way. But Ellsberg had got Henry's blood racing by suggesting that U.S. policy was designed to save American lives but to sacrifice Asians. Kissinger's retort had been to call Ellsberg's argument racist and to declare that he did not consider Vietnamization a racial situation.

Nothing had then been known about the Pentagon Papers; in fact, as we now learned, Kissinger had been about to leave for Los Angeles, on the start of his trip around the world, when the first installment from them had appeared in the New York Times. He merely read the headline and felt so agitated about the "leak" that he called his aide General Haig on the telephone and asked him to find out about its origin. "This time Laird has gone too far," was his instinctive reaction to Haig. "I want you to find out exactly how much has been leaked altogether." Haig, who does not lack appreciation for a funny situation, sheepishly informed his boss that the New York Times had over five thousand classified documents and that Laird was not the source. Kissinger later told this story as a joke about himself and Laird, at least showing he can laugh about himself and his prejudices.

Thinking that after an exhausting tour such talk over lunch was not particularly relaxing and diverting for him, I turned the conversation to the lighter side of Kissinger's life, the girls. A lot had been made of a photograph taken of him and a pretty, blond CBS producer as they left a Paris restaurant; some reports even chided him for spending the evening in such a flippant way, especially when everybody had expected him to seek an opportunity to talk to the North Vietnamese. Again, little did we know that he had done exactly that. "Things have reached ridiculous proportions," Henry said. "I took out a starlet last night in Beverly Hills and there were ten photographers stationed at the door. We left through the back door and my companion was furious." When I suggested that all these shapely girls he enjoyed taking out flocked to him for the power he incorporated, he replied with a shrug, "Oh no—it's for the publicity." And so the conversation rambled on a lighthearted course when his aide appeared to say that the President was on the phone and wanted to talk to him. I suggested jokingly that he take the call on the white telephone on our table, but Henry, with an air of importance, withdrew to the office.

AN INVITATION FROM THE PRESIDENT

A few minutes later he reappeared to say that the President had asked him to bring us over to his villa. Mr. Nixon had asked him with whom he was lunching and on hearing it was us, issued the invitation.

We rushed through the rest of the meal and then went over to a little parking lot of electric golf carts, which seem to be the favored means of transportation within the compound. Henry cautiously sat at the wheel and drove across toward a wide gate in a white stucco wall and to the door of the villa. The offices of the White House West are housed in dull, undistinguishable prefabs, but the private White House West is a Moorish-style house with a retiled roof, in the shade of old palm trees, whose charm and beauty surprised us.

We first entered a Spanish-style courtyard with loggias along three sides and a pretty fountain of Italian tile, in the center a *putti* holding a dolphin. There were large goldfish and floating water lilies in the fountain's pool and blazing scarlet freesias suspended from the arches of the loggias. We walked along one of these and then out toward the swimming pool where Kissinger expected the President to be. Soft music from hidden loudspeakers drifted across the palm trees and as we stood, looking for the President, a lady in a bathing suit raised herself from a deck chair. It was Rose Mary Woods, the President's long-time confidential secretary, who told us that the President had left the pool side and gone to his study. We returned to the patio and entered another part of the building, climbed a few stairs and found ourselves in a pleasant, cool room that gave one the feeling of being on a ship's bridge.

The President got up, we shook hands and were motioned to sit down across from him in simple but comfortable chairs. Henry sat himself a little apart. Mr. Nixon was dressed California-style in a sky-blue linen blazer, gray flannels and black alligator loafers with gold buckles. He seemed a little nervous and gaunt and slightly ill at ease. The quiet restfulness that pervaded the grounds was suddenly mixed with an air of tension. It was difficult to know whether this was due to our arrival or something more important, or just simple shyness. Mr. Nixon had known me since his days as Vice President but had never met my wife before. He sat down again and stretched his legs out on a footstool in front of him. He first enjoined us to look at the beautiful view out of the western windows, explaining that he had these windows enlarged into picture windows when he bought the place after he was elected President. He described how President Franklin Roosevelt had come out to this house in the 1930s on the railroad which used to run below the gardens, between the ocean and the house, and how he had been raised on pulleys from down below up to the house, which at that time belonged to the national Democratic finance chairman for California. They used to play poker in this room, the President said. I ventured to suggest that, maybe, he and Henry were still playing poker in this room, if of a different kind. "That's right," the President replied, with scarcely a smile. "We spend a lot of time here together and we play poker now and then, but it's a different variety."

Sitting here with them, one became acutely aware of their sharing that kind of invisible bond that is special to men who share many very deep, delicate secrets. They did not have to exchange words, a casual glance was enough for each to know what the other was thinking or trying to say. Here were two men who had developed extraordinary collaboration from an appreciation of their mutual need, one for his intellectual power, the other for his political power. It was quite obvious that this was not, to use Mr. Nixon's own words, a "buddy-buddy" relationship. They seemed quite formal with each other, even the teasing about "Henry's girls" on the part of the President seemed more of an act than easy camaraderie. It seemed evident, too, to me in the same room that this was how both preferred it.

Looking over the northern gardens, the President told us that he had invited Britain's Prime Minister Edward Heath to come to San Clemente. "Do you think the Prime Minister would like it here?" he asked me. "I don't know him well, but you do. We could have some good talks here." I suggested that the Premier would love it here, especially since sailing was so close by. The President readily suggested that he could have here all the sailing he wanted. Then suddenly, pointing his long forefinger at me he added, "You can report that I have invited your Prime Minister to come here."

When I reported the invitation the following Sunday, the White House denied the story. In fact, the invitation was never tendered (as Mr. Heath told me later), and when, a little surprised that the most authoritative source should have misled me so, I asked Kissinger about it, he shrugged his shoulders and ventured to guess that perhaps the President had forgotten that he had issued that invitation last year, not this year. The query I received later on from the Prime Minister, no doubt, reflected some doubts about my credibility: such are the journalistic hazards!

As I stood close to the President, in the strong sunlight, I could see a myriad of little lines in his tanned face. His eyelids, as he looked at us, were sometimes closed or flickered nervously. Despite his most courteous manner and the impression he created that he had all the time in the world to spend with us, I couldn't help sensing that both he and Kissinger were anything but relaxed. Was there any reason for tension or was this the President's normal manner?

A VERY IMPORTANT ANNOUNCEMENT

Suddenly the President, looking out over the vast landscape, said, with an underlying excitement in his voice, the words I gave earlier: "We shall have a very important announcement to make this evening. Just remember this room and this view when you hear it."

Then, as if to change the subject, he showed us a sports trophy sitting on a bookshelf, a golf ball perched on a golden tee, a souvenir of a hole in one which he achieved in 1952. My wife, no golfer herself, asked the President whether this was what is also called a birdie, and he, somewhat shocked by such profound ignorance of so hallowed a game, replied by lifting the trophy off the shelf, "Why no. It is one out of thirty thousand chances. There is no name for it!"

Then he asked whether we would like to see the rest of the house. He led us down the stairs to a magnificent begonia plant, tacked against the wall of the loggia. Stopping by the table in the courtyard, he explained that this was where he had breakfast every morning. "My inner time clock never got used to the time difference between Washington and California," he said, "and as a result I have my breakfast usually at 6:30 A.M." He then showed us the small charming mosaic tiles depicting Mexican animals which had been placed on the walls; they were painted about fifty years ago. The President seemed relaxed and now his mood reflected his pleasure in giving us a tour of the house, one of his great prides. A superb red-brown Irish setter, with a beautifully glossy and wavy coat, had joined us. "This is King," the President said. "Isn't he a beauty!" We agreed admiringly and my wife mentioned that we had a bassett hound, but lamented how stupid she was. "It doesn't matter how stupid they are," the President said, "what matters is whether they like you!"

THE PRESIDENT AS A GUIDE

We were led out the western door into the sloping gardens overlooking the beach and the sea. "See those palms," he said with a rising enthusiasm. "Isn't that pine tree grand!" He took great pride in the trees and explained that some of them had been planted seventy years ago. Inspired perhaps by my wife's love of gardens and flowers, he strolled ahead with her, toward the rose garden, leaving Kissinger and me behind. Soon we saw the President trying to pick a specially beautiful rosebud for her. It was a stubborn stem and a struggle between the President and the thorny white Peace rose developed. My wife later reported that the more the rose resisted, the more persistent the President became. "There must be a way of doing this," he exclaimed. Suddenly a gentle-

manly gesture had become a test of power. Finally the rose sur-
rendered and the President graciously presented it.

We re-entered the house through a door that led into the living
room. Before the Nixons bought the house, it had been dark and
austere. Now the walls were white with deep sofas and curtains in
white and yellow and the rug soft and golden yellow. The President led us through the house pointing out some of his favorite
"trinkets." There was a box given to him by Emperor Haile Selas-
sie, done in gold filigree so fine that clumsy handling could bend
it; there was a large, ugly light-green jade incense holder; and there
were two lacquer paintings of two deer on a dark brown background, done in Vietnam. The two most valuable items in the
house, the President explained, were two miniatures given to him
by the Shah of Iran. The frames were inlaid and the scenes de-
picted horsemen hunting. My wife, as she admired them, suggested that they were probably made of ivory. "You would know
more about that than I do," the President suggested modestly. "I
don't know anything about things like that." Later on, as the conversation shifted to art subjects, he reiterated his own lack of
knowledge with deprecating comments. As we passed a cabinet
full of tapes and hi-fi equipment, he pointed at them and said that
he enjoyed music. Then we walked through the dining room, obviously too small for big entertaining, and on to his private bedroom. "I rarely show this room to women," he said to my wife,
"especially if they are unescorted!" The room was low ceilinged
and quite small. The colors were less subdued than in most of the
house; the strong wine red of the carpet and the red-white pat-
terned bedspread gave it a certain challenging gaiety. "It is here
where I do my work," he commented and then explained the origin of yet another Vietnamese lacquer painting, a river scene, that
hung over his bed. When I asked the President whether he had
ever been to Hanoi, where the best Vietnamese lacquer paintings
come from, he said, "Oh yes, it's a beautiful city."

We walked out into the garden again. After the quiet serenity of
the house, its profusion of color had a startling effect. Kissinger
was by this time displaying a certain impatience. Was it because
he simply had to tag along on this house tour wasting his valuable

time? Occasionally he looked at a piece of paper he carried in the palm of his hand. (Later he told us that it listed the telephone numbers of those ambassadors he meant to call before the "important announcement" would be made by the President.) The President, now far more relaxed, finally led us around the house back to the front door. He stopped once more at a gardenia bush and picked another beautiful bud for my wife. We thanked the President for this most unusual occasion and expressed our admiration for the beauty of the house and its lovely setting. "It's all my wife's work," he said, and as we shook hands he added to the farewells: "And don't miss watching television tonight!" Three hours later he announced his most daring policy move yet—his decision to accept an invitation from the People's Republic of China to visit Peking.

CHAPTER TWELVE—THE LONG MARCH
TO PEKING

Mr. Nixon's announcement that he was going to Peking was as unexpected as it was startling, and as brief as it was suspenseful. I had hardly recovered from my surprise when the broadcast was over, leaving me wishing I had had instead of a guided tour of San Clemente a guided tour through the President's thinking that had led to this surprising switch. As so often before, Mr. Nixon left one wondering how to fit this latest move into a coherent picture of his world outlook. He could have used his broadcast as a great opportunity to explain his decision and his vision of the world. Instead, he exploded a bombshell before the amazed gaze of his audience, and then left them gasping to be taken into his confidence about the whys of his astonishing move. I was familiar with the line that he was not a President who liked to explain his thoughts, that he expected people to accept his decision and to follow him in the De Gaulle style. But the Americans are not like the French; they do not see their President surveying them from some Olympian peak, or as some self-sacrificial martyr in the mold of Joan of Arc; they expect to know the whys and wherefores of great national events. It seemed to me that Mr. Nixon had missed an outstanding chance for an act of mutual confidence between himself and the American people.

The fruit of the Sino-American rapprochement took a long time to grow in Mr. Nixon's mind, but I did not realize how long until I found in my own diary a note about a meeting he held in 1954 with half a dozen correspondents during which he remarked that it was important to end the isolation of China gradually and to do this by reopening trade relations and cultural exchanges. (John Foster Dulles' decision to allow American newsmen to go to China in 1957 was more a propaganda gesture, not a serious policy move, designed to show to the press that it was not the U.S. which opposed contacts with China.)

Then, in 1958 during the offshore island crisis, the United States Government considered with horror the possibility of war with China, until the Chinese announced a cease-fire in Quemoy and Matsu. This act deferred but did not resolve the crisis, and was typical of the oblique Chinese diplomatic style. If anyone in 1957 had suggested that fifteen years later the Chinese on every other day would still be lobbing artillery shells on to the offshore islands, he would have been called insane. But that is what they do, in spite of the "cease-fire." Yet, symbolically, they want to make it clear that the battle for these islands now occupied by Chiang Kai-shek's forces is not over but that force would not be used to conquer them. The Communists expect them to fall into their lap together with Taiwan.

Much later, during the election campaign in 1968, I asked Mr. Nixon whether he favored a policy of making common cause with the Soviet Union in containing China. He replied that he disagreed with this idea because it would create the impression in Asia that American policy was influenced by racial considerations.

Inside the United States Government no serious thought, however, was given before 1961 to a change in policy toward China. There was fear of the effect it would have on the many weak countries in Southeast Asia, and there was also a reluctance to take on the powerful so-called "China lobby" in the United States, the sole aim of which was to restore Chiang Kai-shek's leadership on the mainland. What added to this reluctance to initiate any change was that China itself, after the period of the Great Leap Forward, seemed in serious internal disarray. By 1962, refugees were streaming into Hong Kong, and some China experts, especially at Rand, the California think tank which had considerable influence on governmental thinking, thought that China would once again fall apart and be governed by war lords.

President Kennedy expressed the desire to take a new look at the China policy in 1962 and Ambassador Averell Harriman, the then Assistant Secretary for Far Eastern Affairs, thought that maybe the Geneva Conference on Laos might help to make a new beginning possible. This was before the Sino-Soviet conflict over the leadership of the Communist world startled the world and led to an entire new look at the situation. It also wrecked the Geneva Conference because both the Chinese and the Russians were eagerly competing for Hanoi's favors. Still, Harriman began promoting small steps that were designed to help ease relations between Washington and Peking. They included the "releashing" of Chiang Kai-shek, which meant he had to desist from any aggressive actions against the mainland (Admiral Alan G. Kirk, chosen by Harriman as Ambassador to Taiwan, had the task of doing the releashing); other steps involved modifying the foreign assets regulations and easing those for purchasing Chinese goods and so on. By November 1962, the new Office for Asian Chinese Affairs in the State Department had readied a list which included the recognition of Outer Mongolia, freer travel and more trade, and an assurance that the United States had no hostile designs. President Kennedy was inclined to pursue these ideas, though some, including the recognition of Outer Mongolia, were rejected by Dean Rusk.

Kennedy's death left everything lying fallow, and as the Vietnam war assumed greater and greater proportions, so it stayed. Nothing happened until Mr. Nixon became President, except a hint that China also might be doing some rethinking. On November 26, 1968, the Chinese suggested a resumption of the talks between the American and Chinese ambassadors in Warsaw that had been suspended since January 8 of that year. At Dean Rusk's suggestion Robert Murphy, Mr. Nixon's liaison man with the State Department, was informed, but the new Administration obviously needed time to decide what to do next. Nixon, however, was passionately interested in taking a new initiative on this front and twelve days after he entered the White House, on February 1, 1969, he ordered Kissinger to explore all possibilities for reopening relations with Communist China. He was convinced that

China would move faster into the mainstream of world affairs, but even more basically he wanted to create a new and greater flexibility in big-power relations and to broaden his own options. Both he and Kissinger considered predictable positions in diplomacy a handicap, especially in relations with the Soviet Union for whom, they thought, the status quo was a great advantage, for it did not have to worry about the possibility of driving the United States closer to Peking and therefore could afford to ignore U.S.-Chinese relations.

SLOW BOAT TO CHINA

In the U.S.-Chinese minuet Mr. Nixon put his foot forward gently when he explained to General de Gaulle on his first visit to Europe in February 1969 that he was determined to end the war in Vietnam and that he would like to resume relations with the Chinese People's Republic. De Gaulle immediately passed on the news to Peking, but without response.

The first meeting of the National Security Council dealing with China was held in San Clemente in August 1969, and although no decisions were taken, several conclusions were reached. The most important was that an improvement of relations with Peking was possible without abandoning Taiwan and without jeopardizing relations with Moscow. It was also concluded that China was not an aggressively expansionist nation, and anyway a relatively weak one. There was complete agreement about the desirability of the resumption of the Warsaw talks with the Chinese. Then the tactics were developed to thaw out the long-frozen China policy. The guiding thought was summed up by the President when he said later, "We have to live with Communist powers and we have no illusions about communism, but we must accept the realities." It was the true confession of the *Real*politician and the dropping of his old ideological cold-war mantle. In fact, the decline of ideology was not confined to Mr. Nixon and the Americans, but seemed to affect also the Soviet leadership and the Russians generally. Was ideology also declining in China?

Nixon was eager to find out and willing to start the journey in a slow boat, but determined to add sails and if necessary steam. He therefore first instructed Walter J. Stoessel, the U. S. Ambassador to Warsaw, to approach the Chinese Ambassador and to suggest a resumption of the suspended so-called "Warsaw talks." This was in October 1969. The first opportunity Stoessel had to approach the Chinese Ambassador was at a Yugoslav fashion show. He asked his interpreter to convey to the Chinese Ambassador an invitation to "drop by" at the U. S. Embassy. This the Ambassador later did and the resumption of the Warsaw talks was set for the following January. Almost at the same time the United States decided to discontinue the regular naval patrol of the Seventh Fleet in the Taiwan Straits. At least to the Chinese this must have looked like a first confirmation of the changing American attitudes. Although the decision originated in the Pentagon and for budgetary reasons, the State Department quickly consented to the idea and on November 7, 1969, Rogers instructed the American embassies in Tokyo, Seoul and Taipei to convey this decision to the respective governments. Not surprisingly, it caused hard feelings in Taipei.

After the first *prise de contacte* in January, Stoessel was instructed by the White House to tell the Chinese that President Nixon was ready to send a senior official to Peking. He was startled into total disbelief at this turn of American policy, and instead of proceeding with his instructions sent back incredulous inquiries implying that he must have misunderstood. The President finally got a little testy at these anxious questionings. Finally the message got through to Stoessel, but the next meeting, in February, was canceled when a Chinese diplomat defected in the Netherlands and was given asylum in the United States. The third get-together on May 20 was also canceled, because of the American incursions into Cambodia. However, for some months other channels of communications had been established with Peking through third countries and, except for the actual duration of the fighting in Cambodia, these channels remained open. The Rumanians helped to reassure the Chinese that the Americans meant what they were saying, but it was through the Pakistani Government that the Chinese reciprocated with serious and constructive replies.

KISSINGER TURNS HOUDINI

And so the making of the Kissinger mission began and led to one of diplomatic history's most stunning Houdini acts. For an embattled President who was fighting thankless defensive political battles to get American troops out of Vietnam, cut budgets, control inflation and resist American troop cuts in Europe, it was an extraordinary exhilaration to make history rather than be confined by it. Of course, he was also helped by the changing mood inside China. The cultural revolution had lost its momentum and with the domestic situation once again under control, a normalization of foreign relations had begun. The rapprochement with the United States seemed inspired by a variety of circumstances: There was the specter of the Soviet disciplinary action against Czechoslovakia, the threat to Rumania and the growing sense of China's vulnerability along the five-thousand-mile border with the Soviet Union; there was the awareness of Japan rising fast toward world power status and her economic links to Taiwan; there was a feeling of isolation and the growing realization of the need to get out of it; and there were the Nixon Doctrine and various persuasive signs that the United States was indeed initiating a policy of retreat from the Asian mainland. In sum, there was now in Peking what Henry Kissinger described to me later as "a compulsive desire to be more in control of events."

At one point the President considered Rogers for the mission, but decided against him because it would have been hard to keep his visit secret. Also it had become obvious that it would be impossible for the presidential emissary to communicate with Washington from Peking, and only Kissinger really knew what was in the President's mind. The Chinese, as they conveyed through the Foreign Minister of Norway, suggested as their preference Kissinger, most likely because as Edgar Snow wrote in *Life* magazine, "China's leaders respect Kissinger."* Then he quoted a close comrade in arms of Premier Chou En-lai as saying: "There is a man [Kissinger] who knows the language of both worlds—his and

* *Life*, July 30, 1971.

ours. He is the first American we have seen in this position. With him it should be possible to talk."

Kissinger prepared himself with infinite care for this adventure. He even carried with him to Peking ten different versions of a possible communiqué. Later he confessed that "to me it was an adolescent experience. I didn't really know what to expect, what I would be confronted with, in spite of all the diplomatic preparations." He did indeed talk with an almost adolescent enthusiasm about this first forty-nine-hour visit to China. What swept him off his feet was Premier Chou En-lai who, he said, was the most electrifying personality he had ever met. Their shared disdain for bureaucracy no doubt contributed to this liking. Very early in their first meeting Kissinger asked Chou En-lai whether he could call him Mr. Prime Minister, as he had difficulty pronouncing the word "Premier." Chou said, "Of course," and explained that but for a poor translator at the Geneva Conference in 1947 he would now be called Mr. Prime Minister. Then he added, "The translator is now a high official in our Foreign Ministry." Kissinger was impressed with the depth of Chou's psychological insights, his objectivity, candor and subtlety, and his long-range outlook on history. Kissinger explained Chou's approach to me: " 'Here is a problem,' Chou En-lai would suggest. 'It can't be settled now, but such is the possible evolution.' De Gaulle could think that way, but no other leader today can." The intellectual approach, the gentle humor, the thoughtfulness and human quality of the Chinese Prime Minister all made a deep impression on him.

The Chinese today are more opposed to the Russians than to the United States, and this made it easier for them, despite their ideological prejudices, to welcome the American overtures. The depth of their ideological thinking nevertheless surprised Kissinger, as did their conviction that they can prevail in the world through moral superiority. This conviction apparently also leads Chou to believe that the United States is in decline and in the long run destined to collapse. However, in spite of their ideological opposition to the American outlook on life, Chou En-lai convinced him that the Chinese were not out to impose their views on others, that China did not have the kind of expansionist ambitions Kissinger sees in Soviet policy. The Chinese have shown that they are more careful than the Russians and less willing to take risks. Their intervention in Korea was triggered only after American troops had pressed within less than one hundred miles of China's industrial heart; they moved against India only after provocation; and the hostility with the Soviet Union may be more an attempt by the Kremlin to intimidate Peking. Of course, how the Chinese will act if and when they become as powerful as the Russians, Kissinger did not want to speculate on, for this is still too far off in the future. Not even the Chinese seem to be interested in speculating about when they will cease to be a developing country, as they readily admit they now are, for they want to make their industrialization a slow process. They are afraid that if they push too hard some of the virtues of their society, the egalitarianism, the willingness to work hard, the progress already achieved, could be lost. There is still the underlying concern that a majority of the Chinese remain brought up in the classical tradition and not on Mao's teachings, and that it will take much longer until the latter have sunk deep enough into the conscience of the nation. But to be able to afford such a slow industrialization and to be able to concentrate on the needs of their society instead of on their military preparedness, they also need peace.

And so both the United States and China had reached a point in history where they shared an eagerness to start a new relationship, and where both were prepared to pay an ideological price for it. Americans never had with pre- or post-revolutionary Russia the kind of love affair they carried on with China. Certain mementos of the American experience with China have an indelible meaning in the American mind: the Yangtze patrol, Yale in China, Manifest Destiny. That is why the Communist take-over caused such heartache. It is also one reason, now that this shock has waned, why Mr. Nixon's rapprochement with China was welcome to Americans. For the Chinese, reopening Sino-American relations meant compromising their anti-imperialist purity and tarnishing their reputation as revolutionaries which, they have always emphasized, had made them the lone standard-bearers of communism. However, Mao Tse-tung clearly was willing to make the ideological sacrifice, otherwise he would not have told Edgar Snow in his unique interview that he would "be happy to talk with him [Nixon] either as a tourist or as a President." Kissinger, on his return from that first visit to Peking, was able to confirm that such a visit was indeed not only possible but desirable, and would not expose the President to the kind of political risks that could seriously embarrass him. No doubt, Chou En-lai too wanted to reassure himself that militarily President Nixon was determined to end the war in Vietnam, and that politically the problem of Taiwan was also capable of solution acceptable to both sides. And so the first Kissinger mission, followed by another three months later, set the stage for Mr. Nixon's spectacular expedition to China.

MEETING MAO

The absence of a "people's reception" on the President's arrival at the airport in Peking was the Chinese way of demonstrating that there was a contrast between a former "running dog" and a comrade and ally. At least at the start there had to be an indication that supping with the imperial devil was different. When Kissinger on his second preparatory trip remarked to Chou that the sign "Anti-Imperialist Hospital" had been changed to "Friendship Hospital" (it used to be called Rockefeller Hospital in the old days), but some of the other offensive signs had not, Chou said, "Chinese love signs and love changing them. But words are hollow. You can tell more about us by what we do."

This was borne out by the early events of the President's visit. His reception was cool, but a few hours later he saw Chairman Mao and the signals changed. It was as if the Chinese leader had waved a magical wand: The Chinese propaganda machine, proclaiming a new friendship with the United States, went into high gear. Only he could give the signal that would keep at bay whatever internal opposition may have existed to this visit.

The meeting with Mao was set with such speed—it was virtually the first formal appointment—and without any advance indication to the President as to its exact timing, that Mr. Nixon chose to be a few minutes late. The invitation also made it clear that of the Americans only Dr. Kissinger was to be present. It was scarcely the first time that Kissinger and not Mr. Rogers had accompanied the President to meetings with heads of state. This time, though, after the historic photograph of those present was flashed around the globe, it suddenly sprang to people's attention that the Secretary of State was missing, and that this represented a slight. Mr. Rogers, however, seemed unperturbed; he had his own sense of modesty.

What had been expected mainly to be a first ceremonial visit, however, proved the one and only meeting between the two leaders. Mao was still suffering from an attack of bronchitis, still not feeling well, and that may have been one reason why the later meeting that had originally been expected did not take place or was telescoped into this one.

No one except those present really knows what was talked about during the President's interview with Chairman Mao. When I asked one of the State Department's leading China specialists whether he had any idea of what went on, he said that he hadn't, that he was not privy to the transcript of that conversation (nor, as yet, is anyone else apart from the participants). He did have an idea though of Mao's way of conducting such conversations from reports by heads of several governments who had had discussions with the Chinese leader, but not his own; such was the irony of White House-imposed secrecy.

Mao discussed the importance of the President's visit and the excesses of the cultural revolution with considerable candor. The President found Mao's presence impressive. As Kissinger put it later: "He has the quality of being at the center wherever he stood; it moved with him wherever he moved," a quality that he had previously observed only in General de Gaulle. Mao seemed to the President to be one of those rare statesmen who exudes great personal force, and to a man of Nixon's inner insecurities this was perhaps the most striking thing about him. Mao conveyed the serenity of a peasant and the gravity of a rock. He clearly was the fountainhead and the authority. With an uncomplicated mind and an earthy humor he apparently bore down fast on the central issues of Sino-American relations with great lucidity and without wasting time in argument or analysis. Kissinger later said that he thought his earthy, peasantlike strength reminiscent of Khrushchev, but he predicted he would one day be elevated to a position like Confucius rather than suffer the posthumous decline and fall of a Stalin.

Chou En-lai, by contrast, was the man of subtle intellect, with a shrewd, astute mind. He asserted himself not by his physical presence but by his dextrous mental mobility and his electric charm. He was the clever negotiator and diplomatic practitioner—the supermanager. But he was also thoughtful and contemplative. He was deeply concerned about human values, about life in chastened China, which to some of the old China hands in the President's party somehow lacked the vitality it used to have.

On his earlier visits Kissinger had noticed that Chou consulted with Mao on every important subject before discussing it with him. Usually in starting on a new subject for discussion he would begin by saying; "I have the following message from Chairman Mao. . . ."

However, who would issue these "messages" once Mao was gone no one had any idea. No one had the slightest inkling who the new leaders would be or what directions they would want to take. Those Nixon and Kissinger talked to were easier to communicate with because they had some actual acquaintance with the West. None of the younger men they came across had been out of China.

The talks between President Nixon and Chou En-lai were on a philosophical level. Each leader first laid out his view of the world in a broad historical perspective. Specific issues were left to the negotiations that produced the communiqué. But even during these negotiations the Chinese did not make an issue either of Vietnam or Korea, and they never referred to Mao's statement on Indochina of May 20, 1970, in which he pledged the support of the people of Communist China for struggles everywhere against "United States imperialism and its lackeys," and urged the people of the whole world to "unite and defeat the United States aggressors and their running dogs." They restated, as if for the record, their public positions, but delicately did not press them. Vietnam quite clearly was only peripheral in their eyes to the issue of Taiwan, and even that was subordinated to the overarching aim of this great power get-together, the counterbalancing of the Soviet Union.

The communiqué that was issued at the end of the visit was clearly drafted with an eye to one another's public opinion at home, as well as to the sensibilities of each other's allies. Thus the Chinese had to denounce the Japanese as "militarist" and the Americans had to call them "allies." At one point during the negotiations real difficulties developed. But when Dr. Kissinger suggested that this might make it impossible to produce a joint communiqué, the Chinese relented, showing both genuine consternation and also surprising appreciation of U.S. domestic political consideration.

The wordings about Taiwan were particularly carefully and painfully chosen to indicate that the United States agreed to the idea of one China, but also to a peaceful settlement of the problem by letting nature take its course. Taiwan's future was left to direct negotiations between the Nationalists and Peking at some time in the future. The American formula "as tension in the area diminishes" in the joint communiqué, however, left it wide open for U.S. troops to remain on Taiwan for an indefinite period. It is a rider that seems bigger than the horse. Although the press reported a deadlock after the farewell banquet in Peking, this was not correct; what was never reported was that because of complaints by Secretary Rogers, inspired by one of his aides, about the wording of some references to Taiwan in the draft of the communiqué the negotiations had to be reopened, even though Kissinger and Chou had already found each other's text acceptable. In one case the word "stressed" was changed to the word "stated." Some thought later that Mr. Rogers' request had been more embarrassing than useful to the United States. To the Secretary of State, however, the corrected text tasted like a pill easier for Taiwan to swallow. It was one of those rare cases in international negotiations when Secretary Rogers made a show of his authority.

Neither Nixon nor Kissinger was able to assess after the talks how much influence the Chinese had in Hanoi, but quite clearly the one thing that stood out to the Chinese was "the pride" of the North Vietnamese, which probably meant that they were too stubborn, too self-confident to take their advice. "If only," Kissinger said, sighing, during a particularly fruitless period of negotiations with Hanoi, "the North Vietnamese would take the same long-term view of their future relationship with Saigon as the Chinese do in regard to Taiwan, there would be no problem of finding a settlement."

The television coverage of the visit was without precedent and contributed much to reconciling the American public to the new relationship with China, and certainly faster than would otherwise have happened. The Chinese were tolerant of being exposed on television to the entire world after years of isolation and casual about the good and bad comments that appeared in the American press and on television. Chou even apologized for the staging of some children playing near the Wall for the benefit of the TV cameras, to impress American audiences with their clothes and transistor radios. He said it had been thought up by some over-eager officials and did not have his approval.

President Nixon had included William F. Buckley, Jr., the conservative columnist, in the list of accompanying correspondents, in the hope that he might be converted and come to approve his China policy. But Buckley did not submit either to Mr. Nixon's or to Chinese blandishments. He was bitter, almost vengeful in his criticism of the President, yet despite his hatred of the Chinese "Commies" he was said to have spent more dollars in Peking than anybody else and some rumors, no doubt malicious, had it that thanks to his exuberant shopping the price of jade went up by 500 per cent.

Kissinger, who clearly had hit it off well with the Chinese, and especially with Chou, found it more agreeable to negotiate with them than with the Russians. There was a profound difference. The Chinese, he said, would say in an argument, "Do I understand correctly that you believe that etc. . . . ," in order to indicate that they originally made a mistake which they were now willing to correct. The Russians never admitted mistakes and when they made a concession would say that "it was done to be nice to you."

Mao, perhaps more than any other Chinese leader, sees the world from the inside out, with China at its center. Still, there were permanent national interests and certain relatively short-term practical considerations that fell into the scales of decision making. Once he had reached the conclusion that Mr. Nixon's overtures were genuine there were more reasons for accepting than rejecting them. If anything became clear in the various conversations during the visit it was that the principal catalyst for China's changing attitude toward the United States was fear of the Soviet Union. It was both emotional and logical. At various times in Khrushchev's days, and later in 1969, the Russians unofficially threatened preventive war. The Chinese leaders took the threat seriously then and they still do. This is why they have moved many of their important military and industrial installations underground and why they have built air-raid shelters in vast numbers. They must hope that their rapprochement with the United States will serve to make the Kremlin less confident of how Washington would react to a Soviet nuclear or conventional attack against China.

The Chinese at this stage of their nuclear development, as the Russians were twenty years ago, are interested only in total disarmament. They don't mind the SALT talks to the extent that they lead to certain limitations they would profit from. But they are nervous about anything that could strengthen U.S.-Russian relations.

There was also an awareness that China is becoming vulnerable to the growing military power of Japan; and, further, that the old assumption that in the case of Taiwan time was on Peking's side and sooner or later it would fall into its lap might after all be a mistaken notion. Perhaps the longer the island remained economically dependent on Japan the more difficult it would be to reintegrate it into China proper. Worse still, Japan had as much trade with Taiwan as with China, and there was also the possibil-

ity that Japan would attempt to encourage an independence movement there.

Just as the French find it difficult to forget the German occupation, so the Chinese readily remember Japan's behavior during the
Sino-Japanese war. And now with Japan's economic and industrial
capacities greater than ever, its influence again spreading through
Asia, and talk that it might eventually become another nuclear
power, it is not surprising that China's anxieties are reawakened.
With three men still in the Chinese Government who participated
in the Long March and who well remember Japanese aggression,
those memories permeate the thinking at the top and they will
die hard, at least in this generation.

But there were also indirect benefits to China from a rapprochement with the United States. For one, Mr. Nixon's initiative might undermine American relations with Taiwan and Japan,
even with the Soviet Union. All three are now suspicious of American intentions, all three in their different ways somehow consider
Mr. Nixon's move a kind of stab in the back. Mr. Nixon was well
aware of the political drawbacks of his China visit, but he took the
lofty position that the interests of world peace in this case were a
more important factor than special American political advantages,
which, especially after Japan's unwillingness to co-operate with
the United States in matters of trade, had become less compelling.
What made China's decision easier, at least politically, was the
Nixon Doctrine and the fact that American forces were being
steadily withdrawn from Vietnam.

Vietnam as such was not an easy subject to discuss freely with
the Chinese. It was one of those problems both sides mentioned
but preferred to skirt around. It was a problem not only for the
United States but also Peking because of the sense of pride the
Chinese possess and their stubborn sense of independence. The
Chinese repeated what they have been saying publicly for a long
time, that they are against foreign troops being stationed on anybody's territory. And while they made it quite clear that this
applied also to American troops in Vietnam, they also hinted at
their concern that the Russians might be able to exploit the vacuum left behind by departing American forces, thus gaining ex-

cessive influence in Hanoi on the Chinese's very doorstep. They never quite confessed that they would sleep easier while the United States maintained a certain presence in Vietnam, but Kissinger and Rogers thought that this had at times been implied.

Next to the Russians the Chinese dislike the Indians most. After the Indo-Pakistan war, the Indians are stronger today than they were in 1962 when they drove asses across the Chinese border that had the sign "Mao" hung around their necks; in addition, they now have an alliance with Moscow. Pakistan does not impress the Chinese; to them it is an ally *faute di mieux*, whom they will stand by to preserve some sort of influence in the area. In the long run, though, they will be more interested in encouraging the Maoist movement in Bangladesh than in cultivating West Pakistan. They like to talk about sticking to principle and and they therefore expressed their appreciation that the United States in the Indo-Pakistan war also stuck to principle when it backed Pakistan.

Western Europe and NATO may look very remote from Peking, but not if one shares a five-thousand-mile frontier with the Soviet Union. Chou spoke approvingly of the European Common Market as a challenge to American domination of Europe—something of a Gaullist view—and of a unified Europe as an offsetting weight to the Soviet Union. He would regard a withdrawal of U.S. troops from Europe as destabilizing the balance between the Soviet Union's western and eastern frontiers. Anything to keep Russian forces tied down well away from the Chinese borders is acceptable and desirable. The Chinese are well aware that the Kremlin is applying against them a containment policy similar to that which the United States used to apply to the Soviet Union in the cold-war days.

The old struggle beween Peking and Moscow for the leadership of the Communist world is less virulent nowadays, and there is little evidence that the Chinese leadership is inclined to invest much money in spreading its gospel in the developing world.

The Chinese leaders do not refer to themselves as a great power as the Americans, for instance, do now; they call themselves a developing country and in that context they are very proud of their accomplishments in comparison with prerevolutionary days, since they have managed most of them without any outside help. They admit mistakes and they are concerned about economic growth and about improving the living standard of their people, but they insist that progress must be gradual and equally shared.

These distillations from the talks Americans had in China may make it all seem a little tidier than it in fact was. But like all good politicians the Chinese leaders are not argumentative, especially when they are in the process of establishing good relations; they are content with keeping the edges of the arguments fuzzy and with stating their positions; they do not feel they have to get into heated exchanges. However deep the continuing differences in certain areas between the United States and China, there was therefore no sense of hostility. What mattered, as Chou said several times, was "the spirit."

In all negotiations Chou, a thin and delicate, but strong-minded and resilient man, was the central figure, the superman in charge. At one point during a conversation with Mr. Rogers he even managed quickly to re-edit the front page of the China *Daily*, which one of his many aides had put in front of him. In a few minutes he changed some of the headlines and their emphasis without ever having to interrupt the conversation. It was also he who admitted during the negotiations over the wording of the communiqué, when he insisted that the five principles of coexistence formulated at the Bandung Conference be included, that this would "help" him to explain the new *détente* policy to those who opposed it. When he looked particularly worried on the night of the visit to the sports arena, some wondered whether some great new crisis had developed. "No," he said, "I am worried about the weather tomorrow and whether this might not prevent the President from visiting the Wall."

SAFETY IN UNCERTAINTY

Mr. Nixon gained a great deal at home from his Peking visit, especially among Democrats and liberal Republicans. As Senator Frank Church, Democrat, of Idaho, one of Mr. Nixon's sharpest critics on the Senate Foreign Relations Committee, put it to me: "Nixon's great accomplishment is that he has changed the public image of China. No secondary emissary could have achieved what the President did, coming back with a new political posture toward China and Asia as a whole. We must not look narrowly on the communiqué, therefore, and tote up what concessions we made or they didn't make. As regards the war in Vietnam neither Peking nor Moscow can deliver Hanoi, yet I think that the long-term results of this visit will be very good."

The President also paid a certain price for his initiative in bringing China into the scales of world policy. The argument that there was no alternative but absolute secrecy in preparing the reopening of the door to China, which caused so much disappointment, particularly in Tokyo, lacks conviction. It was true that the Japanese Government had not always handled information received from Washington with the discretion expected, but it should not have been beyond the ingenuity of the Administration to give its major allies an inkling of what was in the wind. The news of the President's visit to China came as such a shock in Tokyo because the Japanese always expected to be able to steal a march on Washington by getting to Peking themselves.

But there is enough reason to assume that Mr. Nixon in fact wanted to shock Japan, not only because it stubbornly refused to come to a compromise agreement with the United States on exports, but also in order to shake the Japanese into assuming a more independent role in Asia, in accordance with the Nixon Doctrine. The new U.S. treatment of Japan was not the only thunderbolt that hit Tokyo; there was also the changing American position toward Taiwan, which had lost its role as a floating aircraft carrier to the United States. After all, Japan had been a bigger investor in that island's future than the United States. Suddenly that future looked much more uncertain; a long overdue reality had been brought into this over-all situation. It broke a logjam, and the logs came tumbling down the chutes.

Everybody with interests in the area anxiously looked around to see exactly what had happened, what the consequences were, and how they could re-ensure and protect themselves in this new power constellation. President Nixon had sought to convince the Russians and the Japanese that this new relationship with China was not directed against either, but within days Soviet Foreign Minister Andrei Gromyko flew to Tokyo to see whether he could take advantage of the new virulent anti-American sentiments in Japan. But the Russian image was still tarnished by the way they behaved as occupiers of Japanese territory after the war—indeed, they were still holding to some of it. Because of this, Tokyo had no Soviet option acceptable to Japanese public opinion.

The Japanese may help the Russians to develop some of their Siberian resources, but there is little prospect of their colluding politically with the Russians against the Chinese. Japan is much more concerned with China because of its size and proximity, and its being the historic seat of Japanese culture. They have had a quaint notion that they "understand" China and that they would become its interpreter to the United States. That illusion, of course, is now utterly exploded.

They are aware that China's relations with them have never been placid; they themselves have not yet recovered psychologically from the war with China in 1937, and still feel they have to atone for it. Today the Chinese resent them more than ever and in various ways may try to get their own back. The Japanese also realize that China will increasingly acquire a nuclear capability. Still, Japan will reject nuclear rearmament even though it knows that this will come to hurt its prestige as a world power, and even though a new power complex is creating among some Japanese a growing hang-up about their need for nuclear weapons. To do so, however, it must be certain that the United States will maintain a presence in the Pacific, and this the United States has every intention of doing. As Kissinger put it in August 1970 in a background briefing: "If Japan should draw the conclusion that the United States, for whatever reason, is no longer a factor to be reckoned with in Asia, then Japan has two choices: It can either try to carry the load that we did, in which case we might see a resurgence of Japanese militarism, or it might try to join forces with other Communist countries, in which case we might also see a growth of Japanese military power, but more overtly directed against us. So from many points of view, from the point of view of Japan alone, it is quite important for us to remain a Pacific power so that Japan pursues compatible policies with ours, so that they don't decide to go it alone. They certainly have the industrial capacity to go it alone."

The new Sino-American relationship came as a wrench to most of the U.S. Pacific allies. An old order was suddenly upset, and they were apprehensive of the changes the new fluidity might bring. Indonesia and Thailand were profoundly suspicious of the turn of events, the Philippines were in an uproar, but South Korea and Taiwan maintained a stiff upper lip.

Inevitably, Mr. Nixon's decision to lead China onto the world stage was bound to have far-reaching repercussions on the pattern of relations among the great powers. It created a new flexibility—one can also call it uncertainty—and depending on the situation different power combinations from now on would lead to checks against each other. The rapprochement between the United States and China, for instance, strengthened the American hand with the Russians. It may help to persuade Moscow of the need to continue to seek a *détente* with the United States and Western Europe. The Russians from now on will be as worried about the U.S.-China relationship as the United States used to be about the Sino-Soviet one. In the long run it may even lead the Kremlin to seek a compromise settlement with China. However, this is bound to be much more difficult between two countries which have such drastic territorial claims on each other than between two as distant as the United States and China or the United States and Russia. It also stung Japan into a kind of diplomatic hari-kari. Premier Tanaka's eagerness to establish diplomatic relations with Peking was so precipitous that he had to make for more far-reaching concessions regarding relations with Taiwan than the United States. But whatever the co-operation between these various pairings, they will not lead to formal alliances or even collusion against each other. They will be limited relationships of mutual expediency.

After the overture of the Nixon Doctrine, the trip to Peking was the first act in the application to the seventies of the nineteenth-century concept of balance-of-power diplomacy. The second act, still some way ahead, was to be the President's venture into the Kremlin.

CHAPTER THIRTEEN — THE PENTAGON
ON THE DEFENSIVE

For long enough it seemed that the adage "Nothing succeeds like success" might have been coined for the American military: Anything they wanted, they ask for; everything they asked for, they got. It was odd in its way, because there is a constant element in American thinking that sets uniformed men apart from civilians. In time this is bound to assert itself, and once it does, the military suffer in both standing and influence. Between the world wars those in the armed forces tended to be viewed as having chosen the security of the uniform because they would probably have found it difficult to succeed in the competitive world of private enterprise. Retired officers, except for generals, still rarely continue to attach their rank to their name. Even after World War II, after they had won and become heroes, there was a strong desire to limit their influence and to reduce their power position at home. When in 1946, for example, the admirals revolted against the drastic cuts imposed by the then Secretary of Defense Louis Johnson, President Truman fired the admiral most responsible. What helped the armed forces maintain their strength and influence were anti-communism and the Korean war: Because of them the military got most of the financial support it demanded throughout the fifties. With this acquiescence came a gain in prestige for the military life as a profession and many young and bright men chose the armed forces for their career. Around the world, in spite of the occasional "Yanks Go Home" signs, the

American military were looked on with awe and their protective presence welcomed.

The inevitable erosion of this prestige probably began in 1959 with a misadventure for which they were not directly responsible, but which damaged them none the less. The U-2 plane, which the Russians captured and exhibited, had until then been a secret weapon. Its pilot, Gary Powers, was in the pay of the Central Intelligence Agency, but what mattered was that he was a member of the armed forces, a lieutenant in the U. S. Air Force. The incumbent President was also a soldier. General Eisenhower began by lying about the accident in the belief that he was defending the national interest, but when the Russians proved him a liar the blame again became attached to the military at large. Again, they were mostly on the sidelines when President Kennedy's Bay of Pigs operation came a cropper, but it too did them no good. And then finally and hugely, the military caught the blame—whatever the civilian government's responsibility—for failing to deliver victory in the field in Vietnam.

MCNAMARA'S MASTERY AND TRAGEDY

One of the tragedies of the Vietnam war was that Robert McNamara, who succeeded in reorganizing the U. S. Army into a model fighting machine, with an extraordinarily high *esprit de corps*—restoring the sense of mission largely lost when the Eisenhower administration downgraded its role and proclaimed John Foster Dulles' "massive retaliation" as the military strategy of the fifties—also led it to its undoing.

Soon after he took charge of the Pentagon, McNamara concluded that in both psychological and practical terms, the massive retaliation theory was too rigid and made conventional military force virtually unusable. He therefore developed two new strategic concepts: "flexible response" and "assured destruction." They were based essentially on what seemed to him eminently rational ideas, that you can control the use of force with considerable precision, and that you can apply it in carefully apportioned doses to achieve political ends. At first he ran into heavy resistance from the Air Force and the Navy: They liked the doctrine of massive retaliation, for it gave them a pre-eminence such as they had never before enjoyed. But McNamara persisted and gradually he and his civilian experts succeeded in imposing their will and their ideas. However, he not only built up a strong civilian team to impose control over the military, he also made the Office for International Security Affairs intellectually powerful and thus his own foreign policy arm. His new type of civilian-military bureaucracy soon dominated the creative thinking in the Administration. Hence, whenever McNamara, armed with military and foreign policy advice, sat down in the White House with President Kennedy and later with President Johnson, he was able to assert a powerful influence both on defense and foreign policy, because he had the concrete answers and most of the new ideas. There was no integrated National Security Council system in those days. In fact, McNamara rarely participated in interagency discussions. The big debates took place within the Pentagon, and once the issues had been resolved there, they were transmitted to the President. The close co-operation between the ISA of the Pentagon and several of the State Department policy makers who shared a similar outlook and a similar allegiance to the Establishment made it easier for these policies to find ready acceptance. And since McNamara was the stronger personality, it was he and not Dean Rusk who carried the ball with the President. The Pentagon became the strongest influence on American over-all policy, and it was McNamara who made it so.

THE MYTH OF RATIONALISM

The McNamara idea of limited application of military force, whether actual or psychological, worked successfully in the Dominican Republic in 1965 when the United States intervened militarily to prevent, as President Johnson said, "another Cuba." Earlier, the application of the same theory helped to resolve the Cuban missile crisis. But in Vietnam, which was much farther away, where the enemy were hardened, disciplined, battle-trained guerrillas, the application of limited force for political aims failed when it became clear that a limited application was not good enough. Instead, the identical rationale forced the United States deeper and deeper into an irrational war. And when after 1965 McNamara came to realize that the limited war strategy had more theoretical than practical value, he tried harder than anybody else in the Administration to move away from it. But by then too much prestige was at stake for an imperialist figure such as Lyndon Johnson—who believed, as Philip Geyelin once put it, in "We shall overwhelm"*—to agree to cut his losses. The rationale worked in terms of preventing direct Soviet and Chinese intervention, but it failed in setting a limit to the American involvement. What on paper had looked so rational and logical and convincing, became a myth and a miscalculation. Limited application of the threat or the use of force for political ends can only work in brief and swift and highly circumscribed operations, not in a prolonged guerrilla war, as the history of colonial wars bears out. American technology failed to produce the winning combination: Neither the mobile division concept nor the limited application of air power produced the expected results. The idea that as determined an enemy as the North Vietnamese would have its "will bent" first by the threat of bombing, then by the bombing itself and then by the threat of all-out bombing proved to be a fallacy, and the fact that for humanitarian reasons the United States did not go as far as simply flattening Haiphong and Hanoi does not really weaken this assumption, any more than does General Curtis LeMay's notorious threat "to bomb Vietnam into the stone age."

This leaves the tantalizing question whether or not the United States would have intervened in Vietnam had it remained wedded to a massive retaliation strategy. It is difficult to speculate what might have happened, though we know that John Foster Dulles was ready to intervene, at least with an air strike, in what was then known as the Indochina war, in which the French were still doing the ground fighting. He did not in the end because President Eisenhower refused to act without British support.

* Geyelin, *Lyndon B. Johnson and the World*, Praeger, New York, 1966.

THE ARMY IN DISTRESS

Among the services, the Navy was the least affected by the demoralization the Vietnam war visited on the armed forces. It was never really associated with any serious setbacks, for it was never quite part of the battlefield. With the exception of the river patrols, it stood always at least five miles off the Vietnam coast. The one serious setback it suffered during that period, the capture of the electronic spy ship U.S.S. *Pueblo* by the North Koreans in January 1968, did not belong to the Vietnam war and was not associated with it in people's minds, and the truth as to whether the *Maddox* in August 1964 was attacked by North Vietnamese gunboats came to be regarded as a political dispute between Congress and President Johnson. The Marines negotiated their way out of Vietnam more or less in time; and for the Air Force this war was more a technical than a moral setback, though in many people's minds the moral setback loomed larger. All the experiences of World War II to the contrary, the civilian leadership accepted the idea that air power was a possible key to victory. But the air war did not offer the hoped-for immaculate short cut to victory. Its cost effectiveness was about the worst of any military operation in this war, if not ever. It also exposed the drawbacks of the Air Force's overemphasis on highly sophisticated tactical aircraft, which forced it to resort to costly area bombing.

Worst affected by the war and the public disenchantment with the military was the Army. It suffered the worst loss of prestige, even though it did relatively well considering that it had been neither trained nor equipped for jungle warfare. It was not only the failure to win, however, that hurt it so badly, but other problems that came to haunt it such as the discovery of the murders at Mylai, the widespread drug addiction among drafted men, the rising racial problems within its ranks, the tales of "fragging" (the rolling of hand grenades under unpopular officers' beds), the corruption in its PX establishment, the "gumshoeing" of civilians, especially political radicals, which led to a con-

gressional investigation. All these brought the Army's performance and discipline into disrepute. Every ill, and there were
many, came under the magnifying glass of public scrutiny.

If the Army's loss of public prestige was bad enough, it was
still less serious than its inner demoralization. Thoughtful senior
officers told me that they believed that there was some doubt
whether, as an institution, the Army remained a reliable fighting
outfit, such was the disintegration that had set in within its
ranks. Would it still have the will to fight under real pressure?
That was the question many were posing in the wake of the Vietnam war. A major effort at rebuilding the Army's morale,
therefore, became imperative. Its leadership, too, needed to be
rejuvenated.

It did not help the Army's convalescence that General West-
moreland was made its Chief of Staff, for in the minds of both
the soldiers and the public his name was too closely associated
with a disappointing war. In that sense too the Navy was better
off by choosing as its Chief of Naval Operations Admiral Elmo
Zumwalt, who proved to have the flair and courage to break with
certain outmoded traditions and to give himself the aura of a
reformer.

What has hurt the morale of the uniformed men perhaps most
is not so much what happened in Vietnam as what happened to
them when they came home. Those men, who thought that they
had risked their life in a patriotic cause, in the name of their
government and the American people, found on their return
home that instead of getting recognition for their bravery, they
were treated like outcasts or, as L. James Binder, editor in chief
of the magazine *Army*, put it in the New York *Times*, as "hired
killers" in an "immoral war." Americans look for heroes and like
being heroes, but the war in Vietnam was a war without heroes.
Its only songs have been protest songs. It has added no proud
pages to American history.

It will take a long time until the uniformed men recover some
sort of basic respect in the public mind; it may be even longer
until the Army is restored to a first-rate fighting force. This is a
serious situation, for the stature, prestige and morale of the

Army is what essentially determines the spirit of the armed forces. But it will remain in disarray as long as it is in doubt about its future role. And its future role is in doubt. There is a great deal of talk about "going electronic" and that the Army's future lies with remote-controlled weapons on distant battlefields and not with conventional war. It sounds like a desperate reach for something new, a kind of staff college escapism. It is also born of the realization that the Army, so to say, is pricing itself out of the market. Just as trade union demands for higher and higher wages have led to rationalization, mechanization and automation in industry, so the rising pay scale for men in uniform has made manpower the most expensive item. It is not surprising, therefore, that the Army is thinking of new ways to maintain its role at reduced cost through automation. Paradoxically, perhaps, the younger officers have little faith in these newfangled ideas of some senior officers. They think they will neither work nor help the Army to find its role and morale.

The Army also suffered more than the other services in being behind with the modernization of its equipment. Most of its budget for new matériel had to be spent on helicopter gunships and troop carriers while the rest of its equipment, especially its tank forces, became obsolescent. In fact, experience in this war has raised the question whether the cost of helicopters, which is high, is really worth their effectiveness. The Navy did not fare much better in terms of modernization because it decided to spend most of its funds on doubtful investment in nuclear aircraft carriers. Only the Air Force profited from this war in getting modern equipment. Over-all, therefore, the war has eaten up vast sums that could have been spent on modernization and replacement of equipment. The Soviet Union, which did not suffer such financial drains in the meantime, was able to make much headway in improving the equipment of its forces. It is also true, as some military argue, that the Russians have not fired a shot in anger for many years (except very locally in Budapest and Prague) and that their armed forces, their weapons, their pilots are undertrained, underexperienced, and undertested. The United States has at least the consolation that it has learned a lot about modern weapons and techniques of warfare and that its pilots are well trained.

THE MILITARY'S SHRINKING CONSTITUENCY

What made it so much harder to fight the Vietnam war was that it had to be fought in a climate conducive to a major reassessment of the traditional American values at home. This reassessment would probably have happened anyway, for it was overdue, but the frustrations and the atrocities of the war accelerated it. Certainly, the patience of the blacks was running out anyway, and the young became increasingly hostile as more and more were called by a selective draft to fight in a war that meant nothing to them and whose national interest was difficult to explain to them. Their only hope of bringing this war to an end was to resist it. Therefore, if they resorted to violence it was not surprising, for at least it was violence in their own cause instead of in Vietnam in a cause that was not theirs. This was the stage at which the military's excessive budgetary requests became even more vulnerable than they already were. The constituency defending the interests of the military began shrinking, and is shrinking still. Anti-communism may have been their strongest political ally, but with an American President visiting Peking and Moscow and getting a friendly and hospitable welcome, people will come to be more skeptical even about the dangers of communism.

In Congress, too—the foremost backer of the military-industrial complex, as President Eisenhower called it—support for the military is declining. Some of the most potent defenders of their interests such as Senator Richard B. Russell and Congressman Mendel Rivers have died, and those who are surviving are plainly aware of the growing unpopularity of the Pentagon. Even such stalwart backers as Senator John Stennis, chairman of the Senate Armed Services Committee, spoke of the "general apprehension" in Congress about the Pentagon. In a speech on the Senate floor on January 17, 1972, he critically mentioned "the overly complex weapons," the premature ordering of costly ones while they were being developed and before their needs and performances were established, "the excessive support forces" which amount to more than a million men and women, the questionable usefulness of yet another nuclear-powered aircraft carrier and the contrast between American military manpower costs, which make up 56.8 per cent of the military budget, and those of the Russians, which amount to only 25 per cent. And he wondered "whether we have really gotten through to the Pentagon on all this."

With the political spotlight focused on all the inequalities of American society, on the poor, the hungry, the old and the ill, a major shift of spending priorities from military to social needs is in the making, and Congress, sensitive to these mounting demands, is bound to view defense spending as the one major item where savings are possible. It has not been a "rubber stamp" Congress for some time, but in future it will be even less so, at least as regards the Pentagon's interests.

THE KISSINGER-LAIRD CLASH

The man who warned the military consistently to be more reasonable in their spending was President Eisenhower who, of course, knew what he was talking about and better than any President before him. Lyndon Johnson was much less prejudiced against the military. He had an inborn admiration for raw power; to him, the armed services represented the expression of American might, and he was much more willing to listen to them than either Kennedy or Nixon. He always sought their blessing for almost every decision in order to be able to invoke the fact that he had their support.

Nixon carried to the White House a certain schizophrenia about the military: Some of his instincts led him to be militaristic and aggressive to prove that he was not a coward and the United States not a "helpless giant"; others made him very skeptical about their judgment and performance generally. In the days of McNamara and Clark Clifford, both men with great influence on their Presidents and a strong sense of leadership and self-assertion, the Pentagon dominated foreign policy, but under Nixon's Secretary, Melvin Laird, it learned to play a subsidiary role. Three

months after Mr. Nixon came into power I asked the new Deputy
Secretary of Defense David Packard how he and Laird would divide their functions. "Laird will be the public relations man," he
replied, "he will primarily handle Congress and I'll run the department."

Laird came to the Pentagon after sixteen years in Congress, a totally political man. As a person, he is remarkably devoid of
charm. His bald, oval cranium would make him the perfect model
for an "egghead," but in fact he is about as square and non-in-
tellectual as Middle Americans come. Mr. Nixon appreciated his
political acumen and also the way he astutely defused the issue of
the draft. But at the same time, he was wary of him, for time and
again it became obvious at various critical moments and through
the kind of "leaks" he initiated with the press that he placed his
own interests above his loyalty to the President. It also troubled
Nixon that Laird's military judgment was based on what was
most expedient from a political point of view. Laird's strong point
was his ability to handle Congress and, well aware of this quality,
Laird concentrated quite successfully on re-establishing the kind of
cordiality and co-operation between the Pentagon and Congress
which, he thought, had been lost by his predecessors. As a former
member of the House Armed Services Committee, he knew his
ground in Congress extremely well and carefully tailored his decisions to please his friends on the committees. He also knew how
to keep the military leadership on his side.

Laird and Kissinger were bound to clash. The kind of naked
expediency that the Secretary of Defense often displayed, his
egotism, and his intellectual shallowness were bound to offend
Kissinger. Nixon, also, in his desire to avoid confrontations with
his Cabinet members, used Kissinger as his spearhead in dealing
with Laird and that inevitably led to controversies between Kissinger and the Secretary of Defense. Kissinger, for instance, was
convinced from the first that a negotiated settlement with the
North Vietnamese was possible and, therefore, as did the President, believed in the need to reduce American military strength
from Vietnam gradually. He did not believe in the ultimate success of Vietnamization, but he gave it the benefit of the doubt.

He believed in making every effort to help it succeed. Laird, however, considered it only a propaganda cover behind which the United States could justify a quick withdrawal. He did not believe in a negotiated settlement. Furthermore, his claims in private discussion as to the withdrawal rates he favored were exaggerated, compared to the proposals he submitted to the President. When they are published they will show that at every withdrawal decision the President actually proposed a higher figure than his Secretary of Defense.

McNamara used to be accused of running a "rational war," but in fact, despite the emphasis on systems analysis, its practitioners played a minor role in assessing the war. Kissinger, on the other hand, pushed analysis of the facts underlying the war situation to the extreme limit, some thought even beyond rational limits. He created an analytical framework within which it was easier to assess the prospects of alternative policies, the withdrawal rates and the inherent risks of each phasing-out move. This framework suited neither Laird's character nor his intellect. He was a shrewd operator, who had made a political decision, and the rest he resented. Right or wrong, he thought his way was politically more expedient. The great issues of defense bypassed him; they were simply beyond his comprehension. Laird did not have the intellectual equipment nor did the men around him. It was not surprising, therefore, that he preferred to be the advocate of a simple cause: building more strategic weapons. It suited the Navy and Air Force, whose budgetary requests should have kept them in a happy frame of mind about President Nixon, even if he had strongly reduced their policy-making role. Laird's role during the great crisis discussions was not what he had expected, which led him to see Kissinger as an usurper. When, for instance, during the Jordanian crisis the White House bypassed the Secretary and called on Pentagon experts directly, Laird issued an order that all papers had to go through his office.

LAIRD'S PENTAGON

David Packard, his deputy for three years, had in contrast a towering integrity and a certain raw strength and common sense.

His experience in big business proved an advantage, but it also made him very impatient with the limitations government places on individual decision makers. He had little "feel" for foreign affairs and no real grasp of the great strategic issues, but his instincts were remarkably sound.

The Joint Chiefs of Staff with whom Laird had to deal were relatively tame. His relations with them were better than either McNamara's and Clark Clifford's because he had a shrewd way of making them sympathetic to his problems with the White House. He gave them the feeling that they had greater authority than under his predecessors, yet, in effect, they suffered heavier cuts than under McNamara. However, their voice was better heard in the policy councils, especially the NSC, and their views better known to the President. They have also improved their knowledge of the black art of systems analysis.

One important battle Laird did win against Kissinger, and this was probably crucial for his relations with the JCS, was his determined resistance to Kissinger's attempt to gain control over the Pentagon, as he had over the State Department, through the creation of the Defense Policy Review Board. Laird saw to it that it did not become a potent instrument of presidential leadership. The White House can develop concepts and policies, but it does not have the mechanism to ensure that they will be implemented by the Pentagon. In that sense, the Pentagon remained more or less in control of itself, but in terms of its influence on over-all policy, its power under Nixon declined. Nor was it the free agent it used to be.

This is one of the paradoxes of the Nixon stewardship. Basically, he strongly believed in the display or even the use of power to achieve political ends, yet at the same time he mistrusted the judgment of the military enough to want to restrain their influence. To achieve this he arranged through Kissinger that they be confronted more directly with the civilian views in other parts of the Administration, not just the civilians in the Pentagon, who by Laird's choice, especially in ISA, did not represent a genuinely civilian viewpoint but much more that of the military. What helped Mr. Nixon's relations with the JCS was that, in spite of the drastic military cuts in 1969–70 and in 1971–72 and despite all the talk about "parity," he wanted to maintain a qualitative lead in strategic nuclear weapons. And the President and Kissinger also refrained from meddling with the military and how they spent their money. In 1971 and again in 1972, after Laird had accepted a lower military budget figure suggested by the Bureau of the Budget, Kissinger helped to restore it to the original request by going to the President. Kissinger believed it would be psychologically wrong to reduce military spending at a time when the Russians were increasing their military establishment.

FROM 2½ TO 1½ WARS

In 1969, the Nixon administration took a hard look at how to cut defense costs, so as to be able to trade some of the funds off against higher welfare spending. Options and priority lists were prepared, total revenues for the next three to four years assessed, and finally, agreement was reached on an ambivalent force structure that offered more savings than others by reducing the basic military capacity from being able to fight two and a half wars to one and a half wars. This sounds like a bargain struck on the market in Damascus, but it was nevertheless a serious decision with far-reaching repercussions. In the past, the U.S. planners had to provide for the means to enable the United States to fight two major wars—one in Europe and another in the Pacific—and a local, minor war, say, in Latin America or Africa or somewhere else. This is, of course, a very crude and unsophisticated method of assessing defense needs. It did, however, serve as a rough guide to where reductions could be achieved, even if these were minor by comparison with the total defense budget. Still, it meant that American forces were operating below the resources available to them in 1964. Even if many of the ceilings on defense spending were arbitrary, they did eliminate vague "blue-sky" planning; they forced the military to keep within certain limits and to maintain a proper balance between what was spent on strategic forces and on general purpose forces. In this equation, the allocations for NATO were higher than those for Asia because the President insisted on an effective conventional option in Europe. However, in the American thinking, this option and its effectiveness would depend on the contribution the Europeans were willing to make toward it; if this was inadequate the United States would reduce the high costs of this conventional option by shifting the emphasis to better equipment.

The military have been eager for the last ten years to take at least two divisions out of Europe; it was the civilians who resisted their pressures. McNamara, for instance, favored withdrawing two divisions, but the State Department and President Johnson refused. The military much prefer saving money on manpower costs, which account for half the defense budget, and using it for new weapons. The Laird-Packard stewardship reduced land forces close to the bone, but overinvested in big ships, especially nuclear aircraft carriers, and in too-sophisticated planes such as the F-14 and F-15 tactical fighter bombers. The military's idea is to leave in Europe skeleton forces, which in times of an emergency could be quickly reinforced. The civilians are more concerned with the psychological effect of heavy withdrawals on the allies and on the future of NATO. They also believe that the prospects for negotiating troop reductions with the Russians would disappear if the Russians had no incentive to enter into such negotiations.

However, the pressures for American troop withdrawals from Europe are bound to increase over the next few years. Mr. Nixon with remarkable persistence and stamina resisted these pressures, although in the existing climate he could have carried a lot of favor with Congress and the American public by giving way. But he did not, and American strategy in Europe remained unchanged.

There exist two main strategies: the over-all nuclear strategy of "assured destruction" designed to deter war between the two superpowers, and the "flexible response" strategy which also allows, if necessary, for the use of tactical nuclear weapons to deter a Soviet attack and limit it to Europe. In this over-all strategy the nuclear Polaris submarines play an in-between role; they can be used as part of the superpower deterrent or as part of the European deterrent forces.

The Army remains caught between the military and the civilian outlook, and it dislikes the uncertainty as to how many of its troops Congress will allow to remain in Europe. It is an uncertainty which makes it difficult to plan ahead and develop a new strategy of its own design. Essentially, it is still wedded to McNamara's "flexible response," but this strategy's future is very much in doubt because certainly by the end of this decade there will be insufficient American soldiers left in Europe and not enough Europeans to replace those who have gone.

On the basis of strictly military assessments, the only way to maintain an effective conventional response to a Soviet conventional attack is to maintain the current level of about three hundred thousand American troops in the NATO area. In the age of nuclear parity this American military presence is even more important than it was in the 1960s, for one cannot ignore the thought that one of the consequences of nuclear parity is that an American President will be less ready to strike first against Russian cities in retaliation for a limited Russian attack in Europe and thus risk the destruction of American cities. Robert Ellsworth, who used to be the U. S. Ambassador to NATO, believes that this is an important factor that European politicians and statesmen are still not taking seriously enough. The political consequences on the future outlook of Europe are still difficult to assess, but they could be quite fundamental.

BLUE WATER STRATEGY

In Asia the situation is different. The United States has no vital stake on the Asian mainland. If the war in Vietnam has proved anything, it is that Asia is for the Asians and not for the Americans, and that it is foolish to think that the United States could deploy its army at such geographical distances or even maintain a serious political or military influence on that vast continent.

Even more significant than the withdrawal from Vietnam is the disengagement from Taiwan, which once upon a time John Foster

Dulles and Vice President Nixon saw as their spear pointed at the heart of China. It was the symbol of American power in the Pacific, for there was nothing China could do to dislodge the United States from such a menacing position and to Peking it was a humiliating situation to be in. But in the seventies, Mr. Nixon wisely recognized, Taiwan ceased to be militarily a tenable base. On the question whether it was part of the Chinese homeland there was no difference of view between Peking and Chiang Kai-shek. It was therefore logical for Mr. Nixon to say that future relations between Peking and Taipei were an internal matter to be decided by the two between themselves.

"Blue Water" strategy would mean that the United States would rely on maintaining a certain number of forward air and naval bases, and some Marines on a chain of island bases stretching from Okinawa to the Philippines to Guam to Subic Bay. This would leave the Army without a mission in the Pacific and give the Navy and Air Force a commanding role. The Navy has already discreetly begun to promote the Blue Water strategy by pointing at the costs of land commitments in Thailand, South Korea and Vietnam and the inherent risks. They also diplomatically suggest that there is no need for the United States to stay on the Asian rim, for the combination of floating bases, such as naval ships, and safe island bases is the answer for the future. However much the Army resists the Blue Water strategy, the inevitable withdrawal from Vietnam and the improving relationship between North and South Korea will make it the strategic wave of the seventies in the Pacific.

What will make life particularly difficult in future for the military is the psychological effect of the balance-of-power concept, which tends to blur the distinction between allies and enemies. To the military, who are used to thinking in clear-cut black-and-white terms as to who is on their side and who is not, this is a most confounding concept. It also makes it more difficult for them to obtain public support, especially from the new generation who feel less hostile toward Russia and China and find it difficult to fathom the need for the continuation of vast military outlays. The young do not equate military service with patriotism to the extent young men used to. As a profession the services are now low on the ladder of esteem, which is bound to deprive them of the kind of bright recruits who gave them a special standing in the pre-Vietnam war years.

Mr. Nixon, although he introduced heavy cuts in the military budget, nevertheless went further than Congress in defending the interests of the Pentagon. But his was essentially a rearguard action. The Pentagon will remain on the defensive throughout the seventies as the United States continues to retreat from guard to guardian.

CHAPTER FOURTEEN—THE DOLLAR'S
FALL FROM PRE-EMINENCE

Late in 1964, President Johnson sat by at a meeting in the White House and listened to an exchange between McGeorge Bundy, his National Security adviser, and William McChesney Martin, then chairman of the Federal Reserve Board. Bundy suggested that the United States ought to be able to afford guns *and* butter, but if it found it could not and if in order to carry on the war in Vietnam, devaluation of the dollar proved necessary, it would have to be given serious consideration. To Martin such a course was inconceivable; if he had to choose, he said, between the war and devaluation he would rather get out of the war. No American President, he declared, could politically survive such an admission of financial defeat. President Johnson listened intently but did not comment.

I mention this passing conversation of only a few years ago because of the profound psychological change that has since occurred in the White House. Devaluation of the dollar, unthinkable in 1964, had become not only quite thinkable in the summer of 1971, but was effectively carried out by the year's end and even gained a fair measure of applause. Congress applauded the President's courage, the Washington *Post* (a little ironically but nevertheless approvingly) called the decision the "Midas touch," Wall Street and the business community generally breathed a sigh of relief, and the American public reacted calmly. The fall of the once Almighty Dollar from its uniquely high pedestal thus caused no political shock waves for the President at home, although it caused some around the world. The formal closing of the gold window and the imposition of a 10 per cent surcharge on imports jolted governments and financial and business centers, but at the same time these actions were generally regarded as a first move to face reality. President Nixon's prestige was strengthened rather than weakened.

What had changed? First of all the world, and Americans generally, had come to recognize that the dollar was not what it used to be, that in fact it was an overvalued currency. But it was also a sign that more than the value of the American currency had changed, too. The days when American pride was such that the United States had to be first in everything had gone. Americans had become much less sensitive to the kind of blow to American pride that was, for instance, implicit in the Soviet Union's triumph with the first sputniks, which spurred Kennedy into the space race. Today Americans would shrug off a comparable Russian "first" and do not seem to mind so much if other nations get ahead of the United States, as in the case of the supersonic transport plane. The reason for this change is an acute sense of overstrain and a new perspective on the limits of power brought home with such a vengeance in Vietnam. The old confidence of power, impressive so long as it does not slip over the edge into world weariness, has been replaced by a new maturity, an awareness that even supreme power has its limits.

President Nixon's drastic monetary decisions announced from the presidential retreat at Camp David on August 15, 1971, earned him respect for having the courage to shake the whole world monetary system into an across-the-board revaluation of currencies. It also helped people to forget his obvious failure, at least within the two and a half years he had been in office, to achieve the goals of his domestic economic policies. Throughout all of those two and a half years, conflicting points of view vied with one another in the Administration. Almost unanimously, a policy of gradualism was regarded as desirable in applying the brakes on the sharp inflation which the Nixon administration had inherited; drastic measures, it was feared, might plunge the economy downward so sharply as to make a turnaround difficult to achieve. On the international side, it was believed that success in coping with the inflationary forces at work on the domestic economy would gradually bring about an improvement in the trade picture and in the balance of payments. An assumption which underlay the gradualist approach was that the world would continue to hold large and even increasing amounts of dollars flowing abroad as a result of the adverse balance of trade, foreign investments and other capital movements. In these circumstances, it was believed, the foreigners would be wary of doing anything themselves that might risk pushing the dollar over the brink into devaluation.

By the summer of 1971, however, it was increasingly clear that a gradualist policy of containing inflation was not going to have the desired result, and thus the psychological receptivity to more drastic action on both the domestic and international fronts was much improved. This was a setting to suit a John Connally, who had now been at the Treasury for about six months.

Connally thought that after twenty-two years of balance-of-payments deficits, the emergence of severe trade competition, and permissiveness in allowing other countries to erect trade barriers against the United States, and with no effort having been made to realign the world's currencies, the United States was no longer in its desired position of pre-eminence. There was general agreement within the Administration that with the declining ability of U.S. major industries such as steel and automobiles, not simply to compete in the world's markets, but to withstand imports in the U.S. market, and with the continued freedom of foreign governments to convert dollars into gold, other countries enjoyed a disconcerting whiphand over the dollar. After twenty years of generosity (it was argued) and an outward-looking policy, the United States had to switch to a policy that would give priority to America's own national interests. This feeling was reinforced by the European preoccupation with protecting the interests of its own Economic Community, by the intransigence of Japan in sticking to its import restrictions, and the realization that voluntary revaluation of foreign currencies, especially the yen, came too slowly or not at all. It was clear that the current monetary and trading system simply was not working and that a fundamental change was necessary. The differences that had to be resolved within the Administration thus concerned the specific measures to be taken to deal with such a situation.

Arthur Burns, chairman of the Federal Reserve Board and the President's personal friend of some twenty years, had already been advocating an income policy of a limited price-and-wage freeze, but had failed to get the President's ear. Mr. Nixon's prejudices against such controls dated back to World War II, when he briefly worked for the Office of Price Administration and found them unworkable.

George P. Shultz, then director of the Budget, once dean of the Business School of the University of Chicago, was a disciple of Milton Friedman, the highly articulate, conservative economist who teaches at the University of Chicago. Shultz firmly believed in the wisdom of letting market forces operate freely. He had been an exceptionally good Secretary of Labor who had impressed the President with his knowledge, his strong personality and firm convictions. Allied to the massive powers of Budget director, however, his economic prejudices became a serious liability to the Administration. Yet despite his wrong advice and stubbornly held views, he not only maintained but even increased his influence with the President. Although it had been on Burns's advice that the President chose him, Shultz and Burns had many sharp disagreements and fought bitterly for the President's ear, at least until the fateful Camp David meeting.

THE END OF LAISSEZ-FAIRE

The decision taking actually began a little earlier, on August 2, at a meeting between the President, Connally and Shultz, after Nixon had decided to abandon his unsuccessful "game plan of gradualism" (as it was called), whose authors were Shultz and Paul W. McCracken, chairman of the President's Council of Economic Advisers. At this meeting Nixon decided on the imposition of a limited wage-and-price freeze and the creation of a wage-and-price control board, and certain changes in taxation. What cleared his mind of his long-held prejudice against such measures was the wage settlement in the steel industry, announced that day, increasing wages by 30 per cent over three years, and the industry's instant decision therefore to raise prices by 8 per cent. Quite obviously, inflation could not be allowed to gallop on at such a speed; there was a danger that the country and the world would conclude that control and leadership had slipped from the President's hands.

Already carrying this package, then, President Nixon arrived at Camp David on Friday, August 13, 1971, mentally ready to take some of the most drastic decisions of his career. Several would go against his own basic convictions, but an emergency situation is both a severe examiner of principles and a great inspirer of pragmatism. Besides, Mr. Nixon rather enjoys springing a surprise.

In addition to Connally, Burns, Shultz and McCracken, those summoned to join him there were Herbert Stein, McCracken's deputy; Peter G. Peterson, then the President's adviser on International Economic Affairs; Paul A. Volcker, Under Secretary of the Treasury for Monetary Affairs, and William Safire, Mr. Nixon's speechwriter.

For Shultz, this little weekend trip was his Canossa, a total defeat. Yet as so often happens with men whose judgment has proved to be wrong, he continued to hold one of the most important jobs in the Administration, and after Secretary Connally's resignation was promoted to the Treasury.

For the slow-speaking but quick-thinking Arthur Burns it was a quiet triumph. He was able to puff away at his grandfatherly pipe, look pleased with himself despite his otherwise outward modesty and take satisfaction from having been proved right once again. A few weeks earlier the President had become highly irritated with him, when before the Joint Economic Committee he had criticized Mr. Nixon's economic policy and implied that new measures were needed. Although Connally had tried to dissuade him from criticizing the President's policy, Burns, a crusty, stubborn fellow who likes to say what he thinks, however unpalatable it may be to Presidents, nevertheless went ahead saying publicly what he had been saying privately for many months. But it infuriated Mr.

Nixon and his vindictive streak showed when Charles Colson, one of his aides, leaked the idea that the President was considering broadening the membership of the Federal Reserve Board to make its thinking conform more with the President's, and also suggested that Burns had asked for a raise of his salary by $20,000. The first went against the basic independence of the Fed and disturbed Wall Street, the second offended Burns. Once upon a time, Mr. Nixon had rated Dr. Burns the wisest among economic experts, for he never forgot that in the Eisenhower days he had warned of a recession which later occurred because his advice had gone unheeded and which Mr. Nixon afterward concluded cost him the presidency in 1960. All this made his deafness to Burns's warnings throughout 1970 and 1971 the more baffling.

But by the time he and the President were facing each other across the table at Camp David, the President, by inference, had apologized to Burns for the "leak" at a press conference and strongly praised him. Even more to Burns's satisfaction, the President had also decided to do exactly what the owlish, shaggy economist had asked for months.

The question the assembled company now most hotly debated was whether the convertibility of the dollar into gold be suspended in order to force foreign governments into revaluing their currencies. Connally and McCracken were for it; Dr. Burns argued vigorously that "the closing of the gold window," as it came to be called, would look like the United States murdering the international monetary system without proposing to put anything else in its place. He felt that the surtax on imports and the wage-price freeze would suffice to convince foreigners that the United States was willing to take drastic action to restore the integrity of the dollar, and encourage them to make the needed adjustment in their own monetary exchange rates. The President adjourned the first meeting on Friday night without taking a decision about closing the gold window, but at 4 A.M. on Saturday he told his personal aide Bob Haldeman that he would go "all the way, including the gold window." It was a triumph for Connally.

On Saturday the debate was no longer what to do, but about the timing of the President's announcement. The majority agreed with his preference for Monday night, but the experienced Burns and the mild but persistent McCracken argued for Sunday night because they feared another run on the dollar on Monday would then lead the world to think that the President was reacting to another crisis instead of appearing to be taking a bold, but carefully considered action. The Sunday nighters prevailed, and Burns was instructed to prepare his central banker friends around the world. Volcker was dispatched to Paris to explain to European finance ministers the thinking behind the President's decision. Pierre-Paul Schweitzer, managing director of the International Monetary Fund, was not consulted either by the President or Connally, but (a doubtful form of politesse) was invited to the Treasury to view the President's telecast.

Most of the speech the President delivered that night he had written himself in his big-lettered, nervous, angular longhand. As usual, he started his draft with the hard news and the guts of his arguments. In a marginal comment to his speechwriter Safire he wrote: "I believe that this is the best approach rather than to start with the gobbledygook about this crisis of international monetary affairs, the need for sacrifice, etc., which seemed to be the thrust of Volcker and to a lesser extent Peterson." Later, next to the phrase "stop the rise in the cost of living," he wrote: "This is an overstatement but when we say slow or stop the rate of increase and the rest, it loses impact and has no meaning." His concluding instructions to Safire said: "What I'm interested in in this speech is not fancy words, but emotional feel, lift." He clearly considered himself the best judge of public opinion and his own best public relations man.

A FOUL BLOW BY THE BRITISH?

Fortune magazine the following January claimed that the President's decision was "dictated by the largest money run in history which culminated in a panicked request from the Bank of England for a guarantee against devaluation of its dollar holdings totalling some $3 billion. The British request, viewed as tantamount to a demand for gold, was relayed to the White House on the morning of August 13." The article further stated that the British demand was "considered a distinctly foul blow; after all, the United States had helped rescue sterling at least three times during the 1960s. An outraged Treasury abruptly turned down the British request."

Even earlier, on November 22, 1971, Hendrik S. Houthakker, a former member of the President's Economic Advisory Council, raised the matter in public in a speech at DePaul University. He said, "There is as yet little public knowledge of what exactly led to the President's decision to suspend the convertibility of the dollar into gold. . . . One clue to the developments that precipitated the decision of August 15 may well be the recent disclosure that two days earlier the United Kingdom drew the entire amount of its so-called swap line with the United States, amounting to $750 million. . . . If the British action was indeed the immediate reason for our August 15 decision, it will be interesting to know Britain's motives for thus bringing down the Bretton Woods system of which it had been one of the principal architects."

My own investigation of this grave accusation produced contradictory evidence; only one thing everyone agreed on was that the British request did not "dictate," as *Fortune* magazine had said, the President's decision at Camp David. Secretary Connally with slightly flaring nostrils and considerable emphasis confirmed, when I asked him personally, that the British requested a gold coverage for $3 billion and clearly remembered that he had told the President about it on August 13 during a three-hour talk he had with him in his retreat at the Executive Office Building. He also said that "not any one thing caused the decision to close the gold window. We had talked about this possibility for months." Dr. Burns repudiated the Houthakker accusation and that echoed in *Fortune*. The British request was an "irritant," Dr. Burns said later, "but it did not play a role in the decision to close the gold window, and as far as I can remember, and I participated in all the important discussions at the Camp David meeting, the British action was never mentioned."

British officials in London angrily denied the accusation. Queried as to the exact facts, they replied that they had asked the Federal Reserve Bank of New York shortly before August 12 to activate a reverse "swap" (guaranteeing official dollar holdings against devaluation) and then questioned over the transatlantic telephone as to how much they were asking for, replied that they wanted as much as possible, which meant in effect up to the full amount of the facility they had with them—$2 billion. When the Fed declined to go along with that request and limited the amount to $750 million, which was the equivalent of the inflow of dollars into the United Kingdom since August 1, the British claim that they did not press for more. The reverse swap was carried out on August 13. There was no reference to conversion of gold and the whole transaction was never raised at a political level on either side of the Atlantic; it was treated as a routine exercise. No American reached for the transatlantic telephone to question higher authority in London. Charles Coombs, senior vice president of the Federal Reserve Bank of New York and special manager of the system's Open Market Account, also confirmed that the British Government never formally requested a special amount, and that certainly the figure of $3 billion was never mentioned, and that when the British Government was told that London could have $750 million it did not press for more and appeared satisfied with the American offer.

THE WORLD TAKES A COLD SHOWER

If the world applauded the President's drastic decisions, it did so with all the relish of a bather taking a cold plunge on a December morning. The 10 per cent surtax felt like a gun at the temples of the great industrial powers, and the closing of the gold window, the end of the era of the mystique of gold.

For years American administrations had been warning their allies that the United States in wake of the Marshall Plan had been carrying a heavier burden than was justified and that it could not go on indefinitely. Yet other countries did not listen or did not want to listen to these pleadings. They assumed that the disequilibrium could continue indefinitely and the United States would not dare to devalue the dollar or seriously cut its military and financial commitments. The world's trading nations behaved like players in a poker game in which everybody is expecting to win a hundred dollars. Some countries, especially Japan, carried a policy of economic nationalism to such an extreme that it was bound to bring some kind of retaliation. Both sides really miscalculated. The Americans for too long assumed that to avoid monetary turmoil the leading nations would refrain from pushing the dollar's green back against the walls of Fort Knox, and the Europeans and Japanese calculated that an American President would not want to take the political risk of devaluation.

Japan and Canada were the two countries worst hit by the August 15 decision. The U.S. trade deficit with Japan and with Canada was about $2 billion each; with Europe the United States had a surplus of about $1.5 billion. Japan, the second most important economic power in the free world and the most important in Asia, presented a grave problem for the United States. It had been unwilling to restrict its imports to the United States voluntarily or to allow the yen to float upward, as Germany had done with its mark, and as a consequence had to be forced into doing both through the surtax weapon. Premier Sato failed voluntarily to restrain Japanese textile exports as he had promised, was treated by the President with what Patrick Moynihan might call "unbenign neglect."

CONNALLY: THE ACTOR-MANAGER

The American action could easily be made to seem more like a declaration of economic war than a constructive move to restore the health of the old monetary system. For John Connally, it was exactly that. And he was ready to fight that war with all the cunning and ruthlessness and patriotism he could summon.

Only five weeks before the President's remarkable economic about-face, Connally had told a press conference that there was no need for action. But Connally had the psychological advantage that in financial and monetary affairs he held his convictions less firmly than in political matters, and thus did not find it hard to follow the President loyally down the new road. He is like a brilliant actor, who can play many parts well and when one of his parts has exhausted its appeal, it does not present any problem to him to study a different one and to act it with equal aplomb. He also has the charm, the gall and the persuasiveness to make every new part convincing.

As Secretary of the Navy under Robert McNamara, he was, as McNamara once put it to me, the best administrator he had ever come across. As Governor of Texas he proved to be a virtuoso at playing politics to his best advantage; in that role he was also fortunate enough to survive the assassination of John F. Kennedy, traveling with him in the same car. As Secretary of the Treasury, he was brilliant, though not necessarily wise, forceful though often unpredictable, quick in learning, but not really knowledgeable. He was in many ways a copy of his mentor Lyndon B. Johnson, except that he was more handsome, dressed with better taste, and seemingly much more at ease with the world.

As a bargainer, few could match him. One of his drawbacks in international negotiations was that he previously hardly ever had dealt with foreigners. And since he tended to see everything from his own vantage point, it was not easy for him to sympathize with the problems of others; it made it easier, though, for him to insist that everybody else should hoe to his line. For the members of the Group of Ten, the world's most sophisticated financial managers, he was like a bull at the tellers' windows. They were used to bargaining by raising an eyebrow, not the blunt Texan horse trader's way. Connally was to some of them a figure out of an Edna Ferber novel, a character whose rascality they both admired and loathed, "the bully boy on the manicured playing fields of international finance," as he once enjoyed describing himself.

He was ready to get the best deal he could for the United States and squeeze everybody else until it hurt and until they would give in to the American demands. The financial, economic and political stakes were colossal, and for several months—much longer than anybody expected—the contest raged on.

The relief Americans felt after the President stopped the gold drain and imposed a 10 per cent surtax gradually changed to an uneasy and increasingly worrisome uncertainty about when the United States would end a situation in which the world's currencies were floating against the dollar and agree to a new set of pegged exchange rates. But Connally was adamant. His own view was that currencies should be left to float because this was the best way to obtain a realignment of currencies and also to bring pressure for changes in trading conditions to the advantage of the United States.

For an uncomfortably long time the floating, the continuing uncertainty about American monetary intentions, and the visible concern and irritation in Europe and Japan suited the President politically. His poll ratings went up, he was seen as a hard-to-get defender of American international interests.

Connally, meanwhile, excelled at press conferences and on television and soon became the outstanding member of Mr. Nixon's otherwise lackluster cabinet. He was riding high and enjoying it. He was charming and disarming in public, assertive and intimidating behind the scenes. On the informal, human side, he could be seen holding hands with his wife, even at public occasions. He thrived under the spotlight, in the infighting and in the exercise of power.

His outlook on the world, however, gave American policy a more nationalistic trend than it has ever had since World War II. His desire was to be tough rather than generous with foreigners, for he felt that they had become rich by breast feeding on the American dollar and should now be prepared to be weaned from it. As he saw it, they had taken advantage of the high cost of American production and their own lower standard of living, and yet they were becoming more, rather than less, protectionist. This led him to believe that if Britain failed to get into the Common Market, it should be a welcome development for the United States. To him what mattered was not the political desirability of Western Europe becoming a power to itself, but the economic damage it would cause the United States by widening the area of trade protectionism against the United States. This was a different attitude from Mr. Nixon's public stance or that of previous administrations. But Connally's outlook was symbolic of a new trend in public opinion that should not be under-rated. Even though the President did not share many of Con-nally's attitudes toward foreign economic and monetary policy, he nevertheless gave him an extraordinary latitude to express and pursue them. Mr. Connally, as a consequence, exercised this freedom with all the bravura of a vintage barnstormer. The two saw a lot of each other and seemed to have more in common than they had probably expected. Connally, several men in close contact with him suspected, was playing for high stakes. He had nothing to lose in the Democratic Party he still nominally belonged to. He had no political future within it. None of the Democratic candidates likely to run for the presidency in the spring of 1972 suited his political tastes; none of them would he have wanted to vote for. He was a restless man, torn between his strong urge for a new political future and another, more restful pastime making yet more money at home in Texas. In all probability, however, he dreamed of the vice presidency to give him a chance at the presidency in 1976. The great barbecue he threw for the President in early May 1972, an exhibition of Texas financial power and Connally's command over it, was de-signed to impress the President.

THE CONSPIRACY AGAINST CONNALLY

The uneasiness about the unsettled state of the world's mone-tary system was very much in evidence at the World Bank and In-ternational Monetary Fund meeting late in September 1971. Con-nally superficially tried to fend off these concerns, but in fact had no intention of starting serious negotiations. He wanted to keep the Europeans and especially the Japanese in suspense until they would offer the bargain he considered satisfactory. He was very relaxed and made everybody aware of how little it all worried him. Let the others worry, was his dictum. But among those other people who worried was an increasing number of men in the Nixon administration who were afraid that Connally's tactics could become counterproductive if pushed too far and might seriously erode relations with Canadian, European and Japanese allies and lead to subtle if not overt retaliation instead of to concessions. And so, gradually, those officials in the Administration who had over-all political and foreign policy as well as economic interests to consider began to make common cause against Connally's dangerously nationalistic outlook. Particularly, Dr. Burns, Dr. Kissinger and Nathaniel Samuels, the Deputy Under Secretary of State for Economic Affairs, were watching the situation with growing concern.

Dr. Burns was the first to act. He concluded that an "honest broker" among the governments concerned was needed to avoid another catastrophic failure at the next meeting of the Group of Ten in Rome, planned for the end of Nevember. During the World Bank meeting in Washington in September, therefore, he broached the idea of selecting Dr. J. Zijlstra, the president of the Bank for International Settlements as well as president of the Central Bank of the Netherlands, as the intermediary; the discussions included most of the big Ten ministers of finance and central bankers concerned and also Connally. The idea was for Zijlstra to prepare an over-all plan for a new parity realignment package based on talks he would hold with the key officials in each European capital, in Ottawa, in Tokyo and in Washington. He was by no means to negotiate, but only to explore the area for settlement. Everyone was pledged to secrecy and no one would be committed to accept Zijlstra's plan, which would be his own, but the hope was that it would provide something close enough to acceptability by the finance ministers and central bank governors on which to base the final bargaining round. Burns saw it as a pre-emptive way to avoid the Tower of Babel of the meetings that had already taken place in London and Washington. Everyone co-operated, including Nathaniel Samuels, who before he joined the government was managing partner of Kuhn, Loeb & Co., the U.S. investment bankers, and an old friend of Zijlstra's; his views on the trade and defense burden-sharing elements of a settlement were important to Zijlstra in designing the realignment package.

Everyone, that is, except Connally, who did not want anybody

to interfere with his own negotiating tactics and who refused
to see Zijlstra; when Volcker met Zijlstra for the United States,
he did so on President Nixon's instructions, but the meeting
proved to be only a ceremonial affair. Zijlstra produced a proposal
just before the Rome meeting which might have been more or less
acceptable to all European governments and the Japanese, but well
below what would have been acceptable to Connally. In Burns's
view, however, Zijlstra had greatly advanced the consensus on
which the final solution could be based. It was important at a
given moment to begin to think constructively and in concrete
terms. "Without his preparatory work," Burns said later, "I don't
think the Smithsonian Agreement [in which the new exchange
rates were finally settled] could have been obtained." Others did
not think that the Zijlstra mission had been that influential. But
it was one of those rare secret operations that remained secret
while it mattered.

In the meantime, however, the most difficult and the most
crucial task was to convince President Nixon that Connally's
delaying tactics, which he practiced throughout October and
through much of November, and which left the Europeans and
the Japanese in doubt whether the United States was indeed seeking an equitable solution, were hurting the cause of international
monetary confidence and stability. Burns had been keeping an
inventory on a country-by-country basis of measures that foreign
governments and central bankers were beginning to take to
counter the consequences of the U.S. action, and he found that
some began to look ominous: The possibility of an international
recession began to loom on the horizon. Not only foreign experts
began to express deep concern, but also the heads of great
American corporations. The latter's operations at home had
already suffered a serious decline under the impact of the American domestic situation and if the international monetary uncertainties persisted much longer, their profits from foreign operations too would suffer, and undermine the confidence of the
American investor. American big business had become so globally
expansionist that what was happening abroad had begun to be
also a threat to American domestic economic stability. Soon,

therefore, not only Burns was warning the President of the un-healthy effects a failure to come to a monetary settlement and the 10 per cent surtax could have on the American economy, but also several of his best friends in Wall Street and in the business community generally. They implored him to put an end to the international monetary uncertainties because they feared that a world-wide loss of confidence in U.S. policy could trigger a slump of 1929 proportions.

Reprecussions on the diplomatic front had also begun to build up and aroused Kissinger's attention. Connally's bargaining tactics, he suddenly realized, could imperil American foreign policy on the central diplomatic front. It was a new, unaccustomed problem for Kissinger, because for the first time he sensed that Connally could become a threat to his power at the throne, and he had become more accustomed to threats from the left rather than from the right flank. The great problem became how to avoid a confrontation with Connally in which the President was forced to take sides. Burns and Kissinger were obvious allies in this endeavor to enlighten the President, but two attempts by Burns to make Secretary of State Rogers more than a silent sympathizer failed. Rogers was either unwilling or unable to take a strong position and to help defend against Connally what were obvi-ously State Department interests. Instead of joining the line-up against Connally, he maintained that the President was wise enough to know when to change policy and would do so in due time. Nathaniel Samuels, while earlier in agreement that the time for drastic action was overdue, stood together with Burns on the need for a settlement, but with Rogers taking a passive position, had difficulties asserting the State Department's interests. Because of Samuels' international contacts and experience he was listened to in the interagency meetings, but Connally sat firmly in the sad-dle. What was missing at the White House was an influential "Kiss-inger" concerned with foreign economic policy. In President Johnson's days, for instance, Francis Bator, who knew how to exert influence with discretion, played a powerful and enlightened role as far as foreign monetary and trade policies were concerned. But in Henry Fowler he had had a relatively weak Secretary of the Treasury to contend with. Kissinger himself was not interested in foreign economic policies. He once said to me that "economics bored him," and when Peter Peterson, president of the Bell & Howell Company, was appointed to become a kind of economic pendant to Kissinger in the White House, he did not prove a match for Connally's dynamic, almost despotic personality. Connally resented anyone who even in the slightest contradicted him and would call to complain about anyone almost immediately who had said something publicly that was not in harmony with his own public positions. He would telephone either the critic directly, if he was important enough, or if he was an official, contact his superior. And so the weight of changing the President's mind fell on Kissinger and Burns.

Kissinger, unsure of his economics, consulted experts far and wide. Richard Cooper of Yale University and Francis Bator of Harvard University teamed up to produce a memo for him on what to do next. They stressed the dangers inherent in the United States overplaying its hand by pressing for too much too quickly, and by asking foreign politicians to do things they could not conceivably afford to do. They criticized Connally's refusal to specify U.S. demands more precisely because it made it impossible, in their view, for foreign governments to respond constructively. They drew attention to the dangers of frustrations and the likelihood that foreign governments would fall back on a policy of recrimination and face-saving rhetoric. And they also warned that the malaise could soon impinge on vital American political and security interests, encourage neo-Gaullism in Europe and drive out responsible statesmanship. They argued for the early removal of the surcharge and for approaching the allies informally with proposals for a solution.

Among the experts Kissinger consulted was also the Earl of Cromer, the British Ambassador to Washington, who as a former governor of the Bank of England knew the world of the Group of Ten like his own wine cellar. Burns kept in touch with Cromer to calm the uncertainties and animosities Connally had created in London.

The crisis began to escalate as autumn edged toward winter. The Europeans, especially the French, began talking about a "European solution," and though the Germans were opposed to it since their national security depended so heavily on the American military commitment in Europe, there was a limit to which they could resist French pressures and risk the cohesion of the European Economic Community. The United States was suddenly seen in a very different light. The ruthless use of the surtax weapon in the bargaining had pricked the last balloons of romanticism that were still floating in Europe. It was in mid-October that the President said to some of his aides that the impasse with the Europeans represented a watershed, and they must learn to realize that the United States would pursue its own interests and not give in to the Europeans without their making a necessary contribution to correcting the U.S. balance of payments; in contrast to Connally, however, he excluded the cost of U.S. defense in Europe.

Burns and Kissinger, meanwhile, sought to draw Nixon's attention to the dangers of further delay in a monetary settlement, the damage that could develop to world trading relationships and to American security interests. But nobody at that point knew whether the President wanted a solution of the crisis while its fallout in domestic politics remained so helpful to him. At the Treasury, in a heated meeting during Connally's absence in Japan, Samuels, J. Dewey Daane of the Federal Reserve Board and Carter Murphy of the President's Council of Economic Advisers strongly argued for an end to floating—which did not even have the advantage of a truly free float; only Volcker and his Treasury colleagues still favored it and wanted to concentrate on long-term alternatives for a settlement. Gradually the internationalists succeeded in shifting the President's reflections from the domestic political benefits of his policy to the possible dire international repercussions, and the effect they would have on the domestic economy. Burns and Kissinger both were convinced that once the President looked at the realities he would accept their viewpoint, and Connally, without making a fuss, would also relent.

What Connally did not realize sufficiently was that the President's decisions of August 15 were an aberration from his usual concern for world affairs, and therefore Mr. Nixon would almost necessarily have deep misgivings in due time. Nixon was a convinced internationalist and essentially a believer in a liberal trade policy, and August 15 had caused him some twinges of conscience, however convinced he has tried to appear, for having gone so drastically against his own convictions. For a while showing those foreigners the fist and making them squirm produced a favorable political fallout for him with American public opinion and, inevitably, everything that seemed to improve his chances for re-election had a certain attraction for him. "Most people misunderstand President Nixon," Dr. Burns once said to me, "because they think that this is what matters most to him. It has led many to misjudge him. His rhetoric about foreigners may sometimes sound narrowly partisan and too steeped in political terms, but he is and will always be an internationalist because his greatest aim is to bring peace to the world. Too many people do not grasp this abiding faith and his dream for a place in history."

However, by mid-November the voices of Kissinger, Burns and the President's own friends on Wall Street began to make an impression on Mr. Nixon. They tried to convince him that to continue to follow the Connally policy could have disastrous consequences, that the United States could no longer keep the world on tenterhooks and had to make it clear that it was ready to devalue the dollar in terms of gold and agree to a new set of exchange rates. The President listened and gradually, as is his characteristic way, decided to end the waiting game because it was beginning to be counterproductive. The great confrontation between Kissinger and Burns on one hand and Connally on the other was thus avoided by simply winning the President's support for their point of view. Connally, once he saw that the President's mind was changing, fell in line, at least in principle. He was now willing to announce at the right moment that the United States was ready to devalue the dollar and to negotiate a new set of parities.

CONNALLY SPRINGS DEVALUATION

The right moment occurred at the Rome meeting of the Group of Ten on November 30 and December 1. Shortly before the meeting, Zijlstra delivered his secret memorandum to Burns, Connally and Samuels. But, again, Connally ignored this operation. He did not want to know anything about the results of the mission. However, even if the Zijlstra mission did not provide the ultimate solution, it at least helped to keep the various governments he conferred with under the impression that negotiations were in progress behind the scenes, and that in turn helped to sublimate the growing impatience and uncertainty about the future that had gripped the leaders of finance in the capitals of Europe, in New York and in Tokyo. One major disadvantage for Zijlstra was that he had to assume that the United States would not devalue the dollar.

To Connally the whole exercise was merely an intrusion into what he considered his own preserve. His resentment of sharing responsibility with anyone else also shone through before he left for Rome. At first, for instance, he flatly refused to include the State Department in his delegation. He wanted to make it clear that only he was in charge and informed John Irwin, the Under Secretary of State, that on return he would report on the Rome meeting to Secretary Rogers. It was only after Irwin, a mild, self-effacing but tenacious man, explained to him that it would cause more than raised eyebrows all around if he did not have Samuels on his team that Connally relented. Still, to emphasize his pre-eminence he went so far as to send a cable to the American Ambassador in Rome, Graham Martin, asking that only he be met at the airport by an official black limousine and that the rest of his delegation, which included such limousine-accustomed VIPs as Dewey Daane and Samuels, should travel together with all the secretaries in a bus. Martin, a veteran diplomat, however, did not follow these instructions and sent additional VIP limousines to the airport. Connally, who had little patience with striped-pants diplomats and, above all, did not like to have his instructions countermanded, was highly irritated. But when he heard that Martin was one of Mr. Nixon's favorite ambassadors, the incident was quickly relegated to the dustbin where it belonged.

Another trivial incident occurred at the conference table in Rome when Connally suggested that a meeting be restricted to the principals of the delegations. Pierre- Paul Schweitzer, the executive director of the International Monetary Fund, a sort of neutral fixture to the Group of Ten meeting, was in the room at the time and did not quite know whether this meant that he should leave or stay. Connally had developed a vivid dislike for Schweitzer, a shy, slow-speaking, inarticulate Frenchman, ever since their first private lunch when they quickly ran out of subjects to talk about. Now Schweitzer embarrassedly got up, hesitating as to whether to leave the room, Connally's bête noir Burns, noticing his dilemma, asked him to stay and thus resolved an awkward situation.

The Connally feathers were also ruffled in Rome by the British Chancellor of the Exchequer Anthony Barber. At the earlier London meeting of the Group of Ten, Barber had paid less devoted attention to Connally's arguments than the American Secretary thought they deserved. Connally was overheard saying to his aides before replying to Barber at the conference table, "I'll take his pants off." The remark was undoubtedly overheard by the adjoining British delegation and did not go forgotten. At the Rome meeting, Barber was more European than the Europeans, to the great annoyance of his taunter.

Connally did not like the clubby atmosphere of the Group of Ten. He thought that it had been created to deal with problems of another era, that it was dominated by the Europeans and, in the absence of weighted voting, left the United States at a disadvantage. He felt outnumbered, outvoted and uncomfortable among these smooth-talking financial sophisticates around the table who, he felt, had come together for no other reason than to join in imposing devaluation as an act of humiliation on the United States. They meant to pressure him into paying for the realignment of currencies with the devaluation of the dollar.

Volcker spoke for the United States, Connally being in the chair, and began with his old theme song that the United States favored continued floating of currencies and would not devalue the dollar. He caused consternation and raised hackles, but soon he also began to realize that he was confronted with two major obstacles: First, it was highly questionable whether there could be a clean float because the Europeans were going to set limits to which they would allow market forces to determine the values of their currencies, and, second, all the central bankers simply were against continued floating. Anthony Barber, for Britain, suggested that the conference could not make any further headway until it knew whether the United States was prepared to devalue the dollar. To all the Europeans present this was the key question and so far the answer had always been "never," including an insistence on a sweeping revaluation of other currencies without the United States making any concessions herself.

Connally, speaking slowly and savoring every word, said in the calm, cool tones of a croupier: "What would the gentlemen's reply be if I suggested a devaluation of 10 per cent?"

The "gentlemen," as he had called them with calculated southern politeness, sat around the table startled and speechless. Even though Connally sounded hypothetical, he had broken the ice. It was the first hint that the United States was willing to devalue, though 10 per cent came as a shock, for in everybody's view it was far too much; quite obviously it would give the United States trade advantages no one felt his country could really afford. Still, the magic word had been spoken, the United States had agreed to the principle of devaluation. There was a certain relief about the room, but also awe, for that was the moment of the formal dethronement of the Almighty Dollar.

Connally, who had performed that symbolic act, looked around the table, enjoying the effect. The surprise was so devastating that no one said a word, and many left the table to confer with each other outside the conference room or to telephone their governments. None of the ministers had come with instructions of what to propose in such an event; nobody had expected it would happen.

After more than half an hour's pause, German Finance Minister Karl Schiller was the first to respond. He suggested that his government could not accept a higher revaluation against the dollar than 12 per cent. Others spoke up to say that 5 per cent was the maximum they could accept. Another obstacle was the condition that Connally had attached to the realignment; prompt discussions of modifications in certain trade policies on the part of the Europeans, Japanese and Canadians. Barber claimed that this was an entirely new demand he was not prepared for and could not accept. Connally, correctly, claimed that Barber was wrong, that this was no new demand, and a sharp controversy developed. Barber, quite clearly, was not only speaking as the new good British European (as his French opposite number, Giscard d'Estaing, was delighted to see) but was even *plus français que les français*; not even the remnants of the old special Anglo-American relationship seemed to have survived. The Canadians and the Japanese said nothing, and most of the others, it soon became clear, had come without instructions for the eventuality their governments had most desired.

Connally, with an ironic twist, suggested that everybody stay till midnight if they thought negotiations could be brought to a successful conclusion, but it was quite obvious that no one was ready—not even, truth to tell, Connally himself.

If the Europeans had thought that the United States was negotiating from a position of weakness, they had misjudged Connally. They were stunned and flabbergasted and appalled by his crafty methods. They were used to following certain delicate rules of quiet dignity in their negotiations, of only lifting the corner of each of their cards and letting others just peek under them, but they were not used to having the whole pack thrown at them. Connally, devoid of philosophical fixations about gold and devaluation and the rules of the monetary game, cared only about getting the best possible deal. No one knew what to do next, and so the Rome meeting broke up in disarray.

President Nixon, in the meantime, had set in train a chain of summit meetings, the first one in the Azores on December 14 with President Pompidou of France. He gave it first priority on the assumption that in the field of finance and monetary affairs France was in a position to lead. If he could clinch a deal with France, Britain and Italy would fall into line. Nixon himself did not want to get involved in the details of the bargaining, feeling uncomfortable at discussing monetary affairs with a former head of the Bank of Rothschilds, and so let Kissinger set the stage. It was Connally, however, who sat on Pompidou's left at dinner, with the President on Pompidou's right, so that they could debate the amount by which France was willing to revalue the franc in exchange for dollar devaluation. Both were tough bargainers. Pompidou began by offering to revalue by 6 per cent. Connally countered with a demand for 9½ per cent. Pompidou moved up to 7, and finally 8.57 per cent. Connally tried to hold out for 9 per cent, but the President decided to accept Pompidou's last offer; it seemed reasonable and clearly would be interpreted as a success for Nixon. It was higher than anybody expected Pompidou to go, even his own financial experts, and he was criticized for it at home. Pompidou had made such a substantial concession, not because he thought it was particularly financially advantageous, but because he wanted to make a contribution to U.S.-French understanding. Mr. Nixon on his part agreed to increase the price of gold to $38, an increase of only $3.00, and thereby devalue the dollar, but to Pompidou, and the French mentality generally, it was vitally important that a higher gold price had been agreed on. The French, traditionally, have had a fixation about gold; they still believe in it even though its meaning in international finance has diminished sharply.

The Nixon-Pompidou agreement, it was expected, would make the realignment of all currencies easier when the finance ministers and central bankers of the Group of Ten assembled again at the Smithsonian in Washington. For more than twenty-four hours, however, a solution at the Smithsonian seemed remote; in fact, by lunchtime the second day it looked as if the meeting would break up once again without agreement. Everybody was too concerned with protecting his own position, everybody's own nationalism was shining through—some did not even want to divulge their hands at all. The problem was to find an accord on how the various currencies would be revalued relative to each other. The Germans for a long time refused to go beyond 4 per cent above the franc, the British and the Italians did not want to move at all. The United States was a bystander as the Europeans discussed the troubles they had with each other and with the dollar. Finally, Connally, as the chairman of the meeting, assumed the role of go-between. By 2 P.M. on Saturday, it still looked like a hopeless maze of blind alleys. German Finance Minister Schiller, for instance, had been helpful throughout the proceedings, but remained adamant after having gone to 6 per cent above the French. In between discussions, finance ministers telephoned their heads of government to get new instructions and more negotiations followed. The Japanese did not address the conference, but negotiated directly behind the scenes with Connally and Burns. Connally at first wanted them to revalue the yen by 19 per cent. They refused, but finally agreed to 17.9, more than anybody expected. But they asked Connally not to divulge their decision prematurely. Connally simply reassured the others that the yen would be revalued within satisfactory levels and higher than the German mark, and no one asked any further questions.

Connally was now negotiating country by country; finally he told the Italians as the last holdouts: "It's all right with me if you Italians don't agree because if this meeting breaks up without an accord the United States will no longer be the whipping boy." And so Connally cajoled, threatened, pushed and roughed up these ministers, all anxious to protect their own country's interests to the last, but in the end a new package of exchange rates was agreed on; everybody was pleased, for the world looked suddenly much more stable. Subsequent events, however, proved that monetary agreements arrived at by squeezing everybody else until it hurts are less likely to survive than those attuned to economic realities.

Connally, however much it was against his own convictions, played the loyal servant of his President and pinned the world's leading currencies to new fixed exchange rates. The revaluations against the dollar he had extracted were better than anything anybody, including Zijlstra, had expected. He may not be a monetary wizard, nor a financial strategist, but he proved to be a negotiating tactician par excellence who knew how to squeeze the last drop of blood out of those anemic keepers of their country's treasuries. And so ended the great battle over the dollar. In Anthony Barber's view a lesser man, less tough than Connally, could not have done it. The question still to be answered is whether it was the retreat it seemed to be, or will turn out to have been only a tactical adjustment, which in another few years will make the dollar again the most desirable of currencies.

Implicit in the neo-nationalism that continues to influence American economic policy is the new realism with which the United States views the Common Market. The traditional argument in favor of the EEC, that the United States should accept short-term economic disadvantages for the sake of the long-term economic and political advantages that a strong and united Western Europe would provide to the West, has lost conviction even though it is the American experience that larger trading areas create their own dynamics in international markets and stimulate increased trade.

These reservations were the most extreme in the Treasury, where Under Secretary Volcker even contended that if Britain failed to get into the Common Market, it would not be disadvantageous to the United States. After all, Britain is a large importer of American agricultural commodities, and membership would put Britain behind the European Community's protective wall. At the Department of Agriculture the EEC is a dirty word; in the Department of Labor it is an undesirable magnet attracting big American investments and therefore in their eyes depriving American labor of jobs; in the Department of Commerce it is an uncomfortable trade competitor.

But there was some justification for worrying about the EEC becoming too protectionist and too oblivious to American interests. While its policies on industrial tariffs and investments are liberal, its agricultural protectionism is a serious problem. In their defense, EEC members argue that agricultural policy is basic to the Community and the main reason France went along with it. They are less convincing, though, in defending the special trading arrangements with the Mediterranean, African and Middle Eastern countries which they say help bring these areas closer to Europe and which in turn will have special economic and political benefits for the West as a whole. But to Americans who have lost touch with much of their inner self-confidence, these arrangements, just as the enlargement of the European Community to ten plus inclusion of the former EFTA (Economic Free Trade Area) countries which are not applicants for membership, such as Switzerland, Sweden, Finland, Portugal, Iceland, create a sense that the world is "ganging up" against the United States. Even the State Department, which is the stanchest supporter of the EEC, has been pulled into these countercurrents that developed in the Nixon administration and has tried to impress upon Europe the need to take into account American interests and sensitivities. The Administration is under psychological pressure to avoid the kind of accusation frequently leveled by the Treasury at the State Department, namely, that it "would give the goddamned country away if no one was watching."

To balance the narrow-mindedness of the Treasury, the State Department, however, frequently gets support from the Department of Defense, which is equally anxious for a stable and secure Europe and for a Japan, as the most important power in Asia, that will remain a reliable ally.

The anxieties about the huge balance-of-payments deficit, the enormous dollar balances that have accumulated in foreign countries, the stubborn unemployment at home, all have changed the confident attitude of Americans toward their economic future and well-being. It is not surprising, therefore, that trade matters are nowadays considered in the United States Government at the highest policy levels. The question of what is the role of trade policy, philosophically and realistically, and its relationship to foreign and defense problems, is debated more fiercely than ever before. Strong nationalists such as John Connally, with a certain inborn uneasiness about the Old World, have convinced themselves that large trading blocs will become inevitable, that in fact they already exist in the EEC and the Soviet trade bloc, and that the only way the United States can defend her own interests effectively is by creating her own dollar bloc. Pessimism about the future of American competitiveness in the world's markets is further feeding this kind of defensive mentality where it did not exist in the past. The prospect of the EEC member countries agreeing on a single currency unit, which could become powerful enough to compete with the dollar, is another reason for the new fear of European economic power that is discouraging the search for expansive, liberal trading solutions.

Arthur Burns, as chairman of the Federal Reserve Board, in a crusading speech in Montreal in May 1972, painted the kind of horror world that would develop if the big trading nations fell back on trading blocs. ". . . We might then find the world economy divided into restrictive and inward-looking blocs, with rules of international conduct concerning exchange rates and monetary services altogether absent." And he warned that unless financial leaders correct the "weaknesses" in the present monetary order, the world would lapse again into the kind of "financial manipulations, economic restrictions and political frictions" that followed the presidential decision to break the link between gold and the dollar. It was a warning that the U. S. Treasury's policy of delay in the negotiations for a new over-all monetary system and its advocacy of a dollar trading and monetary bloc carried the dangers of undermining expanding world trade.

There is no agreement within the United States Government as to what kind of monetary system would best secure American interests. The State Department, for instance, in contrast to the Treasury, would get on with reform more urgently because it fears the destabilizing effect on alliance policies and on the less developed countries of monetary instability. It would also get on with the task of squaring America's postwar economic role with the new realities of economic and political power. Japan has become a major economic power and so has the more united Europe. There is, therefore, a new need to redistribute responsibility among the major powers. The basic objectives of the Bretton Woods agreement of 1944 are still valid: to facilitate international co-operation, growth of free trade, and payments based on stable exchange rates and so on. Finally, on the eve of the annual meeting of the International Monetary Fund in September 1972, the reluctant Treasury fell into line and the stage was set for President Nixon and Secretary of the Treasury Shultz to give the leadership and the needed direction to a broad reform plan of the international monetary system.

The world in which the dollar is no longer unique is a different world, but not necessarily a worse one. The dollar is still the world's most important currency and is likely to remain so. It is likely to continue to be the currency in which most transactions will be carried on, for the United States remains economically the most powerful country; American private foreign holdings by themselves, for instance, represent a financial power third only to the United States and the Soviet Union. This also makes it difficult to imagine that the United States will in any wholehearted way adopt a protectionist, inward-looking bloc psychology. Nevertheless, there is the prospect that the seventies will be a period of increased economic rather than military warfare in which the United States will find it harder to fend for her own interests and harder to get others to make concessions, for there will be a new economic as well as political balance of power. Fort Knox has become a symbol of American nostalgia.

CHAPTER FIFTEEN—INDIA: THE END OF
A LOVE AFFAIR

When Dr. Kissinger visited Pakistan on the way to his first reconnaissance in Peking in July 1971, President Mohamed Agha Yahya
Khan offered him a sumptuous state dinner. It reached its climax
when the voluble Pakistani leader, inspired by the sparkle of the
excellent champagne, suddenly got up, looked half seriously, half
smilingly around the table, and offered the boisterous challenge
"Am I a dictator? Am I a dictator?"

He had been already teasing some of his guests, so no one
seemed embarrassed by the question. Everybody took it as a show
of high spirits and a joke at his own expense, though, no doubt,
there was also a strong touch of neurosis behind it. And so
everybody laughed, some with more ease, others with less. Some
shouted, "No," others regarded the question as rhetorical. Then
the commander in chief of the Pakistani armed forces turned to
Kissinger and, apparently for Kissinger's benefit alone, exultantly
repeated the question. All eyes were now on Kissinger. Would he
reply to Yahya's challenging question?

Yahya at that moment felt particularly pleased with himself
and on top of the world, for not only had he been the successful
intermediary between Washington and Peking, but he was also
one of only a handful who knew that the next day's announcement to the press of Kissinger's intestinal upset and stay at a
mountain retreat would be nothing but a cover for his secret
departure for China. He was enjoying the charade no end. Kissinger, too, had entered into the spirit of the dinner party, and

now, ready as ever with the appropriate repartee, smilingly (and diplomatically) replied, "Well, Mr. President, for a dictator you run a lousy election." There was more raucous laughter around the table, then Kissinger added, "Any man who rigged an election that ended up with one hundred thousand votes against him has a few tricks to learn before he could consider himself a dictator!"

Yet diplomatic as he was, Kissinger had hit upon the very situation that ought to have given pause to Yahya's merriment. The genuinely free elections the previous December—for Field Marshal Yahya Khan, with a bow toward democracy, had decided to let the people speak freely on the basis of one man, one vote and vowed to accept their verdict—had heralded Yahya's own downfall and the sundering and military defeat of the nation he ruled.

Pakistan, created by the postwar settlement when the British quit India, was already a geographically divided country. West Pakistan was where the government held sway, but East Pakistan lay a thousand miles away across India and the two states were from the start on anything but the friendliest terms. Their separate creation was an acknowledgment of profound racial and religious differences, but that was between India and Pakistan: What was less appreciated outside Asia was the difference between the Pakistan of the East and of the West. The Islamic religion which linked them was more like a bridge of sand. East Pakistanis (Bengalis) came to resent—a situation with which Americans must historically sympathize—paying taxes to an increasingly remote and inconsiderate government a long way off. The Awami League, the dominant (and Bengali-nationalist) political party in the East, formulated a six-point policy that would have provided the East with a wide measure of autonomy, and left the central government responsible only for defense and foreign affairs.

In the national elections of December 7, 1970, the League, under the leadership of Sheik Mujibur Rahman, won a sweeping victory, 167 seats out of 169 under contest in East Pakistan. Thus seventy-five million people, packed into an area about the size of Illinois, expressed their yearning for the kind of autonomy Mujibur was advocating. At that stage, at least, he was not seeking independence. For President Yahya and the future of Pakistan, it meant that the Awami League would hold a clear majority in the 313-member National Assembly, and that Mujib inevitably would become the new Prime Minister of all Pakistan. Yahya's response to this electoral reverse was to set March 3, 1971, for the convening of a constitutional convention. The man he sent to negotiate with Mujibur was former Foreign Minister Zulfikar Ali Bhutto, whose left-wing People's Party had won a sweeping victory of their own in West Pakistan. He, too, had his eyes on the prime ministership. But when the negotiations between the two were evidently leading nowhere—Yahya claiming that Mujib now wanted independence instead of autonomy, and Mujib countering by claiming that Bhutto wanted separation to ensure the premiership for himself—Yahya himself flew to Dacca to meet with Mujib. Awami officials claim that they were given the impression that the six points had been agreed upon and other differences ironed out, and that a settlement between Yahya and Mujib would be signed a day or two later. Instead, Yahya went home and threw a match into the haystack by ordering his reinforced garrison in the East (composed predominantly of Punjabi West Pakistanis) to crack down on the Awami League and to arrest Mujib. Mujib was taken to West Pakistan and held prisoner.

It is still difficult to establish who caused the break-up of the negotiations, but what followed in that speck on the world map developed into one of the worst genocidal wars in modern times. It shook the watching world; brought India into the conflict and made it the unwilling host to millions of Bengali refugees; precipitated the unilateral independence of Bangladesh and freed Sheik Mujibur Rahman to become its leader; and reduced Pakistan to its defeated western half, when Yahya quit and Bhutto took over.

Kissinger believed in the inevitability of the independence of East Pakistan and made a remark to that effect to the Indian Ambassador to the United States, Lakshmi Kant Jha, in March. Naturally, this was most reassuring to Jha. On April 16, though, at a dinner party at Katharine Graham's house, the one Democratic political salon that had survived under the Republican administration, Jha thought that Kissinger had shifted his ground in the meantime. What mattered to the United States, Kissinger then said to him, was to encourage military disengagement, political accommodation between the two Pakistans, restraint on India's part and to do whatever was necessary to provide humanitarian relief for the refugees. Then, in a bantering exchange, he challenged Jha by predicting that India would attack East Pakistan. India, meanwhile, insisted that no political accommodation was possible, except through direct negotiations between Yahya and Mujib after the latter's release. That remained India's uncompromising position from which it never deviated.

In the 1950s, American policy in the Asian subcontinent was to maintain stability and a relative balance of power based on the assumption that China was the implacable foe. The U.S. aim was to help India, as the strongest power in the area, to contain Communist China or at least act as a buffer to the expansionism then attributed to China. But India also had engendered among liberal Americans deep emotional feelings which developed on the rebound after China (which had been something of a foster child to many Americans for almost two generations) had gone Communist and as such had been disowned. Successive American administrations lavished aid on India. It became something of a monument to American humanitarianism, even though the generosity was underlain with geopolitical considerations. For a long time India could do no wrong and could count on the American cornucopia—and this in spite of a neutralism which gradually become more and more irritating. It was an itch that in the end the United States simply had to scratch: It became too exasperating. On my last visit to India in 1967, it was already evident from my talks with high and low that the Indian Government had decided that its future security depended on the backing of the Soviet Union and that it would not be able any more to rely on American support as it did in 1962 in its conflict with China.

As time went on, Indian politicians became strangers to discretion in commenting on the American role in Korea or in Vietnam. They backed the Arab cause against Israel and sharply criticized the United States on nuclear weapons testing. Yet they practiced much greater restraint, with even a show of reluctance, in expressing disapproval of the policies and activities of the Soviet Union. They used the United Nations to berate the United States, but, American officials felt, hypocritically ignored the UN when India's self-interest was involved. And so Indian policies and attitudes greatly contributed to shaping American prejudices and American policy toward the Asian subcontinent. The bones beneath the skin of U.S.-Indian accord became more and more brittle, and Pakistan a more promising and less complicated ally.

KID GLOVES FOR YAHYA

The Pakistan Army massacred thousands in East Pakistan to subdue the revolt against West Pakistani rule. It displayed a cruelty not even a Himmler could have dreamed up, and millions of refugees poured across the frontier into East Bengal. The Nixon administration was curiously slow to condemn the behavior of the Pakistani troops and reluctant to exert a restraining influence. It claimed that it had stopped all military aid that was not already in the pipelines or for which firm orders had not already been placed and payments made, but it continued to ship ammunition and spare parts for weapons under a program started in 1967. The exceptions aroused Indian and congressional criticism, especially after the State Department conceded that the United States had been selling about 2.5 million dollars' worth of ammunition yearly to Pakistan as "non-lethal" equipment. The one important concession the United States extracted from Yahya, however, was the sparing of the life of Mujib which, according to American officials, would otherwise have been lost. Yahya had come to call him a traitor and was ready to execute him as such. In his bull-headedness, he not only made him a martyr, but he also gave India the ultimate excuse for military intervention.

There were in fact several reasons why the White House insisted on treating Yahya who as a graduate of Sandhurst, Britain's West Point, was assumed to be a gentleman—with kid gloves. There was, first of all, a sense of gratitude and obligation for his having been the *postillon d'amour* for the White House's flirtations with Peking. This service meant an enormous amount to President Nixon. There was also the basic anti-Indian prejudice, dating back beyond the Nixon administration, for what was considered India's arrogant, moralizing attitude in the United Nations against the United States. Furthermore, there was President Nixon's own personal pique with India that shone through everything and was widely attributed to the meager reception he got there on his visit after losing the election against John F. Kennedy in 1960. All he got was a luncheon given by the then Deputy Premier Desai, which was a bland affair not only in terms of conversation but in the fare, for the host was a vegeterian and teetotaler and imposed these disciplines upon his guests. Karachi's reception for the former Vice President and co-architect with John Foster Dulles of CENTO was in contrast spectacular. Mr. Nixon was lionized and feasted by the Pakistanis, and he has always shown a soft spot for those who appreciated him while he was in the political wilderness.

But perhaps more than anything it was the new relationship with China that influenced the President and Dr. Kissinger. It gave them a vested interest in maintaining the integrity of Pakistan, allied with a desire to show Peking that co-operation with the United States can have its advantages. This demonstration probably more than anything determined American policy. The situation also brought out the political theorist in Kissinger, or so he later claimed. As a believer in the global policy of balance of power, he was determined to put theory into practice and to show that the United States stood by the weaker against the stronger in the hope that this would prevent actual conflict. Kissinger, just after Christmas 1971, pointed out to me that in the Pakistani case the United States followed the British example; he drew my attention to a speech by Winston Churchill in 1936, which to him was the best exposition of the balance-of-power principle. In that speech Churchill said:

> We always took the harder course, joined with the less strong powers, made a combination among them, and thus defeated and frustrated the Continental military tyrant who-

ever he was, whatever nation he led. Thus we preserved
the liberties of Europe, protected the growth of its vivacious
and varied society, and emerged after four terrible struggles
with an evergrowing fame and widening Empire, and with
the Low Countries safely protected in their independence.
Here is the wonderful unconscious tradition of British foreign
policy . . . I know of nothing which has occurred to alter or
weaken the justice, wisdom, valour and prudence upon which
our ancestors acted. I know of nothing in military, political
or scientific fact which makes me feel that we are less
capable . . . Observe that the policy of England takes no
account of which nation it is that seeks the overlordship of
Europe. The French Empire or the German Empire, or the
Hitler regime. It has nothing to do with rulers or nations;
it is concerned solely with whoever is the strongest of the
potentially dominant tyrants. Therefore we should not be
afraid of being pro-French or anti-German. If the circumstances were reversed, we could equally be pro-German or
anti-French. It is a law of public policy which we are following
and not a mere expedient dictated by accidental circumstances, or likes and dislikes, or any other sentiment.*

Whether in truth such doctrinal considerations were a decisive
ingredient in the U.S. support of Pakistan is difficult to determine;
what is sure is that it did not prevent war from breaking out. But,
given all circumstances, from prejudices among individuals to the
lack of flexibility of almost all those involved, I doubt whether it
was ever within U.S. capability to do so.

The American retreat from the Indian subcontinent, or perhaps
better, the U.S. declining influence in the area was already obvious
in the mid-sixties. A disenchantment had set in on both sides,
and already under President Johnson led to the United States
showing greater sympathy for Pakistan, which had earned the title
of ally. The American retreat in this area therefore was not a
sudden choice; it was compounded by a mixture of deliberate de-

* Quoted by Hans Morgenthau, *Politics Among Nations*, Alfred A. Knopf,
New York, 1960.

cision, inadvertence, miscalculation and, above all, it was forced by events.

A COLD-BLOODED LADY

"How are you doing with your girl friend?" Secretary Rogers at his staff meeting one morning asked his vigorous Secretary for Near Eastern and South Asian Affairs Joe Sisco. "Golda is . . . ," Sisco began, but the Secretary interrupted him and said, "Oh, no, Joe, I don't mean Mrs. Meir, I mean Mrs. Gandhi!" Fate somehow had chosen Sisco to preside in areas where two powerful ladies ruled two crisis countries, Mrs. Meir over Israel, Mrs. Gandhi over India. It has often been said that if only women ruled the world there would be peace, because of their basic mother instinct; but quite obviously peace and war depend on different criteria. Both ladies were in the American terminology political hawks who didn't shy away from sending their menfolk to war if they thought the national interest required it. Nor was there in their eyes a difference between a man or a woman governing; neither had to worry about a Women's Lib Movement. They were already liberated, and judging by the outcome of the elections in their respective countries, were being judged equal to or better than their male competitors. And if Kissinger or Sisco were asked to give their view of the ability of those two women, both would readily admit the respect they had for the tough and determined ways with which they defended their countries' national interests. But where they would judge Mrs. Meir's toughness, with some compassion, as firm and unvarnished, they would see Mrs. Gandhi with a more jaundiced eye as stubborn and devious; Dr. Kissinger called her "cold-blooded."

When Kissinger stopped off in New Delhi before his visit to Pakistan in July, he was greeted with a fusillade by the Indian press. In his talk with Mrs. Gandhi (at which U. S. Ambassador Keating was not present), he tried to persuade her to look at the larger global picture instead of allowing her view to be distorted by Pakistan. He tried to convince her that he wanted to negotiate with India as a global power about what was a regional issue, because it could have global consequences. He warned that the situation then prevailing along the Indian and East Pakistan border (within which the West Pakistani Army was fiercely at work) could erupt into a major confrontation which could involve even China and Russia. But Mrs. Gandhi would not give him the reassurance he sought, ruling out war between India and Pakistan—the Indian Cabinet on April 28 had secretly decided to prepare for the possibility of war.

MISSED OPPORTUNITIES

What had gone wrong? There was first of all the U.S. failure to condemn Pakistan's tragic misuse of military power in terms impressive enough for Yahya to stop the slaughter before it was too late. To the world at large, it even seemed as if the United States did not care what was happening in the subcontinent. The United States may have at the time underrated the emotional impact the massacres would have around the world and in the press and in the United States Congress. If it could not stop the murderous campaign in East Pakistan, it should at least have halted—then, and not as late as November 8—all military aid, as a powerful warning to Yahya. If it was possible to do so in the autumn, it should have been possible to do it in the spring, especially since the amount of aid was less important than its psychological repercussions. There was also the drain on Indian resources of ten million refugees, who had been given shelter in huge, messy, unhygienic camps, which became more and more intolerable in spite of the aid that came from outside.

There was little doubt that Mrs. Gandhi was determined to bring into existence a separate state of Bangladesh, in the expectation that India would be able to dominate it and perhaps humiliate China (which had continued to back Pakistan) in the process. Thus, the refugees also became the most powerful instrument to fulfill Mrs. Gandhi's aims. On June 16, she said that India is "prepared to go through hell" to look after the refugees. The burden, by then 5.9 million refugees, could not be lifted with economic aid, except on an unprecedented, perhaps inexhaustible scale; and India simply could neither absorb them nor afford to maintain them for any length of time. Too little was done for them by the international community, but it is doubtful whether enough could have been done. The real problem was how to induce them to return to their own homes. And as long as the Pakistani Army raped the people and the country, there was no hope of achieving that. And so India began politically to exploit the presence of the refugees. It did so legitimately to draw world attention to the problems of an independent East Pakistan, and it did so illegally, by training the refugees as guerrillas and helping them back across the frontier with the obvious purpose of establishing an independent Bangladesh.

Thus a momentum was created that was difficult to control. Enormous, unwieldy forces had been unleashed; they suited India's purposes but not those of the United States, which found it increasingly difficult to get a grip on the situation. The UN, which the United States tried to engage in the situation, once more demonstrated its impotence. Neither sanctimonious-sounding India (who did not want to see the guerrilla activity blocked), nor the Soviet Union (whose stance was also to side with the oppressed Bengalis) wished to give it a chance. But if India's hopes were that the guerrillas would engender a concerted uprising in East Pakistan, they were not fulfilled. The military contingency plans which had been under preparation were completed in late August. They called for an attack on East Pakistan by October or November, for by then the monsoon season was over; logistically, it was the most advantageous timing.

Another serious contributory factor in the escalation to war was Yahya Khan's lack of political astuteness in fixing December 20 for the coming into force of a new constitution and civilian government, giving virtual autonomy to East Pakistan. If he had fixed June, as he said he would to Peter Cargill, the World Bank's expert for the area, he might have found it possible, with martial law lifted, to release Mujib freely (and not as part of the price of military defeat) and thus maintain some sort of link with East Pakistan. Mujib had always insisted that he did not want full independence; he was afraid that this would lead to Indian domination. He really preferred autonomy within the framework of Pakistan. (This was apparently one reason why, on release, he chose not to go to India but flew all the way to London. By then the massacres and the war had made independence inevitable.)

Yahya failed to pursue the one real possibility he had of preserving the unity of his country. Nor did he see that the new constitution was the only hope of forestalling India's aims. The U. S. Ambassador to Pakistan Joseph Farland, on the contrary, reassured his friend Yahya that India would not dare to attack Pakistan. If there was a chance of averting what became increasingly inevitable, the United States did not give it the urgent attention it deserved: The Americans thought they had more time to prevent war than they actually had. It was the Soviet Ambassador to India, Pegov, who on August 7 issued the first warning that the situation was "very dangerous" and war a real possibility. He appealed to all nations to counsel restraint on India and Pakistan and added that the Soviet Union had already done so. Foreign Minister Gromyko's arrival in New Delhi on August 8, however, was an obvious gesture of solidarity, and the signing of the Indo-Soviet friendship treaty the next day a signal that in the event of war the U.S.S.R. would stand by India. Indian embassy officials in Washington confided that the friendship treaty was actually negotiated two years earlier at Moscow's suggestion, but Mrs. Gandhi asked the Russians to postpone signing it until a more propitious time.

Nor were the hopes the United States placed in its contacts with the Bangladesh shadow government in Calcutta during August, September and October as promising as Kissinger thought at the time. These men had no authority, no political strength of their own which would have enabled them to translate whatever agreement they might have reached with Yahya Khan into stable results. In fact, they were afraid to negotiate with Yahya Khan for fear that they would be disowned by Mujib and others later.

It is difficult to apportion blame in so complicated a web of events. There were too many imponderables, too much emotion, too many personal antipathies, too many rooted hatreds. Prejudices are a poor guide to policy.

With knowledge of the chaos in Bangladesh after its liberation, one must admit the probable correctness of the Indian assumption that Mujib was the only man with the necessary charisma and popular support to have been able to negotiate a new political settlement—especially since he was not a convinced believer in independence—and carry it through. But Yahya refused to negotiate with him. Perhaps, had he tried, the military would have overthrown him, but the trouble was that he could not bring himself to try, for in his and in American eyes the Indian demand for negotiation meant total capitulation. The Indians never offered any form of compromise. It was Mujib's release, nothing less. As India's President Varahagiri Giri put it: "Only by the release of Mujib and a settlement with him can Pakistan restore normality to India-Pakistan relations."

The more it became clear that the Indian Government would remain inflexible, the more tension grew in the White House. It became obvious to most that India was playing for the highest stakes and was ready to go to war. Some predicted in July that war was inevitable, and most of those who tried to keep an open mind had come around to that view by the beginning of September, when the Indian press reported that the armed forces had been placed on a "general alert." In July, Yahya Khan had told Dr. Kissinger that he was itching to go to war against India, but nobody in the Nixon administration had any doubt that in case of war Pakistan was the certain loser: The CIA gave it three weeks (which as it proved, was generous by 30 per cent). This knowledge, of course, only heightened American nervousness. Both Mrs. Gandhi and Yahya were exasperating, but of the two Yahya elicited more sympathy; after all, he was not only an ally, but he did show a little more flexibility. Under American pressure he consented to the total stoppage of the 4½-million-dollar trickle of arms aid still in the pipelines to him. Indeed, he agreed so readily that there is reason to wonder why it was not possible to cut the aid off months earlier and use that decision to try hard for a settlement at a time when positions were still flexible. To defuse the situation, Yahya also agreed to start withdrawing his troops from his side of the West Pakistan-Indian border if India agreed to reciprocate on its side. And he was also willing to meet with any representative of the Awami League or any other Bangladesh leader the Indians would name, but not Mujib.

AN ICILY INCORRECT OCCASION

These undertakings were intimated to the Indian ambassador shortly before Mrs. Gandhi's arrival in Washington on November 4. The President urged her to start a dialogue on this basis, but all to no avail. Mrs. Gandhi was regarded at the White House as something of a potential Lady Macbeth. The mutual suspicions were virtually insurmountable and her prickly and uncompromising behavior made things worse rather than better. At any rate, expectations were low, for a report which Prime Minister Heath had sent to the President about his meeting with the Indian Prime Minister three days earlier did nothing to raise hopes or to allay suspicions.

President Nixon was at his most formally polite, Mrs. Gandhi icily correct. In their talks they were edgy and unbending. It did not make things easier when in the Rose Garden the President commented on a hurricane that had just hit somewhere and Mrs. Gandhi in reply felt constrained to ad-lib on the man-made disaster of the refugees. At dinner the same exchange repeated itself. But what was worse was that Mrs. Gandhi, instead of toasting relations with the United States, criticized American policy. She said, "It has not been easy to get away at a time when India is beleaguered. To the natural calamities of drought, flood and cyclone has been added a man-made tragedy of vast proportions. I am haunted by the tormented faces in overcrowded refugee camps reflecting the grim events which have compelled the exodus of these millions from East Bengal. I have come here looking for a deeper understanding of the situation in our part of the world, in search of some wise impulse which, as history tells us, has sometimes worked to save humanity from despair."

For the President this was close to a calculated insult, for he had included among the dinner guests some of his Democratic opponents in Congress, as a gesture to Mrs. Gandhi, and she used the occasion apparently to appeal to them over his head. This deliberate playing up to his political opponents only hardened the President's prejudices. No one was surprised, least of all Mr. Nixon, when, after not only urging the start of a dialogue, but offering to oil the wheels of negotiation with $2 million of aid, he was coolly turned down. She insisted that the only hope for a peaceful solution was the unconditional release of Mujib and the complete withdrawal of the Pakistani troops from East Pakistan. But the President wanted, as Henry Kissinger put it to the Washington Special Action Group, "to tilt in favor of Pakistan," and so was unwilling to push Yahya Khan into what was equivalent, at least in Pakistani eyes, to capitulation. Pakistan remained an ally who had helped in the approach to China and even though in Yahya Khan Mr. Nixon was stuck with a non-statesman, he was not going to ditch him, particularly with the Chinese looking on.

Whether Mrs. Gandhi had gone to Washington cynically to create the appearance of having tried her best before launching the war against Pakistan she had already decided on, or whether she had not yet finally made up her mind, hoping that her last attempt to persuade President Nixon to force Yahya Khan to accept her conditions would succeed, is difficult to guess, even now. The majority of the Americans directly involved, though, suspected that she had already decided to go to war, on the fairly obvious assumption that the President would not accede to her inflexible demand. In a private conversation during a reception at the Indian Embassy she confided that she had put it to President Nixon, simply and bluntly, that unless he found a solution she "would have to take things into her own hands." Those present during the conversations in the White House deny having heard her say that to the President.

After she had left, few doubted, though, that war was a foregone conclusion. The United States now abandoned all hope of themselves making the Indians see reason and tried to enlist the Russians, as more influential in New Delhi, to the same end. But these approaches had an air of ritual. Nobody expected them to succeed: They were more an exercise designed to make the Russians aware of the need, in conflicts of a regional character such as this one, for the great powers to follow certain rules and act responsibly, as Kissinger had been preaching, to ensure that neither of them would be drawn into it. Both in the Indian subcontinent and in the Middle East, Russia has now assumed the world-power role which previously it had only played in Europe and in the Far East. It still has only a limited capacity to intervene with non-nuclear weapons, but having ostentatiously concluded a twenty-year pact of "peace, friendship, and co-operation" with India the Soviet Union, quite clearly, was aiming at laying her power in the scales in India's favor. The Kissinger visit to Peking in June may have accelerated India's signing of this formal treaty, for the Indians were afraid that he had reached an understanding with the Chinese that if Pakistan attacked India and China joined in with Pakistan, the United States would do nothing.

AN EMBARRASSING WAR FOR THE UNITED STATES

When war finally did break out, it was impossible to say who in fact committed the first aggressive act. There are ample precedents to similar effect. When, for instance, Indian troops crossed into the Belonia Salient on the eastern border of East Pakistan on November 10 on the grounds that Pakistani forces were shelling Indian villages from positions there, the Indian Government claimed that this was not the start of war, but only a very limited local "incursion." They in turn later insisted that it was Pakistan's attempted aerial blitz against airfields in Indian Kashmir and the Punjab on December 3 which really triggered the war. This totally ineffective attempt at a pre-emptive strike, which succeeded only in confusing the issue of who started the war, was further evidence of how stupidly the Pakistanis were led. The same day Mrs. Gandhi addressed the nation and put India officially on a war footing.

In a controversial backgrounder to the press on December 5, Joe Sisco called the use of force by Pakistan "obviously regrettable and having given rise to a number of difficulties," and added that "even if one assumes, as we do, that the crisis in its initial stages was not really of Indian making, we believe that since the beginning of the crisis Indian policy in a systematic way has led to the perpetuation of the crisis and that India bears the major responsibility for the broader hostilities which have ensued." That statement was an apt interpretation of the U.S. position. But the fat was in the fire, for the United States had taken sides publicly with Pakistan knowing that East Pakistan was lost, but determined to preserve West Pakistan. A day later China accused Moscow in the strongest terms yet of forcing Pakistan to submit to India in order to expand the Soviet sphere of influence in the subcontinent.

On December 7, Henry Kissinger followed up Sisco with a comprehensive "on the record" briefing to defend American policy. It raised many eyebrows and hackles, because he insisted that comments to the effect that the Administration was anti-Indian were "totally inaccurate" which, of course, on his part was itself less than accurate, to say the least, though in the situation in which he found himself, I do not blame him for bending the truth for diplomatic reasons. His was a highly defensive briefing, especially about the inadequacy of the American condemnation of the pogroms in East Pakistan by the Pakistani Army. A few days later Robert McCloskey, a special assistant to Secretary Rogers and one of the best press officers I have ever met, privately remarked that "I have heard more exasperation with India in my time here [and it spanned the time of Dean Rusk] than with any other country—including the Soviet Union!"

What almost lifted the State Department out of its moorings in Foggy Bottom, however, was a warning reportedly given by Dr. Kissinger, on board the President's plane The Spirit of '76, to a five-man pool of correspondents returning from the Azores after Mr. Nixon's meeting with President Pompidou. Under the cover of "deep background," he told them that unless the Russians in the next few days persuaded the Indians to show restraint, "a new look might have to be taken at the President's summitry plans." Dr. Kissinger actually approved the written pool report after making one or two slight changes. Naturally a threat to risk the Moscow summit for a secondary U.S. interest suddenly elevated the stakes in the Indo-Pakistan war far higher than anyone had ever expected. Washington was agog and amazed that the White House was willing to play such a high-risk game with the Russians. Ron Ziegler, the President's press secretary, who is not usually called on to qualify Kissinger's statements, issued a straight denial a few hours later: "The U.S. is not considering canceling the U.S.-Russian summit and no U.S. government official intended to suggest this." He added that Dr. Kissinger's remarks had been interpreted in a "highly speculative way" and had been "taken out of context." Dr. Kissinger's label of "deep background" meant that newsmen were not allowed to identify the source in any way, but both the New York *Times* and the Washington *Post* decided that this was too important a remark for them to assume responsibility for and so they broke the seal of confidentiality and Kissinger made a sizable show of consternation.

CIA'S EXPLOSIVE CHARGE

What was it that had come to agitate the White House to such an extent that it was willing to risk the Moscow summit? Until then one had the impression that the United States had its eye so fixed on the planned summits that nothing was to be allowed to interfere with them. The explanation was a highly confidential Central Intelligence Agency report which claimed that the Indian Cabinet had discussed orders to the Indian armed forces, first, to straighten out the frontier against West Pakistan to India's advantage (this meant liberating the Kashmir territory that India considered to be under Pakistan's "occupation"); and second, to destroy as many Pakistani forces in the West as possible. The report was attributed to a very high level in the Indian Government and was interpreted by Dr. Kissinger as meaning that India was aiming at the destruction of the Pakistan armed forces and hence at the destruction of Pakistan altogether. This he felt had to be prevented. The President clearly was willing to do almost anything short of military intervention—to stop the Indians from executing such a plan. Kissinger was in a state of outrage rarely seen. "I'm getting hell every half hour from the President that we are not being tough enough on India," he was quoted in what became known as the "Anderson Papers"—the secret minutes of White House meetings during the Indo-Pakistan crisis, that fell into the hands of columnist Jack Anderson who published them in his column—as having said to the Washington Special Action Group on December 3. What added to the American suspicions was that the Indian Government refused to reply to an earlier American proposal that Yahya Khan had already accepted, which committed the Pakistan Army to take the initiative in withdrawing from the West Pakistan frontier if the Indians committed themselves in advance to following the Pakistan example. What made these suspicions worse was that when Under Secretary of State John Irwin asked Indian Ambassador Jha to state categorically that India did not want any Pakistan territory, he refused. Asked by Irwin whether he would at least say that India did not want any territory that was under Pakistan occupation, he again refused.

The Indian Government vehemently denied that it planned to extend the war to West Pakistan. The Indian Ambassador, too, was convinced that CIA had been misled or had exaggerated a flimsy rumor because nothing concerning the Indo-Pakistan war preparations, he told me after the war was over, was ever discussed in full Cabinet; these discussions were always limited to the Prime Minister, the Foreign Secretary and the Defense and Finance ministers. The evidence in support of the intelligence report, the CIA admitted, was not conclusive, nor did it say that the decision had been actually taken to attack West Pakistan once Yahya's men had been subdued in East Pakistan. Still, the report was of such far-reaching consequence and apparently from such an important source that it could not be disregarded. CIA, to strengthen its case and to indicate that the report was well founded, let it be known later that they had had a further report stating that Mrs. Gandhi had been so disturbed by the "leak" that she ordered an investigation as to how CIA had been able to obtain the information.

The White House frantically sought Russian co-operation to prevent the Indians from destroying Pakistan altogether: there was good reason to think that this was also considered in the Russian interest. On October 2, Soviet President Podgorny on arrival in New Delhi had asked that "military conflict must be avoided."

It is virtually impossible to establish whether in fact the Russians heeded the American urgings and intervened in New Delhi. By coincidence, Soviet Deputy Foreign Minister Kuznetsov arrived in New Delhi on December 12, and his presence, some believe, was instrumental in taming the Indian appetite. Indian officials confirm that the Russians did press for an early cease-fire.

State Department men like Joe Sisco are convinced that the Indian objectives were limited to shearing off East Pakistan and did not include the total destruction of Pakistan. The British discounted the CIA report but, admittedly, had the luxury of being able to stand aside; they did not play a role in this crisis except in the UN Security Council. British influence in the area, once a part of the Empire, had ceased, and without regret. What worried them, though, was that the United States was backing the wrong horse and that this would lead to an alienation of India difficult to reverse.

The move of the aircraft carrier *Enterprise* and other ships into the Bay of Bengal and close to the Pakistan shores was officially justified as a precautionary move in case the necessity arose to go to the rescue of American citizens stranded in Dacca who would have been lifted by helicopters on to the carrier. In fact, however, it was more an act of psychological warfare and a warning not to expand the war. It, of course, further incensed the Indians who considered it, as the Russians called it, "gunboat diplomacy" and an insult to their pride. Russian warships, of course, immediately tailed the U.S. fleet to prove that the United States does not rule the waves in the Bay of Bengal. Even though the American flotilla packed far more power than the Russian, the American show of force was more a show of vulnerability.

THE CHANGING POWER BALANCE

India's victory within two weeks was impressive in its expert and swift execution. What was even more impressive was that in its wake the Russians emerged as clearly the dominant world power in the area. They had beaten Mr. Nixon at his own game, and at his expense.

India, in her own right, of course, is now the dominant country within the subcontinent and, after ten years of intense economic assistance from the United States, is now freer and less dependent on outside assistance than ever before. Other profound changes occurred. Pakistan has ceased to be a threat to India, and Bangladesh will feel a sense of gratitude toward Russia for a long time, even though the United States in future could become the more important contributor to that unhappy country's economic viability. Politically, however, Russia is bound to remain the more influential—though because of the country's disarray, this may prove to be as much a liability as an asset to Moscow. India and the Soviet Union will continue to have things in common in their attitude toward China, but over Bangladesh their interests will differ. Russian-oriented Communists may gain influence thanks to the support of their comrades in India's West Bengal (and many Indians fear that this could lead to a movement for unification of Bangladesh and West Bengal under a Communist regime). Chinese interest in Bangladesh for the present is only marginal. The Maoists there are very weak compared to the Russian Communists and for the time being there is much "sour grapes" in Chinese propaganda. It is biding its time, saying that what is happening in Bangladesh is a bourgeois revolution supported by bourgeois revolutionaries, but once that changes and true revolutionaries take the lead, China will be with them.

All the three great powers thus will have an interest in maintaining the independence of Bangladesh and soothing its underlying fear that India may want to turn it into a dependency, and this consideration is likely to play an important role in the policies of the Bangladesh leadership. U.S.-Chinese interests in the new state will not coincide because the United States is interested in supporting the kind of moderate leadership that Mujib represents, while China will want to explore the prospects for strengthening the Communist Party there that suits its own aims best and not those of the Soviet Union.

The Soviet Union, of course, is seeking to make India an accomplice in the containment of China, just as the United States used to do, and has also gained an opening into the Indian Ocean.

The American position in Pakistan is no longer of real importance, nor is there likely to be a particular residue of gratitude toward the United States on the part of Mr. Bhutto, Yahya's successor. We may in fact find in future that the Russians themselves will claim that gratitude is due to them, not to the United States. China, apart from a few angry words, did nothing and on this occasion, at least, proved to be a paper tiger. Still, Pakistan has nowhere else to turn and so may even lean more toward China than it did before. In 1962, the Chinese taught the Indian Army some unpleasant and humiliating lessons; now the army is a far more effective fighting machine and, at least in the Tibet area, could become a threat to Chinese interests. More likely, though, the *de facto* border as it was left in 1962 is likely to remain the permanent border for a long time to come.

I doubt whether the Soviet Union will push hard to exploit its new position of influence in India and ask for such special privileges as bases. The Indians are proud and independent-minded. Even Dr. Kissinger is willing to give Indira Gandhi at least that credit. In the now-famous White House meeting on December 8, in discussing the Indo-Pakistan crisis, he said about her, "The lady is cold-blooded and tough, and will not turn into a Soviet satellite merely because of pique" at the United States. Furthermore, her need for Soviet support may be less now after such a clear-cut and decisive victory. He probably sees the Indian natural arrogance, or as Indians would put it, their pride in independence, as an insulating factor against the Soviet Union.

The decline of American power and influence in the subcontinent is not surprising. It is due, first of all, to a basic decision on the part of the Indian Government that in future its most reliable ally against its most dangerous enemy, China, will be the Soviet Union and not the United States. In 1962, during the Indo-Chinese war, the United States became intimately involved and provided not only planes and other weapons but military advice and secret intelligence. But since then, Indo-American relations have deteriorated in direct ratio to the improvement of Indian relations with the Soviet Union. American policy makers have watched India's growing reliance on the Soviet Union with mixed feelings but also with a sense of impotence. On their list of American priorities, India has been downgraded as only of marginal importance. The fact that the United States presented India with a choice between war and a political solution and India chose war has led to a psychological strain between the United States and India that will persist for a long time. India's importance now stands well below that attached to the Middle East.

Viewed from the wider perspective of the Nixon Doctrine and President Nixon's efforts to reduce American commitments on a world-wide scale, the objective on the part of the United States now is to stress the importance of India to the three major powers, the Soviet Union, China and the United States, and the need to reach an understanding among the three to help ensure stability in the subcontinent. In a very tenuous way, without anyone agreeing to anything binding, such a tacit understanding will develop. The American interest within the subcontinent, now that it has lost all illusions that it could play a balancing role together with West Pakistan in maintaining an equilibrium against India, is that the three entities, India, West Pakistan and Bangladesh, should work toward a psychological reconciliation. It is quite certain that the United States will not deploy its own military forces in this area whatever happens. This is a basic decision, even if under the Nixon Doctrine retreat means that the United States wishes to remain engaged in other, more limited ways. However, in spite of the Russians' superior influence in India, in the long run the United States should be able to maintain a certain amount of political leverage because the area cries out for more economic assistance and nobody else can quite assume the economic role the United States can play, even if this economic role will be downgraded too.

In the fifties, the American Government always assumed that it needed India and that therefore it was in its interest to sustain India with economic and military aid. But this attitude has changed. American policy will be based on realism rather than generosity and the assumption will be that it is India that needs the United States. The shoe is on the other foot. The Soviet Union, after hanging around outside the gate for the last ten years, is now the favored suitor, at least so long as India needs her as a balancing agent against China. The United States made it to the parlor but finally ran out of ardor. What Henry Kissinger, a specialist in these matters, once called "a great American love affair," is over.

When Richard Nixon accepted his nomination at the 1968 Republican Convention in Miami and said that he would move from confrontation to negotiation with the Soviet Union, it seemed to many that this was the best promise he could make. Yet, even though some of those close to him suggested to me then that it was less close to his political instincts than to his political calculations, and even though it was one of those vague generalities that are the stuff of convention and campaign speechmaking, he lived up to it more than anybody expected—least of all perhaps, Nixon himself.

The last thing Nixon would want is to go down in history as having retreated before Russian or any Communist power. He is a convinced anti-Communist, seeing communism and Communist dictatorship as something truly evil, an outlook underscored throughout his political career. Indeed, he built the beginning of his public career on his anti-communism, which in the late forties and early fifties was a political trump card; Nixon made ample and indiscriminate use of it. He insinuated that his opponents in congressional elections, Congressman Horace Voorhis in 1946 and Helen Gahagan Douglas in 1950, were crypto-Communists—a fashionably lethal phrase of the time—and many people never forgave him for it. He won fame by exposing Alger Hiss, the State Department official, and his contacts with the Soviets.

If anybody had impeccable anti-Communist credentials, therefore, it was Richard Nixon, and he exploited them adroitly to his political advantage. In the 1968 presidential election campaign, for instance, he hammered home the fact that he, an avowed anti-Communist, had a better chance than any Democrat of getting the U.S. public to accept conciliatory moves toward Communist countries. President Johnson was uncertain in his attitude to the Russians, though he always had the notion that he could make some sort of a deal with them. Dean Rusk, L.B.J.'s Secretary of State, was dovish toward Moscow, but felt hawkish toward the government in Peking; he favored a policy of containing China in collusion with the Soviet Union. Nixon rejected this approach because he thought it would be interpreted in Asia as a racist-influenced policy, and from the start prepared for an evenhanded policy, though one aware of the Russians as the more dangerous because more apt to take military risks.

But Nixon is a realist who recognizes when the public mood changes and enough of a pragmatist to adjust to it. He also was shrewd enough to sense that the Nixon Doctrine could only be applied if he also took advantage of the new opportunities that were beckoning in relations with the Soviet Union. The problem was how to do this without losing his shirt at home or in the Kremlin.

A NEW ERA?

What made some sort of rapprochement with the Soviets look more hopeful than perhaps ever before was that some time in 1970, if not earlier, the Kremlin decided that it wanted to aim at a limited amount of co-operation with the United States and with Western Europe and that it wanted to reduce tension with both. This decision was reflected in Brezhnev's speech at the Communist Party Congress in April 1971 and set the basic direction of Soviet policy.

I remember how at a dinner party at the house of Governor Averell Harriman in June 1971, the then Polish Ambassador George Michalowski admonished everybody present to read the Brezhnev speech carefully, for it represented a very important change in Soviet policy to which, he said, the United States should respond in a conciliatory and understanding way, otherwise an opportunity might be missed that might not return again soon. He argued that since the Russians had more or less achieved nuclear parity with the United States, they were now anxious to commit more of their economic resources to raising their people's standard of living. He admitted that with the tense situation along the Sino-Soviet border, there was a need to shift troops from Western Europe to the East. He also argued that it was not so much the cost of the military forces that mattered—for everybody, whatever his job, was paid by the government anyway—as the fact that a reduction in the number of troops would free manpower, especially technicians, and means of transport needed for civilian use. He also said that the Russians had accepted the existence of the Common Market, as they had not done at first, and that they favored a self-reliant Western Europe because this would make it easier for the United States to withdraw its forces stationed there. What worried Michalowski was whether the United States realized that there was a genuine chance for a new era in East-West relations, and whether it would act accordingly. If the United States delayed too long in reacting to this new situation and if it continued to think that it could afford the arms race while the Russians could not, as used to be argued in earlier administrations, he feared the chance could be missed.

The problem for Nixon, who was quite willing to sound out the prospects, was how to begin. He did not want a summit that would be merely atmospheric and devoid of substance. He also suspected that the Russians were still under the adverse impression that an overeager President Johnson had created with his last-minute appetite for a visit to Moscow. Johnson's excuse for seeking such a trip was to sign an agreement in principle according to which the SALT talks were to proceed. Ambassador Thompson went to see Premier Kosygin several times to promote the visit, but he remained evasive. The Russians clearly did not want to waste time and effort with a President who would soon be out of office. Nixon, therefore, set a cautious pace and a slower one than suited the Kremlin. On his European tour he reassured America's allies that he would not negotiate with the Soviet Union behind their backs.

What added to the difficulties in getting the American-Soviet dialogue started was that the Russians play diplomatic chess while Nixon prefers diplomatic poker. Each game requires a different technique and a different psychology, and so it took longer for both sides to co-ordinate their gamesmanship. The Russians moved a pawn forward, making through Ambassador Dobrynin various approaches to get negotiations going fairly quickly. Nixon simply held his cards close to his chest and pondered his bid in return.

THE PROBLEM OF LINKING "LINKAGE"

Nixon's basic strategy was not to take a quick call, but gradually to build up a good-sized pot on the table—to negotiate with the Russians on a broad front of problems which would be seen to be interconnected. This idea later came to be called the "linkage" principle and was defined by William Safire in his *The New Language of Politics* as "a global negotiations strategy holding that progress on one front is necessary to, or helpful to, progress on other fronts." It was expressed by Kissinger in a background briefing on February 6, 1969, in which he spelled out that the President would like to deal with the problem of peace on the entire front on which peace was challenged and not only on nuclear arms talks, and that a reduction of tension in one area could only be achieved if it also applied to others. It was with linkage in mind that the President sounded an early alarm about the dangers in the Middle East and Berlin. He wanted to make it clear that a *détente*, like peace itself, was indivisible.

More specifically, Nixon and Kissinger laid down, shortly after the inauguration, a basic set of principles on handling the Russians. These were not processed through the NSC machinery, with the result that the NSC never developed a fully fledged over-all policy paper on U.S.-Soviet relations, but instead continued to deal with specific problems—the Middle East, SALT, Berlin and so on—as they came up. The Nixon-Kissinger guidelines went roughly as follows: We want to keep relations on an even keel, we have no illusions on how much can be accomplished, and arms control should not be treated as a "safety valve" (as Kissinger liked to call it) against issues fraught with danger, because it would not in itself alleviate this danger. Individual issues simply were not to be singled out; the key to a better, more stable relationship was a relaxation of tension on all fronts. The behavioral etiquette in dealing with the Russians was to be cool, matter-of-fact, even distant. Public polemics were to be avoided, and so were negotiations that sought only to sweeten the atmosphere.

These guidelines represented a radical change, for under President Johnson the idea was that you should try to do business with Moscow whenever possible. Nixon believed that he could reach an understanding with the Russians, but since the Communists were evil, expansionist and untrustworthy, he had to insist on an *over-all* understanding, and retain the freedom or the will power to use military force if necessary. He thought such a broad understanding could be arrived at by the United States making concessions on SALT and Vietnam, and by the Russians on the Middle East; other issues would have to be resolved somehow by mutual compromise. The idea that a package deal could be negotiated with the Russians on the basis of the "linkage" theory became very controversial among the experts, and many of them viewed it as hopelessly unrealistic, betraying ignorance of the Russian psyche.

The late Llewellyn Thompson, twice Ambassador to Moscow and one of the most respected among the experts, was one of those who dissented. Thompson contended that "linkage" to the Russians meant negotiating from strength, a phrase that went back to John Foster Dulles, one of the many devils in the wax cabinet of the Soviet diplomatic mind. Because they suffered from an inferiority complex, he argued, they would object to the idea and resist it. Thompson once maintained to me, in another gambling analogy, that to the Russians each case for negotiation "was another throw of the roulette ball," and "every time the roulette ball spins, one has to watch how it turns and where it falls. There is no necessary connection between two throws." Thompson continued to defend the idea of simply seeking to improve the atmosphere between the United States and the Russians because once they reciprocated, they always committed themselves a little more, assuming, however slightly, a new attitude. "It does therefore help," Thompson insisted, "to commit the Russians to a trend and direction because they lack flexibility in their propaganda, which makes it difficult for them to reverse it." Thompson developed his view once to Kissinger in the latter's office and, as it happened, the President called on the telephone during their conversation. When he heard that Thompson was in Kissinger's office, he asked both to come and see him. Thompson then explained his views to the President and left feeling that the President had agreed with his interpretation.

Gradually, as Nixon's approach to the Russians evolved, it turned into a mixture of the Kissinger and the Thompson theories, though every time the Russians did something reasonable on one front and something unreasonable on another, the cry of "linkage" was heard from the White House, which put the Kremlin on notice that this was not the way to reach an understanding with the United States. But the mixture was inevitable and Mr. Nixon slowly recognized it. It is one of his eccentricities that he likes to appear more inflexible than he really is. If necessary, though, he can be quite adroitly flexible, especially when the political stakes warrant it. For a long time, for instance, he was convinced that the Russians could help him to persuade Hanoi to make a settlement—which contributed to his slowness about starting the SALT talks—but in the end he recognized that Russian leverage with the North Vietnamese was limited for a number of complicated reasons, and that he had better not make this the stumbling block to a new understanding with the Soviets.

A SUPER AMBASSADOR

Kissinger, from the start, assumed supreme control over diplomatic contacts with the Russians. His first meeting with Ambassador Dobrynin occurred in New York before President Nixon's inauguration, and their meetings after a time became an accepted thing whenever something that could develop into a crisis had to be thrashed out.

Dobrynin is a master of the diplomatic trade, one of the best practitioners in it that I have come across in twenty-five years of international reporting. Thanks to his gift of establishing personal relationships and the apparent confidence he enjoys with the Politburo, he has created for himself a position in Washington that has made him virtually irreplaceable, or at least made him so during the crucial period of the preparation for the Moscow summit. He is tall, almost towering, and his appearance—soft, sensitive, high forehead and gold-rimmed spectacles—combines with a shy charm that makes him seem more a romantic musician than an experienced participant in the roughhouse of superpower diplomacy. Those who have done business with him, however, easy as he is to talk to, consider him a tough bargainer, always in command of whatever business is at hand. He has a fetching smile, a pleasant sense of humor and an inborn civility, but he can also become tough and steely in difficult negotiations; yet he rarely loses his composure and always remains a gentleman. Like all Soviet officials, of course, he is subject to the limitations of the Soviet system, yet some can stretch those limitations and give themselves a little more elbow room under their instructions and Dobrynin probably has done so at times. He once explained to me his guidelines for an ambassador in this way: "To have the courage to tell the facts as they are, and report to his superiors as true and fair a picture as possible; to provide them, when necessary, with honest proposals for action, and to warn them, again courageously if need be, what reactions they must expect to follow certain decisions." The role he was able to play in promoting a policy of easing tensions between the United States and the Soviet Union, despite the many zigs and zags, seems to have suited him temperamentally and intellectually.

Dobrynin, quickly recognizing the uneven balance of power between Kissinger and Rogers and seeing where the center of power really was, lavished attention, as ought any shrewd diplomat in Washington who had the opportunity, on Kissinger. He established easy access to him and soon found out that for quick action, this was the place to call. Dobrynin, as ambassadors go, saw perhaps more of him than most, and soon earned in Kissinger a kind of fond respect. Here were two men who could display an extraordinary amount of charm and wit, but also vie in toughness with each other. Kissinger even had him home for negotiations—and few have seen the Kissinger household from the inside—but only after an electronic sanitizing squad had made certain that the Russians had not bugged the house in advance.

The Russian press had frequently attacked Kissinger's writings, and the new Soviet breed of Americanologists said that they strongly distrusted him, though this did not prevent their according him the respect they give to anyone who wields power. They also distrusted his principal Kremlinologist, the German-born Helmut Sonnenfeldt, because they argued that he and Kissinger, because of their origins, saw the Soviet Union through Euro-American bifocal lenses. They expressed a preference for American-born experts such as Llewellyn Thompson and even Charles Bohlen, both former American ambassadors to the Soviet Union, for they looked at the Soviet Union from a more thoroughgoing vantage point of American power interests. Kissinger and Sonnenfeldt, they believed, were less capable of interpreting those interests and less inclined to deploy the tactical generosity in negotiations Russians have learned to expect from the United States. To them the outlook of the two was molded in their youth in Central Europe and by their experience with European communism. But judging by the fact that more concrete and more positive negotiations were conducted by the two with the Russians than perhaps ever since the end of World War II, and judging by the results, one must conclude that it is less personality than time and circumstance that matter, and for Kissinger and Sonnenfeldt both were propitious.

Both sides recognized that the time was ripe for concrete improvement in American-Soviet relations, and to mutual advantage. Mr. Nixon, for the first time, had admitted that there existed a nuclear weapons parity with the Soviet Union; he had also convinced himself that there would be no war between the United States and the Soviet Union, thanks to the effect of nuclear deterrence and the Russian fear of a Chinese attack. It was not easy for Nixon publicly to accept nuclear parity and for this reason he also said that "we cannot accept to be the Number Two power." He also privately cautioned officials not to emphasize the possibility of the United States dropping behind. The notorious "kitchen debate" with Nikita Khrushchev at the opening of the American Exhibition in Moscow in 1959 had left a deep impression and he has not forgotten it, but, perhaps, the Russians remembered it also, especially the fact that in spite of his sounding so pugnacious in that sharp exchange, he sounded much less combative and hostile in conversation with Russian officials afterward. Nixon is extremely "balance conscious," though, and one of his main concerns was not to create an imbalance for fear that he or his successors could come under pressure from the Soviet Union.

The progression toward serious negotiations with the Soviet Union was slow and various peripheral crises interfered with it at various times. The Russians were at the same time seeking to consolidate their own world-power position, strengthening their influence around the world, accelerating their military build-up (especially their naval program), and creating positions of strength in the Middle East, in India and Vietnam. Still, their main objective was to ease tension in the center of Europe, and when they realized that this was not possible without reaching an accommodation with the United States, to seek that also. The time had come when this was easier to do from the Kremlin's standpoint because the Russians had acquired a new sense of equality, a state of mind that made them easier to negotiate with. The inferiority complex that had been one reason why for so long they were so reluctant to freeze the arms race, and why they were generally so inflexible, had been put aside. With this, it did not take long for the Russians to make it clear to the Americans that they would not accept the idea of an interrelationship between issues, that there could be no preconditions for negotiating one agreement before the United States would be prepared to negotiate another on a different situation. And in that they at first largely prevailed.

What accentuated the Russians' distrust of Nixon—though at the start they were willing to forget his past and judge him on performance—was not only his reluctance actually to begin the SALT discussions, but also his policy in Vietnam and his provocative visit to Rumania. His overtures to China, however, really shocked them. I was not surprised when in September 1969, Mr. Arbatov, the perspicacious deputy director of the Moscow Institute for Soviet-American Affairs, said to me that this was a moment when the United States should try to inspire trust, not the opposite, and that the prospects of improved relations between the United States and the Soviet Union had been endangered. He even hinted that such an American attitude could undermine the position of the current Soviet leadership which favored better relations with the United States.

But Nixon stuck to his own timetable. He did not want to move too fast, for he was afraid Congress would otherwise have refused to approve the Safeguard legislation for a new anti-ballistic missile defense. He also wanted further to test MIRV (Multiple Independent Re-entry Vehicles), which he had no intention of banning,* and to give more time to the new methodical studies of the whole disarmament problem ordered by Kissinger.

John F. Kennedy made the missile gap a big issue during his presidential campaign. But once in power he found that the situation was not so bad after all. Nixon, on the other hand, during his 1968 campaign was led to believe that the United States had a powerful advantage in missilery. Once in office, however, he found that the situation was worse than he had been led to believe and that a serious imbalance in the missile field could develop in half a dozen years. President Johnson had decided on the evidence he was given that the Talinn Line around Moscow was not an ABM defense and that the SS9 intercontinental ballistic missiles were not equipped with maneuverable warheads. But in 1969, Kissinger's verification panel succeeded in injecting doubts into these conclusions, even though CIA continued to support the earlier ones.

In spite of Nixon's orders for everybody to throttle down on anti-Soviet speeches and to exercise restraint, Defense Secretary Melvin Laird accused the Russians of aiming at a first-strike capability. It was the most anti-Soviet statement an American in

* See Chapter Seventeen.

Laird's position could have made, for it implied that the Kremlin had aggressive intentions.

As regards trade, Nixon was again cautious and unco-operative. In his efforts to accumulate as many bargaining chips as possible, this too was to be husbanded for the day when it could be exchanged for something he needed. Contrary to the common assumption, Nixon was convinced that trade could only follow improvements in the political field. This was different from the old theory held by Ambassador Thompson in his Moscow days. The argument then was that since trade between the United States and the Soviet Union would not amount to very much, it would be worth making concessions as a demonstration of good will. But Thompson blamed U.S. industry for the government's reluctance, because it was afraid that the Russians could become serious competitors in the world's markets.

DOUBTS ABOUT RUSSIAN INTENTIONS

Still, Nixon meant to get into serious negotiations with the Russians on a broad front of problems, even though he began to realize that he would not be able to insist on these negotiations being interrelated. He learned it the hard way. His first disappointment was that the Russians could not help him in Hanoi, his second that he could not arrive at an agreed policy with them on the Middle East. It led him to having grave doubts about Russian intentions.

They were sharply accentuated by the so-called "Cuban incident" in September 1970, involving a Soviet submarine tender. Nixon at first did not want to aggravate relations and decided to try secret diplomacy to avoid creating too much of a fuss about it, and to make it clear to the Russians that he was as determined as Kennedy to prevent their establishing an offensive military base at Cienfuegos. But the "incident" broke into the open in a column by C. L. Sulzberger of the New York *Times* on September 25. The same day the Pentagon cautiously confirmed it, and later still the same day, Henry Kissinger at a background briefing on the President's trip to the Mediterranean issued a strong warning that the

United States would consider the establishment of a Soviet strategic base in Cuba a hostile act. The State Department was at first puzzled by these warnings and some of its officials criticized them as a cold-war exercise. But the White House, though it did not want to ring the alarm bell in public, made certain that the full implications of this Russian initiative were understood at least by the press and Congress.

The reason for the American concern stemmed from the presence of the nine thousand ton Ugraclass submarine tender and two barges which, according to an expertly researched story by Benjamin Welles, also in the New York *Times*, had been shipped from the Soviet naval base of Polyarny, near Murmansk, to Cuba. They had no power of their own and were intended as storage space for radioactive wastes which nuclear submarine reactors discharge from time to time.

The initial suspicions that the Russians were building up a new presence in Cuba had been aroused by photographs showing a soccer playing field close to new military barracks, and since it is well known that Cubans do not play soccer but that in Russia this is a very popular sport, a warning signal went up. U-2 photo reconnaissance, which had dropped to one flight a month, was swiftly increased and came up with proof that new communication towers, new barracks and new anti-aircraft sites were under construction, and that two barges and a tender were at anchor at Cienfuegos; it all added up to a potential nuclear submarine base. A nuclear submarine was even identified in the vicinity, though not actually at the harbor of Cienfuegos.

One of the key questions the United States was most anxious to check was whether the submarine and tender would marry up, for that would have been the most conclusive evidence. They never did, though probably would have done, the experts concluded, had not the United States discovered the preparations in time. If it had failed to do so, once the installations were in place the United States would have been presented with a *fait accompli*. The Russians could have said then that because the United States had not raised the issue, they simply assumed it was acceptable and had gone ahead. Once everything was in place, the U.S.S.R.

could have argued that in exchange for a withdrawal the United States had to make a concession, say, by giving up a base in Europe.

What worried the Pentagon was that with a refueling base in Cuba, Soviet submarine strength in the area could be increased, for then the Russians could cut short their patrols and avoid the eight-thousand-mile round trip from their west Atlantic stations back to Polyarny. What worried the White House more, though, was the deception by the Russians just when the two sides were beginning to have serious talks. To some of the Sovietologists it seemed to imply an inherent weakness of the Kremlin leadership, for, they concluded, it must have difficulty in resisting the pressures from the military. Since there was every indication that the facilities to handle nuclear submarines were being built on a crash basis—the new construction had been erected within a month—a speedy intercession with the Russians was imperative.

Kissinger summoned Ambassador Dobrynin to his office and reminded him, after describing the American findings, that the Russian activities violated the Kennedy-Khrushchev understanding which stipulated that the U.S.S.R. would not use Cuba as a base for nuclear weapons. Dobrynin at first expressed surprise but, according to a description in Kissinger's own memo of record, turned "ashen" when the full evidence was presented and the possible consequences of Soviet persistence in these activities were outlined. The Kennedy-Khrushchev understanding of 1962 allowed for defensive ground-based SAM and ABM missiles on Cuba, but not for servicing nuclear submarines, which are offensive weapons. Dobrynin promised to give Kissinger the requested assurances, but did not manage to do so before September 27 when Kissinger left with the President on his second trip to Europe, designed to bolster NATO and to warn the Russians not to overplay their hand in the Mediterranean.

One of the problems at the time was to convince the American public, Congress and the press that the Cuban accusations were not an attempt to "manufacture" a crisis, but a serious controversy with grave implications. The perturbations were set at rest when the Russians, after separate talks between Rogers and Gromyko at the UN, and Kissinger and Dobrynin in Washington, laconically reconfirmed through a *Tass* statement on October 13 that the Soviet Union "has not been and is not building its own military base" in Cuba. In private, Dobrynin confirmed that the understanding of 1962 existed and would be upheld. Even though these Russian assurances were not all that the United States had asked for, the State Department spokesman at a briefing confirmed that the United States considered the Soviet statement as "positive," indicating that it was satisfied. It was a textbook case of preventive secret diplomacy which succeeded in averting the build-up of a really serious crisis. Nevertheless, the White House privately suggested to the press that it would prefer no victory to be claimed and the case considered as closed.

When the President officially instructed Kissinger to warn the Russians of the gravity of the situation and to imply that the United States could not allow the Russians to carry out their intentions, he had to weigh the possibility that the Kremlin would test his implied threat. This aspect of the crisis had been carefully considered and the risks weighed—fortunately, the Russians did not let it come to a test.

And so between the summer of 1970 and the autumn of 1971, U.S.-Soviet relations underwent important tests of strength: in the Jordan crisis, the Cuban incident, the cease-fire confusion along the Suez Canal. In each case the United States remained firm. There was also what one could call an internal Communist crisis, the workers' rebellion in Poland which must have made quite an impression in Moscow. Then in January 1971, began the secret dialogue between President Nixon and Chairman Brezhnev concerning the stalled SALT talks with which neither side allowed any of the various crises to interfere. These talks had continued despite many bitter public accusations over the Jordan and Suez Canal crises, and despite the poisonous war in Vietnam. The SALT negotiators, like miners, continued to chip their way toward a gold mine. In April 1971, came the much-delayed Communist Party Congress in Moscow where Brezhnev signaled the basic decision in favor of a *détente* policy and a new approach to domestic economic development. It was a far-reaching decision and it led to increasingly more businesslike negotiations—as the Russians like to call useful and realistic negotiations—between the White House and the Kremlin.

NIXON WINS HIS BIGGEST GAMBLE

Chairman Brezhnev, for the first time, moved to the forefront as the man behind the forceful *détente* policy when he invited Chancellor Willy Brandt to the Soviet Union. It was on this occasion that Gromyko, with his sardonic humor, expressed Russia's unconcern about the Common Market by remarking to Brandt, "It is a tame animal, a dinosaur born in captivity." Brezhnev during this visit exposed himself to the press and candid photography as never before. His private exchanges with President Nixon also gained frequency and led to the first agreement in principle on SALT and later to the clinching of the Berlin agreement. Other Russo-American bilateral interests began to be more carefully defined and worked over, as were the plans for a summit meeting which, the Russians insisted, was first suggested by President Nixon. But from the Russian viewpoint, it virtually became a must after Mr. Nixon's voyage to China, for the Russians were far too concerned about the possibility of a U.S.-Chinese collusion directed against them.

It even withstood the most daring decision President Nixon had yet taken. When he announced the mining of Haiphong Harbor as a counterthrust against the North Vietnamese May offensive, it scared the Americans more than the Russians. This was a decision President Johnson had never risked taking; it was a slap in the face for the Russians and a challenge to their ideological relationship with Hanoi. It created suspense in the White House, where the possibility of postponement or cancellation of the summit suddenly looked more likely than its being held on time. It created suspense in Congress and in the press, where Mr. Nixon was widely criticized for risking a SALT agreement for the sake of an intensification of the war. It created suspense in Moscow, where the Politburo obviously saw itself confronted with an extremely embarrassing decision. But President Nixon had talked himself into white anger. The North Vietnamese offensive had upset all his calculations. It proved to pack a far greater punch than anybody in the United States Government had anticipated, thanks to the heavy and more sophisticated weapons the Soviet Union had provided—the tank and artillery strength, particularly, were well above American intelligence estimates. As a consequence, the South Vietnamese Army was put to a much more difficult test than it had been prepared for and would have been destroyed without the enormous panoply of American air power. In this situation Nixon was prepared seriously to consider risking the Moscow summit and the consequences for his election campaign.

When Kissinger flew to Moscow on Brezhnev's invitation to set the stage for the summit conference, the President had not yet actually decided to order the mining, but he was very close to it. Not unexpectedly, the subject of Vietnam occupied almost half the time of the discussions between Kissinger and Brezhnev, who surprised Nixon's emissary because he proved to be much smarter, much more intelligent, much better informed than he had expected from everything he had heard about him. It only went to prove that, although Brezhnev is a creature of the Soviet bureaucracy, to become *primus inter pares* nevertheless requires outstanding leadership qualities. Kissinger found him tough, but capable of greater informality than he had expected. Brezhnev needed no coaxing or coaching by aides in discussing the issues at hand and dealt with most of them personally and knowledgeably. But in contrast to Mao's or Chou En-lai's mind, his was non-conceptual; it was also difficult to discuss with him internal political problems that had direct bearing on foreign affairs. For instance, during Kissinger's first stay in Peking, Chou En-lai suggested that he wanted to tell him about the cultural revolution. His enraptured guest indicated that he need not if it were at all embarrassing to him, but the Chinese Premier simply set aside this courtesy with a wave of his hand and insisted that he wanted to explain this very significant development in Chinese history because it was essential to an understanding of Chinese policy today. The Russians, on the other hand, never brought up their internal political affairs; they avoided them, and when Kissinger once or twice tried to raise questions about events that went back fifteen to twenty years, they behaved as if they had not heard his question. It was as if a collective authorization were needed before such matters could be discussed.

However, as far as the agenda for the summit was concerned, much progress was made in preparing the key issues at least close enough to a promise of success. Half a dozen difficult points in the SALT agreement still were left open, but the inclusion of sea-based Polaris missiles, to which the Russians had previously objected strenuously, was accepted by Brezhnev within a day after Kissinger further explained a new compromise proposal he had forwarded ten days in advance via Ambassador Dobrynin. No decision was taken on whether to include the agreed "principles" which the Russians had originally proposed as part of the package of agreements; the problem of Vietnam also remained essentially unresolved. The general framework for the summit, however, was agreed on, and there was a good understanding as to the emphasis to be given to various issues. A new tone for negotiations had been set, and a readiness on both sides to talk informally achieved that nobody had held possible.

Most disappointing, but not surprising, was the Russian refusal to stop supplying North Vietnam with more arms. But there was ample evidence that Mr. Brezhnev was unhappy about the timing and even the launching of North Vietnam's massive offensive. With the U.S. forces withdrawing, it looked inevitable, at least to the Russians, that Hanoi would gain its objectives within a very few years; the enormous losses in men and matériel, therefore, seemed to them a sign of stubborn foolishness. The Russians had taken that view for a long time. As far back as the time of Kosygin's visit to London in February 1967, when Prime Minister Harold Wilson thought he had detected a willingness on the part of the Russian Premier to intervene in Hanoi, the Russians argued that if the North Vietnamese were only smarter and not so bloody-minded they could have conquered South Vietnam without bloodshed.

When Henry Kissinger left after four days of private talks with Mr. Brezhnev, he was toasted shortly before his departure by Deputy Foreign Minister Kuznetsov, a man of considerable charm and sense of humor, in the name of the State of the Soviet Union. Antonov, the man in charge of VIP security, whose ward

Kissinger was wherever he went, was pleased that everything had gone well, and also raised his glass to their American guest, toasting him in the name of the State Secret Police. Kuznetsov, a little surprised at Antonov's toast, asked, "Do you mean to say that the Secret Police is not part of the State?" But Antonov simply repeated that he wanted to add his toast in the name of the State Secret Police!

The secret meeting between Kissinger and Le Duc Tho, Hanoi's chief negotiator in Paris, shortly after his talks with Brezhnev, which the Russian leader had said could hopefully be more productive, was somewhere between a fiasco and a charade. The North Vietnamese, with their military offensive in full swing, wanted to gain time for Hanoi's forces to occupy as much territory as possible before accepting anything resembling a cease-fire, and Kissinger did not want to wait for the situation on the battlefield to get worse, knowing that the President was ready to play a trump card of desperation and order the mining of Haiphong. If Le Duc Tho had some concessions up his sleeve, he did not produce them at the first meeting and Kissinger did not give him a second chance.

On the old target list prepared by the Joint Chiefs of Staff in President Johnson's days, after the bombing of Haiphong Harbor was the mining of the harbor, and President Nixon, desperate to prove that the Vietnamization he had praised so often was not a failure, decided to play the riskiest card yet. He hardly batted an eyelid. He had considered the consequences and was willing to accept them. His advisers were unanimous that the Russians would not go ahead with the summit as planned. Indeed, some would have welcomed a Russian postponement or a cancellation to avoid Mr. Nixon's arriving in Moscow with his position in Vietnam eroding. Serious consideration was given to an American cancellation of the summit—a speech to announce the cancellation had already been prepared—but then that idea was rejected in favor of testing the Russian "manhood" first. No doubt, if the summit had been canceled or postponed Mr. Nixon would have tried to wrap himself in the American flag and claim he had acted in the defense of American honor.

But the Kremlin saw the situation quite differently. They had bigger stakes in mind. After several days of hard deliberations whether to proceed with the summit, Chairman Brezhnev carried the day; it soon became clear, to the surprise of the White House and Mr. Nixon's critics, that there would be no change in the timing or in the arrangements for the visit. The last thing his critics had expected was to be disarmed by the Kremlin.

Several Soviet trade and maritime officials who were in Washington for negotiations at the time spent a day or two of uncertainty but then continued to smile and to negotiate. When Comrade Pyotr Y. Shelest was demoted a few days later, it became very obvious that there had been a bitter controversy and that Mr. Brezhnev had made certain that he had the unanimous backing of the entire leadership. The lone dissenter was not allowed to disturb this unanimity. Two weeks later, *Pravda* went a long way toward admitting that a controversy had taken place in the Politburo: "The dialogue took place despite the complexity of the international situation and in the face of the sometimes direct opposition of those who like to warm their hands by fanning the fires of hostility and tension." *Pravda* sounded like Senator Fulbright putting Senator "Scoop" Jackson in his place. Nikita Khrushchev had been willing to rupture relations with President Eisenhower after the U-2 incident in 1959 and had broken up the Paris summit meeting; but he knew the President had only another year in office. Mr. Brezhnev did not want to take the same risk with President Nixon. A cancellation of the summit would almost certainly have jeopardized ratification of the Soviet-West German treaties. It would have left the United States seemingly with better relations to China than to the Soviet Union. And it would have delayed prospects for trade expansion and put the question of a *détente* with the West into doubt, the *détente* on which Mr. Brezhnev had staked his place in history. Compared with these objectives, Haiphong Harbor was only a passing incident.

PEACEMAKING FOR POSTERITY

The validity of these considerations was confirmed in various ways by Mr. Brezhnev in his private talks with the President.

Brezhnev, who is sixty-five but looks like fifty-five, has most likely only another five years at the top, and there were ample indications that he hoped to be remembered as neither a Stalin nor a Khrushchev, but as a peacemaker who also wanted to improve the life of his people. From remarks such as "the terrible things people say about me," the chairman of the Communist Party showed that he was aware of having the reputation of being crude and brutal—a reputation that seemed partly to go back to the punitive expedition into Czechoslovakia in 1968—and that he wanted to erase it. He has even gone to such extremes as shaving down his bushy eyebrows because they give him a somewhat sinister look and make him an easy target for cartoonists. He pays much attention to clothes: To the earlier Kissinger meetings he sported a light blue jacket and flamboyant tie, but for the President he preferred the sober-suited look of the trade-union boss in his Sunday best. Socially, he is surprisingly at ease, and he exudes a dynamic bargaining technique in business discussions. In various small ways during the Moscow summit he went to great lengths to show that he has good simple human qualities. Quite obviously, he is a man with a much more balanced temperament than Khrushchev who, had he been confronted with the mining of Haiphong Harbor, undoubtedly would have volleyed his shoes against the wall in anger and canceled the summit.

Brezhnev, it soon became clear to the President and Kissinger, was much more deeply committed than they had assumed to a *détente* not only with the United States but also with Western Europe. He recognized correctly that he could not obtain what Kissinger liked to call a "selective *détente*," that there had to be a parallel reduction of tension with each.

The profound emotional antagonism toward China exuded by Brezhnev clearly also influenced the decision not to abandon the meeting with Mr. Nixon. The Soviet Union wanted to prove to its own people, to the world and, above all, to the Chinese that Moscow had more important business with the United States than had Peking. This competitive feeling toward China was not only conditioned by ideological and security considerations, but went much deeper, and those who had a chance to listen to Mr. Brezhnev came away with a feeling that it might be rooted in some sort of ethnic prejudices, certain cultural inferiority complexes and possibly also a feeling of guilt about past relations with China. "For a European mind like mine," the Communist Party chairman once remarked with a tone of quiet exasperation, "the Chinese are impossible to understand."

During most of the private conversations the President had with Mr. Brezhnev, no other members of the Politburo were present, only Foreign Minister Gromyko, the veteran expert in foreign affairs who has survived some twenty years in key positions and on whom Mr. Brezhnev relied for technical advice. To the surprise of the President, Mr. Brezhnev insisted that the only interpreter allowed to be present at this talk was to be Suchodrev, the charming and adroit Russian who can put on an American as well as an English accent. Brezhnev was obviously distrustful of an American interpreter and refused to accept one. Mr. Nixon had to rely on the minutes dictated by a Russian. Once, in talking to Dr. Kissinger, Brezhnev seemed to share President Nixon's ideas about the dispensability of foreign secretaries. "Maybe we should send Messrs. Gromyko and Rogers first to Mars to see what it's like up there," he suggested, "and if they don't come back we shouldn't go." Then he teased Kissinger about how much better university professors are treated in the U.S.S.R.

Gromyko, too, showed not only his impressive qualities as a foreign policy expert, but also his puckish sense of humor. When Kissinger wondered whether it was better for him to speak close to the orange or the apple, implying that he assumed that one or the other contained a miniature microphone, Gromyko looked up to the ceiling from where a sculpture of a heavy-bosomed woman looked down on them. He pointed at one of her breasts—word of Kissinger's interest in the ladies had obviously reached the Kremlin—and said, "No, I believe it is in there."

Brezhnev, though appearing to be always acting within the guidelines agreed on by the Politburo, clearly had a strong hand in formulating them. He also seemed to have more rapid access to information than the others; in the main negotiating sessions, Messrs. Kosygin and Podgorny accompanied the chairman.

During the summit meetings Brezhnev seemed much calmer and more at ease than when he met with Kissinger in late April.

Then he seemed nervous, something seemed to worry him. He played constantly with his watch chain, tapped the table with his cigarette holder, got up at intervals and walked around restlessly. Now he seemed jovial and in a joking mood. Several times he put his arm around Kissinger's shoulders as a kind of gesture of welcome, and altogether proved to be a much more likable person than the Americans had expected. With Mr. Nixon, though, he kept a formal and respectful distance.

THE BENEFITS OF MUTUAL SELF-RESTRAINT

But it was not only the factual negotiations or their results that mattered; above all, an American President and the Soviet leadership took full advantage of an opportunity really to discuss their mutual problems and their outlooks on the world in a relaxed and informal manner. They were able to feel each other out and to lose some of those preconceived views, which on Mr. Nixon's side had been expressed in his book *Six Crises:* "The Communist threat is indivisible. . . . The Communist threat is universal. . . . Our failure to meet a Communist probe in Asia or Africa or Latin America only increases the probability that we will be forced to meet such a probe in Europe. . . . The Communist threat is total. . . ." etc., etc. Since then, Mr. Nixon has modified his ideas about communism, especially since communism has proved, surprisingly, not to be indivisible. And the Soviet leaders, who used to regard Mr. Nixon as the capitalist devil incarnate and a mediocre politician with a badly distorted view of world affairs, were said after the summit to see him as a shrewd, enlightened, skillful statesman who has succeeded in transforming American foreign policy in a surprisingly constructive manner. To the Americans Brezhnev had become a more sympathetic and less formidable figure. Moreover, the White House saw a link between his leadership and *détente:* They therefore began to wonder about the extent to which the opponents to his *détente* policy might thrive on any further blows to his prestige like the mining of Haiphong Harbor or, later, the eviction of Russian troops from Egypt. The catastrophically bad harvest, no doubt, gravely accentuated his problems. For President Nixon it meant an unexpectedly lucky windfall in the midst of his election campaign: a Russian purchase of about $1 billion of wheat. It gave trade negotiations a certain added momentum and whetted the appetite of those Americans who hoped to do business with the Russians. The prospects for much increased trade between the United States and the Soviet Union suddenly looked more promising than before.

Obviously, the mountains of suspicion accumulated over two decades of cold war cannot be blasted away in one meeting; many will persist and on the periphery of the direct bilateral interests between the United States and the Soviet Union dangerous situations will continue to exist. No progress, as expected, was made about coming closer to a solution for the Middle East, but it was important and reassuring to know that both sides considered this area as the most explosive one, that both were well aware that they did not fully control it, and that they shared a mutual concern about its dangers. They found no formula for translating this mutual concern into policy, but there was good reason to believe that the Russians would exercise retraint in the kind of weapons they would sell to the Egyptians to prevent them from going off the deep end. (This was so, as the anger and frustrations in Cairo later confirmed.) The same applied to Cuba, where the United States accepted a limited Soviet presence, but where the Russians knew what the United States would tolerate. There were no accords as regards third countries, but there was an understanding on both sides to exercise self-restraint. It was a promising sign— that both seemed to recognize the importance of keeping third countries from interfering with the basic interests of the two superpowers.

What was most reassuring to the President was that the Soviet leadership had finally come to understand the full implications of nuclear war, the need for imposing controls on the arms race, for redoubling the efforts to widen those controls and to grapple with the conceptual problem—irrespective of their ideological view of the world, of which there continued to exist strong vestiges that assert themselves from time to time—of how to live with the most powerful enemy in a way that will not jeopardize each other's and everybody else's survival; in short, how to maintain order in the world. Like everybody else, though, the leaders of the Soviet Union remain very much confused on that score.

And so the summit produced a new understanding as never before of each other's interests and made some progress, too, on how to protect them without running the risks of confrontation. In psychological terms, though, the Moscow talks from the U.S. viewpoint represented something of a plateau, hopefully for a long respite before a slow descent.

The NATO allies watched Mr. Nixon's dazzling acrobatics in Moscow with mixed feelings. On the one hand, they could not object to the President's promoting a *détente* policy they themselves had advocated. On the other, they felt like uncomfortable onlookers, who could not see most of the game, at what they feared might be a new and exclusive duopoly: Was this to be the new diplomacy?

The United States for two decades climbed and climbed to become the world's supreme power; it accepted responsibilities much against its traditions and habits of thinking, and with a certain amount of guilt as well as ambition. Both the political Right and Left, due to the fear of communism and a missionary zeal, were united in their desire to bring a new deal to the many downtrodden around the world. It was the only way for a number of successive administrations to maintain public backing for foreign policy that was new and alien to most Americans. Now the traditions and the guilt and a reassessment of American values and a disillusionment with the results of that policy are asserting themselves, and as a consequence, the consensus that sustained it has disintegrated.

The Soviet leadership, on the other hand, though it has come to recognize a certain community of interest with the United States, shows a new dynamism that animates its foreign policy and continues to propel it toward more ambitious geopolitical goals. In other words, while the Soviet Union has acquired a new zest in establishing itself as a world power more or less equal to the United States, the United States has become a reluctant world power.

President Johnson used to say, "If you have a new weapon, you use it." Instinctively he wanted to do something about the arms race but he did not really understand its complexity; but even now, few people do. Everybody has a vague feeling that it is dangerous, that it costs excessively much money, that this money could be put to far more constructive uses, and that therefore every effort should be made to halt it. But only the experts (and even among them there is much disagreement) understand the intricacies of what constitutes the "balance of terror," as Sir Winston Churchill put it so graphically, that prevents war between the superpowers.

It makes the layman cringe to think that he must rely on a relatively small band of experts—often at loggerheads among themselves—for finding a safe solution to the problem that may well be the most important one of the seventies. This is an issue on which our survival depends.

The central stage for dealing with this problem between the United States and the Soviet Union is the so-called SALT (Strategic Arms Limitation Talks) which alternately take place in Helsinki and Vienna. The only look behind the scenes and this the merest glimpse, was at the preparations for these talks in the Kissinger policy kitchen, the National Security Council. However, I have had unusual opportunities to learn about the complex evaluations that went into the policy making for these SALT talks, and these offer perhaps a better insight into what it all means to our security than has yet been given.

At the start of what were at first called "disarmament talks," beginning in the early fifties and for a long time thereafter, there was a lot of empty and meaningless propaganda talk at the United Nations about general disarmament. The reason was that the Russians then were not ready to enter into serious arms control discussions because they were far behind the United States and wanted to be able to negotiate from something close to nuclear arms parity with the United States. It took the Soviet Union almost twenty years to establish this position. During those twenty years, the U.S. aim was to stay ahead of Russian developments, and time and again, the alleged failure to do so became a searing political issue. In 1960, John F. Kennedy, for instance, made the "missile gap" a big campaign issue in his fight against Richard Nixon. But as soon as he came into power, his Secretary of Defense Robert McNamara discovered that Kennedy had grossly exaggerated the problem.

By 1962, however, McNamara became more concerned with getting the strategic arms race under control than with the United States staying ahead, for by then he had convinced himself that the United States had bought a far larger strategic force than was necessary for deterrence of the Soviet Union. It was late that year that, under the skillful handling of Ambassador Averell Harriman and the then Moscow-based Ambassador Llewellyn Thompson, the agreement on a Nuclear Test Ban Treaty was reached and McNamara succeeded in persuading the Joint Chiefs of Staff to support it in their testimony before Congress. For almost a month he debated the issues and their original opposition to the Treaty, but in the end they accepted McNamara's arguments that the Treaty would not weaken American security—and General Curtis LeMay was a hard man to convince. Congress ratified the Treaty, though such influential figures in matters of national security as Senators Richard Russell, John Stennis and Scoop Jackson voted against it.

The question that developed was to what extent the United States was stimulating a Soviet arms build-up that was in turn constantly forcing the United States to step up its arms race yet again—the classic arms race spiral. McNamara became a passionate believer in the need to bring what he called the "mad momentum of the arms race" under control, and historically, thanks to him, a turning point was reached by the end of 1966 that gave American thinking a new direction. Anti-ballistic missile systems became to him the key to the arms race. He had no doubt that the correct decision was not to deploy one; but in the end in order to resist the pressures for proceeding with an anti-Soviet ABM system for which the House had already appropriated an initial sum, he agreed to an anti-Chinese ABM system. As Morton H. Halperin, one of his former assistants and now a senior fellow of the Brookings Institution of Washington, D.C., devoted to nonpartisan research, put it in a brilliant analysis of how bureaucratic and domestic politics interfered with his conviction: "In the end, he was not prepared to push the argument to the point of a break with President Johnson, who did not share his view that an American ABM deployment would make agreement with the Russians more difficult. He managed, however, to persuade the President to accept a compromise, and to begin with only a small anti-Chinese system. Still, Johnson also saw the dangers of the arms race and was anxious to do something to bring nuclear weapons under control."*

DISAPPOINTMENT AT GLASSBORO

McNamara's hopes were high at the meeting between President Johnson and Soviet Premier Kosygin at Glassboro, New Jersey, on June 23 and 25, 1967, that he could persuade the Soviet leader to set a date for arms limitation talks, but the Russian in the end proved unyielding; he considered ABMs as defensive and therefore unobjectionable. Disappointed, Johnson decided to go ahead with what came to be known as the Sentinel defense system. Halperin drew the following conclusions:

> Shared images which officials believed dominated American society also biased the system toward an ABM deployment. There was a widely accepted view that the United

* Halperin, World Politics, Princeton University Press, Princeton, N.J., 1972.

States needed to have strategic superiority over the Soviet Union and that the United States needed to match any system which the Soviet deployed. . . . Given this situation the President had to be concerned with the domestic political effects, particularly on his re-election prospects in 1968, if he appeared to be opening an ABM gap, failing to match the Soviet system, and giving up American nuclear superiority. . . . Although McNamara lost the short-run battle to prevent a deployment and to deploy a system which could not grow into a large anti-Soviet system, his efforts to change the terms of the debate within the bureaucracy, with Congress and with the public, were considerably more successful. Thus by 1969 President Nixon accepted nuclear sufficiency rather than superiority as the American goal. . . . Perhaps the most successful conversion came with the Russians. Kosygin was arguing at Glassboro that ABMs were purely defensive weapons and that the American effort to prevent their deployment was immoral. However, by 1971, the Russians were pressing for an agreement at the strategic arms talks simply to limit ABMs.

THE ERA OF PARITY

In the spring of 1968, the Russians for the first time began to respond more positively to the American urgings for arms limitations talks, and after much to-ing and fro-ing, an announcement was made in July of that year that they were ready to enter into discussions to limit offensive and defensive missiles. They said privately that their military had become less adamant and their civilian leadership had reached a better understanding of the issues involved. Of course, they were also more confident that a relationship of nuclear parity now existed with the United States, and that no harm and some good could come from exchanging ideas on this complex problem. To give their decision a spectacular send-off the Russians even agreed to a visit by President Johnson to Moscow around October 15, 1968, which he, in turn, hoped would end his first term with a historic high point.

But at that time, the clouds over Czechoslovakia had been darkening fast. Undeterred by the possibility of upsetting the prospect for the President's visit, which obviously had a low priority compared to events in Czechoslovakia, the Soviet military forces moved to discipline an ally which had become too daring in seeking its own ideology.

ARMS LIMITATIONS WITHOUT TEARS

The announcement of the Moscow visit, set for August 21, consequently was never made. On August 20, the Soviet Ambassador asked to see Mr. Johnson and gave him the news of the invasion of Czechoslovakia. The euphoria that a few hours earlier had pervaded the White House about the forthcoming visit was such that the President still hesitated to cancel it, but he soon realized with a heavy heart that he had no choice.

The Johnson administration had by then developed a still-secret, agreed "initial presentation" of the objectives and the rationale for the arms limitations discussions. These aims were:

1. To limit and subsequently to reduce both offensive and defensive strategic armaments.

2. To maintain a stable mutual deterrent.

3. To demonstrate American and Soviet willingness to limit their armaments.

4. To provide mutual assurance that security will be maintained and to improve the understanding of common strategic issues.

The Russians replied on September 16, 1968, proposing four basic principles to guide future arms limitations talks:

1. The establishment of a stable U.S.-Soviet strategic deterrent.

2. The need to enhance the credibility of the U.S.-USSR effort to prevent destabilizing actions by other nations.

3. Mutual assurances to each other that equal security be-

tween the two will be maintained while at the same time the tensions, costs and uncertainties of an unrestrained arms race will be avoided.

4. Improvements of U.S.-USSR understanding by establishing a continuing process of discussion of issues arising from the strategic situation to include both offensive and defensive weapons.

These principles sounded reasonable for a start and persuasive enough to convince the Johnson administration that the Russians meant business. Even the inevitable reference to the war in Vietnam read inoffensively: "The achievement of progress toward a peaceful settlement of the Vietnam problem would be highly desirable."

In November, President Johnson tried to revive the summit meeting with the agreement of President-elect Nixon, and more position papers for the talks were exchanged which showed that both sides were in agreement on the basic essentials. The Russians added to the American proposals only the possibility of discussing ways of reducing the risks of nuclear war in crisis situations and of using the agreed principles as guidance for the actual arms talks which Johnson hoped could be started at Geneva. However, by December the Kremlin was no longer interested in talking to a "lame duck" President and Mr. Nixon did not want to be committed to anything by an outgoing President without having studied the American proposals carefully himself.

Still, as late as January 13, three cables, all related to the opening of arms talks with the Russians, were approved by Secretary of State Dean Rusk, Secretary of Defense Clark Clifford, Chairman of the Joint Chiefs of Staff General Wheeler, Walt Rostow and Adrian Fisher, head of the Disarmament Agency; they sought to elicit the views of the NATO Council on the statements agreed between the United States and the U.S.S.R., but they also instructed the American Ambassador to NATO not to mention that the text had already been submitted to the Soviet Union and no mention was made of the Soviet message. It was a curious attempt to mislead the allies as to the extent to which the United States had already been in touch with Moscow and as to the progress the consultations had made before word was passed on to them.

The initial position paper worked out by the Johnson administration in preparation for the opening of the SALT talks was similar in principle to that developed later by the Nixon team, but it lacked, at least at that stage, the thorough studies initiated by Kissinger and the technical detail. It did not include specific limits on intercontinental ballistic missile systems and sea-based ballistic missiles, although there was of course every intention of negotiating such specific limitations; it did not deal with intermediate ballistic missiles and no limitations were imposed on the number of aircraft. In regard to the ballistic missile system, it considered levels for ABMs acceptable between 100 and 1,000 in view of the Sentinel ABM system that had been programmed for 672 launchers. But it banned the enlarging of the silos, the relocation of launchers, land mobile strategic offensive missiles and the deployment of surface ballistic missile ships, and limited quantitatively sea-based missiles, both on nuclear submarines already built and those still under construction. The proposals did not allow, however, for the freedom to mix what Kissinger came to call "building blocks": for instance, balancing more missiles on land against fewer at sea or vice versa. It was an inflexible position built around an "assured destruction" capability, carrying through to the end of 1976, based on a capacity to destroy all major Soviet cities in a retaliatory strike. What mattered was to make the Russians realize that launching an attack ("a first strike") would be national suicide. Even if the Soviets violated a treaty based on these proposals, their authors argued, it would not have made any difference to the destructive capabilities on either side.

That, at least, was the theory on which McNamara based his thinking. The Nixon administration saw flaws in it. It saw a danger that as Russian and American strategic power came close to parity, the strategic relationship could become less stable.

WHY "ASSURED DESTRUCTION" WAS NOT ENOUGH

The Kissinger analysts, delving as they believed deeper into specifics than was the practice in the Johnson days, concluded, according to Dr. Larry Lynn, that the Johnson proposals had built into them a progressive deterioration of the survivability of American land-based missiles as the Russians caught up with MIRV† developments. The revised thinking focused on whether the United States had enough missiles to attack enemy cities and thereby create a stable nuclear relationship in which a balanced threat existed with neither side able to take advantage of the other. "Assured destruction" was dropped from the vocabulary and replaced by President Nixon in his first press conference with the doctrine of "sufficiency."

One of the most striking missing ingredients in the Johnson plan was MIRV. The reason was that it would have led to a bitter fight with the military and until a first agreement was in sight, the civilians concluded, why spill a lot of blood possibly to no avail? Whether or not to proceed with this system later became one of the most controversial issues in Congress and in the scientific community, and led to massive attacks on the Nixon administration because of its unwillingness to halt MIRV testing.

In the Johnson days the issue had not yet aroused such attention; one reason was, as Morton Halperin, a student of the games bureaucrats play,‡ says, that the bureaucracy had not yet thought it necessary to evoke a response on the domestic scene. One of its powers, Halperin maintains, is to arouse public opinion either through testimony before Congress, through indiscretions to members of Congress or the press, or through its former members, who, as experts, can have sufficient authority to contest policy in learned articles or public speeches before informed and influential audiences.

The original argument, still shrouded in secrecy, whether or not to build MIRV was carried out in the Pentagon. It centered on the best way of getting the widest coverage of targets—was it by building more launchers, more warheads or to MIRV the war-

† MIRV: Multiple Independently targeted Re-entry Vehicle, a horror of a warhead, which divides into up to twelve smaller warheads which confuse the defense because they can be independently guided to twelve targets and because the "bouquet" also includes decoys. MIRV represented a major technical breakthrough, in fact a new stage in the arms race.

‡ Halperin, *Why Bureaucrats Play Games*, the Brookings Institution, Washington, D.C., 1971.

heads? The intelligence estimates in 1963 concluded that the "greater than expected" likelihood was that within five years the Soviet Union would be able to deploy up to eight thousand long- and short-range interceptors. Consequently, a debate developed behind the scenes as to the best means of penetrating the Soviet ABM defenses that "could happen" by 1970. McNamara, influ- enced by the desire to find a nuclear strategy that would not rely on the destruction of cities, by the intelligence estimates—which in retrospect proved grossly exaggerated—by a concern that the military, who then still packed a wallop in Congress, would chal- lenge him if he rejected MIRV, decided in favor of it.

When he began to fund research and decided to test and par- tially deploy MIRV in 1965, there was lengthy discussion as to whether its existence should be made public or not. Despite the argument that it would spur the Russians into proceeding with the same idea, the only case against disclosure, the decision was made to reveal its existence; the chosen instrument was an inter- view with Robert McNamara in *Life* magazine.* He had devel- oped, from the basis on which the military rested their advance planning, the concept of "greater than expected threat," but in his view the more sensible basis for advance calculations was the threat the intelligence community accepted as probable. However, he decided to proceed with MIRV to meet the basis of both. In the 1968–69 posture statement he unobtrusively referred to this deployment by stating that "we can convert the entire force to Minuteman III, increase the number of warheads each Minute- man can carry . . ."

THE QUIET BIRTH OF MIRV

Curiously enough, MIRV at this stage aroused no opposition either in the press or in Congress. No one warned publicly that the United States was critically accelerating the arms race. Only a few inside the Administration drew attention to the fact that a major escalation was being prepared to limit a much less dangerous weap- ons escalation. The same situation prevailed when it was de-

* September 29, 1967.

cided in 1968 to test MIRV for the first time. By design or coincidence—depending on which partisan view one listens to—the first test took place just before the date the SALT talks with the Russians were expected to begin. Morton Halperin then sent a memo to Paul Nitze, Deputy Secretary of Defense, suggesting a postponement of the test, and so did William Foster, who then headed the U. S. Disarmament Agency. The systems analysts in the Pentagon were also against testing, but did not make an issue of it within the government; once out of the Pentagon, though, they began to beat their breasts both in guilt and new zeal. At the State Department, Leonard Meeker, the legal adviser, and Henry Owen, then head of the State Department Planning Staff, tried to persuade Dean Rusk to oppose a decision to test, but Rusk refused. President Johnson was kept informed about the progress of MIRV development; however, he was not asked for any specific new authority by Clark Clifford (who by then had succeeded McNamara) to clear the way for the first test. Clifford, in explaining his decision, which he knew had far-reaching implications for the weapons race, said to me later that "the development of MIRV at that time had reached a point where the United States needed to know what we had and how to carry on from here."

And so, without a great debate, the testing of MIRV began, an act which greatly complicated the problem of the strategic relationship with the Soviet Union. It made it much more difficult to calculate and structure this relationship in any future negotiations, and it added the possibility that the other side would feel compelled to take countermeasures, for if MIRVed warheads become too accurate they destabilize the arms race. They then provide counterforce capability and a first-strike threat. The original purpose, of course, was not to aim for a first-strike capability, but to improve the American ability to penetrate the Russian ABM defenses; it was not thought at that time that an agreement with the Soviet Union to limit ABM deployment was likely. However, those involved in the original decision to test MIRV, such as Paul Nitze, believe that the development of MIRV was inevitable because the United States could not risk losing an important advantage in the inexorable arms race, that in fact it stabilized "assured destruction" and offered a hedge against the other side building a counterforce capability. Gerard Smith agreed with Nitze that without the U.S. advantage in warheads given by MIRV, the Phase I SALT agreement might not have been possible. But there are many equally qualified experts who maintain that MIRV accelerated the arms race and made it open-ended.

The existence of MIRV aroused intense public attention only in 1969 after President Nixon had moved into the White House, and mainly because some of the experts then newly out of office felt free to speak their minds. Also the climate had changed. The public emphasis was on the importance of reaching an arms limitation agreement with the Russians and to avoid anything that might jeopardize it. An anti-MIRV test campaign began in Congress and in the press, and the President was bitterly attacked and exhorted to halt the testing and to propose a moratorium on testing to the Russians. The Soviet Union had publicly repeated its willingness to start arms control talks in January 1969, but Nixon wanted to chart his own approach to these negotiations. He decided not only to go on testing but also to deploy MIRV, and, furthermore, not to proceed with SALT negotiations where the Johnson administration had left off.

VERIFICATION BEFORE NEGOTIATION

The delay, as it lengthened, aroused growing public criticism. But Nixon, a believer in the "linkage" theory, wanted to wait until it became clearer whether the Soviet Union would indicate her desire for *détente* on a broad front.

And he wanted to learn to understand the essentials of the problem involved and to think them through. After all, he was facing up to one of his most fateful decisions, one that would influence U.S. military power and possibly national survival far into the future.

The behind-the-scenes preparations Kissinger organized in his meticulousness and intellectual sagacity were unprecedented; he marshaled and co-ordinated every possible source of information with a bearing on the subject. The NSC's initial task was to develop alternative approaches, consisting of different "packages" of arms limitations and their evaluation for their strategic effect and the strategic capabilities of both sides. There was, furthermore, the need to find out how verifiable these limitations were and to what extent compliance could be monitored with means under American control. In addition, it was necessary to be able to estimate the variety of weapons developments the Soviet Union had under way, the inherent risks of an arms limitation agreement and the consequences of having no agreement at all.

What seemed to Kissinger's staff people missing in the Johnson approach was that the verification analysis lacked adequate detail, especially as to the degree of certainty about what the Russians were doing. For that reason the Verification Panel was created, which assumed a central role in guiding the SALT studies. "Before we can convince ourselves, the Senate and our allies that a strategic arms limitation treaty is in our interest, we must have a full and detailed understanding of how well we will be able to determine Soviet compliance with an agreement," Kissinger told an early meeting of the National Security Council. "This had always been the great obstacle in the U.S. mind, but needs to be determined now that we have agreed to place maximum reliance on unilateral verifications." American willingness to accept the latter was based on:

1. The belief that the Russians would not accept intrusive on-site inspection—President Johnson and Llewellyn Thompson, Ambassador to the Soviet Union, had emphasized that the United States was prepared to accept inspection by national means.
2. The conviction that the enormous growth in U.S. intelligence capabilities made such acceptance feasible.

Soon the Verification Panel got embroiled in the big disputes that raged in the bowels of government about whether the Soviets were developing a simple or triple warhead, what their potential was for independently targetable warheads and whether the SS9s were designed for a knockout first strike. The differences among the experts were monumental, the range of controversies almost infinite. Here are a few examples: In the case of intercontinental ballistic missiles, the problem was not simply to decide on the maximum number to be permitted, but what one should control, how to distinguish between missiles of different ranges (for small missiles might get advanced propulsion which could give them transatlantic range, etc.) and how to prevent their deployment being concealed in other programs. Or in the case of ABMs, the difficulty was that it would not be enough to control numbers, but also necessary to impose qualitative restrictions. In the case of MIRV, the conclusion was reached that it was simply impossible to use national means to detect whether a warhead was MIRVed or not. Furthermore, as Mort Halperin puts it: "The banning of MIRV is impossible because a MIRV test can be camouflaged as a MRV† test and as a consequence, in monitoring it, it becomes impossible to distinguish it from any other multiple warhead. One of the basic truths is that you cannot control technology, only the number of weapons on each side and their location."

Each option was examined as to whether it helped to preserve or improve U.S. security, whether it would be convincing enough to Congress, the UN and the Russians should Soviet violations occur, and how the United States would react to it. Studies were developed of the impact of each option on future U.S. strategy, and whether the option was in fact negotiable and how much money it would save.

As regards ballistic missile submarines, the CIA, the State Department and the Disarmament Agency agreed that an illegal increase in submarines could be detected within a year and certainly within two years, but the Joint Chiefs of Staff disputed this and called it an overoptimistic assessment.

One of the liveliest debates developed around the question of how vulnerable Polaris nuclear submarines were likely to become in future, for they represented for the present the least vulnerable nuclear deterrent. Most of the experts agreed that they would remain "sufficiently invulnerable" for the United States to rely safely

† Missile with multiple but not independently guided warheads.

on this system throughout the seventies. The Chinese threat, another controversial issue, was not expected to amount to much beyond twenty ICBMs by the late seventies.

Basic to the ideal of controlling these weapons by national means, as against on-site inspection are, of course, the overhead satellites which both the United States and the Soviet Union use to observe each other's activities. Some of these satellites can cover over five million square miles per mission and stay in orbit for two to three weeks. The Russians, of course, are well aware of the American monitoring system but probably not of the quality of the data obtained. Since a time could come when one side might be tempted into shooting down the other's celestial watchdogs, much thought was also given to the idea of proposing a private understanding with the Soviet Union which would declare such overhead reconnaissance by satellite legitimate for verification purposes and commit each side not to interfere with the other's reconnaissance system.

BUILDING BLOCKS

And so, only after intensive discussions, the options for the SALT talks were laboriously and carefully worked out. They consisted of the building blocks, the detailed studies of individual weapons systems which, combined in various packages, provided the negotiating options. To give an example of how these options were composed, here are a few examples:

> *Option 1:* Proposed limiting the number of ICBMs and IRBMs, banned mobile land-based offensive missile systems, limited fixed ABM launchers and radar, but imposed no constraints on sea-based offensive missiles and MIRV.
> *Option 2:* Limited the number of land and sea-based ICBMs, permitted mobile ICBMs on land, but banned mobile IRBMs, prohibited construction and relocation of fixed launchers.
> *Option 3:* Differed in that it allowed each side to substitute sea-based missiles for ICBMs, and limited heavy bombers.

Option 4: Prohibited the deployment of MIRV and MIRV testing, etc.

Options 5, 6, and 7: Specifically limited various weapons by numbers.

These options were later whittled down to four—named A,B,C,D —and then to two before plan E was put together (described later) and became the first detailed proposal the United States submitted in the summer of 1970.

On November 17, 1969, the much delayed SALT talks with the Russians finally got under way in Helsinki. The U.S. team was led by Gerard Smith, a cautious, meticulous, level-headed lawyer (who actually prefers to be called a bureaucrat) with extensive previous experience in the State Department, who believes in the cause of arms control without being a crusader. The Russian delegation was led by Vladimir Semyonov, an intelligent man at ease in contacts with foreigners and a shrewd bargainer, who was obviously under instructions to negotiate with the aim of reaching an agreement. And so a momentous discussion began in the strange jargon of missile technology that few people understand. Except for its military members, the Russian delegation, it turned out, knew very little about Soviet strategic weapons; and the military kept themselves apart. Gradually, however, the Russian civilians came to realize how much more the United States knew about their weapons than they did themselves. Gradually, also, both sides got used to delving into information neither side would have dared to mention to the other only a year or two earlier.

It also became evident that the Russians in their scheme of things wanted to limit the talks to putting a ceiling on ABMs, which used to be the U.S. principal aim, while the United States was now insisting on the need to include ICBMs. The Russians had become afraid that the U.S. ABM system might be broadened into a city defense to protect the population and thus deprive them of a retaliatory capability; the United States, on the other hand, feared that the SS9s, more powerful than anything in the U.S. arsenal, could give the Russians a first-strike capability once their number reached 420.

And so each was anxious to compel the other to hold down its massive nuclear arsenal at a level that would prevent a surprise attack that could destroy the other's capability to strike back; in short, each wanted to make certain that a balance of power could be preserved indefinitely. This balance, when the SALT talks began, consisted of 1,054 land-based ICBMs, 656 submarine-based missiles and 450 B-52s on the part of the United States; and a Soviet total of just under 1,200 land-based ICBMs, with about 200 submarine-based missiles and 200 heavy bombers. Their ABM system, protecting Moscow and parts of European Russia, had 64 launchers. They were building, on U.S. intelligence estimates, 8 nuclear submarines a year.

With neither side having as yet a first-strike capability and both sides aware what a nuclear war would mean for them and the world, with the pressures both in the United States and the Soviet Union for more to be done at home to raise the standard of living, both governments had decided that the time had come to genuinely seek an accommodation.

Two months after the start of the talks in Helsinki, which led the Nixon administration to the conclusion that the Russian intentions were serious, Kissinger sent a memo on December 30, 1969, to the Verification Panel which asked some of the key questions in preparation for a concrete U.S. proposal:

Should the United States enter the next round of SALT with a simple position or with several options?

What levels of ABMs are required for protection against accidental and third country attacks, for protection of the U.S. bomber force, for defense of Minutemen and for the defense of the National Command Authority (the capital)?

What are the verification problems and strategic implications of possible upgrading of Soviet air defense missiles to give them ABM capabilities and of their ABM systems to give them more extensive capabilities?

What would be the consequences for the United States and allied security of an agreement which does not place limits on intermediate range missiles?

What are the strategic and verification problems of various possible controls on U.S. overseas-based nuclear forces, especially carrier-based aircraft?

What are the strategic and verification implications of restricting ballistic missile submarine patrols and the overseas flights of strategic aircraft?

What are the strategic, verification and political problems presented by transfers of strategic systems and technology to third countries and by possible restrictions upon them?

This memo gives an idea of the many-sided problems that had to be taken into consideration in preparation of the kind of detailed proposals the United States placed before the Russians in spring and later on in August 1970. These were Plan E, covering both defensive and offensive missiles, including SLBMs (submarine-launched), ICBMs and bombers. Plan E excluded Forward Based Systems, which the United States did not want to discuss, but which the Russians insisted on including, because from the start they based their proposals on the principle that all strategic weapons systems must be included as long as they could hit the Soviet Union, regardless of their location. They had a plausible argument for including FBS, since U.S. forward based missiles are indeed quite capable of dropping nuclear weapons on the Soviet Union; but the United States did not accept the Soviet definition of "strategic weapons." The FBS have a dual conventional and tactical role and there is no way of limiting their strategic role without losing their tactical capability. The U.S. counterproposal that the United States would be prepared to discuss FBS if the Russians would include their IRBs in Eastern Europe was rejected by them; according to their definition, they were not strategic weapons capable of hitting the United States. Indirectly, though, the United States conceded that FBS had a strategic value when, after the Moscow summit, to fend off congressional accusations that the United States had accepted "inequality," Kissinger argued that this was not the case because the United States had its B-52 fleet, more warheads than the Soviet Union, and FBS aircraft. The problem of how to meet Soviet insistence to include FBS in any future agreements will be one of the difficult issues in SALT's Phase II.

Plan E set a limit of 1,900 offensive strategic missiles, including bombers, with sublimits of 1,710 ICBMs plus SLBMs; and either 100 ABMs for the defense of the capital or no ABMs at all, with limitations on radars in both cases. Land mobile ICBMs, the modification of silos and new hardened silos were to be forbidden. Since the Russians showed no interest in a MIRV ban, most likely because the United States was ahead in MIRV development but also because the United States had tied it to the need for on-site inspection, MIRV was excluded from the proposals. But by late 1970, it became clear that the Russians were not going to negotiate on the basis of Plan E. Instead, they pressed for an agreement limited to ABMs. The United States, on the other hand, firmly adhered to the principle that there could be no ABM agreement that was not linked to offensive missiles.

The arguments in favor of zero ABM used in the searing debate in Congress in 1969 over whether to proceed with Safeguard still make sense, but not if seen in the light of the eventual SALT agreement. It is quite correct that the best world is one without any ABMs but, as it turned out during the SALT talks, Safeguard became a decisive incentive for the Russians to seek an arms limitation agreement. What worried the Russians about the American ABM system was the awareness of their intelligence that it is better than theirs and that it can be improved.

HOW TO RESOLVE A DEADLOCK WITH THE RUSSIANS

There is a difference between seeing a problem purely from a theoretical viewpoint and seeing it from the White House, where the shrewd use of power must sometimes be allowed to prevail over logic and theory. When the Russians seemed hopelessly adamant about wanting only an ABM treaty, and continued to insist on the inclusion of Forward Based Systems in an offensive missile agreement, President Nixon decided to get in touch with the Kremlin directly. Whether or not he followed an idea put forward by Dean Rusk in December 1970, at a meeting of the General

Advisory Committee is not clear, but the President certainly thanked him for the suggestion.

In reply to the President's invitation, the Russians a few weeks later agreed to highly secret discussions to be conducted between Dr. Kissinger and Ambassador Dobrynin. These talks were limited to the terms on which an agreement in principle could be arrived at. The specifics in technical terms, however, continued to be hammered out between Smith and Semyonov. Smith, head of the American delegation to the SALT talks, knew nothing about the secret talks until about a week before the actual announcement on May 20 of the so-called agreement "in principle"; by contrast, the Russian delegation knew about them, but did not let on when they realized that their American opposite numbers had no inkling. It leads one to the fascinating speculation that in the Nixon administration the distribution of official documents is much more restricted than in the otherwise much more secretive and dictatorial regime in Moscow. Could it be that Soviet security arrangements were more secure? Secretary of Defense Laird for instance, who had a reputation for being indiscreet with the press, only heard about these negotiations a day before the agreement in principle was announced; and so did Secretary Rogers, though he may have had an earlier hint from the President.

In any event, the negotiations between Kissinger and Dobrynin remained an extraordinarily well-kept secret as they dragged on through four months. It was only after Kissinger had made it absolutely clear that the United States, for technical and political reasons, could never agree to the Russian demand for an ABM-only agreement—though there was public pressure for accepting such a limited agreement—that the Kremlin agreed to commit itself to discuss offensive missiles subsequently. Kissinger, however, insisted that this was not enough, that they would have to accept a ceiling on offensive missiles, including the SS9. The formal agreement of May 20, 1971, in principle firmly limited ABMs on both sides, but made such an agreement dependent on freezing ICBMs at their existing numbers, with an understanding that it would include a specific subceiling on the dreaded SS9, on which the ultimate survivability of the American Minuteman force depended.

The Kissinger-Dobrynin talks proved that deadlocks can be broken, if the situation is ripe, by an appeal to the very top. Dobrynin was given direct access to the Kremlin, though most likely via the Foreign Ministry, while Kissinger had the advantage of being able to get quick approval from the President without having to go through the State Department. Gerard Smith had to follow the strict instructions he received from Washington; the same was true for Semyonov and Moscow. The President accepted a serious risk when he agreed to the May 20 agreement, because he gave up a comprehensive treaty and went for a lesser goal without knowing what offensive missile arrangement he would be able to obtain.

THE DEADLOCK OVER SUBMARINES

The new negotiations after the breakthrough began with a sharp disagreement. The Russians insisted that submarine-based missiles had not been included in the freeze of offensive missiles, while the United States claimed that the whole history of the talks made it clear that they were included. It was a difficult impasse because the issue had not been clearly defined at the time the May 20 agreement of principle was concluded. At the White House, in fact, there had been doubts as to whether it was desirable to include the SLBMs in an initial agreement or whether it would be better to wait for a permanent accord of offensive missiles. No one quite knew what was the missile-submarine program of the Joint Chiefs of Staff for the late seventies. When questioned whether in view of the huge Soviet submarine program they wanted to start a crash program, as the United States had stopped building Polaris submarines five years earlier, they replied that they were against building more such submarines based on a 1950 technology. Moreover, they would have had to give up building attack submarines, to which they now attached greater importance than to Polaris. Thus, there was every reason for limiting the Russian submarine program. In fact, the Joint Chiefs of Staff made it clear that they would reject any agreement that did not include submarine-based missiles, and subsequently this issue became one of the most difficult to resolve—it almost wrecked the final SALT agreement.

In the eyes of some Disarmament Agency staffers Kissinger was a hardliner. At least he gave that impression because he tended to agree on many issues with the Joint Chiefs of Staff, who were of course a much more powerful group in government than the "disarmers," and needed extremely shrewd handling in a field they were unfamiliar with and which was altogether against their tradition. As were their Russian counterparts, they were at first against any agreement that might limit their own freedom to deploy new weapons, and everybody is well aware that they can still muster formidable congressional support whenever they choose to, particularly as regards new weaponry. But gradually they became more pliable, especially after they had extracted from Secretary Laird and the President a high price for their co-operation—support for the B-1 bomber and a new generation nuclear submarine, the Trident.

Another major point of disagreement that was resolved before the Moscow summit was the Russian objection to an asymmetrical limitation on ABMs, with the United States having four (later reduced to three and then two) Safeguard sites as against the Russian defense around Moscow which was still quite primitive. It consisted of sixty-four interceptors which could at maximum be destroyed by sixty-four re-entry vehicles: the sixty-fifth of course would then get through. The radar units were still mechanically operated, not electrically automated, and all the land-based missiles lacked hard fortifications. It would actually have taken only ten U.S. warheads to put the Russian radars out of action. The Soviet ABM defense, to the experts, was designed to maximize the coverage of the principal components of the armed forces and of the defense industries. The population coverage did not seem to be a decisive consideration and the main areas protected were in widely separated clusters, often only sparsely populated.

Smith and his team labored with extraordinary patience and skill, and gradually the outline for an eventual ABM treaty began to take shape during the sixth round of talks from November 1971 to February 1972. An agreement was reached for each side to have two ABM sites; the question, though, whether one would be to protect the capital—the Russians firmly insisted that one site must be around Moscow—was left open until the last round when the Joint Chiefs of Staff opted for two sites, one to protect Minuteman and another around Washington. One of the most remarkable achievements, and proof that the Russians were serious about a SALT agreement, were the strict limitations they accepted on radar developments. Without those strict limitations the ABM agreement would have been a sham.

When Kissinger flew to Moscow on the eve of the Moscow summit, the problem of the inclusion of the SLBMs, which had come to haunt him, was still deadlocked. Two weeks earlier he had given a new compromise plan to Dobrynin, who had shown himself to be more like a plenipotentiary than an ambassador and who, as he proved during the Moscow summit, knew how to explain the American point of view fairly. In that plan the United States did not insist on limiting the Russians to an equal number, but allowed them a substantial numerical advantage subject to their agreeing to reduce their obsolescent land-based SS7s and SS8s and their H-class submarines in ratio. This was to give the JCS the necessary lead time to complete the research and development for, and to start, the Trident program. One argument in favor of Trident was that it would give the Russians an incentive to negotiate a permanent offensive missile agreement, another that it was necessary for the 1980s, because by then Minutemen would be too vulnerable to the SS9 and the Russians might have made enough progress with their ASW (Advanced Anti-submarine Warfare) to expose Polaris submarines to detection. Having a much longer missile and cruising range, the Trident would be virtually invulnerable and would no longer need refueling bases in Scotland and Spain.

When Kissinger began to discuss the SLBM problem with Brezhnev, the Soviet leader replied with startling frankness that if the United States was worried about the Russian submarine program he would tell him that it aimed at sixty-two Polaris-type submarines and that he would not accept an agreement that called for an equal number on both sides. However, in many ways the latest U.S. compromise proposal was close to what Brezhnev was willing to settle for—in fact to the surprise of the Americans this was less than they had expected. Brezhnev had one important reservation—there had to be some compensation to make up for the British and French Polaris submarines. Kissinger rejected this, and then an argument developed about how many submarines the Soviet Union already owned and how many were under construction. This was important, so as to establish the base figure on which the agreement could be calculated, i.e., how many more would be built. American intelligence is confident that it has accurate information about the number of Soviet submarines already in service. It is quite uncertain about the number of those under way before they are moved into the assembly sheds, more certain about the number under construction once they are in the sheds, fairly certain about the number once they are actually taken out of the sheds. Brezhnev refused to accept the U.S. estimate of how many Polaris submarines the U.S.S.R. had in operation or under construction, but in the end he accepted a compromise figure for the eventual Russian submarine force. He also agreed to destroy SS7s and SS8s as well as the H-class submarines as the new Soviet Polaris submarines entered service.

Kissinger returned to Washington with this compromise, but still no agreement on what this meant in terms of the number of submarines the Russians would be able to build in future. It was a crucial issue, for quite obviously if the United States had accepted a Russian claim of forty-eight, while U.S. intelligence believed it should be forty, it would have enabled the Soviet Union to build eight submarines "for free."

SALT ON THE BRINK

Smith in his negotiations with Semyonov had virtually clinched the ABM limitation treaty—the most significant achievement of the SALT talks to date—but nothing was agreed until everything was agreed. And to overcome the very last hurdles the President's intervention had become indispensable.

Such was the situation when Mr. Nixon arrived in Moscow. Important progress was made in breaking a few of the deadlocks during the first long session between him and Chairman Brezhnev on Tuesday. They related to the missile silo size and the base figure for ballistic missile launchers on nuclear submarines. But important disagreements remained still unresolved. On Wednesday, after a long meeting at Mr. Brezhnev's *dacha*, dealing entirely with Vietnam, Dr. Kissinger met with Mr. Gromyko and Mr. Smirnov, a Deputy Prime Minister in charge of weapons production, at the Foreign Ministry. There they succeeded in whittling down the disagreements left to two issues: The question whether land-based ICBM silo launchers could or could not be increased in size—this was perhaps the most hotly contested—and what should be the clear and unambiguous definition of the base figure to avoid a debate over how many submarines were "under construction," since the Russians still refused to divulge exact numbers. The deadlock continued, especially over the second issue, and was once again tackled when everybody returned to the Foreign Ministry after the *Swan Lake* performance at the Bolshoi Theater. The meeting lasted until well after midnight and for the first time it looked as if the issues had been narrowed far enough to warrant a final decision from the Politburo. According to all indications available, it met, in fact, on Thursday morning and possibly once more later that day.

Time was running out. It looked as if this issue would hold up the signing of the agreement, until on Friday morning Mr. Smirnov brought news from the Kremlin that an agreement had been reached on the basis of the American suggestions of Wednesday evening. Thus the green light came only two and a half hours before the time set for the signing of the agreement.

Nixon knew the outer limits to which he could compromise. He was in daily touch with the civilian and military experts in Washington to check on any new wrinkle proposed by the Russian negotiators. He wanted a SALT agreement badly; it would not only make a great difference in U.S.-Soviet relations, it would not only help him politically at home to say that he had smoothed the way for "a generation of peace" at the Moscow summit, but it would also ensure that his name would go down in history as the man who laid the cornerstone for international arms control. During the Thursday night impasse, however, the President determined that he could go no further and that if necessary he would accept failure. He expected that the country would back him up if he explained that a SALT agreement had foundered because he had refused to risk the future of U.S. security. But he also hoped, having gained the impression that the Russians too wanted a SALT agreement badly, and having seen the Politburo swallow the mining of Haiphong, that the odds on the Russians accepting the final terms, which looked to him fair to both sides, were good.

Both sides renounced the option of a nationwide ABM defense system and agreed to limit deployment of ABMs and associate systems to two sites. The second Russian ABM site would be to protect their population and their industrial centers near the Urals against the Chinese. Both sides, however, retained the freedom, though with some important reservations, to modernize their weapons. Offensive missiles were frozen at their existing levels, including those already under construction. MIRV was not banned, but after ABMs had been limited to two hundred, there was no really convincing reason to proceed with MIRVing. No one, however, in the Pentagon accepts this argument and the Soviet "military-industrial complex" probably does not either. The United States does not want to give the appearance of "inferiority"; the Russians probably want to prove that they are "can do" people who can MIRV equally well.

The danger that the Russians might gain superiority in warheads was farfetched. What could happen, though, is that, thanks to their heavier ICBMs, they may gain something close to a 4-to-1 superiority in "throw-weight." That is why the United States put the Russians on notice that it would want to move toward numerical parity of ICBMs in Phase II of the SALT talks. Historically, one of the most important limitations agreed on, despite initial opposition by the Pentagon, was the banning of the testing and deployment of future sea-, air- and space-based and mobile land-based missile systems, for governments have never before agreed in such a precisely worded form to forgo the deployment and development of weapons systems which do not yet exist, yet which, like ABMs relying on laser beams, are not beyond fantasy and are on the verge of getting onto the drawing boards. The American and Russian military disliked the idea of a ceiling on technological developments; they were up till then willing to talk only about numerical, not qualitative, limits.

The extent to which suspicions between these two countries have subsided was reflected in the special accord that neither side would interfere with the other's observation satellites: This is a far cry from the days when one U-2, as it did in 1960, led to the cancellation of a summit meeting. It shows how sophisticated both sides had become in assessing the value of overhead reconnaissance. Already in 1969, just before the start of the SALT talks, the United States had concluded that by combining satellite, aircraft and other technological means of reconnaissance it would be able to monitor a strategic arms limitation program. It was a key conclusion that paved the way for a general acceptance of the SALT talks throughout the United States Government.

The debate about whether Mr. Nixon had negotiated an agreement that had protected American interests or whether he had, in fact, conceded "inferiority" began almost as soon as the ink dried on the parchment. In Congress, Senator Scoop Jackson, Democrat from Washington, a much listened-to critic in national security affairs, complained, for instance, that the United States had failed to get the Russians to specify the exact number of ICBMs they had in operation and under construction. The United States used the number 1,618 in its calculations, confident that it could discover with national means of verification any new ICBM construction built in violation of the agreement. What really mattered, however, was that the Russians had agreed to a subceiling for heavy missiles of 313. It did not seem, therefore, worth risking the entire agreement for the sake of a figure that was not essential. The criticism voiced by Senator Jackson that the offensive missile agreement did not prohibit specifically enough a "significant" increase in the size of heavy missile launchers for the freeze period had some validity. However, the Russians argued that the freeze was only a short-term agreement, a kind of moratorium, and that specific restrictions were only appropriate to a treaty, and, furthermore, the freeze on heavier missiles than the SS-11, in fact, applied only to them. There was some logic in their argument, for they had given proof that in the ABM treaty they had accepted highly specific limitations. In the last stretch, however, during the Moscow summit negotiations, they did accede at least to a ceiling on the size of heavy launchers. While Senator Jackson's criticisms were essentially technical, those of Senator James Buckley, Republican from New York, were total. Buckley questioned the "basic doctrine" underlying the SALT agreement.

On the left of Mr. Nixon, everybody praised the importance of the ABM agreement, but denounced the requests for the next generation nuclear weapons, the B-1 bomber and the Trident. I doubt whether a President less known for his anti-Communist bias could have gained the broad acceptance for the SALT agreement Mr. Nixon obtained. It was a pity that Secretary Laird, even as he defended the SALT agreement, took advantage of it to exert alarmist pressure on Congress to get approval for Trident and the B-1, which he had already forced into the military budget for 1972–73. Whether or not these two new weapons were essential, it struck altogether the wrong note for the Nixon administration to allow this move toward peace to be used in this way to further an escalation of the arms race.

The NATO allies, of course, watched the SALT negotiations and the American behavior with bated breath and an eagle eye. They were anxious, however well briefed at intervals, that the United States should not give away something that would in any way affect their own interests. Nothing of the kind occurred, and the comforting conclusion they could draw from Phase I was that because of the low level of permitted ABM deployment and the geographical separation of the two sites, the British and French nuclear deterrents have remained unimpaired. Both still have the power at least theoretically, to threaten Moscow, which they would have lost had the SALT agreement permitted a major Russian ABM deployment.

In Phase II, however, it will be difficult not to come to grips with Forward Based Systems, which form an important part of the defense of Western Europe and include all nuclear weapons and their delivery vehicles, mainly fighter bombers, based outside the continental United States and which have the capability of attacking targets in the U.S.S.R. The "no-transfer" clauses in the ABM Treaty and their interpretive statements create no problems for NATO. They could, however, do so later if, following this precedent, these same clauses were included in an offensive missile treaty; for the nuclear exchange agreement between the United States and Britain will expire in 1974, and if Britain decides to proceed with building a Poseidon warhead it will need continued co-operation from the United States. In that case, I doubt whether the White House, by refusing to co-operate, would want to deprive Britain of its own very limited deterrent. Yet the decision will not be up to the President alone. He will not be able to offer continued co-operation on the quiet on his own authority. A bitter and complex debate is bound to develop within the Administration and in Congress, and even if the President makes it clear that he favors a continuation of the nuclear exchange arrangement with Britain, the outcome of this debate is difficult to predict. What will further complicate it is the relevance of the French nuclear deterrent, the possibility of an Anglo-French deterrent and the effect of both on the U.S.-Soviet nuclear relationship.

IS IT WORTH ITS SALT?

Phase I of SALT turned out to be a much more promising beginning than most people had expected, even only a year previously. It will help to maintain a certain balance of power, but it will not halt the nuclear arms race or save as much money as was hoped, because it does not ban major "qualitative" improvements of offensive weapons systems. More money will also be needed to improve the collection of intelligence as a protection against any temptation on the part of the Soviets to cheat.

The United States continues to have a second-strike capability of such overwhelming power that no rational adversary would want to risk starting up the kind of conventional war that could quickly escalate to battlefield nuclear weapons and then to triggering the nuclear strategic arsenal. A recent National Security Council study on U.S. strategy endorsed the view, and the Joint Chiefs of Staff accepted it, that the Triad, which embraces ICBMs, SLBMs and bombers, should be considered as a whole and that each arm need not be "sufficient" in itself. There is also agreement that to launch a second strike, only one arm is needed to survive a Soviet first strike. The time will come, probably by 1980, when Minutemen will have become so vulnerable that they could be phased out and when the United States will be relying on SLBMs and, maybe, bombers. But for the time being, there should be no problem in maintaining the ICBM forces, which are comparatively cheap to keep up.

The Americans are not absolutely certain to what extent the Russian Chiefs of Staff have explicitly accepted the doctrine of "assured destruction" and the idea of sufficiency, but it is believed that the civilians concerned most likely have. They sometimes seemed to be almost eager to make common cause with the American negotiators against the Soviet military, especially after they realized how much more their counterparts knew about the scope and character of Soviet weaponry than they themselves did.

One of the controversies that continues on both sides between those favoring arms control and those in charge of new weapons development is whether a ban on testing would or would not be feasible. It was an important issue that surfaced time and again during the Phase I SALT talks. Much will depend on whether subsequent phases of the SALT talks merely develop into a competitive race as to who can better improve the quality of weapons and surpass the other in inventing new and exotic arms systems not yet banned, or whether they succeed in strangling the arms race.

A disturbing turn in the race, for instance, came to light when the highly reliable Pentagon correspondent of the New York Times, William Beecher, reported in August 1972 that the Nixon administration, contrary to earlier denials, was seeking to develop warheads accurate and powerful enough to destroy Russian missile silos, what are called "hard targets." He also reported that the Administration was seeking funds for a development that has been on the "wanted list" of the Joint Chiefs of Staff for a long time—a nuclear-tipped cruise missile that could even be fired from the torpedo tubes of non-missile submarines, one of those destabilizing weapons that was bound to arouse fears in Moscow.

These revelations startled not only the press, but agencies within the government such as the State Department. Highly placed officials, dumbfounded by the report and annoyed by having been kept in the dark, called for a meeting of the Defense Program Review Committee to find out what was actually going on. "Such surprises are the result of overcentralization," one enraged high official complained. "Too few guys are doing too many things. These issues have not been discussed, nobody knows much about them." The suspicion was that Secretary Laird must somehow have obtained presidential consent, obviously without proper consultation within the government.

Kissinger reported after the Moscow summit that the Russians had made it clear during the negotiations that they would proceed with building yet bigger missiles than they already had in their arsenal and which, of course, if MIRVed could offer a first-strike capability. Whether the recognition of this threat led the President to give the green light to Secretary Laird, or whether it was a move to gain a new "bargaining chip" for Phase II of SALT whose principal objective, at least from the American viewpoint, will be to reduce the danger of a counterforce threat against American land-based missiles, was not clear.

But the decision, seemingly carelessly taken, was a clear illustration of the vicious circle of the nuclear arms race: First the United States decided to proceed with MIRV for protective reasons, and the Russians to build heavier warheads than the United States to keep the deterrent stable. Then, when the Russians perceived that MIRV could not only be protective but with sufficient accuracy represent a first-strike threat, they began to experiment with MIRV themselves. American intelligence at the time this chapter was written was convinced that the Russians had no MIRVed warheads yet. But with the prospect of the Russians' bigger missiles being MIRVed sooner or later, the United States perceived a new danger to its land-based ICBMs and began to get ready to leap up one more rung on the ladder of escalation: warheads against "hard" targets and—for a time, even further in the future—the cruise missile. This escalation brings home not only how important it will be to prevent the nuclear balance from being destabilized in Phase II, but also how limited were the results of Phase I. The long history of the cold war, the mutual suspicions and the fears on either side that the other may gain an advantage die hard. Both the United States and the Soviet Union publicly claim that they are restraining themselves to pursue only stabilizing strategic policies, but these claims do not ring true.

The SALT Phase I accord was an agreement without precedent, and as such worth taking. Though it was only a first step, it led to the hope that a new rationality is entering international relations, at least between the United States and the Soviet Union, and that President Nixon may indeed have shown a way that would begin "to free us from perpetual confrontation." It codified a principle that matters greatly to the pride and self-confidence of the Soviet Union, that parity now exists between the two superpowers. But there is a real danger that both sides will now try to race each other through the doors left open and unguarded by the new agreements. There is no reason to believe that President Nixon has accepted inferiority. This is one area where the United States is not retreating in terms of actual power, but where it continues in fact to maintain a qualitative advantage, even if this cannot be exploited politically. Whatever one may think of Mr. Nixon's negotiating techniques, whether it is the controversial linkage theory or "negotiating from strength" or the often criticized "bargaining chip" approach, the fact remains that he did succeed in concluding a vital, workable and substantial agreement as a first step toward the dispersal of that cloud of ultimate doom that has hung over the world ever since Hiroshima.

CHAPTER EIGHTEEN—A LACQUER
PAINTING AND THE VIETNAM WAR

It cannot be quite by accident and without significance that in Mr. Nixon's own private bedroom in his villa in San Clemente, and directly above his bed, hangs a typical Vietnamese lacquer painting, a river scene. It was presented to him when, as Vice President, he and his wife visited Vietnam and one of the many refugee camps. The refugees had pooled their pennies, he likes to recall, and bought this Vietnam scene as an expression of their welcome to the Nixons. As lacquer paintings go, it is not a masterpiece, and quite obviously Mr. Nixon hung it in this privileged position not for its artistry but because it symbolized his very personal, perhaps even emotional, attachment to Vietnam. One cannot altogether resist speculating on what influence this picture hanging over his bed for years has had on his dreams.

It was not surprising, therefore, that he more than anybody else in his Administration insisted, as he put it in his impassioned appeal on national television on November 3, 1969, on "an orderly scheduled timetable" for the withdrawal of the American forces from Vietnam. "If a vocal minority, however fervent its cause," he then said challengingly, "prevails over reason and the will of the majority, this nation has no future as a free society." His aim was, as he explained privately to the visiting New Zealand Prime Minister Jack Holyoake, to prevent South Vietnam coming under communism, and he claimed to be convinced that Vietnamization could succeed, that there was no need to change the Thieu regime and that American public opinion would remain patient for long enough. He banked on being able to consolidate the majority of Americans who, he thought, preferred an honorable gradual withdrawal to the humiliation of a hurried escape which would be equivalent to a defeat. By polarizing the so-called "Silent Majority" against the vocal minority opposing the war, he hoped to isolate the liberals and radicals. To a surprising extent, he succeeded in buying time for his strategy. The protesters with their mass marches on Washington helped rather than hindered him, even though they succeeded in drawing attention to the revulsion against the war among the young.

For almost a year, the White House was uncertain about the military situation on the ground, but by starting to withdraw troops and announcing that 115,000 would leave Vietnam by April 1970, and by renouncing the use of biological weapons, he created a climate of public patience, however unstable. Nixon sounded to people as if he had a disengagement plan, and so they tended to give him a chance to carry it out. The country was still cruelly divided, but violence had 'abated.

DIVIDE AND GOVERN

No serious ghetto riots occurred in 1969 and the turbulence on the campuses, too, had declined. But did the Silent Majority, which lacks understanding of social problems and of the world beyond American shores, represent a broad enough political base to enable him to govern? Could he have done better if, instead of accentuating the bitterness among the eastern Establishment, which still had its sources, though declining, of strength and influence in the country, he had encouraged it to co-operate? Could he, instead of shouldering much of the blame for Vietnam and making it gradually his war, have pinned it on the Establishment that bore a major responsibility for it, by accepting its demands for a quick withdrawal? At least until the Cambodian operation, he seemed to have gained their grudging sympathy, almost admiration. President Kennedy, after the Bay of Pigs catastrophe, went out of his way to appeal for support from the Establishment and succeeded. Mr. Nixon would have found it much more difficult to win over his natural enemies, although several intellectuals suggested to Henry Kissinger that Mr. Nixon should at least try.

But Mr. Nixon and Kissinger were less afraid of the liberal Establishment than of the emergence of a Caesar of the right in the wake of a precipitous withdrawal from Vietnam which would ravage American pride and outrage patriotism. In fact, they were incensed by what they considered irresponsible demands by the Establishment which, they felt, was more interested in undermining the President than keeping the country together. They saw extremism growing on the Right and the Left, and the middle weakened as a consequence. They did not believe that to appease the Establishment would help strengthen the presidency. In any case, Mr. Nixon did not simply want to throw in the towel in Vietnam, which was what more and more Democrats and some liberal Republicans were proposing; he wanted to make the best possible effort to organize the withdrawal so as to ensure that the American blood spilled in Vietnam would not have been spilled altogether in vain. The great and unresolved question was whether such a controlled retreat was politically and military feasible. However, he was confident that by demonstrating that he was winding down the war, he could gather enough support in Congress and in the country at large. Could he have saved American lives by withdrawing faster? The analysts concluded that given the goal of wanting to avoid defeat, he could not.

KISSINGER AND LAIRD IN CONFLICT

His closest advisers differed on his prospects with this plan. Kissinger thought that if it had a chance of success, it would have to be through a negotiated settlement, and he hoped that an equitable one was possible; he had little confidence in Vietnamization. Defense Secretary Laird, whose task it was to transform the ineffective de-Americanization programs of the Johnson administration into Vietnamization—the difference in the Madison Avenue approach was telling—considered it more as a clever cover behind which to manage a rapid American disengagement. Mr. Rogers did not come forward with any concrete proposals for withdrawal, but, at least initially, he was thoroughly in favor of it.

The President decided on a withdrawal strategy in February, but he did not tell anybody except one or two of his closest advisers. It was more than a tactical decision, though for about a year no one could give him an estimate of the military situation on the ground with any assurance of reliability. The big question was how fast troops could be withdrawn without seriously jeopardizing South Vietnam's internal security. To reach more reliable conclusions, Kissinger decided to send his own team to Vietnam, headed by Major General Haig, who combined the knowledge of a military with an intelligent civilian mind. They culled all the existing studies, checked them carefully to see to what extent they could corroborate their findings, and concluded that by carefully meshing the withdrawal rate with the military risks involved a policy could be developed to sustain the President's strategy. The NSC staff then created an analytical base and framework for the phasing out of U.S. forces and for estimating the risks to security in the Vietnamese countryside.

McNamara and the Johnson administration used to be accused of running too much of a rational war, but actually the systems analysts played a minimal role. Kissinger, however, pushed systems analysis to the limit with his use of Dr. Larry Lynn, who used to be one of Robert McNamara's whiz kids, as his chief expert. This brought him into collision with Secretary Laird, who became a tireless advocate of withdrawal but did not want to devote much effort toward finding a carefully calculated basis for it; he was more interested in the political implications for himself and the President.

The conclusion of the field investigators was that the North Vietnamese had indeed suffered unconscionable losses of life in the Tet offensive and that the consequent gains for the American and South Vietnamese forces had been preserved. Without the North Vietnamese guerrilla forces, with the village leadership gone and the main-force elements decimated, the enemy was forced to change from a main-force war to a protracted war strategy.

However, by April 1970, the gains from the Tet offensive began to level off, and one of the secret, so-called "countryside" papers produced by the Vietnam Special Study Group in that month raised warning signals.

A DISTURBING FIELD ANALYSIS

These field studies covered the over-all situation in Vietnam, the consequences of the redeployment of U.S. forces, how a cease-fire would affect security in Vietnam, the state of the war and of Vietnamization, and a report on the economic situation.

The April 1970 report, for instance, showed that the leadership of the Thieu government was improving but that serious weaknesses remained, and that it was mainly accepted as the lesser of two evils. It concluded that if the U.S. troop withdrawals continued at the currently planned rates through to July 1971, the control of the Thieu governmental machine would suffer, especially in two provinces, Binh Dinh and Quang Nam.

In case the North Vietnamese accepted the President's "leopard" cease-fire proposal (so-called because it would have left the GVN in control of some parts of South Vietnam, the Vietcong of others, depending on where each dominated the area), the report concluded, the GVN would gain in three provinces, while two would be a tossup. In terms of population, the GVN was in control of 62 per cent of the population, and though this represented "dramatic progress," the analysts nevertheless concluded that they were not confident that the GVN could significantly increase its control during 1970. One reason was that the Vietcong infrastructure, they estimated, was largely intact. They ventured to predict, however, that a cease-fire a year ahead, with Vietnamization expected to gain further ground, would be to the advantage of the GVN in five provinces instead of the mere three of April 1970. The enemy force structure was estimated at 340,000 to 485,000 men, of whom 220,000 to 290,000 were part of the North Vietnamese Army. This was a decline of 100,000 men or around 25 per cent. The guerrilla forces had declined by 50 per cent to about 50,000.

Still, in April 1970, they concluded, a formidable enemy main-force threat existed in four provinces in the Mekong Delta region.

Allied ability to meet this threat would almost certainly decline as U.S. forces continued to be withdrawn. Detailed recommendations as to which units in what provinces could be withdrawn followed. As an example: in Thua Thieu Province, one or two of the three U.S. brigades were thought to be dispensable; in Quang Nam, however, any U.S. withdrawal within the next eighteen months was seen as raising difficulties in preserving the gains achieved so far. In Bien Hoa, for instance, the situation deteriorated after the withdrawal of the U.S. brigade, and the same applied to Dinh Tuong.

In many ways, the above facts from this field report, prepared by Kissinger's men on the basis of their own studies and not on reports from province chiefs, as had been the method under the Johnson administration, created a good deal of uneasiness about the future of the Nixon withdrawal policy. It was one of the contributing factors in the decision to clean out the enemy sanctuaries across the border in Cambodia, and early the following year to invade Laos and to cut across the Ho Chi Minh Trail. It is generally claimed that the Cambodian operation gained one year; the Lam Son operation into Laos, however, was a letdown. Some simply blamed its failure on the fact that the GVN were outnumbered 2 to 1 and that U.S. intelligence, while warning that two enemy regiments were in readiness close to the Demilitarized Zone, did not expect both of them to move into Laos and leave the DMZ altogether defenseless. Others blamed the poor performance of the GVN and President Thieu's refusal to throw another four thousand men into the battle as he had originally promised. He got cold feet when the staggering losses of the GVN threatened to hurt him politically.

TRAPPED BY WESTERN LOGIC

Now that the withdrawal of American troops began to reach a critical level, the debate as to the pace of the withdrawal began to get more heated. The Joint Chiefs of Staff and General Abrams began to fight for every resource to be kept in Vietnam and strongly recommended a slowing down. Secretary Laird held to his view that the forces should be withdrawn as fast as possible; his military aide General Robert Pursley had always been a great protagonist of a fast withdrawal.

Kissinger maintained that the two-track approach of linking negotiations with troop withdrawals he originally designed should be adhered to. The President agreed that he had to take whatever risks it involved and stepped up the pace of withdrawal to preserve public support for his policy at home.

To counter the military advice, the President was able to cite a new analysis produced by the NSC which showed that South Vietnam was under much better control than had been admitted and that the ARVN was by now ready to assume responsibility for the fighting. Furthermore, in terms of supplies and logistical support, the North Vietnamese did not have the capability to stage another Tet offensive, with the supply route from Sihanoukville dried up and the Ho Chi Minh Trail pipeline temporarily disrupted. Kissinger, in the meantime, tried to keep the second track lubricated—the Paris negotiations with the North Vietnamese. During his secret trips to Paris, he had a try at tackling the hard issues with Hanoi's Le Duc Tho, a member of the Politburo and hence a man of some authority, and for a while it looked as if some progress was being made. The Americans committed themselves for the first time to a definite date of withdrawal for all troops and to President Thieu's stepping down one month in advance of new elections, but to the North Vietnamese Thieu's readiness to resign looked like an empty gesture and nothing more than a stepping stone to perpetuating his rule. Then came the sudden announcement of Kissinger's trip to China. The White House had hoped it would impress Hanoi sufficiently to make it soften its stand, but it seemed to have the opposite effect. Also, the North Vietnamese had by then decided to stake everything on military victory. Le Duc Tho broke off the secret negotiations in the autumn, which puzzled and disturbed Kissinger. The North Vietnamese, not for the first time, refused to follow the logic of the Western mind.

The intelligence that came in from the field was also disturbing. There were worrisome signs of road building through the

DMZ and the launching of an offensive between January and July 1972 was seen as a serious possibility by the Vietnam Review Group. A plot to embarrass Mr. Nixon either during his stay in Peking or later in Moscow or during the election campaign seemed in the making. By January, an unusually heavy flow of supplies and manpower, quite inconsistent with previous patterns, was discovered and reinforced the prognostication for a new offensive. CIA estimates, which had come under White House criticism for a few earlier misjudgments, were fairly accurate in predicting the general perimeter of the offensive, though its main thrust came across the DMZ and not against the highlands near Kontum; the use of much mechanized equipment to back it up was also expected, but not to the extent that quickly became apparent.

The offensive was quite different in character from any previous one. It was much more mobile and instead of relying on mortars and rockets, as in the past, it was led by hundreds of tanks and supported by heavy artillery barrages. It looked as if the North Vietnamese had decided to gamble everything on a military decision, and it confirmed the suspicion that their earlier offers at the negotiating table were a feint behind which this big military gamble was being prepared. The Russians had provided them with masses of sophisticated weapons, from 600–1,000 T-54 tanks to 130 tube artillery pieces to anti-tank weapons to heat-seeking anti-aircraft guns. The war had changed its character; the ambiguities of the past as to whether it was still a civil war or an invasion from the North had suddenly been discarded. Saigon was convinced that the GVN had made enough progress to defend itself against the guerrilla-type warfare of the past, but it was doubtful whether it had enough strength to withstand such a powerful conventional and yet highly sophisticated onslaught. To President Nixon this was the ultimate challenge. Were the North Vietnamese trying to prove that he had been bluffing? He had threatened many times that he would find ways of retaliating if the North Vietnamese took military advantage of the withdrawal of the American forces. They did not realize how implacable he could be. Nor did they know about the lacquer painting over his bed.

Kissinger told me in August 1971 that he thought everything then depended on whether the North Vietnamese believed they could gain by waiting until the United States was down to a residual force in the South; or whether they had decided they could not wait because Saigon would then be able to preserve the independence of South Vietnam on its own. At one point in the secret negotiations in the summer of 1972, the North Vietnamese proposed to Kissinger a settlement that would have meant a camouflaged American acceptance of Hanoi's terms, a face-saving device, or what Joseph Kraft had called a "fig leaf." But Kissinger rejected the offer. Mr. Nixon did not just look for a sham agreement, he insisted on one that would meet his basic minimum conditions. Kissinger continued to assume that Hanoi would prefer a negotiated solution to another military confrontation. But once again the North Vietnamese were not willing to play the game by the rules thought up by others and by more logical minds than theirs. Nixon, however, insisted that the game be played by the rules he set, though he had also shown considerable readiness to make concessions. He also resented being pressed with his back against the wall. As he saw it, Hanoi was trying to take military advantage of the departure of the American troops, which he had warned them not to do, and of his summitry which they thought would tie his hands politically.

CALLING A BLUFF THAT WASN'T

If President Nixon did not share President Johnson's view about winning the war, he nevertheless was convinced that he must avoid losing it. But unlike Mr. Laird, who invented Vietnamization as an excuse for getting out as fast as possible, he really believed in it and in the possibility that President Thieu could prevent South Vietnam from going Communist. The trouble was that even Hanoi believed in it. The mounting of the big military offensive in the spring of 1972 was proof that it was afraid the Nixon strategy could succeed. To accept a military solution that excluded the overthrow of Thieu, therefore, looked to them like defeat and like twenty-five years of fighting in vain. But Mr.

Nixon flatly refused to agree to the one condition that remained the great stumbling block between him and Hanoi—to impose a coalition of the kind Hanoi demanded, which entailed the removal of Thieu; in his mind this could only lead to a Communist take-over and he did not want to be party to such a betrayal of his own goals.

Therefore, when the North Vietnamese launched their powerful attack in three regions, clearly designed to knock out the South Vietnamese Army and with it the Thieu regime, he ordered virtually the full panoply of sea and air power, short of nuclear power, into the area not only as a show of force, but to unleash it if necessary. The North Vietnamese, attacking in unexpected strength, found that Mr. Nixon had not been bluffing. Once again the fires of this tragic war were feeding on a chain of miscalculations. It seemed reasonable for Hanoi to assume, at least on past experience, that Mr. Nixon's options for retaliation against their most powerfully armed offensive were very limited. Probably the last thing they expected was his daring to mine Haiphong Harbor on the eve of the Moscow summit. He had threatened *ad nauseam* that if they changed the ground rules, so would he, but quite obviously they did not believe him.

Actually the President surprised not only the North Vietnamese and the Kremlin, but also most members of his own Administration. The latter and the critics outside the Administration judged the situation from the strategic perspective of 1968, which had become, at least in the President's and Kissinger's mind, totally fallacious. They faulted the McNamara school of systems analysis for being excessively mechanical and for imposing the test of "worst assumption," which meant that there was no choice between defeat and 100 per cent foolproof, guaranteed success. Under the Kissinger option method, the assumption was that a sound decision could not simply be restricted to these two extremes, that there was a need to consider all factors and to assess the various risks they involved.

According to the Pentagon Papers, the Joint Chiefs of Staff urged on President Johnson as early as October 1966 that the ports be mined and a "naval quarantine" be imposed to "decrease the Hanoi and Haiphong sanctuary areas." Secretary McNamara in a draft memorandum in May 1967, however, rejected the military demands for intense bombing of the North and the mining of enemy harbors. "No combination of actions against the North short of destruction of the regime or occupation of the North Vietnamese territory will physically reduce the flow of men and matériel . . . needed by enemy forces to continue the war in the South," he wrote, and later again he argued: "The picture of the world's greatest superpower killing or injuring 1,000 noncombatants a week, while trying to pound a tiny backward nation into submission on an issue whose merits are hotly disputed, is not a pretty one. It could conceivably produce a costly distortion in the American national consciousness and in the world image of the United States—especially if the damage to North Vietnam is complete enough to be 'successful.'" But there was also the added consideration that mining North Vietnam's ports would be seen in Moscow and Peking as a challenge to their prestige and a test of the extent to which they were willing to support an ally. At that time also, neither Ambassador Llewellyn Thompson nor Allen Whiting, the State Department's leading China specialist, excluded the possibility that such action would provoke both the Soviet Union and China into war; in fact, Whiting was convinced that it would as far as China was concerned. In early 1969, NSSM-1 showed that the views had not really changed. The military favored a blockade because it would reduce North Vietnam's capacity to reinforce aggression in South Vietnam; the Central Intelligence Agency, in contrast, argued that the effect of a blockade "would be widespread but temporary" until alternative supply routes by road and rail were organized, and that experience had shown that air attacks alone could not interdict ground transport routes over an extended period.

In early 1972, the situation was quite different. The United States by then had established a new relationship with China, and was in process of doing so with the Soviet Union, which raised the common interests among the three into a different range. The Nixon administration had produced proposals for a peace settlement—none had existed in 1967—and had already withdrawn close to five hundred thousand men. Both the Kremlin and Peking seemed to be fed up with the military strategy pursued by Hanoi and would not intervene directly. The three great powers, each for their own reasons, had reached the conclusion that it was better for everybody to bring this ill-fated war to an end. The Chinese most likely preferred a neutral buffer to unification and did not want South Vietnam to be destroyed by sophisticated Russian military equipment, which made Hanoi even more dependent on Moscow. The Russians were losing their keenness as Hanoi's appetite for newer and better weapons grew.

When President Nixon actively began to consider the possibility of imposing a blockade and requested the principal agencies concerned to submit their recommendations, the NSC staff committee, which had studied the issue once before in 1970, expressed a view strongly in favor of the operation. Only one staffer dissented. Kissinger himself, in contrast, was so skeptical of the idea that he was considered as being against it. His reservations were based on the old theory that it would not make a great deal of difference to the outcome of the war and that it would unnecessarily upset the extraordinary progress he had made in preparing the Moscow summit meeting. The military, including Kissinger's deputy, General Haig, were in favor of the operation; Secretary Laird, however, disliked it because of the dire repercussions, he thought, it would have in Congress and among the public. Secretary Rogers also had very little stomach for this venture; in fact, his intervention delayed the final decision by one day. There was one member of the Cabinet, though, who strongly and unequivocally urged the President to proceed with the mining—John B. Connally. It gave him a great deal of satisfaction later on to have outmaneuvered Kissinger on a foreign policy issue and to have the President follow his recommendation. What created so much apprehension was the risk to the newly created relationships with Peking and Moscow, and to the SALT agreement which, rationally, looked to most a much more important development in the history of the Nixon administration, and in history generally. But there was that lacquer painting above the President's bed.

With so much coolness throughout the Administration toward

the idea of a blockade, the President decided to wait until there was no ambiguity about what the enemy was up to. Once he made his decision, however, he poured in all the resources necessary to give the blockade every chance of success. Then in cold blood and with steely determination he ordered the mining of all North Vietnamese harbors and an intensified bombing campaign against all important military targets. There was still a great deal of skepticism and no enthusiasm within the bureaucracy, but by now the President had built up a certain equity with decisions he took against official advice and proved right, and so everybody closed ranks, loyally accepted his judgment and backed it without either hidden or carefully leaked dissent.

A NEW WAR

Suddenly, it was a new and quite different war. The North Vietnamese had set the pace, but the United States was catching up fast and getting ahead. B-52s were used as never before to stem the tide of the attack, and the Phantoms were given "smart bombs" that hit targets with an accuracy not previously achieved. Fire power was unleashed as never before in history, and the American public watched the spectacle with awe and mortification. The peace movement Hanoi had relied on in the past to force the President's hand failed to gain momentum for another protest wave. The President's withdrawal policy and the virtual end of the draft had deprived it of its emotional propellant. The young, having been unsuccessful in influencing the war decisively (though they should be credited with having left the President no alternative but to hurry up with the withdrawal of American forces), turned to the presidential campaign to sublimate their drive to change things. It was a new turn of the protest movement, a return to work within the "system," which they first tried, but failed, to destroy. Hanoi was suddenly not only bereft of one of its most effective political weapons, but it also could not help but sense the new detachment in Moscow and Peking. The North Vietnamese offensive was in full swing when Kissinger suddenly flew to Moscow on April 20. The main purpose was to prepare the

summit meeting, though by then he had an inkling that the prospects for the meeting actually taking place had become tenuous.
In his meetings with Chairman Brezhnev, therefore, Kissinger took
care also to indicate the concern the new North Vietnamese offensive was causing President Nixon. He even gave the Russian
leader a highly confidential advance look at the latest proposals for
a cease-fire and a peace settlement that the President had decided
to offer Hanoi. (The speech in which he did so, then still not announced, was given on May 8.) Kissinger wanted to stress to
Brezhnev that, in spite of the turn of events, the United States
remained genuinely anxious to end the war, and that the conditions it would offer were reasonable. Brezhnev seemed impressed
by the new propositions.

By the time the President got ready to leave for Moscow, Quan
Tri had fallen, but the spearhead of the attacks seemed to have
been halted before Hue, Kontum and An Loc. It was in the middle
of the offensive, as if to prove that nothing could divert him from
his withdrawal policy, that the President announced another reduction of twenty thousand men. Secretary Laird immediately
sent a cable to General Abrams, the commanding general of the
U.S. forces in Vietnam, that he was sorry this had to be done at
this awkward moment, but he hoped he would accept this decision
without protest. When Abrams in his reply agreed, symbolically
clicking his heels and saluting like a good soldier, Laird was so
moved that he called in his private staff and read the cable to
them. Abrams was not a political soldier, he was a commander
of men. When he got orders, he accepted them; he did not try by
more or less devious means to get his resentment out into the
public.

And so the struggle reached its last crucial stage. The ARVN,
supported by American air power, held its ground better than
Hanoi had expected, and once again the war stood at stalemate.
Between this and a similar situation in 1968 thousands more lives
had been lost and vast amounts of money squandered, and huge
areas of both Vietnams had been pushed back toward the Stone
Age. The North Vietnamese were not much closer to gaining control over South Vietnam, and Vietnamization, the United States

could claim, had passed its test. In the White House the feeling was, and more strongly than ever before, that only the presidential election was delaying the end of the war. Did Americans really care about preventing South Vietnam from going Communist? Mr. Nixon did and more than most. Time and again, with steely eyes, he said to his aides that he would rather lose the election and not be President than accept terms which would mean an American defeat in Vietnam. Nor could he wish it on to any successor, because he would not want to dishonor the American presidency. Most of his aides were convinced, too, that—however much of a politician Nixon is—American Presidents are different from most other heads of government. They think that they are a very special clan, that something binds them, irrespective of party, for they have gone through an experience, and they know things that nobody else knows and nobody else can appreciate. Mr. Nixon certainly thinks this way, and Presidents Eisenhower and Kennedy used to speak in the same terms about the presidency.

The Vietnam policy, was run and supervised by the President himself. Not surprisingly, he became increasingly impatient with the lack of progress of the Paris negotiations the closer the presidential election date approached. To Kissinger, the negotiations in Paris and the impatience of the President added up to a nightmare.

The Kremlin's interest in the continuation of the war and that of Peking had sharply declined; the Peking and Moscow summits had been held in spite of Hanoi's undisguised outrage; on the battlefield the North Vietnamese had failed to score a decisive victory; and the expected internal uprising against the Thieu regime had not materialized. Even the public pressures on President Nixon in the United States to end the war before Election Day were far from what Hanoi had hoped for. Yet, the North Vietnamese remained hard bargainers. One thing, though, had become obvious to both sides: The war could not be decided by military means nor could either side expect to win at the conference table what it had failed to achieve on the battlefield.

On October 8, the long-awaited breakthrough occurred. The North Vietnamese made the admission on October 26 when they became fearful that President Nixon would not initial the draft peace settlement before Election Day. Their revelation hit the White House like a "smart bomb" and forced Kissinger, a few hours after his return from strenuous talks in Saigon, to face the press and to counter Hanoi's accusations that Mr. Nixon was delaying peace. Thus, a situation that he had hoped to iron out in secret became a dramatic and public deadlock. Now Kissinger had to steer a tricky course in public between the Scylla of Hanoi and the Charybdis of Saigon, to prevent the "peace at hand" from slipping through his fingers.

And so the greatest moment of Kissinger's White House career turned into a period of greatest agony. Nothing had mattered to him more than to bring the war to an end. He had favored a carefully controlled withdrawal, not a surrender; nevertheless, his objectives were more limited than Mr. Nixon's. He had always been aware of the very uncertain future an independent non-Communist South Vietnam would be facing. Only President Thieu's stubbornness now stood in the way of his ultimate triumph. Somehow with an unusual lack of foresight Kissinger had overrated his ability to persuade the South Vietnamese leader to accept the terms he had negotiated; not even the verdict of General Abrams, who by then had become the Army's Chief of Staff, that the terms were "manageable" from South Vietnam's point of view helped to budge Thieu. Thus, Thieu's obstinacy robbed President Nixon of the chance to announce his success on Election Eve and Kissinger of another personal spectacular, the initialing of the accord in Hanoi. In electoral terms, though, Mr. Nixon no longer needed to pull this rug from under his opponent, Senator McGovern; his victory looked, and was, assured.

What troubled the White House was whether Thieu was simply playing a skillful hand of poker to position himself politically in the most favorable way or whether he was courting suicide.

The cease-fire "in place," the so-called "Leopard" cease-fire, originally conceived by Cyrus Vance, deputy to Ambassador Harriman during the Paris peace talks under President Johnson, but never tested by him at the conference table, was bound to be messy, even dirty, with some inevitable bloodletting. However, since the North Vietnamese had accepted a council subject to the veto of any of its three factions instead of the coalition government they had previously demanded, it was fairly safe to assume that it would not be able to exert authority to govern. Thieu's prospects, therefore, to keep Vietnam indefinitely divided were fair, especially since Hanoi had conceded him continued control of the Army and the police. Kissinger did not share Thieu's insistence that there was no justification for northern troops to stay in the South. First of all, the North Vietnamese had tacitly agreed to pull out all but thirty-five thousand of them and, secondly, Kissinger sympathized with their argument that they must have some leverage to ensure that Thieu keep to the bargain of accepting some Vietcongs into the political structure. What emboldened Thieu to reject the terms Kissinger had negotiated was, no doubt, the assumption that his own survival meant symbolic proof to Mr. Nixon that the United States had obtained peace "with honor." Kissinger's return to the Paris peace table after the election was a bitter pill he had to swallow and a public demonstration that Thieu, at least temporarily, had carried more conviction with Mr. Nixon than Kissinger. But the Paris talks were to clarify the terms of the agreement not to reopen them. What would matter in the end was when President Nixon would begin to make Mr. Thieu understand that these were the best terms attainable.

The terms Kissinger had found acceptable did not represent a withdrawal with "honor"; nor did they imply the kind of humiliation that a simple acceptance of Hanoi's terms, as advocated by Senator McGovern, would have meant. Nor did the peace settlement herald peace. It did, however, create conditions that offered President Thieu a lease on his political life and thus fulfilled one of Mr. Nixon's basic criteria. In many ways it was an invitation for continued political deadlock between Saigon and Hanoi, and for a continued division of Vietnam. To Americans it meant that at long last the U.S. military role in Vietnam was coming to an end.

What no one really could be certain of was whether Hanoi had accepted the settlement to seek a respite to restore its shattered army and economy in order to resume the struggle a few years hence or whether it had acquiesced in the concept of an Indochina that would remain divided into four independent states—North and South Vietnam, Laos and Cambodia—a concept that the leaders in Peking favored to prevent the Soviet Union from using a united Indochina to encircle China.

Whether or not Mr. Nixon succeeded in delaying the eventual Communist take-over, however, one thing was always beyond doubt—that the North Vietnamese would remain in the area long after the United States had gone. In the perspective of history the American attempt to rescue South Vietnam is bound to look an even greater waste of American lives and resources than it does now.

CHAPTER NINETEEN—THE BALANCE
OF MUTUAL WEAKNESS

In the preceding chapters are the threads out of which the tapestry of American foreign policy in the seventies will be woven: a clearer understanding of the limitations of American power, whether military, financial or economic; a fatigue with foreign commitments and a disenchantment with the world; a rebellion against the American values of the last fifty years, noisy on the Left, quiet in the center, resisted on the Right; a despair about the intractability of domestic problems; an over-all disposition to retrench and retreat.

President Nixon shifted gears into reverse, but at the same time he put his foot on the brakes to slow the backing up when his Democratic critics would have had him step hard on the accelerator. The actual pace of the American retreat will be faster than he was willing to admit and slower than they wanted it to be. But the President's sense of pace—typified by the stop-go retreat from Vietnam—was confirmed by his overwhelming election victory.

The first half of the seventies will be a period of transition and experimentation, a search for new fixed points of orientation. It will be a period of uncertainty as to the role the American public wishes the United States to play in the world, the amount of influence it wants to preserve. The intellectuals, when President Nixon came to power, withdrew to their ivory towers to contemplate the mistakes of the past and the lessons to be drawn from them for the future. And the indications are that the foreign policy elite, having found overseas affairs their undoing, are now turning inward and are more interested in becoming a domestic policy elite, under the impulse of the overriding problems that any American government will be facing at home in the seventies. Europeans and the Japanese tend to underestimate these problems; Americans perhaps tend to overestimate them.

The new generation of Americans is coming to power with a different experience and a different outlook. It is hardly aware of the Communist coup in Czechoslovakia in 1947, it has no memory of the Berlin blockade, the invasion of Korea or the suppression of Hungary. Uppermost in its mind is the catastrophe of Vietnam. The poison from that war will circulate in the American body and the American conscience for some time to come; the war's character and conduct are bound to remain part of the American experience and may leave an imprint as lasting as that of the Civil War. To this new generation it is damning evidence that the far-flung responsibilities of the United States have been executed in a reckless manner, that the limitations of American power have been incorrectly assessed and that American domestic needs have been badly neglected. The aim of this new generation will be to change the priorities of the past. Between those who do not understand the game of world power politics and those who exaggerate the need for overkill capacity, a great political struggle is developing in the seventies. There are many eloquent spokesmen among this new generation for the urgent American domestic needs, but as yet none for internationalism who can command the respect of this generation as well as of Congress. The kind of last-ditch defense the Nixon administration mounted by sending the old guard of internationalists to do battle against Senator Mansfield's attempt to drastically cut American troop commitments in Europe will be difficult to repeat.

THE LOST CONSENSUS

This new generation became the engine behind the shifts and changes in the Democratic Party for the presidential campaign, and by 1976, with many more million young people enfranchised, its impact, of course, will become increasingly effective. Their influx into active politics has profoundly upset many political assumptions, and the consensus that for twenty-five years gave American foreign policy continuity, bipartisan support and a remarkable stability has, as a consequence, been badly undermined. There are many who believe that an entirely fresh start has to be made, that every priority, every commitment, every assumption needs to be re-examined. The very idea of continuity, which has been the basis on which the world viewed American foreign policy with either confidence or awe, has become an albatross around the neck of the United States.

Some revered and idealistic concepts such as the Atlantic alliance have lost their significance. The United Nations, one of those great idealistic hopes that rose from the destruction of World War II, strongly promoted by the United States, has been shunted onto the side tracks of history. As a guardian of international security it has lost its significance. It will linger on as an international meeting ground and, who knows, could once again become a useful instrument when the challenge of the Third World to the industrial world becomes more acute.

The momentum for big ideas which accompanies the aftermath of great catastrophic wars has petered out. The young of today may be idealistic but it is with an inner-directed idealism. They have no feeling for, no understanding of, no commitment to the world that created the United Nations.

Americans are now sharply divided on the U.S. role in the world and any President in this decade will find it difficult to enter into new commitments, least of all any that could lead to sending American fighting forces abroad again, short of a very drastic change in the international situation. Such change seems to me to be unlikely because, despite their overweening power, the United States and the Soviet Union are confined by a mutual vulnerability of which they have become well aware. It is this balance of mutual weakness that has raised hopes around the world that the seventies will be a period of relative peace and stability. Not only are there the weapons of infinite power, which compel the superpowers to co-exist because neither can use them to impose its will on the other, there is also the lesson the superpowers are beginning to grasp: that it is in their own interest to keep tension down and to avoid getting too deeply involved in peripheral conflicts. Diplomacy, as Kissinger defines it, "is the art of restraining the exercise of power."

In that sense President Nixon's foreign policy has been extraordinarily successful. And success very much affects the way the public views foreign policy. Had the American intervention in Vietnam, for instance, ended in victory, it would not have aroused the opposition and revulsion it has and American foreign policy would not have come under the kind of barrage of criticism it has. Whatever public controversy it engendered would have been soon forgotten in the wake of a successful conclusion. The old memento against appeasement, "Munich," that dragged the United States into Vietnam will now be replaced by the new memento, "Vietnam," a warning against military involvement.

THINKING IN TERMS OF EQUILIBRIUM

Nixon met the public desire for a shift away from the cold-war outlook that had dominated American foreign policy throughout the post-World War II period by actively pursuing a *détente* with Moscow and Peking. In the process he and his impresario Henry Kissinger introduced a new diplomatic approach, balance-of-power diplomacy, at least as far as the United States, Russia and China were concerned. It meant a far more radical change in the conduct of American diplomacy than is as yet fully recognized. The acknowledgment of the existence of a mutual weakness, the fading of the cold war, the weakening of the old rigid framework of coalition diplomacy, and the public pressures everywhere for exploring a *détente* policy, all contributed to this new approach. Kissinger described it in 1968 as follows: ". . . Political multipolarity, while difficult to get used to, is the pre-condition for a new period of creativity. . . . The shape of the future will depend ultimately on the conviction which far transcends the physical balance of power . . . part of the reason for our difficulties is our reluctance to think in terms of power and equilibrium."

By opening up relations with China Nixon made the Soviet

Union suspicious and jealous, sufficiently eager to hold the Moscow summit to swallow the affront of the mining of Haiphong Harbor. It became important to the Soviet leaders to make certain that the balance of power in the seventies would be three cornered, and to demonstrate that the relationship between the United States and the Soviet Union was more important than that between the United States and China. When Kissinger squared the triangle by returning to Peking after the Moscow summit, he wondered, as he flew toward the China coast, whether he would get the same cordial reception as previously. But in spite of Moscow's smiles and Haiphong's mines, he was received even more warmly than before.

The world of the seventies is not so compact as the early nineteenth-century political world, which has been Kissinger's life study, and it is accordingly much more difficult, in his own phrase, "to respond to change with counteradjustment." He readily admitted this when he told members of Congress in June 1972:

This Administration's policy is occasionally characterized as being based on the principles of the classical balance of power. To the extent that that term implies a belief that security requires a measure of equilibrium, it has a certain validity. . . . But to the extent that balance of power means constant jockeying for marginal advantages over an opponent, it no longer applies. The reason is that the determination of national power has changed fundamentally in the nuclear age. Throughout history, the primary concern of most national leaders has been to accumulate geopolitical and military power. It would have seemed inconceivable, even a generation ago, that such power once gained could not be translated directly into advantage over one's opponent. But now both we and the Soviet Union have begun to find that each increment of power does not necessarily represent an increment of usable political strength.

This became painfully obvious during the Indo-Pakistan crisis, when all the counteradjustments were not enough to prevent war from breaking out. Still, as Nixon and Kissinger have shown, at least as regards the United States, Russia and China, scales for balancing relations can be a valid instrument in the diplomatic toolbox, even in the complex world of today.

However, to pursue a balance-of-power concept, a clear definition of basic interests is needed. Britain, at the height of its Empire days, was ruled by an elite which could forge its foreign policy on the basis of what it thought was in Britannia's interest —irrespective of public opinion. These interests were so clearly defined that even after the introduction of universal suffrage, the British public had an instinctive understanding of what was best for the Empire. No similar instinctive understanding is to be found in the United Stated today. The Nixon Doctrine is too vague a definition of American interests and priorities. It does not offer enough guidance as to how new priorities should be adjusted between U.S. domestic and international responsibilities and commitments, how to marshal resources to maintain the balance-of-power equation with the Soviet Union, even if it is only a balance of mutual weakness. What complicates these calculations and adds to the pressures for a new approach is the recognition that has begun to sink in among economic planners—the fact that economic growth, which used to absorb the rising social costs of government, cannot do so any more, and that new ways must be sought of finding the resources for the kind of new undertakings that are increasingly being talked about by leading politicians, from a new welfare program and a national health scheme to income redistribution, to mention the costliest. Americans have come to accept a much more massive interventionist policy by the federal government in dealing with social problems, but they have not yet found ways to fund them appropriately.

The most obvious target in the search for funds for domestic needs is the defense budget. Half of that budget goes to paying for the forces on active duty. The conventional force structure therefore is constantly eyed for possible savings. It means that the defense requirements of Western Europe are increasingly exposed to attacks, especially as the *détente* becomes a settled state of mind. American interests and defense commitments therefore are under review, the cost of the so-called "bargaining chip" policy is frowned upon, and the margins of safety are bound to be narrowed. But there is something of a vicious circle between the security that is desirable and the cost of military expenditures to ensure it. The views as to how large an insurance premium the United States should pay vary enormously if one compares, for instance, the Nixon and McGovern views. The Nixon Doctrine, being designed for all seasons, offers arguments to justify defense cuts, but that aspect of it has been obscured for the present by the requests for new weapons, included in the defense budget. Even sympathetic critics at the Brookings Institution wonder whether these new weapons systems are not being determined before the nature of the threat is fully analyzed, in other words, whether they are not pressed prematurely.*

It has become obvious, therefore, that with American economic means limited, greater stringencies will have to be imposed and they will have their effect not only on defense and foreign policy, but also on American foreign economic policy.

ECONOMIC NATIONALISM

A much more pervasive economic nationalism is making itself felt as a consequence of the costs of American defense commitments abroad, the heavy balance-of-payments deficits, and the influence foreigners can exert on the dollar. But just as the liberal Establishment has lost influence because of its misjudgments in Vietnam in the past ten years, so the international economic Establishment is now coming under increasing criticism for not deploying enough of its financial resources in the United States, for not being nationalistic enough.

John Connally, when he was Secretary of the Treasury, reflected the revival of economic nationalism, which had not been respectable for a generation or more. Even an internationalist such as Senator Hubert Humphrey thought it expedient to adopt an economic nationalist slogan during the California primary of 1972;

* *Setting National Priorities, the 1973 Budget,* the Brookings Institution, Washington, D.C., 1972.

he admonished American investors to "make the dollar more patriotic." What he meant was that Americans should invest at home rather than abroad, so that Americans rather than foreigners would benefit.

Connally's outlook was not isolationist, but a mixture of nationalism and protectionism. It troubled not only foreign governments but also American business corporations which are, with their multinational operations and vast holdings overseas, the last American globalists. His views were not typical, but they nevertheless reflected the views in the U. S. Treasury and of many in Congress. Mr. Nixon considers himself an expert in foreign policy, and so does Kissinger, but neither has a real understanding of overseas economic affairs. As a consequence, there has been an unfortunate lack of American leadership in this field. Mr. Connally, while in power, was primarily interested in tactics, not long-term strategy. Still, he presented the President with a highly controversial, still unpublished, proposal for a dollar bloc as a counter to the potential power of the European Economic Community. The EEC, he was convinced, would increasingly threaten American interests and exploit weaknesses in the over-all American economic situation. What he underrated was the extent to which these weaknesses were mutual and therefore created an interdependence. He saw the harnessing of dollar power as the best way to stave off the threat. It was difficult, however, to see the practicality of a dollar bloc, and easy to predict that to play the balance-of-monetary-power game would lead to trade and monetary wars and inevitably jeopardize not only international economic but political relations as well. It was an idea that certainly did not fit the Kissinger scheme of things.

WESTERN EUROPE—ALLY OR COMPETITOR?

There was anyway a danger of relations between the United States and the Western European alliance deteriorating. Nixon and Kissinger, preoccupied with their diplomatic forays to Peking and Moscow, had little time—except during the dollar crisis after August 15, 1971—to think about future economic, financial, military and nuclear relations with their European allies. They did not matter much in connection with the overarching balance-of-power maneuvers they were engaged in, because Western Europe did not figure as a great power. What added to the Europeans' feeling of being on the outside was the realization that, in order to gain a freer hand for this great-power diplomacy, the Nixon administration tended to behave like a mother bird toward its allies and friends to make them more aware of the future need to fly on their own wings. They wondered whether the Gaullist view —that it was interests, not friends, that mattered—had come to inspire American diplomacy. The American view of the world, in the quest for flexibility, seemed to have become an extension of the weaknesses that Mr. Nixon and Kissinger share—a difficulty in committing themselves intimately to other people, a desire to have no firm commitments and to have the freedom of several options. The European allies made their own contribution to the alienation with Washington by being too insensitive on their part to American problems. As a result allied relationships have deteriorated and have been unnecessarily hurt. Kissinger once quipped that "the worst fate that can befall one is being an ally of the United States." Even if this should not be read too literally, the detached U.S. attitude toward her allies came as a surprise after the impressions Mr. Nixon left behind on his first European tour in February 1969. There was also an implicit assumption that countries like West Germany (and Japan) had nowhere else to go, so had to stay, in their own interests, close to the United States, and an assumption, too, that self-interest was a more enduring basis for relationships between governments than the sentimentality of a feeling of friendship. But mutual confidence, I believe, being a bit of a romantic, does play a role in international relations and to undermine it is a loss to both sides. The British in their Empire days ruled supreme, convinced they did not need to consult with anybody. But when the Empire was transformed into the Commonwealth and Britain became *primus inter pares*, it consulted more and more because it correctly concluded that a co-operative Commonwealth would help to make up for Britain's declining influence. The United States, however, is consulting less and less.

The continuing American interest in the Western alliance is

to make certain that the most powerful industrial complex out-side the United States does not come under Soviet control, but Americans also have a cultural conscience about the fate of Europe, and with so many other U.S. interests at stake they want to keep their oars in European affairs.

One of the serious dangers, as the spirit of the Atlantic alliance continues to fade in the seventies, is that the United States and Western Europe will come to see each other as competitors and not as allies. There are important men on both sides who are either anti-European or anti-American, and an unfortunate coincidence of chain reactions could play into the hands of those so prejudiced. A major American troop withdrawal, for instance, without proper consultation with NATO, a breakdown in the negotiations about EEC preferential tariffs, followed by new protectionist legislation in Congress, just to dip into a basket of eels, could set in motion forces on both sides of the Atlantic that would be difficult to restrain.

Western Europe cannot become a military equal to the United States or the Soviet Union and should not even try to. What will decide its power position in the seventies, whatever efforts are made to create a European Defense Community, is whether it can acquire a unified foreign, economic and monetary policy. Whether it will have the political will to achieve that remains uncertain, but in seeking it, the Europeans will have to be careful not to overplay their hand in dealing with American interests. There is an interdependence between economic and security relationships, and alienating one could lead to alienating the other.

The United States is not prepared any more to pay a high economic price for the political benefits of European unity. A growing number of Americans have strong reservations about how desirable a new independent European power is, especially from the U.S. economic point of view. There is almost no area where the United States feels a more acute sense of vulnerability than in its economic relationship with Western Europe and Japan. The danger exists that the unco-operative behavior of the U.S.'s main trading partners or of the United States in monetary affairs, with both blaming each other, will make for transatlantic and transpacific friction. Moreover, the United States, which for so many years shunned trading with Communist countries, will become a major competitor for Europeans who used to have this market virtually to themselves. The United States also enjoys better communications with Russia today than most European governments, and American interests in preserving this duopoly are also bound to conflict at times with the interests of the Western alliance.

The pressures at home for withdrawals of American troops from Europe will add to the strains between the United States and the rest of NATO. There is no evidence that these pressures reflect a desire for change in the relationship toward Western Europe. When the most vocal senators such as Mansfield, Fulbright or Church raise the issue they see it more as a housekeeping problem. Nor are there any public pressures for a change in the relationship. What troubles Congress is the disparity between the American defense effort and that of the Europeans, and the cost of maintaining that many troops under arms. One way to delay the congressional pressures for a troop withdrawal from Europe (which are mainly budgetary) would be to deactivate those forces stationed in the United States that are assigned for the defense of Europe; they represent about half of the expense, and it costs the United States as much to keep them in uniform at home as it would in Europe. Withdrawing the troops actually in Europe would not in itself save money. And since there is logic in maintaining American troops in Europe as a "bargaining chip" for the negotiations with the Russians about mutual and balanced force reductions, this would be a practical way for the United States Government to approach this problem. Furthermore, there is a new reason for maintaining sufficient conventional forces in Europe: The advent of nuclear parity between the two superpowers could become a temptation to the Russians to use their conventional forces, if not for military ends then for political pressures.

The advocates of troop withdrawals reject the accusation, usually from across the Atlantic, that they would throw doubts on the reliability of the American security guarantee. They are believers in the trip-wire theory, which holds that even a handful of American soldiers in Europe would be enough to activate the guarantee. Still, this accusation raises a more fundamental question—how reliable, in fact, is this guarantee in the era of mutual weakness? Men like Kissinger believe that the Europeans, to be safer, should create their own nuclear deterrent. The British, in contrast to the French, used to oppose this in the belief that it would give the Americans a tempting escape clause, or that at any rate it would lessen the psychological deterrence of the American commitment. Kissinger is a *Realpolitiker*; the British tend to believe more in the mystique of power, though Prime Minister Edward Heath is the first British prime minister also to favor a European nuclear deterrent. It is impossible to decide who is right. Kissinger and Heath may be, in the light of the balance of mutual weakness and vulnerability between the great powers; but then it may be more important to preserve the psychology of the American guarantee in the Russian mind; the best hope of course is that the test as to which is the better choice will never occur.

Europe in many ways has become politically more stable. Written agreements usually are nothing more than the codification of an already existing situation, but the treaty on Berlin and the agreements of the Federal Republic of Germany with the Soviet Union and with Poland are the equivalent of a peace settlement of the Second World War. The territorial gains made by the Soviet Union and Poland are now legally confirmed and, since the Russians attach great importance to legality, they will help to lessen tension in the center of Europe. Berlin, the symbol of these tensions for so many years, is likely to become more a symbol of relaxation, and as the frontiers between the two Germanys harden, will become something of a bridge. The psychology of the division of Germany is changing. What used to be regarded as a forcibly imposed division, arousing frustrations and illusions about the unrequited promises of unification, will be viewed instead as a recognition of the existence of two German states with two different and deepening identities. This is not likely to be a permanent solution, but probably one that will last through the seventies, and one that will be equally welcome to the Russians and the West Europeans. It will help the Russians to maintain control over Eastern Europe and at the same time strengthen West Germany's sense of belonging to the European Community.

Unquestionably, therefore, the United States will want to maintain an influence in Western Europe, though the relationship will come to rest more on psychological than institutional foundations. As the power of NATO declines and the U.S. security guarantee seems to become open to question, this psychological relationship will provide the necessary index. If it is good, then so will be the deterrent value of the guarantee; if it deteriorates, then the guarantee will be devalued with it. The growing fluidity in international relations will not make all this any easier.

THE REGIONAL PROBLEMS OF GREAT POWERS

In the Middle East the Israelis, though lacking a formal guarantee, will continue to rely on the United States to counterbalance Soviet power. When Egypt's President Sadat told Mr. Rogers in 1971 that he would never allow the Russians to remain in his country indefinitely, the American Secretary of State was encouraged and impressed, but his elation was met with skepticism inside and outside the Administration. Yet a year later, to everybody's surprise, the Russians had been "expelled." The Middle East, with so many irreconcilable elements, so many people driven by emotion, so much smoldering hatred, is bound to remain a crisis area. But Mr. Nixon's luck in foreign affairs held even in this unpredictable area, and he and Mr. Rogers can take solace in the fact that they were able at least to begin the seventies by preserving a cease-fire along the Suez Canal. However simple it seems to many Israelis that the status quo is better than any settlement Israel could negotiate with its neighbors, the Arab-Israeli territorial conflict cannot go on indefinitely. It is an enormous drain in men, material and money to Israel, and it perpetrates the dangers of conflict—something will have to give somewhere sooner or later. American policy will continue to aim at preserving a balance of power to prevent Israel from being destroyed. The Israelis would feel readier to give up territory that reinforces their security and their frontiers if they were more certain about the extent and consistency of this U.S. protection.

What Israeli policy makers must take into consideration, and American planners increasingly talk about, is that by the end of this decade the United States will be facing a very serious energy crisis. And since so much of the needed oil comes from the Middle East, the Arabs will by then be in a powerful bargaining position with the United States.

In Asia, U.S. and Chinese interests are nowhere in serious conflict, except for Taiwan, and that problem has been defused. The Chinese do not mind the world behaving as it pleases as long as it does not impinge on their interests. The two powers that could impinge on them are the Soviet Union and Japan, and with both of them the United States can exert an important influence, mainly to reassure the Chinese that neither will attack China.

The Chinese, for instance, were very much concerned about the outcome of the Indo-Pakistan war, which involved Chinese interests, but Peking proved unable to give the support its Pakistani allies expected. The United States, whose interests were also involved, was not able to prevent the war from truncating Pakistan, but it nevertheless played an important hand, much more than China. In Washington the United States was seen as defending American interests, but in Peking it also seemed to be defending Chinese interests in this situation. Thus Peking does not mind the United States maintaining a position in Asia because it imposes certain limitations on Russia's freedom to extend her influence. Actually, the Russians have been careful enough not to get tied too closely to a weak country like India; what probably matters most to them is to ensure that India does not fall under Chinese influence.

It was not surprising that the Indo-Pakistan war was compared to the old Balkan wars and the roles of the United States, Russia and China to those that Austria, Prussia and Russia played then. What actually happened to India and Pakistan seemed of lesser interest to the observers of big-power play. It was the maneuvers among the big powers that aroused the greatest attention, and not in the sense of who was gaining geographical advantages, but who was cleverer in preventing the other from gaining any. The Indo-Pakistan war experience points at the danger of small, limited wars among minor powers, as did the Israeli-Arab war, and the risks and temptations they create for the great powers. It may be even more difficult to prevent them, now that big-power intervention is fraught with so much danger, and therefore cannot dictate their settlement. The great powers are also learning that the developing world is hard to deal with. The Russians have learned that lesson in Indonesia, in the Sudan and, above all, in Egypt; the United States in Vietnam. It is bound to moderate their outlook and appetite.

If the Russians desist from moving against China—and they may already be too late—then China, probably with some technological support from the United States, will gradually move toward great power status (Chou En-lai still refers to China as a developing country). If the United States continues to play her cards well and does not try to play off China against the Soviet Union, then it will place the Russians in a position where they will want to maintain not only the *détente* in Europe but also a *modus vivendi* in the gray areas where American and Russian interests overlap.

U.S.-Japanese relations have markedly deteriorated under the Nixon administration, and although the United States would like Japan to assume the leading role in the Pacific region, no well-defined concept for this has yet developed in either country. Certainly in Washington the war in Vietnam and the initiative toward China took up too much of the time and effort of the Kissinger operation to leave room for much else. Whatever frustrations were caused by the Vietnam war were compensated for by the exhilaration of the new relationship with China. For the rest of Asia, as for the Third World, no time was left on Kissinger's calendar which, he once quipped, "was so crowded that it left no time for war."

HOW MUCH IS ENOUGH?

The majority of Americans, despite the new relationship with the Kremlin and Peking, remain very conscious of the risks and dangers of cutting too deeply into the muscle of American power. Just as the forces for change in the United States are formidable, so are the forces of resistance. Robert W. Tucker in his small book *A New Isolationism*—which he advocates with so much persuasiveness to American ears—admits that "the mood of the public is clearly ambivalent, the American people show little propensity to impose a massive veto on presidential action on foreign policy, at least so long as this action avoids a repetition of the events associated with Vietnam."† Whether interventionist or isolationist, Americans remain power conscious and power proud. A drastic reduction of the military budget soon is therefore unlikely; even if desired it could not be accomplished except over a period of three to five years. The trade unions, the military-industrial complex, the military and congressional forces will slow it down. After all, the U.S.S.R. is not sitting complacently on its achievement of nuclear parity. What the great debate in Washington will be about is not whether the United States should protect whatever qualitative lead it has in nuclear weapons, but the degree to which it should try to keep ahead. Hopefully, the next phase of the SALT talks will make this easier to decide.

But I have no doubt that the United States will, in the next few years, cut its overseas commitments more closely according to the cloth at its disposal. Nixon and Kissinger became very conscious of the fact that the United States no longer had the capacity to fulfill the range of commitments it had acquired after World War II, when the balance of power among the leading nations was quite different. There were commitments the United States was bound to live up to, but there were others it was prepared to jettison if necessary. The two therefore came to feel that they were acting from a hand that was, as they saw it, vulnerable. It is not impossible that in the recesses of his mind Kissinger occasionally compared his own situation to that of the Iron Chancellor Bismarck, who, at least after 1871, applied his mastery of the balance-of-power game to protect a vulnerable Prussia against any hostile coalition. The feat of developing good relations with China and the Soviet Union at the same time was alone one that would have been quite a challenge to Bismarck or Metternich; Kissinger succeeded because he knew how to restrain the contending forces by manipulating their antagonisms and how to exploit their aspirations.

What presents a serious problem for the future is the intricate

† Tucker, A New Isolationism, Potomac Books, Inc., Washington, D.C., 1972.

weave of the Nixon and Kissinger diplomacy and the difficulty of anybody else's assuming its management. Abram Chayes, the Harvard Law professor who headed a task force to develop McGovern's foreign policy during the election campaign, called Kissinger a virtuoso for whom there was no obvious successor because there was simply no one, he thought, who had the same command of diplomacy and who could play the balance-of-power game with the same skill and success. Nothing worries Kissinger more than the fear that a President will come to power in this decade who will not understand his scheme of things, who will see the world quite differently and tear down the pillars of the power relationship he built. Essential to his thinking is the belief that you do not cut your strength and then fashion policy accordingly, but that you maintain or build up your resources and then negotiate about limiting or reducing them, if they can be limited or reduced. He has more faith in the power than in the prospects of limiting it—he is convinced of human fallibility. But it is a policy that increases rather than decreases budgets, and therefore will become increasingly more difficult to follow.

What may alleviate this problem is that the two superpowers have in common the urgent need to deal with demands for domestic reform, as have China and Japan. This *Drang* for reform is most obvious, though, in the United States and the Soviet Union, the two societies that have prided themselves for so long on being "classless." They have become more class-ridden than they are willing to admit, and the leaders in both countries have come to recognize that they must do more to alleviate these pressures for the sake of internal peace and order. It is a vital element in the balance of mutual weakness. The rebellions in the American ghettos and among the workers in Poland were signals no government could ignore. What happened in Poland, where police power is almost as strict as in the Soviet Union, could happen in the Soviet Union itself tomorrow.

In the Soviet Union the raising of the standard of living is still a relatively simple problem of more and better consumer goods; in the United States the problem is how to restrain the glut of inessential consumer goods that eat up an inordinate amount of raw materials, and how to reduce the ever-widening gap between the rich and the poor. Americans could say with Churchill, "We are stripped bare by the curse of plenty." The focus may shift between the schools, the cities, the environment, the welfare program, but all are aspects of the redistribution of wealth, which will be the great social struggle in the United States in the seventies. What this requires is a Kissinger for domestic policy who can undertake the kind of long-term economic planning that this requires; Mr. Nixon lacked such an equivalent.

The retreat of American power will continue to prove a traumatic experience for Americans, their friends and even their enemies. This does not mean, however, that the Western world will not continue to look to the United States for leadership, or will not watch with some anxiety whether the retrenchment will be managed wisely and how much the polarization of forces on the Right and Left will be kept under control. The stability of the Western world will continue to depend on the quality of American leadership. In a period of *détente*, which hopefully the seventies promise to be, and in an even more complex world than the one we are used to, it will be more difficult to keep a steady rudder than it was in a period of tension when the answers often imposed themselves automatically. It will require a careful balancing between preserving the essentials of the older policy principles and making sufficient allowances for the new public mood. Whoever is in charge during the rest of this decade will have to remember that people do not forgive their leaders when they err, even if their errors reflect the popular preferences.

The seventies will go down in history as representing a watershed in the American relationship to the rest of the world. This relationship will prove to be more restrained, more impersonal, more detached, more self-centered. After a period when everyone knew where everyone else stood, when diplomacy was played to well-established rules, and a certain intimacy and interdependence were observed within the alliance, the world of the seventies will be less predictable. But the basic design of the retreat of American power is already drawn. Only its pace and its limits remain in doubt. Both, I hope, will be moderate.